Thou Shalt Do These Things

A Study of the Commands
In the New Testament

For the Glory of the Lord
Pastor Scott Markle

Shepherding the Flock Ministries

7971 Washington St. ❖ Melvin, MI 48454
(810) 378-5323
www.shepherdingtheflock.com

Thou Shalt Do These Things:
A Study of the Commands in the New Testament
by Pastor Scott Markle

Printed in the United States of America

ISBN 978-1732166608

Shepherding the Flock Ministries
7971 Washington St.
Melvin, MI 48454
(810) 378-5323
www.shepherdingtheflock.com

TABLE OF CONTENTS

THE EXHORTATION

W e live in a time when some (even many) would teach us that we New Testament believers are no longer under the Law of Moses, but are now under the grace of God, such that we have few (if any) Biblical rules and regulations by which we are required to govern our lives. Indeed, they would teach us that being under God's grace, we possess the God-given freedom to live primarily according to our own interests with very little restriction thereof. Yet with a careful study through the New Testament Scriptures themselves, we find over three hundred different commands for us New Testament believers to follow. Even so, although we may not be bound under all of the details in the Law of Moses, we certainly are still bound under the absolute authority of the Lord our God and Savior over our daily living.

Although we are not under the law, but are under God's grace, yet we are the children of God our heavenly Father and the servants of the Lord our God. Thus we are to obey the authority of our heavenly Father and to serve under the authority of our divine Lord. We are to walk "*as obedient children*," seeking to be holy as our heavenly Father is holy, and passing "*the time of our sojourning here*" in the fear of the Lord. (See 1 Peter 1:14-18) We are to walk as good and faithful servants, yielding ourselves as "*a living sacrifice, holy, acceptable unto God*," and yielding our members "*as instruments of righteousness unto God.*" (See Romans 12:1 & 6:13)

Due to our Lord God's abundant grace and mercy in saving us, this is only our "*reasonable service*" unto Him. (See Romans 12:1) Indeed, the love of Christ for us "*constraineth us*," such that we should no longer live unto ourselves, but unto Christ Jesus our Lord who died for us and rose again. (See 2 Corinthians 5:14-16) We are no longer our own, for we have been bought with the price of Christ's blood. Therefore, we should live unto the glory of God in both our body and our spirit; for they are both God's ownership. (See 1 Corinthians 6:20) We should cleanse ourselves *"from all filthiness of the flesh and spirit, perfecting holiness in the fear of God."* (2 Corinthians 7:1)

Without Obedience, There Is No Abiding in Christ

Faithful obedience unto our Lord's commandments is an essential ingredient for spiritual success in our daily Christian walk. In fact, apart from faithful obedience there is no daily abiding in Christ. In John 15:4-5 our Lord Jesus Christ gave instruction, warning, and promise, saying, *"Abide in me, and I in you. As the branch cannot bear fruit of itself, except it abide in the vine; no more can ye, except ye abide in me. I am the vine, ye are the branches: He that abideth in me, and I in him, the same bringeth forth much fruit: for without me ye can do nothing."*

Now, bringing forth spiritual fruit in our daily Christian walk is the reason that our Lord has chosen us and ordained us. In the opening portion of John 15:16, our Lord Jesus Christ proclaimed, *"Ye have not chosen me, but I have chosen you, and ordained you, that ye should go and bring forth fruit, and that your fruit should remain."* Furthermore, bringing forth spiritual fruit in our daily Christian walk is the way that we bring glory unto God our heavenly Father. In John 15:8 our Lord Jesus Christ declared, *"Herein is my Father glorified, that ye bear much fruit; so shall ye be my disciples."* Yet the only way that we can bring forth spiritual fruit in our daily Christian walk is through abiding in Christ and allowing Christ to abide in us. "As the branch *cannot* bear fruit of itself, except it abide in the vine," no more can we, except we abide in Him.

So then, what does it mean to be abiding in Christ and allowing Him to abide in us? First, it means that we walk in humility, fully recognizing that apart from Him we are, can be, and can do nothing of spiritual value before God. Second, it means that we walk by faith, wholly trusting in our Lord's spiritual provision, loving care, and wise guidance for our daily living. Third, it means that we walk with surrender, completely yielding ourselves to obey our Lord's will, rule, and leadership in our daily living. Indeed, concerning this third truth, the opening portion of 1 John 3:24 states, *"And he that keepeth his commandments dwelleth in him, and he in him."* In order to be abiding in Christ and have Christ abiding in us, we must be obeying His commandments. Even so, the truth is this simple – If there is no obeying Him, then there is no abiding in Him.

Without Obedience, There Is No Love for the Lord

In John 14:15 our Lord Jesus Christ proclaimed, *"If ye love me, keep my commandments."* Again in verse 21 our Lord proclaimed, *"He that hath my commandments, and keepeth them, he it is that loveth me: and he that loveth me shall be loved of my Father, and I will love him, and will manifest myself to him."* Yet again in verse 23 our Lord proclaimed, *"If a man love me, he will keep my words: and my Father will love him, and we will come unto him, and make our abode with him."* In all three of these verses, our Lord clearly revealed the truth that those who walk in love for Him demonstrate their love by walking in obedience to His commands.

Furthermore, in 1 John 5:3 God's Word declares, *"For this is the love of God, that we keep his commandments: and his commandments are not grievous."* Finally, Deuteronomy 11:1 declares, *"Therefore thou shalt love the LORD thy God, and keep his charge, and his statutes, and his judgments, and his commandments, alway."* Yes, love for God is demonstrated through faithful obedience unto His requirements, His rules, His regulations, and His responsibilities. Even so, the truth is this simple – If there is no obeying Him, then there is no loving Him.

Without Obedience, There Is No Fellowship with the Lord

In John 15:9-10 our Lord Jesus Christ proclaimed, *"As the Father hath loved me, so have I loved you: continue ye in my love. If ye keep my commandments, ye shall abide in my love; even as I have kept my Father's commandments, and abide in his love."* Herein our Lord revealed that we abide in the love of His daily fellowship and friendship just as we walk in obedience to His commandments.

11

Thus in John 15:14 our Lord proclaimed, ***"Ye are my friends, if ye do whatsoever I command you."***

Finally, in 1 John 2:3-6 God's Word declares, ***"And hereby we do know that we know him, if we keep his commandments. He that saith, I know him, and keepeth not his commandments, is a liar, and the truth is not in him. But whoso keepeth his word, in him verily is the love of God perfected: hereby know we that we are in him. He that saith he abideth in him ought himself also so to walk, even as he walked."*** To know the Lord our God is not simply to know information about Him. Rather, it is to know Him Himself. It is to have a relationship of growing fellowship with Him. Even so, we experience this relationship of fellowship with Him only "if we keep his commandments." On the other hand, if we claim to have such a walk of fellowship with Him, but do not keep and obey His commandments, we are actually lying about our spiritual walk. So then, the truth is this simple – If there is no obeying Him, then there is no fellowship with Him.

Without Obedience, There Is No Right Heart before the Lord

In Deuteronomy 5:29 the Lord God Himself exclaimed concerning His people, ***"O that there were such an heart in them, that they would fear me, and keep all my commandments always, that it might be well with them, and with their children for ever!"*** Again in Deuteronomy 6:25 the message was delivered unto God's people, ***"And it shall be our righteousness, if we observe to do all these commandments before the LORD our God, as he hath commanded us."*** Yet again in Deuteronomy 10:12-13 the message was delivered, ***"And now, Israel, what doth the LORD thy God require of thee, but to fear the LORD thy God, to walk in all his ways, and to love him, and to serve the LORD thy God with all thy heart and with all thy soul, to keep the commandments of the LORD, and his statutes, which I command thee this day for thy good?"*** Through these passages we understand that a right heart before the Lord is one that fears the Lord so as faithfully to keep His commands. Yea, a heart that walks in righteousness before the Lord is one that observes to do all that the Lord has commanded. It is a heart that fears the Lord, that walks in all of the Lord's ways, that loves the Lord, that serves the Lord with all of the heart and soul, and that keeps the Lord's commands and statutes. Even so, God's Word declares in Ecclesiastes 12:13-14, "***Let us hear the conclusion of the whole matter: Fear God, and keep his commandments: for this is the whole duty of man. For God shall bring every work into judgment, with every secret thing, whether it be good, or whether it be evil.***" Even so, the truth is this simple – If there is no obeying Him, then there is no right heart before Him.

Without Obedience, There Is No Wisdom in the Lord

In Matthew 7:24-27 our Lord Jesus Christ declared, "***Therefore whosoever heareth these sayings of mine, and doeth them, I will liken him unto a wise man, which built his house upon a rock: and the rain descended, and the floods came, and the winds blew, and beat upon that house; and it fell not: for it was founded upon a rock. And every one that heareth these sayings of mine, and doeth them not, shall be likened unto a foolish man, which built his house upon the sand: and the rain descended, and the floods came, and the winds blew, and beat upon that house; and it fell: and great was the fall of it.***" Herein our Lord made it clear that those who hear His Word and obey are walking in spiritual wisdom. However, He also made it clear that those who hear His Word, but do not obey are walking in spiritual foolishness. As such, the key ingredient between spiritual wisdom and spiritual foolishness is a walk of obedience or disobedience unto God's Holy Word.

In like manner, James 1:22 gives the warning, "***But be ye doers of the word, and not hearers only, deceiving your own selves.***" Hearing God's Word, but not obeying it is not the way of spiritual wisdom, but is the way of self-deception. Furthermore, in Deuteronomy 4:5-6 the message was delivered unto God's people, "***Behold, I have taught you statutes and judgments, even as the LORD my God commanded me, that ye should do so in the land whither ye go to possess it. Keep therefore and do them; for this is your wisdom and your understanding in the sight of the nations, which shall hear all these statutes, and say, Surely this great nation is a wise and understanding people.***" Indeed, obedience unto the statutes and

13

standards of God's Holy Word *IS* our wisdom and understanding. Even so, Psalm 111:10 proclaims, *"The fear of the LORD is the beginning of wisdom: a good understanding have all they that do his commandments: his praise endureth for ever."* So then, the truth is this simple – If there is no obeying Him, then there is no wisdom from Him.

Without Obedience, There Is No Blessing from the Lord

In James 1:25 God's Word gives the promise, *"But whoso looketh into the perfect law of liberty, and continueth therein, he being not a forgetful hearer, but a doer of the work, this man shall be blessed in his deed."* The one who is an obedient doer of the work, this very one alone, "shall be blessed in his deed."

In Deuteronomy 4:40 the message was delivered unto God's people, *"Thou shalt keep therefore his statutes, and his commandments, which I command thee this day, that it may go well with thee, and with thy children after thee, and that thou mayest prolong thy days upon the earth, which the LORD thy God giveth thee, for ever."* Again in Deuteronomy 5:32-33 the message was delivered unto God's people, *"Ye shall observe to do therefore as the LORD your God hath commanded you: ye shall not turn aside to the right hand or to the left. Ye shall walk in all the ways which the LORD your God hath commanded you, that ye may live, and that it may be well with you, and that ye may prolong your days in the land which ye shall possess."* Yet again in Deuteronomy 11:26-28 the message was delivered unto God's people, *"Behold, I set before you this day a blessing and a curse; a blessing, if ye obey the commandments of the LORD your God, which I command you this day: and a curse, if ye will not obey the commandments of the LORD your God, but turn aside out of the way which I command you this day, to go after other gods, which ye have not known."*

Even so, in Joshua 1:8 the Lord God delivered His instruction and promise unto Joshua, saying, *"This book of the law shall not depart out of thy mouth; but thou shalt meditate therein day and night, that thou mayest observe to do according to all that is written therein: for then thou shalt make thy way prosperous, and then*

thou shalt have good success." Even so also, Psalm 19:10-11 states concerning God's Word of truth in relation to all of us who are the Lord's servants, "***More to be desired are they than gold, yea, than much fine gold: sweeter also than honey and the honeycomb. Moreover by them is thy servant warned: and in keeping of them there is great reward.***" Again Psalm 103:17-18 gives the promise, "***But the mercy of the LORD is from everlasting to everlasting upon them that fear him, and his righteousness unto children's children; to such as keep his covenant, and to those that remember his commandments to do them.***" Yet again Psalm 112:1 gives the promise, "***Praise ye the LORD. Blessed is the man that feareth the LORD, that delighteth greatly in his commandments.***" Finally, Psalm 119:1-2 gives the promise, "***Blessed are the undefiled in the way, who walk in the law of the LORD. Blessed are they that keep his testimonies, and that seek him with the whole heart.***"

So then, the truth is this simple – If there is no obeying Him, then there is no abiding in Him, no loving Him, no fellowship with Him, no right heart before Him, no wisdom from Him, and no blessing from Him.

THE
INSTRUCTION

As we have noted, faithful obedience unto our Lord's commands is Biblically important for abiding in Him, for loving Him, for walking in fellowship with Him, for walking in righteousness before Him, for walking in wisdom from Him, and for receiving blessing from Him. Yet how can we walk in faithful obedience unto our Lord's commands if we do not even know what those commands are? So then, let us consider the following list of commands from the New Testament. (Note: The page number reveals the corresponding portion for the given point in the meditation section of the book.)

1. The lost sinner must repent of sin and believe the gospel of Jesus Christ unto eternal salvation. (Matthew 3:2; Mark 1:14-15; John 6:29; 7:37-38; 12:35-36; Acts 3:19; 16:31; 17:30; Revelation 22:17) (See p. 53)

2. We must bring forth fruits worthy of repentance. (Matthew 3:8; Luke 3:7-14) (See p. 56)

3. We must follow our Lord's leading without delay (even if it seems unreasonable to our own thinking). (Matthew 4:19; 8:21-22; 9:9; Mark 1:16-20; 2:14; Luke 5:27-28; 9:57-62; John 1:43; 21:18-22) (See p. 58)

4. We must "rejoice and be exceeding glad" when we are persecuted for our Lord's sake. (Matthew 5:11-12; Luke 6:22-23; 1 Peter 3:14; 4:12-16) (See p. 60)

5. We must "so shine" our spiritual light before the lost of this world. (Matthew 5:14-16) (See p. 62)

6. We must get right with those against whom we have done wrong. (Matthew 5:23-24) (See p. 63)

7.   We must agree quickly to make right with those against whom we have committed a civil infraction. (Matthew 5:25-26; Luke 12:58-59) (See p. 64)

8.   We must sever and cast away anything in our lives that leads us unto sexual lust. (Matthew 5:27-30) (See p. 65)

9.   We must not be swearing to the truth of things, but must just be faithful to our word. (Matthew 5:33-37; James 5:12) (See p. 66)

10. We must not retaliate against evil, but must show kindness instead. (Matthew 5:38-42; Luke 6:29-30; Romans 12:14, 17, 19-21; 1 Thessalonians 5:15; 1 Peter 3:9) (See p. 67)

11. We must love our enemies, blessing them, doing good to them, and praying for them. (Matthew 5:43-48; Luke 6:29-30, 32-35) (See p. 96)

12. We must not do "right things" to "be seen of men" that we "may have glory of men." (Matthew 6:1-2, 5, 16) (See p. 71)

13. We must do "right things" only to be seen of our heavenly Father. (Matthew 6:3-4, 6, 17-18) (See p. 73)

14. We must not use vain repetitions when we pray. (Matthew 6:7-8) (See p. 74)

15. We must pray with adoration, reverence, hope, surrender, trust, confession, forgiveness, consecration, and praise. (Matthew 6:9-13; Luke 11:1-4) (See p. 76)

16. We must not set our affection upon or lay up for ourselves "treasures upon earth," but must set our affection upon and lay up for ourselves "treasures in heaven." (Matthew 6:19-24; Luke 12:33-34; Colossians 3:2-4) (See p. 80)

17. We must not be worried about the matters of this life. (Matthew 6:25-34; Luke 12:22-30; Philippians 4:6) (See p. 84)

18. We must seek first "the kingdom of God, and His righteousness." (Matthew 6:33; Luke 12:31-32; Colossians 3:1) (See p. 88)

19. We must not be judgmental toward others, but must humbly seek after their spiritual growth. (Matthew 7:1-5: Luke 6:37, 41-42) (See p. 89)

20. We must not give that which is holy and precious unto those who fiercely oppose it. (Matthew 7:6) (See p. 93)

21. We must continue in a fervent and faith-filled prayer life. (Matthew 7:7-11; Luke 11:5-13; 18:1-7; Romans 12:12; Ephesians 6:18; Philippians 4:6; Colossians 4:2; 1 Thessalonians 5:17; James 1:6-8; Jude 1:20) (See p. 93)

22. We must do unto others what we would want them to do unto us. (Matthew 7:12; Luke 6:31) (See p. 99)

23. We must examine ourselves and be certain that we have entered in at the narrow gate through faith and are truly saved in Christ. (Matthew 7:13-14; Luke 13:23-30; 2 Corinthians 13:5) (See p. 100)

24. We must beware of false prophets, who will appear good outwardly, but who will inwardly be as "ravening wolves." (Matthew 7:15-20; Jude 1:17-18) (See p. 102)

25. We must learn the heart of our Lord to show compassion and mercy toward those in sin. (Matthew 9:9-13; Jude 1:22) (See p. 104)

26. We must be praying that our Lord will send forth more laborers into His harvest. (Matthew 9:37-38; Luke 10:1-2) (See p. 107)

27. We ourselves must go forth as laborers into our Lord's harvest, preaching the gospel unto the lost. (Matthew 10:6-7; Mark 16:15; Luke 24:47-48; Jude 1:23) (See p. 108)

28. As we go forth with the gospel, we must be "wise as serpents," but "harmless as doves." (Matthew 10:16) (See p. 109)

29. As we go forth with the gospel, we must beware the persecutions of men, fleeing these persecutions and preaching the gospel in the new places into which we flee. (Matthew 10:17-18, 21-25) (See p. 110)

30. As we go forth with the gospel, we must trust the Holy Spirit to guide our words when we are delivered up before governing officials. (Matthew 10:19-20; Mark 13:11; Luke 12:11-12; 21:10-15) (See p. 111)

31. As we go forth with the gospel, we must be on our guard over our hearts and behavior that we might not walk in fear of the oppositions and persecutions of men. (Matthew 10:26, 28-31; Mark 13:9-10; Luke 12:4-9; 21:16-19; Philippians 1:28; Revelation 2:9-10) (See p. 113)

32. As we go forth with the gospel, we must boldly preach the truth of the Lord our God and Savior. (Matthew 10:27) (See p. 116)

33. As we go forth with the gospel, we must walk in the fear of the Lord our God and heavenly Father. (Matthew 10:28-31; Luke 12:5) (See p. 117)

34. We must come unto the Lord Jesus Christ in faith as our only spiritual Help and Hope. (Matthew 11:28) (See p. 118)

35. We must actively and purposefully take our Lord's yoke upon us and learn of Him in our daily Christian walk. (Matthew 11:29-30) (See p. 119)

36. We must understand that what comes out of our hearts and mouths is that which defiles us. (Matthew 15:10-20; Mark 7:14-23) (See p. 121)

37. We must take heed and beware of the doctrine of the Pharisees and Sadducees, that is – the doctrine of hypocrisy. (Matthew 16:1-12; Mark 8:11-15; Luke 12:1) (See p. 124)

38. We must deny ourselves, take up our cross daily, and follow our Lord. (Matthew 16:21-27; Mark 8:31-38; Luke 9:23-26; John 12:23-26) (See p. 125)

39. We must sever and cast away anything in our lives that would cause a little child to stumble spiritually. (Matthew 18:1-9; Mark 9:42-48) (See p. 130)

40. We must take heed that we not despise one of these little ones. (Matthew 18:10-14) (See p. 133)

41. We must follow our Lord's proscribed pattern for reconciliation when a fellow believer has trespassed against us. (Matthew 18:15-17) (See p. 134)

42. We must ever be willing to forgive our fellow believers who sin against us. (Matthew 18:21-35; Luke 17:3-4; Ephesians 4:32; Colossians 3:13; Philemon 1:18-21) (See p. 136)

43. We must not allow anything of this world to divide our marriage relationships. (Matthew 19:4-6) (See p. 138)

44. We must ever help the little children to come unto Christ and never hinder them from coming unto Him. (Matthew 19:13-15; Luke 18:15-17) (See p. 140)

45. When we are in a leadership role, we must lead by being the minister and servant of others. (Matthew 20:20-28; Mark 9:33-37; 10:35-45; Luke 22:24-27) (See p. 141)

46. We must pay our taxes. (Matthew 22:15-22; Mark 12:13-17; Luke 20:20-26) (See p. 143)

47. We must love the Lord our God with all our heart, soul, mind, and strength. (Matthew 22:37-38; Mark 12:29-30) (See p. 145)

48. We must love our neighbor as ourselves without hypocrisy, working no ill whatsoever to our neighbor. (Matthew 22:39-40; Mark 12:30; Romans 12:9; 13:8-10; 1 Timothy 1:5) (See p. 147)

49. We must keep the religious standards that are set before us, but must not be hypocrites in so doing. (Matthew 23:1-7) (See p. 150)

50. We must not seek to be exalted before others, but must humble ourselves to serve others. (Matthew 23:8-12; Luke 14:7-14; John 13:12-17) (See p. 151)

51. We must repent of our hypocrisy and must seek to be cleansed from the heart out. (Matthew 23:25-26) (See p. 153)

52. We must not be deceived by anyone into following a false Christ. (Matthew 24:4-5; Mark 13:5-6; Luke 21:8) (See p. 154)

53. We must not be troubled in heart at the signs of the times. (Matthew 24:6-8; Mark 13:7-8; Luke 21:9) (See p. 156)

54. We must watch and be ready for our Lord's coming through faithful obedience to His will. (Matthew 24:42-46; Luke 12:35-40; 21:34-36; 1 Thessalonians 5:1-6; Titus 2:11-13; Jude 1:21) (See p. 157)

55. We must regularly practice the Lord's Supper in remembrance of His death until He come. (Matthew 26:26-28; Mark 14:22-24; Luke 22:19-20; 1 Corinthians 11:23-26) (See p. 159)

56. We must faithfully watch and pray so that we do not fail in the time of temptation. (Matthew 26:41; Mark 14:38; Luke 22:40, 46) (See p. 161)

57. We must go forth as laborers into our Lord's harvest, teaching others to follow our Lord Jesus Christ from conversion to spiritual maturity. (Matthew 28:18-20) (See p. 162)

58. We must take heed that we hear the message of God's Word with honest and good hearts. (Mark 4:1-25; Luke 8:4-18; Revelation 2:7, 11, 17, 29; 3:6, 13, 22) (See p. 165)

59. At times we must come apart from the ordeals of public ministry in order to rest. (Mark 6:30-32) (See p. 169)

60. We must not forbid those who truly minister for Christ's sake, even though they may not directly join with us in ministry. (Mark 9:38-41; Luke 9:49-50) (See p. 170)

61. We must maintain a spiritually pure and morally preserving character in the attitudes and motives of our hearts. (Mark 9:50) (See p. 171)

62. We must have peace one with another as much as we are able. (Mark 9:50; Romans 12:18; 14:19; 2 Corinthians 13:11; Colossians 3:15; 1 Thessalonians 5:13; Hebrews 12:14; 1 Peter 3:11) (See p. 172)

63. We must pray with fullness of faith in God our heavenly Father. (Mark 11:19-24) (See p. 174)

64. We must have a heart of forgiveness toward others when we pray. (Mark 11:25-26) (See p. 175)

65. We must beware of those who love the recognition and honor of others, who take advantage of others for selfish gain, and who are hypocritical in religious matters. (Mark 12:38-40; Luke 20:45-47) (See p. 176)

66. We must watch and be ready for our Lord's coming through a faithful and fervent prayer life. (Mark 13:32-37; Luke 21:34-36; 1 Peter 4:7) (See p. 178)

67. We must be merciful, even as our heavenly Father is merciful. (Luke 6:36; 10:37; Colossians 3:12) (See p. 179)

68. We must have a forgiving heart toward those who sin against us. (Luke 6:37) (See p. 181)

69. We must have a giving heart toward those in need. (Luke 6:38; Romans 12:13; 2 Corinthians 8:1-15, 24; 9:6-11; Hebrews 13:16) (See p. 181)

70. We must rejoice above all else because our names are written in heaven. (Luke 10:17-20) (See p. 185)

71. We must take heed to our heart attitude and beware that covetousness not enter therein. (Luke 12:13-21; 1 Timothy 6:9-11; Hebrews 13:5) (See p. 185)

72. We must recognize that a life of obedient service to our Lord is nothing more than our duty. (Luke 17:7-10) (See p. 188)

73. We must not allow the place in which God's people assemble for worship to become a place for merchandizing. (John 2:15-17) (See p. 189)

74. We must decrease, while our Lord must increase. (John 3:27-30) (See p. 190)

75. We must worship the Lord our God "in spirit and in truth." (John 4:21-24) (See p. 193)

76. We must love one another as our Lord Jesus Christ has loved us, with purity and fervency of heart. (John 13:34-35; 15:12-13, 17; Ephesians 5:2; Colossians 3:14; 1 Thessalonians 4:9-10; Hebrews 13:1; 1 Peter 1:22; 2:17; 4:8; 1 John 3:10-18, 23; 4:7-11; 16-21; 2 John 1:5-6) (See p. 195)

77. We must not allow our hearts to become troubled, but must set our trust in our Lord. (John 14:1, 27; 16:33; 1 Pet. 3:14-15) (See p. 199)

78. We must keep our Lord's commandments to demonstrate our love for Him. (John 14:15, 21, 23) (See p. 201)

79. We must be abiding in our Lord Jesus Christ through faith, and must allow Him to be abiding in us. (John 15:4-6; Romans 13:14; Colossians 2:6; 1 John 2:27-28) (See p. 202)

80. We must abide in our Lord's loving fellowship by keeping His commandments. (John 15:9-10; Jude 1:21) (See p. 204)

81. When the world hates us who serve our Lord, we must not be surprised, but must remember that it first hated our Lord Himself. (John 15:18-25; 1 Peter 4:12-14; 1 John 3:13) (See p. 204)

82. When we pray, we must ask of the Father in our Lord's name. (John 16:24-25) (See p. 206)

83. The lost sinner must know and believe that Jesus Christ is the only Savior. (Acts 4:10-12; 13:38-39) (See p. 207)

84. We must choose out Spirit-filled men of godly wisdom and integrity to serve as deacons. (Acts 6:3) (See p. 207)

85. We must repent of the wickedness of selfish thinking rather than spiritual thinking, and must seek God's forgiveness thereof. (Acts 8:14-24) (See p. 208)

86. As we go forth with the gospel, we must trust the Holy Spirit to guide us unto the right place and the right people. (Acts 8:26-29; 10:19-20; 16:6-10) (See p. 209)

87. We must be willing to separate unto the ministry those whom the Holy Spirit calls. (Acts 13:1-3) (See p. 210)

88. Those who are called unto pastoral ministry must take heed to themselves and to the flock that they feed the flock according to the Word and will of God, taking the spiritual oversight thereof with a willingness of heart and with a burden to edify. (Acts 20:28-31; Colossians 4:17; 1 Peter 5:1-2) (See p. 211)

89. We must recognize that we are spiritually "dead indeed unto sin, but alive unto God through Jesus Christ our Lord." (Romans 6:11) (See p. 212)

90. We must not yield ourselves and our members to obey the lusts of sin in our daily living. (Romans 6:12-13; 1 Thessalonians 4:4-5) (See p. 216)

91. We must yield ourselves and our members to obey the will of God in our daily living. (Romans 6:13; 6:19; 12:1; 1 Thessalonians 4:4; 1 Peter 3:15) (See p. 217)

92. We Gentiles must not be high minded against the unbelieving nation of Israel. (Romans 11:18-25) (See p. 218)

93. We Gentiles must walk in the fear of the Lord our God, beholding His goodness and severity in relation to our salvation. (Romans 11:20-23) (See p. 219)

94. We must not be conformed unto this world. (Romans 12:2; Ephesians 4:17-19; 5:3-7) (See p. 220)

95. We must be transformed by the renewing of our mind. (Romans 12:2) (See p. 222)

96. We must not think highly of ourselves. (Romans 12:3) (See p. 223)

97. We must be both dependent and diligent in fulfilling the ministry responsibility unto which the Lord our God has called us, doing all for the glory of the Lord our God. (Romans 12:3-8; 1 Timothy 4:14; 2 Timothy 1:6; 1 Peter 4:10-11) (See p. 226)

98. We must "abhor that which is evil" and "cleave to that which is good." (Romans 12:9; 1 Peter 3:11) (See p. 231)

99. We must have kind affection for our fellow brothers and sisters in Christ. (Romans 12:10) (See p. 232)

100. We must prefer others in honor. (Romans 12:10) (See p. 233)

101. We must not be slothful in our responsibilities, but fervent, ever motivated by service to our Lord. (Romans 12:11) (See p. 233)

102. We must ever rejoice in our hope as believers. (Romans 12:12) (See p. 236)

103. We must patiently and joyfully remain faithful in the will and work of God through the tribulations of this life. (Romans 12:12; Hebrews 12:1; James. 1:2-4; 5:10-11) (See p. 238)

104. We must be "given to hospitality." (Romans 12:13; Hebrews 13:2; 1 Peter 4:9) (See p. 242)

105. We must maintain a unity of care and compassion for one another as fellow believers. (Romans 12:15; 1 Peter 3:8) (See p. 243)

106. We must maintain a Spirit-filled unity of mindset and love for, toward, and with one another as fellow believers in accord with the will of our Lord Jesus Christ. (Romans 12:16; 1 Corinthians 1:10; 2 Corinthians 13:11; Ephesians 4:3; Philippians 2:1-2; 3:15-16) (See p. 244)

107. We must not set our focus upon high honors among men, but must willingly abide with the lowly. (Romans 12:16) (See p. 248)

108. We must not think highly of, or trust in our own wisdom. (Romans 12:16) (See p. 249)

109. We must purposefully pursue and perform that which is good, right, true, and honest in the sight of all men. (Romans 12:17; Galatians 6:10; 1 Thessalonians 5:15; Titus 3:1, 8, 14; 1 Peter 2:11-12, 17; 3:11) (See p. 250)

110. We must submit ourselves unto our government authority. (Romans 13:1-5; Titus 3:1; 1 Peter 2:13-17) (See p. 251)

111. We must render unto our government authority what is due unto them in tribute, custom, respect, and honor. (Romans 13:6-7) (See p. 254)

112. We must cast off all the works of our sinful flesh. (Romans 13:11-13; Ephesians 4:22, 25, 31; 5:3-4; Colossians 3:5-10; Titus 2:11-12; Hebrews 12:1, 15-16; James 1:21; 1 Peter 2:1, 11) (See p. 255)

113. We must put on the spiritual armor of righteousness. (Romans 13:12; Ephesians 4:24; 6:11, 13-17; 1 Thessalonians 5:7-8) (See p. 259)

114. We must walk honestly (or, honorably) before our Lord and toward others, having a good conscience before God and having a good conversation (behavior) before others. (Romans 13:13; 1 Peter 3:16-17) (See p. 265)

115. We must not make any provision for the flesh to fulfill its sinful lusts. (Romans 13:14) (See p. 266)

116. We must not be judgmental toward others over questionable matters. (Romans 14:1-4) (See p. 267)

117. We must each have full faith before the Lord concerning a questionable matter. (Romans 14:5-9, 22-23) (See p. 268)

118. We must never cause "a stumblingblock or an occasion to fall" for a fellow believer by participating in a questionable matter. (Romans 14:13-18, 20-21; 15:1; 1 Corinthians 8:4-13) (See p. 269)

119. We must ever pursue the spiritual edification of our fellow believers. (Romans 14:19; 15:1-3; 1 Corinthians 10:23-24) (See p. 271)

120. We must receive one another as fellow believers with an attitude of godly love and unity. (Romans 15:7; 16:1-2, 16; 2 Corinthians 13:12-13; Philippians 4:21; Colossians 4:15; 1 Thessalonians 5:26; 2 Timothy 4:19; Titus 3:15; Hebrews 13:24; 1 Peter 5:14; 3 John 1:5-8, 14) (See p. 271)

121. We must fervently and faithfully pray for those who minister in the work of the Lord. (Romans 15:30-32; Ephesians 6:18-20; Colossians 4:3-4; 1 Thessalonians 5:25; 2 Thessalonians 3:1-2; Hebrews 13:18-19) (See p. 273)

122. We must mark and avoid those who "cause divisions and offenses" that are contrary to the truth of God's Word. (Romans 16:17-18; 1 Timothy 6:3-5; 2 Timothy 3:1-9; 4:14-15; Titus 3:10-11; 2 John 1:7-11) (See p. 274)

123. We must not glory in ourselves, but must glory alone in the Lord Jesus Christ our Savior. (1 Corinthians 1:17-31; 2 Corinthians 10:17-18) (See p. 277)

124. We must take heed how we build upon the foundation of our salvation in Christ. (1 Corinthians 3:5-15) (See p. 278)

125. We must become foolish in the wisdom of this world that we may grow in the wisdom of God. (1 Corinthians 3:18-20) (See p. 280)

126. We must not glory in the human leadership that the Lord our God has placed over us, but must view them simply as the servants of Christ and the stewards of God's Word. (1 Corinthians 3:21 - 4:6) (See p. 280)

127. We must be followers of our God-given leadership and of other faithful believers as they follow after our Lord Jesus Christ. (1 Corinthians 4:14-17; 11:1; Philippians 3:17-19; 4:9; Hebrews 13:7) (See p. 282)

128. We must put away from among us and not keep company with fellow believers who are living a lifestyle of immorality. (1 Corinthians 5:1-13) (See p. 283)

129. We must flee the sin of fornication. (1 Corinthians 6:12-20; 10:8; 1 Thessalonians 4:3) (See p. 285)

130. We must glorify God in our bodies and in our spirits because they are God's. (1 Corinthians 6:20; 10:31) (See p. 287)

131. Married couples must regularly render unto one another the due benevolence of sexual relations. (1 Corinthians 7:1-5) (See p. 287)

132. Divorced individuals must remain unmarried or be reconciled to their original spouse. (1 Corinthians 7:10-11) (See p. 289)

133. A believer who is married to an unbeliever must not pursue after a divorce, but must not fight against a divorce if the unbeliever desires it. (1 Corinthians 7:12-16) (See p. 289)

134. We must materially take care of those who minister God's Word unto us. (1 Corinthians 9:3-14; Galatians 6:6; 1 Timothy 5:17-18) (See p. 290)

135. We must pursue the Christian life with spiritual discipline, keeping the desires of our body under subjection to our Lord's cause. (1 Corinthians 9:24-27) (See p. 291)

136. We must not lust after evil (selfish) things. (1 Corinthians 10:6) (See p. 292)

137. We must flee the sin of idolatry. (1 Corinthians 10:7, 14; 1 John 5:21) (See p. 294)

138. We must not tempt (provoke) our Lord Jesus Christ by questioning His presence, His purpose, His power, or His promise. (1 Corinthians 10:9) (See p. 294)

139. We must not murmur or complain about anything. (1 Corinthians 10:10; Philippians 2:14-16) (See p. 295)

140. We must not think highly of our spiritual condition lest we fall through the sin of pride. (1 Corinthians 10:12) (See p. 296)

141. We must limit our personal rights and liberties by the conscience of the lost around us that we might not offend them spiritually and thus hinder them from coming unto salvation. (1 Corinthians 10:25-33) (See p. 296)

142. A woman who ministers in the public services of the church must do so in a manner that honors the headship of her husband. (1 Corinthians 11:3-10) (See p. 297)

143. We must be motivated by charity (godly love in behavior toward others) in all of our ministry efforts. (1 Corinthians 14:1; 16:14) (See p. 298)

144. We must use our gifts of ministry for the purpose of edification. (1 Corinthians 12:31; 14:1-5, 12, 26) (See p. 300)

145. We must do all things "decently and in order" in the ministry of the church. (1 Corinthians 14:40) (See p. 301)

146. We must awaken out of our spiritual lethargy unto a committed pursuit of righteousness. (1 Corinthians 15:34) (See p. 301)

147. We must be "stedfast, unmoveable, always abounding in the work of the Lord." (1 Corinthians 15:58; 16:13; 2 Timothy 4:5; Hebrews 6:10-12; Revelation 2:24-25; 3:11) (See p. 302)

148. We must give materially unto the work of the Lord "upon the first day of the week" according as God has prospered us. (1 Corinthians 16:1-2) (See p. 304)

149. We must not despise faithful ministers of the Lord, but must conduct them forth in peace. (1 Corinthians 16:10-11) (See p. 305)

150. We must submit ourselves to those who are faithful ministers in the work of the Lord. (1 Corinthians 16:15-16; Hebrews 13:17) (See p. 306)

151. We must highly commend and honor those who are faithful ministers of the Lord. (1 Corinthians 16:17-18; Philippians 2:25-30; 1 Thessalonians 5:12-13; Hebrews 13:24) (See p. 307)

152. We must consider those who do not love our Lord Jesus Christ to be accursed. (1 Corinthians 16:22) (See p. 308)

153. We must forgive repentant believers, comforting them and confirming our love toward them. (2 Corinthians 2:6-11) (See p. 309)

154. We must not be joined in fellowship and communion with unbelievers. (2 Corinthians 6:14-18) (See p. 310)

155. We must have no part whatsoever with spiritually unclean things. (2 Corinthians 6:17-18; Ephesians 5:11-12; 2 Timothy 2:19, 21-22; Jude 1:23) (See p. 311)

156. We must cleanse ourselves through repentance from all spiritual filthiness in our actions and attitudes. (2 Corinthians 7:1; James 4:8-9) (See p. 312)

157. We must be perfect by surrendering to our Lord's perfecting work within us. (2 Corinthians 13:11) (See p. 312)

158. We must be of good comfort by receiving our Lord's gift of comfort for us. (2 Corinthians 13:11) (See p. 313)

159. We must consider those who preach any "gospel" other than the Biblical gospel to be accursed. (Galatians 1:8-9) (See p. 314)

160. We must stand fast in the spiritual liberty of salvation through faith in Christ alone, and not be entangled with the spiritual bondage of justification through the works of the Law. (Galatians 5:1-6) (See p. 315)

161. We must not use our spiritual liberty for an occasion to the flesh. (Galatians 5:13) (See p. 317)

162. We must serve one another by love. (Galatians 5:13-14) (See p. 318)

163. We must take heed that we "be not consumed one of another" through backbiting and harshness. (Galatians 5:15) (See p. 319)

164. We must walk after the Holy Spirit in order not to fulfill the desires of our flesh, but in order to walk in the wisdom of our Lord. (Galatians 5:16-25; Ephesians 5:18) (See p. 320)

165. We must not be "desirous of vain glory," and thereby "provoking one another" and "envying one another." (Galatians 5:26) (See p. 321)

166. We who walk in the Spirit must restore in the spirit of meekness a fellow believer who is overtaken by sin. (Galatians 6:1) (See p. 322)

167. We must lovingly bear one another's burdens. (Galatians 6:2) (See p. 323)

168. We must prove our own work before the Lord in bearing our own responsibilities from the Lord. (Galatians 6:3-5) (See p. 324)

169. We must not be deceived into thinking that we can get away with sowing unto our sinful flesh. (Galatians 6:7-8) (See p. 324)

170. We must not be weary in well doing because in due season we will reap reward. (Galatians 6:8-9; 2 Thessalonians 3:13; Hebrews 12:12-13) (See p. 326)

171. We must remember our lost spiritual condition before we were saved, and the way by which we were saved from that lost condition. (Ephesians 2:11-13) (See p. 327)

172. We must walk worthy of our eternal calling into the family and fellowship of God. (Ephesians 4:1, 17-21; 5:8) (See p. 328)

173. We must walk "with all lowliness and meekness." (Ephesians 4:1-2; Colossians 3:12; 1 Timothy 6:11; 1 Peter 5:5) (See p. 330)

174. We must walk "with longsuffering, forbearing one another in love." (Ephesians 4:1-2; Colossians 3:12-13; 1 Thessalonians 5:14) (See p. 330)

175. We must be renewed in the spirit of our mind. (Ephesians 4:23) (See p. 331)

176. We must put away all falsehood and "speak every man truth with his neighbor." (Ephesians 4:25; Colossians 3:9) (See p. 333)

177. We must be angry at unrighteousness, in a God-honoring manner, not in a self-serving manner. (Ephesians 4:26) (See p. 334)

178. We must not allow any anger to germinate through even one day into the sin of bitterness. (Ephesians 4:26-27; Hebrews 12:15) (See p. 335)

179. We must not steal, but must work with our hands "the thing which is good" in order that we might give to the needs of others. (Ephesians 4:28) (See p. 336)

180. We must not speak with corrupt communication, but only with "that which is good to the use of edifying." (Ephesians 4:29-30; Colossians 4:6) (See p. 337)

181. We must be kind to one another. (Ephesians 4:32; Colossians 3:12) (See p. 339)

182. We must be tenderhearted toward one another. (Ephesians 4:32) (See p. 340)

183. We must be followers (or, imitators) of the Lord our God. (Ephesians 5:1) (See p. 341)

184. We must reprove the works of darkness through our walk in light. (Ephesians 5:11, 13) (See p. 341)

185. We must walk carefully in wisdom and thereby redeem the time from this evil world. (Ephesians 5:15-16; Colossians 4:5) (See p. 342)

186. We must understand the will of our Lord in order to walk in wisdom. (Ephesians 5:17) (See p. 343)

187. We must not be drunk with alcohol. (Ephesians 5:18) (See p. 343)

188. We must sing in joyful praise unto the Lord our God, both with one another publicly and from our hearts privately. (Ephesians 5:19; Colossians 3:16) (See p. 344)

189. We must give thanks always in and for all things unto God our heavenly Father in the name of our Lord Jesus Christ. (Ephesians 5:20; Philippians 4:6; Colossians 3:17; 4:2; 1 Thessalonians 5:18; Hebrews 13:15) (See p. 346)

190. We must submit ourselves "one to another in the fear of God" and in godly humility. (Ephesians 5:21; 1 Peter 5:5) (See p. 347)

191. The wife must submit herself under her husband's headship in everything as unto the Lord with a meek and quiet spirit of reverence toward her husband. (Ephesians 5:22-24, 33; Colossians 3:18; Titus 2:5; 1 Peter 3:1-4) (See p. 348)

192. The husband must love his wife as Christ loved the church, giving up of himself to nourish her, cherish her, dwell at harmony with her, and give honor unto her. (Ephesians 5:25-33; Colossians 3:19; 1 Peter 3:7) (See p. 352)

193. Children must ever maintain a spirit of honor toward their father and mother, obeying their parents while they abide under their parents' authority. (Ephesians 6:1-3; Colossians 3:20) (See p. 357)

194. Fathers must not provoke their children to wrath, lest they be discouraged, but must "bring them up in the nurture and admonition of the Lord." (Ephesians 6:4; Colossians 3:21) (See p. 359)

195. Servants (or, employees) must be obedient and submissive to their masters (or, employers) in all things as unto the Lord with honor and respect, not argumentatively or grudgingly, but pleasantly and heartily, not with eye service, but with commitment of heart, not embezzling, but with faithful responsibility. (Ephesians 6:5-8; Colossians 3:22-25; 1 Timothy 6:1-2; Titus 2:9-10; 1 Peter 2:18) (See p. 362)

196. Masters (or, employers) must treat their servants (or, employees) with good will in submission to the Lord their Master, not being quick tempered or mean spirited, but being just and fair. (Ephesians 6:9; Colossians 4:1) (See p. 367)

197. We must be "strong in the Lord, and in the power of His might." (Ephesians 6:10; 2 Timothy 2:1) (See p. 369)

198. We must be persevering in prayer for our fellow believers. (Ephesians 6:18) (See p. 372)

199. We must have our love toward one another to abound yet more and more in Spirit-filled discernment. (Philippians 1:9; 1 Thessalonians 3:12; 4:9-10) (See p. 374)

200. We must approve with full conviction of heart and with full commitment of life those things that are spiritually excellent. (Philippians 1:10; 1 Thessalonians 5:21) (See p. 375)

201. We must walk in Spirit-filled sincerity (as opposed to flesh-filled hypocrisy), being filled with the fruits of righteousness. (Philippians 1:10-11) (See p. 376)

202. We must conduct ourselves in a manner that is worthy of and adorning to the gospel of our Lord and Savior Jesus Christ. (Philippians 1:27) (See p. 377)

203. We must stand fast in Spirit-filled unity against suffering and persecution for our Lord's sake. (Philippians 1:27-30) (See p. 380)

204. We must strive together in Spirit-filled unity "for the faith of the gospel." (Philippians 1:27) (See p. 381)

205. We must do nothing "through strife or vainglory." (Philippians 2:3) (See p. 382)

206. We must in godly humility esteem others as better than ourselves. (Philippians 2:3) (See p. 382)

207. We must not be self-centered, but must be others centered. (Philippians 2:4) (See p. 383)

208. We must have the same servant-mindedness as our Lord Jesus Christ. (Philippians 2:5-8) (See p. 384)

209. We must work out of our own salvation with fear and trembling by serving the Lord our God "with reverence and godly fear." (Philippians 2:12-13; Hebrews 12:28-29; 1 Peter 1:17-19; 2:17) (See p. 385)

210. We must rejoice in our Lord always. (Philippians 3:1; 4:4; 1 Thessalonians 5:16) (See p. 388)

211. We must beware of those who put their confidence in the flesh. (Philippians 3:2-14) (See p. 388)

212. We must help and assist fellow believers who faithfully labor in the ministry of evangelism and edification. (Philippians 4:3) (See p. 390)

213. We must maintain a moderate attitude of gentleness toward and before every one. (Philippians 4:5; Titus 3:2) (See p. 391)

214. We must set our thoughts on whatever things are true, honest, just, pure, lovely, of good report, and of true virtue and praise. (Philippians 4:8) (See p. 392)

215. As we abide and walk in our Lord, we must be rooted and built up spiritually in Him. (Colossians 2:6-7; 2 Peter 3:18) (See p. 393)

216. As we abide and walk in our Lord, we must be established in the faith. (Colossians 2:6-7; Jude 1:20) (See p. 393)

217. As we abide and walk in our Lord, we must be abounding with thanksgiving. (Colossians 2:6-7) (See p. 394)

218. We must beware lest anyone spoil us "through philosophy and vain deceit." (Colossians 2:8) (See p. 395)

219. We must not allow anyone to judge us according to the Old Testament religious system. (Colossians 2:16-17) (See p. 396)

220. We must not allow anyone to deceive us out of our spiritual reward through the false humility of man-made religious regulations. (Colossians 2:18-23) (See p. 397)

221. We must be thankful toward one another. (Colossians 3:15) (See p. 398)

222. We must "let the word of Christ dwell" in us "richly in all wisdom." (Colossians 3:16; 1 John 2:24) (See p. 399)

223. We must spiritually teach and admonish one another through the ministry of singing. (Colossians 3:16) (See p. 400)

224. We must give attendance unto reading God's Word in our church services. (Colossians 4:16; 1 Thessalonians 5:27; 1 Timothy 4:13) (See p. 400)

225. We must "abound more and more" in a walk of obedience that pleases the Lord our God. (1 Thessalonians 4:1-2) (See p. 401)

226. We must not defraud (cheat) our fellow believers in any matter. (1 Thessalonians 4:6, 8) (See p. 401)

227. We must study to be quiet in doing our business and working for our own provision. (1 Thessalonians 4:11-12; 2 Thessalonians 3:10-12) (See p. 402)

228. We must comfort and exhort one another through the truth of our Lord's coming for His own in the rapture. (1 Thessalonians 4:13-18; 5:9-11) (See p. 403)

229. We must warn our fellow believers who are "unruly." (1 Thessalonians 5:14) (See p. 404)

230. We must comfort our fellow believers who are discouraged. (1 Thessalonians 5:14) (See p. 404)

231. We must support our fellow believers who are weak. (1 Thessalonians 5:14) (See p. 405)

232. We must not quench the work of the indwelling Holy Spirit in our hearts. (1 Thessalonians 5:19) (See p. 405)

233. We must not despise the truths of God's Word, but must desire and receive the truths of God's Word wholeheartedly and submissively. (1 Thessalonians 5:20; Hebrews 13:22; James 1:21; 1 Peter 2:2) (See p. 406)

234. We must abstain from every appearance by which evil may seek to enter our lives. (1 Thessalonians 5:22) (See p. 407)

235. We must not become deceived, shaken in mind, and troubled in heart that the day of Christ has already come upon us. (2 Thessalonians 2:1-3) (See p. 407)

236. We must stand fast upon and hold firm to the truths that we have been taught from God's Word. (2 Thessalonians 2:15; 2 Timothy 1:13-14; 3:14-17; Hebrews 2:1-4) (See p. 409)

237. We must withdraw ourselves from fellow believers who walk disorderly, living a lifestyle that is not in accord with the teachings of God's Word. (2 Thessalonians 3:6, 14) (See p. 410)

238. We must not view fellow believers who walk in a disorderly, disobedient lifestyle as enemies, but must admonish them as brethren in Christ. (2 Thessalonians 3:15) (See p. 411)

239. Those in pastoral leadership must authoritatively forbid anyone from teaching anything contrary to the doctrine of God's Word in the ministry for which those leaders have God-given responsibility. (1 Timothy 1:3-4; 2 Timothy 2:14, 16-18, Titus 1:10-14) (See p. 411)

240. We must faithfully fight the good fight of faith, "holding faith and a good conscience," enduring hardness "as a good soldier of Jesus Christ," and not being entangled "with the affairs of this life." (1 Timothy 1:18-19; 6:12-16; 2 Timothy 2:3-4) (See p. 413)

241. We must fervently and faithfully pray and give thanks for all of the people around us in our lives. (1 Timothy 2:19) (See p. 415)

242. We must fervently and faithfully pray and give thanks for all of our government officials. (1 Timothy 2:1-2) (See p. 415)

243. Men of God must take the leadership in public prayers with holiness of character and "without wrath and doubting." (1 Timothy 2:8) (See p. 416)

244. Women of God must "adorn themselves in modest apparel, with shamefacedness and sobriety." (1 Timothy 2:9; 1 Peter 3:3-4) (See p. 417)

245. Women of God must adorn themselves with godly behavior and good works. (1 Timothy 2:9--10; Titus 2:3-5) (See p. 418)

246. Women must not teach or have authority over men within the church ministry, but must learn from and submit to the male leadership of the church ministry. (1 Corinthians 14:34-35; 1 Timothy 2:11-15) (See p. 419)

247. We must choose for the office of the pastorate those who meet the Biblical qualifications. (1 Timothy 3:1-7; Titus 1:5-9) (See p. 421)

248. We must choose for the office of the deaconate those who meet the Biblical qualifications. (1 Timothy 3:8-13) (See p. 422)

249. We must refuse to involve ourselves with doctrines that are rooted in philosophical speculations, rather than in Biblical revelation. (1 Timothy 4:7; 6:20-21; 2 Timothy 2:16-18; 2:23; Titus 3:9; Hebrews 13:9-10) (See p. 423)

250. We must exercise ourselves unto and follow after godliness and true holiness, ever remembering that this world shall be consumed with fire and that we look forward to "new heavens and a new earth," and ever seeking to be found of our Lord "in peace, without spot, and blameless." (1 Timothy 4:7-10; 6:11; 2 Timothy 2:22; Titus 2:11-12; Hebrews 12:14; 1 Peter 1:14-16; 2 Peter 3:11-14) (See p. 425)

251. Those who are called to pastoral ministry must preach and teach the whole counsel of God's Word, reproving, rebuking, and exhorting "with all longsuffering and doctrine." (1 Timothy 4:11, 13; 6:2; 2 Timothy 4:1-4; Titus 2:15; 3:8) (See p. 427)

252. Those who are called to pastoral ministry must not allow anyone in the flock to despise them as the ministers of God's Word. (1 Timothy 4:12; Titus 2:15) (See p. 429)

253. Those who are called to pastoral ministry must be an example of godliness unto the members of the flock. (1 Timothy 4:12; Titus 2:7-8; 1 Peter 5:3) (See p. 429)

254. Those who are called to pastoral ministry must meditate daily upon the truths of God's Word and must give themselves wholly to learn the wisdom of God's Word. (1 Timothy 4:15) (See p. 430)

255. Those who are called to pastoral ministry must take heed unto themselves to continue learning, obeying, and teaching the doctrine of God's Holy Word. (1 Timothy 4:16) (See p. 431)

256. We must not verbally beat down one another in correction, but must lovingly entreat one another as family members. (1 Timothy 5:1-2) (See p. 432)

257. As a church body, we must financially support those widows who meet the Biblical qualifications. (1 Timothy 5:3-16) (See p. 432)

258. Personally, we must financially help the older members of our family who are in financial need. (1 Timothy 5:4, 7-8, 16) (See p. 433)

259. Younger widows and younger women should pursue marriage and home responsibilities. (1 Timothy 5:11-14) (See p. 434)

260. We must regard pastoral leadership who are godly in leadership and faithful in ministry as being worthy of both spiritual and financial honor. (1 Timothy 5:17-18) (See p. 434)

261. We must not receive a public or official accusation against a pastoral leader unless it is accompanied by two or three witnesses. (1 Timothy 5:19) (See p. 436)

262. We must publicly rebuke pastoral leadership that is found guilty of significant (especially disqualifying) sin. (1 Timothy 5:20) (See p. 436)

263. We must not handle matters either of honor or of rebuke for pastoral leadership with partiality. (1 Timothy 5:21) (See p. 436)

264. We must be slow and careful in ordaining men for roles of pastoral leadership. (1 Timothy 5:22, 24-25) (See p. 437)

265. We must be content with such things as we have, recognizing that we cannot take the things of this life with us into the life to come, and recognizing that our Lord Himself is all-sufficient for our lives. (1 Timothy 6:6-8; Hebrews 13:5-6) (See p. 438)

266. Those who are rich in the things of this world must view their riches as a gift from God to be used according to the will of God. (1 Timothy 6:17-19) (See p. 439)

267. We must not be ashamed "of the testimony of our Lord" or of those who are suffering for that testimony. (2 Timothy 1:7-8) (See p. 439)

268. We must be willing partakers "of the afflictions of the gospel according to the power of God." (2 Timothy 1:7-8) (See p. 440)

269. Those who are called to pastoral ministry must commit the truths of God's Word unto other faithful men, who may in turn teach others also. (2 Timothy 2:2) (See p. 441)

270. We must be diligent in studying and rightly dividing God's Word of truth. (2 Timothy 2:15) (See p. 441)

271. We must not strive with a contentious spirit about Biblical doctrine. (2 Timothy 2:24) (See p. 442)

272. We must teach the truths of God's Word unto others with a spirit of gentleness, patience, and meekness. (2 Timothy 2:24-26) (See p. 443)

273. We must conduct ourselves in a manner that is adorning to the sound doctrine of God's Holy Word. (Titus 2:1-6) (See p. 443)

274. We must consider and meditate upon the truth of our Lord Jesus Christ. (Hebrews 3:1; 12:2-3) (See p. 446)

275. We must take heed to our heart character and beware that our hearts not become hardened by a spirit of unbelief. (Hebrews 3:7-13) (See p. 449)

276. We must exhort one another daily not to be "hardened through the deceitfulness of sin," but to cleave unto our Lord and to pursue godly love and good works. (Hebrews 3:13; 10:24-25) (See p. 451)

277. We must take heed unto our heart that we not come short of our Lord's promised rest unto our souls due to our unbelief. (Hebrews 4:1, 9-11) (See p. 452)

278. We must hold fast the full assurance, daily walk, and public testimony of our faith in the Lord without wavering. (Hebrews 4:14; 10:23) (See p. 452)

279. We must come boldly unto God's throne of grace through prayer, "that we may obtain mercy, and find grace to help in time of need." (Hebrews 4:15-16) (See p. 453)

280. We must grow forward unto spiritual maturity by using God's Word to exercise our spiritual discernment. (Hebrews 5:12 - 6:2) (See p. 454)

281. We must draw near unto the Lord our God in spiritual fellowship "with a true heart in full assurance of faith." (Hebrews 10:19-22; James 4:8) (See p. 455)

282. We must not "forsake the assembling of ourselves together" for church services. (Hebrews 10:25) (See p. 456)

283. We must not cast away our godly confidence concerning the rewards of the life to come. (Hebrews 10:32-36) (See p. 456)

284. We must not despise or faint at the chastening of our Lord in our lives. (Hebrews 12:5-6) (See p. 457)

285. We must not rebel against the authoritative Word of our Lord Jesus Christ. (Hebrews 12:25-27) (See p. 458)

286. We must remember with compassion fellow believers who are suffering in prison or under persecution for the cause of Christ. (Hebrews 13:3) (See p. 460)

287. We must willingly and purposefully bear the reproach of Christ in being separated unto Christ and apart from the world. (Hebrews 13:12-14) (See p. 461)

288. We must purposefully allow God's work of patience to accomplish its perfecting work in our lives. (James 1:4; 5:10-11) (See p. 462)

289. We must ask humbly of God in prayer for wisdom when we recognize our lack thereof. (James 1:5) (See p. 463)

290. Believers who have learned humility through being materially poor must rejoice in the Lord's promise of exaltation for the humble. (James 1:9) (See p. 463)

291. Believers who are materially rich must rejoice when they experience circumstances that may teach them godly humility. (James 1:10-11) (See p. 464)

292. We must never indicate or imply that the Lord our God is the source for our temptations unto sin. (Also, by implication, we must never accept when any other indicates or implies that the Lord our God is the Source for temptation unto sin.) (James 1:13-14) (See p. 464)

293. We must not go astray into error in relation to the doctrine of God's goodness and the doctrine of sin's corruption. (James 1:16) (See p. 465)

294. We must be swift to hear, slow to speak, and slow to wrath. (James 1:19-20) (See p. 466)

295. We must be doers of God's Word, and not hearers only. (James 1:22-25) (See p. 466)

296. We must not attempt to join our walk of faith in our Lord Jesus Christ with the practice of showing partiality against others due simply to external considerations. (James 2:1) (See p. 467)

297. We must be careful both to speak and to act toward others in accord with God's law of love. (James 2:9-13) (See p. 468)

298. We must not pursue greater leadership and teaching authority than the Lord our God has granted to us. (James 3:1) (See p. 469)

299. We must not allow our communication both to be filled with praises toward God, yet also harsh words against others. (James 3:9-10) (See p. 470)

300. If we think ourselves to possess spiritual wisdom, then we must demonstrate it through the reality of good behavior and a meek spirit. (James 3:13) (See p. 471)

301. If we possess "bitter envying and strife" in the character of our hearts and lives, then we must stop glorying in our supposed wisdom, and thus lying "against the truth." (James 3:14) (See p. 472)

302. We must humbly submit ourselves in dependence upon and obedience to the Lord our God. (James 4:6-7; 10; 1 Peter 5:6-7) (See p. 473)

303. Having submitted ourselves unto the Lord our God, we must faithfully resist the spiritual attacks of our adversary the devil. (James 4:7; 1 Peter 5:6-9) (See p. 474)

304. We must not speak evil, harsh, biting words against one another. (James 4:11; Ephesians 4:31; 1 Peter 2:1; 3:10) (See p. 475)

305. We must not be presumptuous concerning our plans for the future, but must ever recognize the sovereignty of the Lord our God concerning the circumstances of our lives. (James 4:13-17) (See p. 475)

306. The wealthy of this world that have become arrogant in their wealth and oppressive over others should take serious heed concerning their future judgment (even to take heed unto repentance). (James 5:1-6) (See p. 477)

307. We must establish our hearts in patient endurance under the afflictions of this life with a focus upon the return of our Lord. (James 5:7-8) (See p. 478)

308. We must not hold grudges against one another. (James 5:9) (See p. 479)

309. We must follow the example of the Biblical prophets in suffering affliction with patient endurance. (James 5:10-11) (See p. 479)

310. If we are in circumstances of affliction, we must pray unto the Lord about it. (James 5:13) (See p. 480)

311. If we are in circumstances of happiness, we must sing psalms of praise unto our Lord. (James 5:13) (See p. 480)

312. If we are in circumstances of significant illness, we must call for the leadership of the church to pray over us. (James 5:14-15) (See p. 480)

313. We must confess unto one another the sinful faults that we have committed against them. (James 5:16) (See p. 481)

314. We must pray for the healing of our fellow brothers and sisters in Christ. (James 5:16) (See p. 481)

315. We must maintain a mindset of confident hope in our Lord's promises concerning our eternal future. (1 Peter 1:13) (See p. 482)

316. We must follow our Lord Jesus Christ's example of taking it patiently when we suffer wrongfully for righteousness' sake. (1 Peter 2:19-25) (See p. 483)

317. We must "be ready always to give an answer" concerning "the hope that is in us with meekness and fear." (1 Peter 3:15) (See p. 484)

318. We must maintain a Christ-like willingness to suffer for righteousness' sake in refusing to join in with the fleshly lusts of this world. (1 Peter 4:1-5) (See p. 485)

319. We must not behave so as to suffer punishment as a murderer, thief, evil doer, or "busybody in other men's matters." (1 Peter 4:15) (See p. 486)

320. When we suffer for righteousness' sake, we must "commit the keeping of our souls" unto the Lord our God "in well doing," completely trusting in His everlasting faithfulness and almighty power. (1 Peter 4:19) (See p. 487)

321. Those believers who are younger in age must submit themselves unto the spiritual maturity and wisdom of those believers who are older in age. (1 Peter 5:5) (See p. 487)

322. We must be diligent to grow forward unto spiritual maturity through the development of virtue, knowledge, temperance, patience, godliness, brotherly kindness, and charity. (2 Peter 1:5-7) (See p. 488)

323. We must remember that our Lord's longsuffering in not yet returning is because He is concerned for the repentance and salvation of lost souls. (2 Peter 3:15) (See p. 489)

324. We must beware that we not be "led away with the error of the wicked," and thereby fall away from our steadfastness in walking with and for our Lord. (2 Peter 3:17) (See p. 489)

325. We must walk after the example of our Lord Jesus Christ's walk, ever obeying God's Word and will in everything. (1 John 2:6) (See p. 490)

326. We must not love the world around us or the principle of selfishness that governs the world around us. (1 John 2:15-17) (See p. 490)

327. We must not be deceived into thinking that a person can be right with the Lord while walking in sin. (1 John 3:7) (See p. 491)

328. We must not believe every teaching or teacher, but must test every teaching and teacher by the doctrine of God's Word, whether they are the truth of God or the error of the antichrist. (1 John 4:1-6) (See p. 492)

329. When we see a fellow believer in sin, we must pray for his or her repentance, in order that he or she might be restored unto the abundant life. (1 John 5:16-17) (See p. 494)

330. We must not follow the example of believers who are evil, but must follow the example of believers who are good. (3 John 1:9-12) (See p. 494)

331. We must "earnestly contend for the faith which was once delivered unto the saints," that is – for the sound doctrine of God's Word. (Jude 1:3) (See p. 495)

332. We must repent of leaving our priority love for the Lord, and must return unto a faithful walk therein. (Revelation 2:5) (See p. 496)

333. We must repent of allowing false teachers to have freedom to teach their falsehood within our churches. (Revelation 2:14-16) (See p. 496)

334. We must repent of becoming spiritually dead, and must pursue spiritual revival in our lives. (Revelation 3:1-3, 15-20) (See p. 496)

THE
MEDITATION

This section provides some explanation and meditation for each of the commands that are listed in the instruction section of the book. I pray that all will be found "good to the use of edifying."

1. The lost sinner must repent of sin and believe the gospel of Jesus Christ unto eternal salvation.

Matthew 3:1-2 – "*In those days came John the Baptist, preaching in the wilderness of Judaea, and saying,* **Repent ye***: for the kingdom of heaven is at hand.*"

Mark 1:14-15 – "*Now after that John was put in prison, Jesus came into Galilee, preaching the gospel of the kingdom of God, and saying, The time is fulfilled, and the kingdom of God is at hand:* **repent ye, and believe the gospel***.*"

John 6:26-29 – "*Jesus answered them and said, Verily, verily, I say unto you, Ye seek me, not because ye saw the miracles, but because ye did eat of the loaves, and were filled. Labour not for the meat which perisheth, but for that meat which endureth unto everlasting life, which the Son of man shall give unto you: for him hath God the Father sealed. Then said they unto him, What shall we do, that we might work the works of God? Jesus answered and said unto them, This is the work of God,* **that ye believe on him whom he hath sent***.*"

John 7:37-39 – "*In the last day, that great day of the feast, Jesus stood and cried, saying,* **If any man thirst, let him come unto me, and drink. He that believeth on me***, as the scripture hath said, out of his belly shall flow rivers of living water. (But this spake he of the Spirit, which they that believe on him should receive: for the Holy Ghost was not yet given; because that Jesus was not yet glorified.)*"

John 12:35-36 – *"Then Jesus said unto them, Yet a little while is the light with you. Walk while ye have the light, lest darkness come upon you: for he that walketh in darkness knoweth not whither he goeth. While ye have light, **believe in the light**, that ye may be the children of light. These things spake Jesus, and departed, and did hide himself from them."*

Acts 3:19 – *"**Repent ye therefore, and be converted, that your sins may be blotted out**, when the times of refreshing shall come from the presence of the Lord."*

Acts 16:29-31 – *"Then he called for a light, and sprang in, and came trembling, and fell down before Paul and Silas, and brought them out, and said, Sirs, what must I do to be saved? And they said, **Believe on the Lord Jesus Christ, and thou shalt be saved, and thy house**."*

Acts 17:30 – *"And the times of this ignorance God winked at; **but now commandeth all men every where to repent**: because he hath appointed a day, in the which he will judge the world in righteousness by that man whom he hath ordained; whereof he hath given assurance unto all men, in that he hath raised him from the dead."*

Acts 20:20-21 – *"And how I kept back nothing that was profitable unto you, but have shewed you, and have taught you publickly, and from house to house, testifying both to the Jews, and also to the Greeks, **repentance toward God, and faith toward our Lord Jesus Christ**."*

Acts 26:19-20 – *"Whereupon, O king Agrippa, I was not disobedient unto the heavenly vision: but shewed first unto them of Damascus, and at Jerusalem, and throughout all the coasts of Judaea, and then to the Gentiles, **that they should repent and turn to God**, and do works meet for repentance."*

Revelation 22:17 – *"**And the Spirit and the bride say, Come. And let him that heareth say, Come. And let him that is athirst come. And whosoever will, let him take the water of life freely**."*

Yes, the Lord our God and Savior has commanded all lost sinners everywhere "to repent" of their sins and of their sinfulness. This is the message that every lost sinner must hear and heed – repent and believe. Repent of your sinfulness before God, and believe on the Savior Jesus Christ. Acknowledge that you are a sinner before God, worthy of God's eternal judgment in hell and unable to save yourself from your own sin and its judgment. Then place your trust in Jesus Christ as God the Son who died on the cross to save you from your sin and its punishment.

Yet in our day and time there are those who preach a so-called gospel message that speaks nothing of sins and sinfulness. It does not speak about the utter abomination and offense that our sin is in the presence of our holy Lord God. It does not speak about mankind as utterly and thoroughly sinful. It does not speak about how our sin is worthy of God's eternal judgment and wrath. It does not speak about mankind's complete inability to save itself from its sins and its sinfulness.

Yet the true gospel of our Lord Jesus Christ that we have received through God's Holy Word is all about our sins and our sinfulness. It is our sin that has separated us from the Lord our God. It is our sin for which we should be cast into hell-fire forever. It is our sin for which God the Son, the Lord Jesus Christ, shed His precious blood and died upon the cross. It is our sinfulness and guiltiness from which we must be saved. Therefore, it is because of our sinfulness that the Lord our God and Savior has commanded all lost sinners everywhere "to repent." The true gospel of our Lord Jesus Christ requires repentance of sin and faith in Christ. Even so, our Lord Jesus declared in Luke 13:3, "*Except ye repent, ye shall all likewise perish.*"

Indeed, each lost sinner must turn his or her focus from that which might be obtained through self-effort, whether in material things or in religious things, and must set his or her focus upon the eternal salvation and eternal life that may be received only from God the Son, the Lord Jesus Christ, through faith in Him. God the Son, the Lord Jesus Christ, alone can meet the spiritual need of this world, yea of each and every lost soul in this world. He alone can meet their hunger for eternal salvation and their thirst for eternal life. He is the Light of the world. In Him alone may be found deliverance from the darkness of sin. Through faith in Him alone may a lost sinner be made a child of light and a child of God.

2. We must bring forth fruits worthy of repentance.

Matthew 3:5-8 – "*Then went out to him Jerusalem, and all Judaea, and all the region round about Jordan, and were baptized of him in Jordan, confessing their sins. But when he saw many of the Pharisees and Sadducees come to his baptism, he said unto them, O generation of vipers, who hath warned you to flee from the wrath to come?* **Bring forth therefore fruits meet for repentance**."

Luke 3:7-14 – "*Then said he to the multitude that came forth to be baptized of him, O generation of vipers, who hath warned you to flee from the wrath to come?* **Bring forth therefore fruits worthy of repentance**, *and begin not to say within yourselves, We have Abraham to our father: for I say unto you, That God is able of these stones to raise up children unto Abraham. And now also the axe is laid unto the root of the trees: every tree therefore which bringeth not forth good fruit is hewn down, and cast into the fire. And the people asked him, saying, What shall we do then? He answereth and saith unto them, He that hath two coats, let him impart to him that hath none; and he that hath meat, let him do likewise. Then came also publicans to be baptized, and said unto him, Master, what shall we do? And he said unto them, Exact no more than that which is appointed you. And the soldiers likewise demanded of him, saying, And what shall we do? And he said unto them, Do violence to no man, neither accuse any falsely; and be content with your wages.*"

Acts 26:19-20 – "*Whereupon, O king Agrippa, I was not disobedient unto the heavenly vision: but shewed first unto them of Damascus, and at Jerusalem, and throughout all the coasts of Judaea, and then to the Gentiles, that they should repent and turn to God,* **and do works meet for repentance**."

The phrase, "meet for repentance," refers to that which is "worthy of repentance." It is not the repentance itself, but is that which flows out of the repentance. If there is true repentance, then there will be some change in the life. True repentance brings forth works that are worthy of that repentance.

What then are some of the works that are worthy of repentance? For one who repents and comes to the knowledge of the truth for salvation such would include the public acknowledgement and confession of sinfulness and the public profession of faith in Christ through baptism. In Matthew 3:5 we find that many of those who came out to John the Baptist *"were baptized, confessing their sins."*

Another work that is worthy of repentance would be a change in our attitude and behavior toward others around us and toward the things of this world. In Luke 3:10-14 John the Baptist instructed the people to bring forth the works of generosity, contentment, and honesty.

Yet another work that is worthy of repentance would be a change in our attitude and behavior toward sin itself. In 2 Corinthians 7:10-11 we read, *"For godly sorrow worketh repentance to salvation not to be repented of: but the sorrow of the world worketh death. For behold this selfsame thing, that ye sorrowed after a godly sort, what carefulness it wrought in you, yea, what clearing of yourselves, yea, what indignation, yea, what fear, yea, what vehement desire, yea, what zeal, yea, what revenge! In all things ye have approved yourselves to be clear in this matter."*

Godly sorrow over sin will bring forth true repentance of sin, and true repentance of sin will bring forth a change in one's attitude and behavior toward sin. It will bring forth a "carefulness" toward sin, that is – a burden over the sin in our lives. It will bring forth a "clearing" of ourselves concerning our sin, that is – a confession of our sin to the Lord and to those against whom we have sinned. It will bring forth an "indignation" against sin in our lives. It will bring forth a "fear" of returning to sin and of committing sin. It will bring forth a "vehement desire" to flee any and all sin and to follow after righteousness. It will bring forth a "zeal" to serve the Lord and to walk in His will. It will bring forth a "revenge" in our attitude against any sin that may yet enter our lives.

Finally, when we believers walk in sin and then repent thereof, true repentance will cause us to return unto "the first works" of surrender and obedience. Even so, in the first portion of Revelation 2:5 our

Lord declared to the church of Ephesus, "*Remember therefore from whence thou art fallen, and repent, and do the first works.*" Also in Luke 21:28-30 our Lord gave the parable, saying, "*But what think ye? A certain man had two sons; and he came to the first, and said, Son, go work to day in my vineyard. He answered and said, I will not: but afterward he repented, and went. And he came to the second, and said likewise. And he answered and said, I go, sir: and went not.*"

⌒⌒⌒

3. We must follow our Lord's leading without delay (even if it seems unreasonable to our own thinking).

Matthew 4:18-22 – "*And Jesus, walking by the sea of Galilee, saw two brethren, Simon called Peter, and Andrew his brother, casting a net into the sea: for they were fishers. And he saith unto them,* **Follow me, and I will make you fishers of men.** *And they straightway left their nets, and followed him. And going on from thence, he saw other two brethren, James the son of Zebedee, and John his brother, in a ship with Zebedee their father, mending their nets;* **and he called them.** *And they immediately left the ship and their father, and followed him.*" (See also Mark 1:16-20)

Matthew 8:19-22 – "*And a certain scribe came, and said unto him, Master, I will follow thee whithersoever thou goest. And Jesus saith unto him, The foxes have holes, and the birds of the air have nests; but the Son of man hath not where to lay his head. And another of his disciples said unto him, Lord, suffer me first to go and bury my father. But Jesus said unto him,* **Follow me;** *and let the dead bury their dead.*" (See also Luke 9:57-62)

Matthew 9:9 – "*And as Jesus passed forth from thence, he saw a man, named Matthew, sitting at the receipt of custom: and he saith unto him,* **Follow me.** *And he arose, and followed him.*" (See also Mark 2:14; Luke 5:27-28)

John 1:43 – "*The day following Jesus would go forth into Galilee, and findeth Philip, and saith unto him,* **Follow me.**"

John 21:18-22 – *"Verily, verily, I say unto thee, When thou wast young, thou girdedst thyself, and walkedst whither thou wouldest: but when thou shalt be old, thou shalt stretch forth thy hands, and another shall gird thee, and carry thee whither thou wouldest not. This spake he, signifying by what death he should glorify God. And when he had spoken this, he saith unto him, **Follow me**. Then Peter, turning about, seeth the disciple whom Jesus loved following; which also leaned on his breast at supper, and said, Lord, which is he that betrayeth thee? Peter seeing him saith to Jesus, Lord, and what shall this man do? Jesus saith unto him, If I will that he tarry till I come, what is that to thee? **Follow thou me**."*

The best way, yea the only way, to truly bring forth fruits that are worthy of repentance is to follow our Lord wherever He leads us. We must learn the commands and counsels, precepts and principles, statutes and standards, wisdom and warnings of our Lord through His Holy Word and His Holy Spirit; and we must walk therein. Our Lord is willing to instruct us, teach us, and guide us in the way that we should go. Even so, we must be willing to follow His instruction, teaching, and guidance without stubbornness. He will lead us *"in the paths of righteousness for His name's sake."* (Psalm 23:3) Even so, we must be willing to follow His leading, and to walk in such paths of righteousness, and to bring glory unto His name. If we will, our Lord has promised to make us "fishers of men," that we might reach many more lost souls "for His name's sake."

Yet in Matthew 8:21 we encounter a disciple who was seeking to postpone and put off his following of the Lord in obedience. He had some things that he wanted to do first. Although we may not know all of the details of the case, it is certain that whatever was involved in this man's desire was not right with the Lord. Indeed, our Lord Jesus Christ rebuked this man's desire, saying, *"Follow Me; and let the dead bury their dead."*

Herein our Lord was revealing the truth that we should follow Him in obedience to His will immediately and without delay. We should not seek to postpone and put off our following of our Lord until we have first accomplished our own will, or until things are more personally convenient and comfortable. In fact, in Matthew 8:20

our Lord had already indicated that the way of following Him was a way of personal sacrifice, not necessarily a way of personal comfort and convenience.

There are those who say – I am willing to follow and serve the Lord with my life; but I just want to have some fun first to live a little bit for myself first. To such our Lord gives answer – Follow Me in obedience now, immediately, without delay. There are others who say – I am willing to follow and serve the Lord in obedience; but I just want to make a little bit of money first or to get my business stable and established first. To such our Lord gives answer – Follow Me in obedience now, immediately, without delay. Yea, to all of us our Lord declares – Follow Me in obedience now, immediately, without delay!

Indeed, in Matthew 9:9 we find an example of one who did follow the Lord in obedience immediately, without delay. When the Lord called him, Matthew did not hesitate to obey. He did not delay. He did not hold back. He did not even try to hold onto anything behind him in his life. Matthew had been a publican, that is – a tax collector for Rome. As such, he lived a fairly sinful lifestyle. Yet when the Lord called him to follow, this man Matthew immediately turned his back upon his old, sinful life and wholly gave himself to follow and serve the Lord in obedience. Even so, day after day our Lord and Savior Jesus Christ passes by us spiritually and calls unto us, saying, "Come, follow Me." Will we do as Matthew did? Will we follow the Lord immediately in obedience without delay?

4. We must "rejoice and be exceeding glad" when we are persecuted for our Lord's sake.

Matthew 5:10-12 – "*Blessed are they which are persecuted for righteousness' sake: for theirs is the kingdom of heaven. Blessed are ye, when men shall revile you, and persecute you, and shall say all manner of evil against you falsely, for my sake. **Rejoice, and be exceeding glad**: for great is your reward in heaven: for so persecuted they the prophets which were before you.*"

Luke 6:22-23 – "*Blessed are ye, when men shall hate you, and when they shall separate you from their company, and shall reproach you, and cast out your name as evil, for the Son of man's sake.* **Rejoice ye in that day, and leap for joy***: for, behold, your reward is great in heaven: for in the like manner did their fathers unto the prophets.*"

1 Peter 3:14 – "*But and if ye suffer for righteousness' sake,* **happy are ye***: and be not afraid of their terror, neither be troubled.*"

1 Peter 4:12-16 – "*Beloved, think it not strange concerning the fiery trial which is to try you, as though some strange thing happened unto you:* **but rejoice, inasmuch as ye are partakers of Christ's sufferings; that, when his glory shall be revealed, ye may be glad also with exceeding joy***. If ye be reproached for the name of Christ,* **happy are ye***; for the spirit of glory and of God resteth upon you: on their part he is evil spoken of, but on your part he is glorified. But let none of you suffer as a murderer, or as a thief, or as an evildoer, or as a busybody in other men's matters. Yet if any man suffer as a Christian, let him not be ashamed;* **but let him glorify God on this behalf.**"

In 2 Timothy 3:12 God's Holy Word informs us with absolute certainty, "*Yea, and all that will live godly in Christ Jesus shall suffer persecution.*" If we follow the Lord as He has called us to follow Him, we shall suffer some form of persecution. If we walk "in the paths of righteousness for His name's sake," we shall be reviled, and reproached, and rejected, and hated, and persecuted, and falsely spoken against at some point. We shall "suffer for righteousness' sake" at some point. We shall "be reproached for the name of Christ" at some point. We shall suffer the "fiery trial" of persecution at some point.

What then will we do when that time comes? Will we quit walking "in the paths of righteousness for His name's sake"? In order to relieve the pressure of persecution, will we make some compromises in our walk "in the paths of righteousness for His name's sake"? Will we continue walking "in the paths of righteousness for His name's sake," yet do so with a bitter attitude? None of these things are the will of our Lord for us in such matters. Rather, our Lord commands us, *"Rejoice, and be exceeding glad."* Rather, our Lord commands us, *"Rejoice ye in that day, and leap for joy."* Rather, our Lord commands us to *"glorify God on this behalf."*

When we are reviled, reproached, rejected, hated, persecuted, and falsely spoken against "for righteousness' sake," for the name of Christ, for faithfully following our Lord's will in our lives, then we are to continue walking faithfully "in the paths of righteousness for His name's sake." Indeed, then we are to continue faithful with rejoicing and exceeding gladness, glorifying God. This we are to do because our reward "is great in heaven." This we are to do because we are "partakers of Christ's sufferings." Thus we are to do because at such times "the spirit of glory and of God resteth upon [us]." This we are to do because the Lord our God is glorified through our faithfulness unto and through our persecution.

<hr>

5. We must "so shine" our spiritual light before the lost of this world.

Matthew 5:14-16 – *"Ye are the light of the world. A city that is set on an hill cannot be hid. Neither do men light a candle, and put it under a bushel, but on a candlestick; and it giveth light unto all that are in the house.* **Let your light so shine before men,** *that they may see your good works, and glorify your Father which is in heaven."*

We who are the children of God are the spiritual "light of the world." Even so, as "the light of the world" we are commanded to "so shine before men," that is – before the lost souls of this world. Yea, we are to "so shine" before these lost souls, "that they may see our good works," and that they may glorify our heavenly Father by bowing in humble faith to receive the Lord Jesus Christ, God's only begotten Son, as their personal and eternal Savior. Indeed, even in those times when we are reviled, and reproached, and rejected, and hated, and persecuted, and falsely spoken against for our Lord's sake and "for righteousness' sake" – even then we are yet to "so shine" before the lost of this world.

6. We must get right with those against whom we have done wrong.

Matthew 5:21-26 – "*Ye have heard that it was said by them of old time, Thou shalt not kill; and whosoever shall kill shall be in danger of the judgment: but I say unto you, That whosoever is angry with his brother without a cause shall be in danger of the judgment: and whosoever shall say to his brother, Raca, shall be in danger of the council: but whosoever shall say, Thou fool, shall be in danger of hell fire. Therefore if thou bring thy gift to the altar, and there rememberest that thy brother hath ought against thee; **leave there thy gift before the altar, and go thy way; first be reconciled to thy brother, and then come and offer thy gift. Agree with thine adversary quickly, whiles thou art in the way with him**; lest at any time the adversary deliver thee to the judge, and the judge deliver thee to the officer, and thou be cast into prison. Verily I say unto thee, Thou shalt by no means come out thence, till thou hast paid the uttermost farthing.*"

The case is set before us in verse 23 where we read, "*Therefore if thou bring thy gift to the altar* [that is – when you come to a place of worship before the Lord], *and there rememberest that thy brother hath ought against thee* [that is – there you remember that you have actually done some wrong against another person] . . . ." Then in verse 24 follows a series of four commands, "*Leave there thy gift before the altar, and go thy way; first be reconciled to thy brother, and then come and offer thy gift.*"

First, we learn that there is something more important to the Lord our God than our gifts of sacrifice and worship. Through four commands our Lord instructs us, saying – If you remember that you have done wrong to another, leave your gift of sacrifice, go your way, first be reconciled to that other one, and then come and offer your worship. Unto the Lord our God, our being reconciled to those against whom we have done wrong is more important than our giving to Him gifts of worship. Unto our Lord, our being reconciled and right with one another is more important than our offering up worship through financial giving, or thanksgiving and praise, or prayers, or works of ministry. Yea, our Lord directly commands us – "*First, be reconciled to thy brother, and then come and offer thy gift.*"

Second, we learn that we must get right with those against whom we have done wrong. The phrase in verse 23, *"And there rememberest that thy brother hath ought against thee,"* means that we ourselves recognize and know that we have actually done some wrong unto another. When such is the case, we must not just "shrug it off." Rather, we must get it right. We must go to that other one and must "be reconciled" to that other one. We must confess our wrongdoing and must seek forgiveness; and as much as we are able, we must make right any damages that we have caused by our wrongdoing.

What all does this include? This includes any wrong attitude that we have committed against another; for in verse 22 our Lord gives the example of one who "is angry with his brother without a cause." Furthermore, this includes any wrong words that we have spoken against another; for again in verse 22 our Lord gives the example of one who says to his brother, "Raca," or who says to his brother, "Thou fool." Finally, this includes any wrong actions that we have done against another; for in verse 25 our Lord gives the example of one who has created an "adversary" because of his wrong actions.

7. **We must agree quickly to make right with those against whom we have committed a civil infraction.**

Matthew 5:25-26 – *"**Agree with thine adversary quickly, whiles thou art in the way with him**; lest at any time the adversary deliver thee to the judge, and the judge deliver thee to the officer, and thou be cast into prison. Verily I say unto thee, Thou shalt by no means come out thence, till thou hast paid the uttermost farthing."*

Luke 12:58-59 – *"When thou goest with thine adversary to the magistrate, as thou art in the way, **give diligence that thou mayest be delivered from him**; lest he hale thee to the judge, and the judge deliver thee to the officer, and the officer cast thee into prison. I tell thee, thou shalt not depart thence, till thou hast paid the very last mite."*

The case described in these two passages is that of some civil offense against another. It is something for which we could be brought before a civil judge and could be found guilty of a civil infraction. It may be something committed accidentally. It may be something committed purposefully. It may be something committed maliciously. Yet it is some civil offense that we have committed. Even so, in such a case our Lord commands us to "agree with [our] adversary quickly." In a sense our Lord is commanding us to "settle out of court" by quickly accepting whatever "deal" our adversary is willing to make. Why should we do this? Why should we not try to fight the case? Ultimately it is because our Lord would have us to get right and reconcile with anyone against whom we have done wrong. Such is our Lord's command.

8. **We must sever and cast away anything in our lives that leads us unto sexual lust.**

Matthew 5:27-30 – "*Ye have heard that it was said by them of old time, Thou shalt not commit adultery: but I say unto you, That whosoever looketh on a woman to lust after her hath committed adultery with her already in his heart. **And if thy right eye offend thee, pluck it out, and cast it from thee**: for it is profitable for thee that one of thy members should perish, and not that thy whole body should be cast into hell. **And if thy right hand offend thee, cut it off, and cast it from thee**: for it is profitable for thee that one of thy members should perish, and not that thy whole body should be cast into hell.*"

First, our Lord presents the spiritual truth that sexual lust in one's mind and heart is equivalent in the sight of the Lord our God to the sin of adultery. Sexual lust in our minds and hearts is not a light matter. Rather, it is a very serious spiritual matter in the sight of the Lord our God.

Therefore, our Lord adds a serious and severe instruction on this matter in verses 29-30, stating that we should pluck out our right eye or cut off our right hand if they offend us in this matter. Now, let us take note that this instruction is not primarily about the sin of adultery, but is primarily about the sin of sexual lust. Furthermore, I do not believe that our Lord literally intends for us to pluck out an eye or to cut off a hand. However, I do believe that our Lord was using this severe illustration in order to make a very serious point. So then, what is our Lord's point? It is that anything which might lead us unto sexual lust and impurity should be severed and cast away from our lives, and that such should be done without mercy. Yea, in the intensity of our Lord's instruction and illustration, He indicated that it would be far better for us to lose some element of perceived importance from our lives, even if it might be some body part, than it would be for us to lose our whole life to the devouring and destroying power of sexual impurity.

Even so, Proverbs 2:18 speaks concerning the adulterous woman, saying, *"For her house inclineth unto death, and her paths unto the dead."* Again Proverbs 5:3-5 declares, *"For the lips of a strange woman drop as an honeycomb, and her mouth is smoother than oil: but her end is bitter as wormwood, sharp as a twoedged sword. Her feet go down to death; her steps take hold on hell."* Yet again Proverbs 6:32 declares, *"But whoso committeth adultery with a woman lacketh understanding: he that doeth it destroyeth his own soul."* Finally, Proverbs 7:24-27 warns, *"Hearken unto me now therefore, O ye children, and attend to the words of my mouth. Let not thine heart decline to her ways, go not astray in her paths. For she hath cast down many wounded: yea, many strong men have been slain by her. Her house is the way to hell, going down to the chambers of death."*

9. We must not be swearing to the truth of things, but must just be faithful to our word.

Matthew 5:33-37 – *"Again, ye have heard that it hath been said by them of old time, Thou shalt not forswear thyself, but shalt perform unto the Lord thine oaths: but I say unto you, **Swear not at all**; neither by heaven; for it is God's throne: nor by the earth; for it is* *his footstool: neither by Jerusalem; for it is the city of the great King. Neither shalt thou swear by thy head, because thou canst not make one hair white or black.* **But let your communication be, Yea, yea; Nay, nay**: *for whatsoever is more than these cometh of evil.*"

James 5:12 – "*But above all things, my brethren,* **swear not**, *neither by heaven, neither by the earth, neither by any other oath:* **but let your yea be yea; and your nay, nay**; *lest ye fall into condemnation.*"

Some individuals are regularly swearing to the truth of things. They might say, "Cross my heart; hope to die; stick a needle in my eye," or, "I swear on a stack of Bibles," or, "I swear on so-and-so's grave." Yet our Lord instructs and teaches that such things should not be a regular part of our speech. Now, such does not necessarily mean that it is wrong to "swear to tell the truth, the whole truth, and nothing but the truth" in a court of law. Yet it does mean that our regular communication should not require such "swearing." Why not? It should not be required because our regular communication should be true and faithful at all times. Even so, through such constant truth and faithfulness, we will be known as those who always speak truthfully and faithfully. We will be known as those who are true to their word. Our "yea" will always be "yea," and our "nay" will always be "nay." Indeed, no one will have a need to question the truth and faithfulness of our words. Such is the desire of our Lord.

10. We must not retaliate against evil, but must show kindness instead.

Matthew 5:38-42 – "*Ye have heard that it hath been said, An eye for an eye, and a tooth for a tooth: but I say unto you,* **That ye resist not evil: but whosoever shall smite thee on thy right cheek, turn to him the other also. And if any man will sue thee at the law, and take away thy coat, let him have thy cloke also. And whosoever shall compel thee to go a mile, go with him twain. Give to him that asketh thee, and from him that would borrow of thee turn not thou away**."

Luke 6:29-30 – "***And unto him that smiteth thee on the one cheek offer also the other; and him that taketh away thy cloke forbid not to take thy coat also. Give to every man that asketh of thee; and of him that taketh away thy goods ask them not again.***"

Romans 12:14 – "***Bless them which persecute you: bless, and curse not.***"

Romans 12:17 – "***Recompense to no man evil for evil.*** *Provide things honest in the sight of all men.*"

Romans 12:19-21 – "***Dearly beloved, avenge not yourselves,*** *but rather give place unto wrath: for it is written, Vengeance is mine; I will repay, saith the Lord.* ***Therefore if thine enemy hunger, feed him; if he thirst, give him drink****: for in so doing thou shalt heap coals of fire on his head.* ***Be not overcome of evil, but overcome evil with good.***"

1 Thessalonians 5:15 – "***See that none render evil for evil unto any man;*** *but ever follow that which is good, both among yourselves, and to all men.*"

1 Peter 3:9 – "***Not rendering evil for evil, or railing for railing: but contrariwise blessing****; knowing that ye are thereunto called, that ye should inherit a blessing.*"

In that day a slap on the cheek was considered a grave insult. Yet our Lord commands us not to retaliate against such insults, but to give way unto them, even to the point of allowing for further insults. In that day one's coat could be taken forcibly in payment for a civil debt; whereas the cloak could not be taken, but could only be given voluntarily. Yet our Lord commands us to give voluntarily both our coat and our cloak, that is – to sacrifice our rights in the fulfillment of our responsibilities. In that day a Roman soldier had the legal right to require a civilian to carry his pack for a mile. Now, the Jews despised the Roman soldiers because they were a symbol of the hated Roman oppression over their nation. Yet our Lord commands us to go the extra mile, even for the benefit of our oppressors. In addition, our Lord commands us to give unto the aid of others and not to turn them away. In all of these things we find that our Lord would have us not to fight for our rights, but to give in kindness and even in sacrifice for the benefit of others.

Furthermore, when we are directly mistreated, it is not our place to avenge ourselves. It is not our place to return "evil for evil, or railing for railing" unto anyone. Vengeance is the possession of our Lord. It is His place to return punishment for evil. For us to seek to avenge ourselves and to repay evil for evil is for us to steal the rightful place of the Lord our God. It is for us to seek to take the place of sovereignty from Him. This ought not so to be. We must not seek to avenge ourselves. We must not seek to repay evil for evil in any form, whether verbal or physical. Rather, we must get out of our Lord's way in the matter and must give place unto Him to repay in His wrath as He so wills.

Yet our Lord's command unto us requires even more. We are not simply to withhold our own vengeance and repayment in such matters. We are actually required to return blessing and kindness unto such individuals. We are not to be overcome with the evil of bitterness, anger, wrath, cursing, evil speaking, malice, and vengeance toward those who mistreat us. Rather, we are to overcome their evil toward us through our goodness and kindness toward them.

11. We must love our enemies, blessing them, doing good to them, and praying for them.

Matthew 5:43-48 – *"Ye have heard that it hath been said, Thou shalt love thy neighbour, and hate thine enemy. But I say unto you,* **Love your enemies, bless them that curse you, do good to them that hate you, and pray for them which despitefully use you, and persecute you;** *that ye may be the children of your Father which is in heaven: for he maketh his sun to rise on the evil and on the good, and sendeth rain on the just and on the unjust. For if ye love them which love you, what reward have ye? Do not even the publicans the same? And if ye salute your brethren only, what do ye more than* others? Do not even the publicans so? Be ye therefore perfect, even as your Father which is in heaven is perfect.*"*

Luke 6:27-28 – "***But I say unto you which hear, Love your enemies, do good to them which hate you, bless them that curse you, and pray for them which despitefully use you***.*"*

Luke 6:32-36 – "*For if ye love them which love you, what thank have ye? For sinners also love those that love them. And if ye do good to them which do good to you, what thank have ye? For sinners also do even the same. And if ye lend to them of whom ye hope to receive, what thank have ye? For sinners also lend to sinners, to receive as much again.* **But love ye your enemies, and do good***, and lend, hoping for nothing again; and your reward shall be great, and ye shall be the children of the Highest: for he is kind unto the unthankful and to the evil. Be ye therefore merciful, as your Father also is merciful.*"*

Romans 12:20 – "***Therefore if thine enemy hunger, feed him; if he thirst, give him drink***: *for in so doing thou shalt heap coals of fire on his head.*"*

The love of God should flow from our hearts, not only toward our family and friends, but also toward our enemies and persecutors. When our enemies curse us and speak against us, we should respond, not by speaking back against them, and not by an angry silence, but with sincere blessing upon them. When our enemies pour out their hatred against us, we should respond, not with hatred and bitterness back against them, but by doing good things toward them, such as giving them food and drink when they are hungry and thirsty. When our enemies despitefully use us and persecute us, we should respond, not with spite and malice back against them, but with prayer on their behalf. Even so, we shall demonstrate ourselves to be the children of our heavenly Father; for He Himself "maketh his sun to rise on the evil and on the good, and sendeth rain on the just and on the unjust." Even so, we shall demonstrate ourselves to be perfect even as our heavenly Father is perfect, and to be merciful even as our heavenly Father is merciful. Yea, by so doing we walk in the holy character of "our Father which is in heaven."

12. We must not do "right things" to "be seen of men" that we "may have glory of men."

Matthew 6:1-2 -- "***Take heed that ye do not your alms*** [acts of mercy, such as giving to help the poor and needy] ***before men, to be seen of them***: *otherwise ye have no reward of your Father which is in heaven. Therefore when thou doest thine alms, **do not sound a trumpet before thee, as the hypocrites do** in the synagogues and in the streets, **that they may have glory of men**. Verily I say unto you, They have their reward.*"

Matthew 6:5 – "*And when thou prayest, **thou shalt not be as the hypocrites are**: for they love to pray standing in the synagogues and in the corners of the streets, **that they may be seen of men**. Verily I say unto you, They have their reward.*"

Matthew 6:16 – "*Moreover when ye fast, **be not, as the hypocrites**, of a sad countenance: for they disfigure their faces, **that they may appear unto men to fast**. Verily I say unto you, They have their reward.*"

The issue here is not simply that others see us doing such good and right things; for then there would be contradiction with the instruction of Matthew 5:16 – "*Let your light so shine before men, **that they may see your good works**, and glorify your Father which is in heaven.*" Rather, the issue here is the motivation for doing such good and right things. The issue is whether we do such good and right things in order that we ourselves might receive the glory, or whether we do such good and right things in order that God our heavenly Father might receive the glory. We must take notice that according to Matthew 6:2 the hypocrites do such good and right things before men, "*that they may have glory of men.*" They do such good and right things with a wrong and sinful motive, that they themselves might receive the glory. Yet according to Matthew 5:16 we are to let our light "*so shine before men, that they may see our good works, **and glorify our Father** which is heaven.*" We are to do such good and right things, not so that we ourselves might receive the glory, but so that God our heavenly Father might receive the glory.

So then, are we doing good and right things that we "may have glory of men"? If we are, our Lord declares that we are hypocrites. In Matthew 6:2, 5, 16 our Lord attributes this motivation of heart unto "the hypocrites." Yet what does it mean that such individuals are hypocrites? It means that while the outside actions may appear unto men to be good and right, the internal heart attitude is not actually good and right with the Lord our God. This is the way of the hypocrite – apparently "right" actions with a wrong and sinful heart. What then is so wrong and sinful about this heart attitude? It is so wrong and sinful because it is a desire to receive unto one's self the glory that is due unto the Lord our God Himself. It is also so sinful and wrong because it is all focused upon self; whereas we have been called to deny ourselves and to exalt our Lord.

Furthermore, if we are doing good and right things that we "may have glory of men," then our Lord declares that we have our reward. At the end of Matthew 6:2, He declared, *"Verily I say unto you, They* [the hypocrites] *have their reward."* Again at the end of both verse 5 and verse 16, He declared the same, *"Verily I say unto you, They have their reward."* When we do good and right things to "have glory of men," then whatever glory we receive of men is our only reward. We shall receive nothing more than this.

Even if we receive very little "glory of men," if we did such good and right things with the motive to "have glory of men," then that little bit of glory is all of the reward that we shall receive. Even if the glory that we receive passes away quickly (and it will), if we did such good and right things with the motive to "have glory of men," then that quickly passing glory is all of the reward that we shall receive. Even if we receive no glory at all for what we have done, if we did such good and right things with the motive to "have glory of men," then there is no other reward that we shall receive. Yea, in the second half of Matthew 6:1 our Lord warns us that if we do such good and right things with the motive to "have glory of men," then we shall "have no reward" at all from our heavenly Father.

So then, are we hypocrites? Are we doing the good and right things that we do with the motive that we "may have glory of men"?

13. We must do "right things" only to be seen of our heavenly Father.

Matthew 6:3-4 – *"But when thou doest alms, **let not thy left hand know what thy right hand doeth**: that thine alms may be in secret: **and thy Father which seeth in secret** himself shall reward thee openly."*

Matthew 6:6 – *"But thou, **when thou prayest, enter into thy closet**, and when thou hast shut thy door, **pray to thy Father which is in secret; and thy Father which seeth in secret** shall reward thee openly."*

Matthew 6:17-18 – *"But thou, **when thou fastest, anoint thine head, and wash thy face; that thou appear not unto men to fast, but unto thy Father which is in secret**: and thy Father, which seeth in secret, shall reward thee openly."*

Again the issue here is not simply that others must never see us doing such good and right things; for according to our Lord's instruction in Matthew 5:16, there are appropriate times and ways for others to see our "good works," and thereby to glorify our heavenly Father. In addition, according to other portions of Scripture, there are indeed appropriate times for us to pray together with other believers as a group.

Rather, the instruction of our Lord in these verses (that in our alms-giving we are not even to let our left hand know what our right hand is doing, and that we are to pray in our closet, and that in our fasting we are not to appear openly to fast) is intended to indicate that we are to do such good and right things only to be seen of our heavenly Father. Our motive must not be to "be seen of men" that we "may have glory of men." Rather, our whole motive must be to do that which is pleasing in our Lord's sight without any concern whether others will see us and give us credit.

Even so, if we are doing such good and right things only to be seen of our heavenly Father and only to be pleasing in His sight, then our Lord gives us this promise at the end of verse 4 – *"And thy Father which seeth in secret Himself shall reward thee openly.*" Again the promise is given at the end of verse 6 and verse 18 – "*And thy Father which seeth in secret shall reward thee openly.*" First, we must remember that our heavenly Father sees and takes notice of our good and right behavior even when others do not see or do not take notice. Indeed, if we are doing good and right things with the right motive, then such is all that should matter to us. Second, we must rest assured that our heavenly Father shall certainly reward any and all of the good and right things that we do with the right motive. Not a one shall go unseen by our heavenly Father, and not a one shall go unrewarded by our heavenly Father. This is His promise. Finally, we may realize that our heavenly Father shall openly reward any and all of the good and right things that we do with the right motive.

14. We must not use vain repetitions when we pray.

Matthew 6:7-8 – "***But when ye pray, use not vain repetitions, as the heathen do****: for they think that they shall be heard for their much speaking. **Be not ye therefore like unto them****: for your Father knoweth what things ye have need of, before ye ask him.*"

The issue here is not simply the repetition of some prayer need or request. In fact, in Luke 11:5-8 our Lord Jesus Christ presented a parable with the specific purpose of teaching us to continue with perseverance in our praying. So then, in Matthew 6:7-8 our Lord is not speaking against our praying for or about the same things more than once. Rather, in this passage the key word is that word "vain." Our Lord is not speaking against our praying with repetitions. Rather, He is speaking against our praying with "***vain*** repetitions."

So then, what is praying with "vain repetitions"? In verse 7 our Lord indicated that it is praying "as the heathen do." How then do the heathen pray? Our Lord further revealed that they pray with the thinking "that they shall be heard for their much speaking." They pray with the thinking that they will somehow earn a hearing with God through "their much speaking." Yet this is wrong thinking. We do not earn a hearing with God through our "much speaking" in prayer. In fact, we do not earn a hearing with God at all. Rather, we have access unto God's throne of grace in and through our Lord and Savior Jesus Christ.

In addition, such "vain repetitions" are empty repetitions. The "much speaking" of such "vain repetitions" often become ritualistic. They often become an external ritual that is empty of any meaning from the heart. Yet the ritual continues because there is some thinking that this ritual will somehow earn the favor of the Lord our God. However, the Lord our God is not at all pleased with our rituals. Rather, our Lord is only pleased when we give Him our hearts.

Finally, such "vain repetitions" may involve the thinking that the Lord our God requires a continual reminder of our needs. Thus our Lord Jesus Christ gives warning in Matthew 6:8, "*Be not ye therefore like unto them* [like unto the heathern]*: for your Father knoweth what things ye have need of, before ye ask Him.*" Our heavenly Father does not require our continuing prayers in order to remind Him of our needs. In fact, our heavenly Father does not need our prayers at all in order for Him to know the things that we "have need of." Yea, He knows the things that we "have need of," even before we ask Him.

Thus our continuance in praying is not in order to inform our heavenly Father or in order to earn a favorable hearing with Him. Rather, our continuance in praying is in order to keep us in the place of humility before Him. Our continuance in praying is to be done with the continual recognition that we ourselves are desperately poor and needy, and that we desperately and continually need the grace and care of our heavenly Father. "*For God resisteth the proud, and giveth grace to the humble.*" (1 Peter 5:5)

15. We must pray with adoration, reverence, hope, surrender, trust, confession, forgiveness, consecration, and praise.

Matthew 6:9-13 – "***After this manner therefore pray ye****: Our Father which art in heaven, hallowed be thy name. Thy kingdom come. Thy will be done in earth, as it is in heaven. Give us this day our daily bread. And forgive us our debts, as we forgive our debtors. And lead us not into temptation, but deliver us from evil: for thine is the kingdom, and the power, and the glory, for ever. Amen.*"

Luke 11:1-4 – "*And it came to pass, that, as he was praying in a certain place, when he ceased, one of his disciples said unto him, Lord, teach us to pray, as John also taught his disciples. And he said unto them,* **When ye pray, say***, Our Father which art in heaven, Hallowed be thy name. Thy kingdom come. Thy will be done, as in heaven, so in earth. Give us day by day our daily bread. And forgive us our sins; for we also forgive every one that is indebted to us. And lead us not into temptation; but deliver us from evil.*"

In these passages of Scripture our Lord Jesus Christ commands us to pray "after this manner." First, let us recognize that the words of this prayer are not to be used in "vain repetitions." Our Lord's command and instruction just previous to this, in verses 7-8, was that we should never use "vain repetitions" when we pray. Second, let us recognize that our Lord is not instructing us to pray with these exact words when we pray. Rather, our Lord is giving us a model prayer, that is – a prayer which includes the various elements that ought to be a part of our praying. Thus our Lord is commanding us to be certain to include these particular elements in our praying – "after this manner," not necessarily with these very words.

So then, what are these elements? First, we are to pray with adoration, even as this model prayer begins with the words, "*Our Father which art in heaven.*" If we have received the Lord Jesus Christ through faith as our Savior, then the Lord our God is our heavenly Father; and we are His dear children. He is our heavenly Father who cares for us. He is our heavenly Father who cares about us. He is our heavenly Father who will take care of us. He is our heavenly Father who has bestowed upon us such wondrous love "*that we should be called the sons of God."* (See 1 John 3:1) Even so, we ought to love Him with all of our hearts "because he first loved us" and because He continues to love us and care for us. Yea, we ought to approach unto Him in prayer with our hearts full of love and adoration, crying, "Abba, Father." (See Galatians 4:6) *"Our Father which art in heaven."*

Second, we are to pray with reverence. As this model prayer continues, we find that the very first request which should come forth in our praying is one of reverence unto the Lord our God and unto His holy name. Indeed, our Lord instructs and teaches in verse 9, *"After this manner therefore pray ye: Our Father which art in heaven, hallowed be thy name."* Although we may approach unto the Lord our God as our heavenly Father, we must never approach unto Him as an equal. Certainly, we must never approach unto Him as one whom we may direct according to our own will and way. He is the Lord God of heaven and earth. He is the most high God. He is *"the high and lofty One that inhabiteth eternity, whose name is Holy."* (Isaiah 57:15) Never, NEVER, **NEVER** are we to approach unto Him in a "common" way. Always, ALWAYS, **ALWAYS** we are to approach unto Him in prayer with our hearts full of "reverence and godly fear." (See Hebrews 12:28) *"Hallowed be Thy name."*

Third, we are to pray with hope. As this model prayer continues into the beginning of verse 10, we find that the next request which should come forth in our praying is one of a hopeful looking for our Lord's coming kingdom – *"Thy kingdom come."* Our Lord has promised to come again that He might receive us unto Himself and that He might establish His kingdom upon this earth forever and ever. Although many scoffers, who walk *"after their own lusts,"* may mock and say – *"Where is the promise of His coming?"* – we ourselves should continue in faith and hope *"looking for that blessed hope, and the glorious appearing of the great God and our Savior Jesus Christ."* (See 2 Peter 3-4; Titus 2:13) Oh yes, we should be looking in hope for that day when *"we shall be like Him, for we shall see Him as He is."* (See 1 John 3:2) Yea, we should be praying, *"Even so, Lord, come quickly."* (See Revelation 22:20) *"Thy kingdom come."*

Then with this hope in our Lord's coming, we should purify ourselves *"even as He is pure."* (See 1 John 3:3) Thus we come to the fourth matter of the model prayer – that we are to pray with surrender. Even so, verse 10 continues, *"Thy kingdom come. Thy will be done in earth, as it is done in heaven."* Indeed, if we pray in this manner with sincere hearts, then the first focus of our request will be – "Oh Lord, Thy will be done in my own heart and life, even as it is done in heaven." This is the prayer of one whose heart cries out – "Not my will, but Thine be done." This is the prayer of one who is presenting himself or herself as *"a living sacrifice, holy, acceptable unto God"* to live wholly unto the Lord, and not unto themselves. (See Romans 12:1; 2 Corinthians 15) This is the prayer of one who is denying himself or herself, taking up his or her cross daily, and following the Lord. (See Luke 9:23) Oh brethren, how we must learn to pray with the surrender of ourselves unto our heavenly Father. *"Thy will be done in earth* [in my own heart and life]*, as it is done in heaven."*

Fifth, we are to pray with trusting dependence; even as the model pray continues in verse 11, *"Give us this day our daily bread."* Now, this is the prayer for daily provision, not only concerning our physical food, but also concerning our every need. Throughout our days we find ourselves in many a place of need. We have physical needs. We have financial needs. We have circumstantial needs. We have mental and emotional needs. We have spiritual needs. Even so, we must learn to come unto our heavenly Father in prayer, with the full realization that He is the One and only One who can truly meet our every need. Furthermore, we must learn to pray with trusting dependence, in full assurance of faith that our heavenly Father will meet our every need in the best possible way for His own glory and for our own good. We must come boldly, in full assurance of faith and trust, unto His throne of grace in prayer, *"that we may obtain mercy, and find grace to help in time of need."* (See Hebrews 4:16) *"Give us this day our daily bread."* "Yea, Lord, meet our every daily need."

Sixth, we are to pray with confession; even as the model pray continues into the beginning of verse 12, *"And forgive us our debts* [that is – our transgressions and sins]*."* Every day we commit transgressions and sins of attitude, word, and action in the sight of our heavenly

Father. Therefore, every day confession of sin must be a part of our praying if we are to be cleansed of our unrighteousness and if we are to continue walking in fellowship with our heavenly Father. We must not seek to excuse our sins, or to cover over our sins, or to lighten the blackness of our sins, or to shift the blame of our sins. Rather, we must acknowledge and confess our sins with a broken and a contrite heart. Then our heavenly Father will be *"faithful and just to forgive us our sins, and to cleanse us from all unrighteousness."* (1 John 1:9) *"And forgive us our debts* [our transgressions and sins against Thee]."

Seventh, we are to pray with forgiveness; even as the model prayer continues in verse 12, *"And forgive us our debts, as we forgive our debtors."* Even so, our Lord Jesus Christ gives us the promise and the warning in verses 14-15, *"For if ye forgive men their trespasses, your heavenly Father will also forgive you: but if ye forgive not men their trespasses, neither will your Father forgive your trespasses."* If we desire for our heavenly Father to forgive us our trespasses against Him, then we must be tender hearted and forgiving of others' trespasses against us. On the other hand, if we will not forgive others of "their trespasses" against us, then our heavenly Father will not forgive our trespasses against Him. In addition, if our trespasses against our Lord are not forgiven, then they will separate between Him and us so that He will not hear our prayers. Therefore, we must pray with forgiveness in our hearts toward others. *"And forgive us our debts, as we forgive our debtors."*

Eighth, we are to pray with consecration; even as the model prayer continues in the opening portion of verse 13, *"And lead us not into temptation, but deliver us from evil."* Such is the prayer of one who sincerely desires to be consecrated, that is – to be set apart unto the Lord and His righteousness. Such an individual desires not to yield himself or herself unto sin, not to *"obey it in the lusts thereof."* (See Romans 6:12) Such an individual desires not to yield his or her members *"as instruments of unrighteousness unto sin."* (See Romans 6:13) Such an individual desires to *"stand against the wiles of the devil"* and to resist temptations unto sin. (See Ephesians 6:11) Yet such an individual also recognizes that victory over temptation and sin can only be found in and through the grace and power of God our heavenly Father. Thus such an individual, with a sincere heart of consecration unto the Lord, will pray unto our heavenly Father to grant Him such victory and deliverance for each moment of the battle against temptation and sin. *"And lead us not into temptation, but deliver us from evil."*

Finally, we are to pray with praise unto the Lord our God and heavenly Father; even as this model prayer closes at the end of verse 13, *"For Thine is the kingdom, and the power, and the glory, for ever. Amen."* Oh brethren, how very much should our prayers be filled with the praises of our heavenly Father!

<hr>

16. We must not set our affection upon or lay up for ourselves "treasures upon earth," but must set our affection upon and lay up for ourselves "treasures in heaven."

Matthew 6:19-24 – *"**Lay not up for yourselves treasures upon earth**, where moth and rust doth corrupt, and where thieves break through and steal: **but lay up for yourselves treasures in heaven**, where neither moth nor rust doth corrupt, and where thieves do not break through nor steal: for where your treasure is, there will your heart be also. The light of the body is the eye: if therefore thine eye be single, thy whole body shall be full of light. But if thine eye be evil, thy whole body shall be full of darkness. If therefore the light that is in thee be darkness, how great is that darkness! No man can serve two masters: for either he will hate the one, and love the other; or else he will hold to the one, and despise the other. Ye cannot serve God and mammon."*

Luke 12:33-34 – *"**Sell that ye have, and give alms; provide yourselves bags which wax not old, a treasure in the heavens that faileth not**, where no thief approacheth, neither moth corrupteth. For where your treasure is, there will your heart be also."*

Colossians 3:2-4 – *"**Set your affection on things above, not on things on the earth**. For ye are dead, and your life is hid with Christ in God. When Christ, who is our life, shall appear, then shall ye also appear with him in glory."*

80

In these passages we find a two-fold instruction. We are instructed both concerning what we must not do and what we must do. On the one hand, we are instructed not to set our affection upon or lay up for ourselves "treasures upon the earth." On the other hand, we are instructed to set our affection upon and lay up for ourselves "treasures in heaven." As long as we live upon this earth we shall be required to deal with physical "things." In addition, there is some element within all of our hearts that drives us to seek after, obtain, take pleasure in, and hold onto the "things" of this life. Yet God's Word instructs us not to allow the "things" of this life to become the treasure of our hearts and lives.

We must not set the affections of hearts upon "things on the earth." We must not covet after the money and the treasures of this life. We must not set our trust, hope, and confidence in "uncertain riches;" and such "treasures upon the earth" are indeed "uncertain riches." Upon this earth "moth and rust doth corrupt," and thieves do "break through and steal." As Proverbs 23:5 indicates, such treasures and riches "*certainly make themselves wings; they fly away as an eagle toward heaven.*" They are "here today and gone tomorrow." We must not seek and labor "to be rich." (See Proverbs 23:4) Such is often the direction and driving motive for those of this lost world. Yet such must not become the direction and driving motive of our hearts and lives as God's own dear children.

Rather, God's Word instructs us to "lay up" for ourselves "treasures in heaven," to make the things of heaven to be the treasures of our hearts and lives. We are to "seek those things which are above," and to set our "affection on things above." We must seek first "*the kingdom of God, and His righteousness.*" (See Matthew 6:33) We must view the things of our Lord Jesus Christ as far "*greater riches than the treasures*" of this earth. (See Hebrews 11:26) We must come to understand and know with full assurance of faith that we "*have in heaven a better and an enduring substance*" (See Hebrews 10:34), that is – "in heaven, where neither moth nor rust doth corrupt, and where thieves do not break through nor steal."

Now, such does not mean that it is wrong for a child of God to have some "things" of this world, or even for a child of God to be "rich in this world." Indeed, the Lord our God is willing at times to bless some of His dear children with such wealth and riches. However, this does mean that we must never seek after such riches, nor trust in such riches, nor hoard such riches unto ourselves. Rather, we must *"be content with such things"* that our Lord has graciously given us, and must trust in our Lord and give thanks unto Him in all things. (See Hebrews 13:5-6) In addition, if our Lord does graciously bless us with *"this world's good,"* then we must be *"rich in good works, ready to distribute"* and willing to give of our good to help those in need. (See 1 John 3:17; 1 Timothy 6:17-19)

So then, having given to us the warning and instruction of Matthew 6:19-20, in verse 21 our Lord reveals the principle upon which these things are founded – *"For where your treasure is, there will your heart be also."* Then in explanation of this principle, our Lord first gives an illustration and then an admonition. We find the illustration in verses 22-23, *"The light of the body is the eye: if therefore thine eye be single, thy whole body shall be full of light. But if thine eye be evil, thy whole body shall be full of darkness. If therefore the light that is in thee be darkness, how great is that darkness!"*

Herein our Lord used our physical eye as an illustration for the focus of our hearts. It is only by our physical eyes that we can experience physical light. If we close our eyes, or if our eyes become blinded, then no matter how much physical light may be around us, we ourselves will not be able to experience that light. Our physical eyes must be focused upon the light in order to experience that light. Even so, in the spiritual realm, if our hearts are focused upon the things of our Lord, who Himself is the light, then our whole lives "shall be full of light." However, if our "eye be evil," that is – if our hearts are focused upon the "treasures" of this dark world, then our whole lives "shall be full of darkness." Indeed, Proverbs 28:22 declares, *"He that hasteth to be rich hath an evil eye, and considereth not that poverty shall come upon him."* On the other hand, Proverbs 22:9 declares, *"He that hath a bountiful eye shall be blessed; for he giveth of his bread to the poor."*

Then in Matthew 6:24 our Lord delivered His admonition, *"No man can serve two masters: for either he will hate the one, and love the other; or else he will hold to the one, and despise the other. Ye cannot serve God and mammon* [that is – the "things" of this world]." It is spiritually impossible for us both to give our lives in service to the Lord our God and Savior and to seek after the riches and treasures of this life at the same time. It is spiritually impossible for us both to "lay up" for ourselves "treasures in heaven" and to "lay up" for ourselves "treasures upon the earth" at the same time. It is spiritually impossible for us to set our affection both "on things above" and "on things on the earth" at the same time. It is spiritually impossible for us to set the focus of our hearts both upon the "things" of our Lord and light and upon the "things" of this world and darkness at the same time.

Two "masters" stand before us seeking to direct our lives according to their own ways. On the one hand is the Lord our God and Savior who is seeking to direct our lives according to His light and righteousness. On the other hand is the "things" of this world that seeks to direct our lives according to its darkness and unrighteousness. We cannot follow and serve both of these "masters" at the same time. We must choose one or the other to follow and serve. Either we "will hate" the "things" of this world as a master, "and love" the Lord our God and Savior as our Master; or else we "will hold to" the "things" of this world as the master of our hearts and lives, "and despise" the Lord our God and Savior as a Master for our hearts and lives.

Even so, Colossians 3:2-4 presents four motivations which should move us to love and serve the Lord as the Master for our hearts and lives. First, we are to be motivated by the truth that at our salvation in our regeneration, we were made spiritually dead unto this present, evil world. Indeed, by *"the cross of our Lord Jesus Christ," "the world is crucified"* unto us; and we unto the world. (See Galatians 6:14) Second, we are to be motivated by the truth that our spiritual life is now "hid with Christ in God." Third, we are to be motivated by the truth that our Lord and Savior Jesus Christ is the very Source of our present spiritual life. Finally, we are to be motivated by the truth that our Lord Jesus Christ is coming again to take us out of this world and to receive us unto Himself. Therefore, our affection should be set on the things of our Lord, our Savior from sin, our Source of life, and our coming Lord, not on the things of this world.

17. We must not be worried about the matters of this life.

Matthew 6:25-34 – *"Therefore I say unto you,* **Take no thought for your life, what ye shall eat, or what ye shall drink; nor yet for your body, what ye shall put on.** *Is not the life more than meat, and the body than raiment? Behold the fowls of the air: for they sow not, neither do they reap, nor gather into barns; yet your heavenly Father feedeth them. Are ye not much better than they? Which of you by taking thought can add one cubit unto his stature? And why take ye thought for raiment? Consider the lilies of the field, how they grow; they toil not, neither do they spin: and yet I say unto you, That even Solomon in all his glory was not arrayed like one of these. Wherefore, if God so clothe the grass of the field, which to day is, and to morrow is cast into the oven, shall he not much more clothe you, O ye of little faith?* **Therefore take no thought, saying, What shall we eat? or, What shall we drink? or, Wherewithal shall we be clothed?** *(For after all these things do the Gentiles seek:) For your heavenly Father knoweth that ye have need of all these things. But seek ye first the kingdom of God, and his righteousness; and all these things shall be added unto you.* **Take therefore no thought for the morrow**: *for the morrow shall take thought for the things of itself. Sufficient unto the day is the evil thereof."*

Luke 12:22-30 – *"And he said unto his disciples, Therefore I say unto you,* **Take no thought for your life, what ye shall eat; neither for the body, what ye shall put on.** *The life is more than meat, and the body is more than raiment. Consider the ravens: for they neither sow nor reap; which neither have storehouse nor barn; and God feedeth them: how much more are ye better than the fowls? And which of you with taking thought can add to his stature one cubit? If ye then be not able to do that thing which is least, why take ye thought for the rest? Consider the lilies how they grow: they toil not, they spin not; and yet I say unto you, that Solomon in all his glory was not arrayed like one of these. If then God so clothe the grass, which is to day in the field, and to morrow is cast into the oven; how much more will he clothe you, O ye of little faith?* **And seek not ye what ye shall eat, or what ye shall drink, neither be ye of doubtful mind.** *For all these things do the nations of the world seek after: and your Father knoweth that ye have need of these things."*

Philippians 4:6 – "***Be careful for nothing***; *but in every thing by prayer and supplication with thanksgiving let your requests be made known unto God.*"

Three times in Matthew 6:25-34 our Lord instructed us to "take no thought" for the matters of our lives, concerning our daily food, concerning our clothing and shelter, and concerning tomorrow's events. In like manner, in Philippians 4:6 God's Word instructs us to "be careful for nothing." These instructions do not mean that we are never to think about our lives, our way, or our future. Nor do these instructions mean that we are never to pay careful attention in the steps and activities of our lives. Rather, within the context of Matthew 6:25-34, the phrase, "Take no thought," means that we should not be anxious or worried about the matters of this life. Also the "carefulness" about which Philippians 4:6 speaks refers, not unto attentive care, but unto anxious care. Thus we are not to be filled with a spirit of anxious worry about what we shall eat or drink or wear, or about how we shall take care of ourselves. Indeed, as the children of God our heavenly Father, we are never to be filled with a spirit of anxious worry about anything of this life.

We are to be full of anxious care and worry "for nothing" whatsoever at all. On the other hand, in Philippians 4:6 God's Word instructs that "in every thing" we are to let our "requests be made known unto God." We are to take every matter, every care, every problem, every situation, every issue, every need, every decision, everything, no matter how small or big, no matter of what sort, unto the Lord our God "by prayer and supplication." We are to make our "requests known unto God" by the heart-expression of prayer and by the heart-fervency of supplication; and we are to do so with the heart-gratitude of thanksgiving. We are to enter into prayer and supplication "with thanksgiving," giving thanks that the Lord our God graciously cares for us so as to hear our prayers and to answer them according to His righteous will and perfect wisdom. Then the anxieties and worries of our hearts will be replaced with the perfect peace of God. Even so, Philippians 4:7 delivers the promise, "*And the peace of God, which passeth all understanding, shall keep your hearts and minds through Christ Jesus.*"

Such is our Lord's instruction and promise unto us. Furthermore, with this instruction our Lord included various reasons for its value in our lives. First, we find that we should not be filled with anxious worry about the matters of life because such worrying demonstrates a wrong focus. This truth is revealed to us through the first word of Matthew 6:25, that is – through the word *"therefore."* Certainly, the word "therefore" leads us back unto the command to "take no thought for your life." Yet this word "therefore" also directs us back to the instruction and warning that our Lord had just delivered in verses 19-24.

The instruction was that we are not to lay up for ourselves "treasures upon earth," but to lay up for ourselves "treasures in heaven." The warning was that we cannot serve both the Lord our God and the things of this world. "Therefore," because of this very instruction and warning, we are not to be worried about the matters of this life. Yet how are these things so connected? Our worrying reveals the focus of our hearts. Yea, our worrying about the things of this life reveals that our hearts are focused upon the world and the things of this world, rather than upon our Lord and the things of our Lord. This truth and principle is also presented through the parenthetical statement of verse 32 where our Lord proclaims, *"For after all these things do the Gentiles seek."* The lost of this world seek after the things of this world. Yet we who are the children of God are to seek after the things of our Lord. "Therefore," we are not to set the focus of our hearts upon the things of this world; and "therefore," we are not to be worried about the things of this world and of this life.

Second, we find that we should not be filled with anxious worry about the matters of this life because our lives are more (much more) than just about the things of this life. At the end of Matthew 6:25, our Lord asked the rhetorical question, *"Is not the life more than meat, and the body than raiment?"* To this question our Lord's intended answer is – "Yes, certainly our lives are more than such things." Our Christian lives are not defined by food, and clothing, and the things of this world. Rather, our Christian lives are to be defined by our fellowship with, obedience to, service for, and fruitfulness in our Lord.

Third, we find that we should not be filled with anxious worry about the matters of this life because such worrying is a waste of our time and energy. This is so because our worrying can do nothing to change our situation. In Matthew 6:27 our Lord asked another rhetorical question, *"Which of you by taking thought* [that is – by worrying over it] *can add one cubit unto his stature?"* Let us image a young man who has come to the conclusion that he is just too short and that he needs to grow taller. So then, this young man begins to worry, and worry, and worry, and worry some more over his short stature. Here is the question – How many inches will this young man's worrying add to his stature? The obvious answer is that all of his worrying will not do a single thing to help his situation. In like manner, all of our worrying about the matters of life will not do a single thing to help our situation.

Fourth, we find that we should not be filled with anxious worry about the matters of this life because such worrying demonstrates a lack of faith in the Lord our God. In Matthew 6:26 our Lord declared, *"Behold the fowls of the air: for they sow not, neither do they reap, nor gather into barns; yet your heavenly Father feedeth them. Are ye not much better than they?"* Certainly, we are "much better" than "the fowls of the air." So then, if our heavenly Father feeds and takes care of the birds, certainly our heavenly Father will feed and take care of us who are His very own dear children. Again in verses 28-30 our Lord declared, *"Consider the lilies of the field, how they grow; they toil not, neither do they spin: and yet I say unto you, That even Solomon in all his glory was not arrayed like one of these. Wherefore, if God so clothe the grass of the field, which to day is, and to morrow is cast into the oven, shall he not much more clothe you, O ye of little faith?"* Certainly, if the Lord our God clothes and cares for the flowers of the field, then He will "much more" clothe and care for us who are His own chosen people. Yet our worrying over such things demonstrates that we have a lack of faith in our heavenly Father's concern for us and in His willingness to take care of us. Certainly, such a lack of faith in our Lord is an offense and sin against our Lord and heavenly Father.

Fifth, we find that we should not be filled with anxious worry about the matters of this life because our heavenly Father, who cares for us, already knows all of our needs. In Matthew 6:31-32 our Lord gave the instruction and truth, *"Therefore take no thought, saying, What shall we eat? Or, what shall we drink? Or, wherewithal shall we be clothed? (For after all these things do the Gentiles seek:) For your heavenly Father knoweth that ye have need of all these things."* So much of our worrying is over the unknowns, the "what-ifs," of life. Yet such unknowns should not overcome us who are the children of God because we know that our caring heavenly Father does know all of these things.

Finally, we find that we should not be filled with anxious worry about the matters of tomorrow and following because we have plenty of responsibility for the present day. In Matthew 6:34 our Lord gave the instruction and truth, *"Take therefore no thought for the morrow: for the morrow shall take thought for the things of itself. Sufficient unto the day is the evil thereof."* If we spend our time and energy worrying about the things of tomorrow, we will not have the time and energy to deal with the responsibilities of today.

18. We must ever seek first "the kingdom of God, and His righteousness."

Matthew 6:33 – *"**But seek ye first the kingdom of God**, and his righteousness; and all these things shall be added unto you."*

Luke 12:31-32 – *"**But rather seek ye the kingdom of God**; and all these things shall be added unto you. Fear not, little flock; for it is your Father's good pleasure to give you the kingdom."*

Colossians 3:1 – *"If ye then be risen with Christ, **seek those things which are above**, where Christ sitteth on the right hand of God."*

To be risen with our Lord Jesus Christ means that spiritually our old man has been crucified with Christ and that spiritually we have been raised with Christ unto newness of life. This occurs at the moment of our faith in Christ for salvation. So then, if we are saved, if we have been raised up with our Lord and Savior Jesus Christ unto newness of spiritual life, then we should no longer seek after the things of this world. Rather, we should seek first after the things of our Lord in heaven. Our citizenship is there. Thus our interests should be focused there.

Instead of seeking after and worrying over the things of this life, we are to be seeking after the kingdom and righteousness of the Lord our God. The things of the Lord are to have first place in our hearts and lives. Furthermore, our Lord has promised that if we will seek first His kingdom and righteousness, then He most certainly will meet our needs. This is His promise, *"And all these things shall be added unto you."* Now, this promise only stands true for those who will seek "first the kingdom of God, and His righteousness." Yet for such individuals this promise stands absolutely true. For such individuals this promise is absolutely solid ground. If we will set our focus upon the kingdom and righteousness of our Lord in our service for Him, then He will provide for all of our needs in His care for us.

19. We must not be judgmental toward others, but must humbly seek after their spiritual growth.

Matthew 7:1-5 – *"**Judge not**, that ye be not judged. For with what judgment ye judge, ye shall be judged: and with what measure ye mete, it shall be measured to you again. And why beholdest thou the mote that is in thy brother's eye, but considerest not the beam that is in thine own eye? Or how wilt thou say to thy brother, Let me pull out the mote out of thine eye; and, behold, a beam is in thine own eye? **Thou hypocrite, first cast out the beam out of thine own eye**; and then shalt thou see clearly to cast out the mote out of thy brother's eye."*

Luke 6:37 – *"**Judge not**, and ye shall not be judged: **condemn not**, and ye shall not be condemned: forgive, and ye shall be forgiven."*

Luke 6:41-42 – *"And why beholdest thou the mote that is in thy brother's eye, but perceivest not the beam that is in thine own eye? Either how canst thou say to thy brother, Brother, let me pull out the mote that is in thine eye, when thou thyself beholdest not the beam that is in thine own eye?* **Thou hypocrite, cast out first the beam out of thine own eye**, *and then shalt thou see clearly to pull out the mote that is in thy brother's eye.*"

In these passages our Lord presented a two-fold command. On the one hand, He presented a command of warning; and on the other hand, He presented a command of practice. In Matthew 7:1 our Lord delivered the command of warning – "*Judge not, that ye be not judged.*" (See also Luke 6:37) Then in Matthew 7:5 our Lord delivered the command of practice – "*Thou hypocrite, first cast out the beam out of thine own eye; and then shalt thou see clearly to cast out the mote out of thy brother's eye.*" (See also Luke 6:42) Thus we find a two-fold command concerning that which we should not do and that which we should do.

First then, we consider that which we should not do. In Matthew 7:1 our Lord declared, "*Judge not, that ye be not judged.*" Does this mean that we are never to be discerning and never to make discerning judgments concerning the spiritual condition of others? By removing this command from the entire context of the passage, many have used this command in just such a manner. However, through the context we find that our Lord does not intend such an application. In fact, in Matthew 7:5 our Lord Himself gives us instruction on the manner by which we are to seek "*to cast out the mote out of* [our] *brother's eye.*" Even so, such a practice certainly requires for us to make some form of discerning judgment concerning our brother.

So then, what does our Lord mean with the command that we should "judge not." Our Lord's intent is to warn us against maintaining a judgmental spirit against others. Our Lord is warning us against the spirit of looking for faults in others and of looking down upon others for their faults. Our Lord is warning us against always criticizing and condemning others for their faults. Such a judgmental spirit is completely without any element of godly love one for another. In Galatians 5:14-15 we are given the instruction and warning, "*For all the Law is fulfilled in one word, even in this; Thou shalt love thy neighbor as thyself. But if ye bite and devour one another, take heed that ye be not consumed one of another.*" The way of "biting and devouring" one another is contradictory to the way of loving one another. Thus we are not to engage in a judgmental spirit against one another.

In fact, in Matthew 7:1-4 our Lord provided two reasons that we should not be judgmental against one another. The first is that we ourselves shall receive the same measure of judgmentalism (that is – of criticizing and condemning) that we have meted out against others. In verses 1-2 our Lord gives the warning, "*Judge not, that ye be not judged. For with what judgment ye judge, ye shall be judged: and with what measure ye mete, it shall be measured to you again.*" If we mete out loving edification, and even loving correction, toward others, then we ourselves shall receive back such loving edification and correction. Yet if we mete out criticizing and condemning, then we ourselves shall receive back just such criticizing and condemning. If we follow the way of "biting and devouring" others, then we shall find others "biting and devouring" us. Such is our Lord's principle and warning. Sowing love reaps love; and sowing loving correction reaps loving correction. On the other hand, sowing judgmentalism reaps judgmentalism. "*Judge not, that ye be not judged.*"

The second reason that our Lord gives against such judgmentalism is that we ourselves should not walk in hypocrisy. In Matthew 7:3-4 our Lord gives this warning in the form of some rhetorical questions, saying, "*And why beholdest thou the mote that is in thy brother's eye, but considerest not the beam that is in thine own eye? Or how wilt thou say to thy brother, Let me pull out the mote out of thine eye; and, behold, a beam is in thine own eye?*" A mote is a small speck of wood; whereas a beam is like an entire four-by-four post. What right would an individual have to be pointing out the small speck of wood that is in another's eye while that same individual is completely ignoring the wooden post that is in his own eye? Yea, how could that individual even be able to help the other remove the small speck of wood from his eye while he himself still has that wooden post in his own eye? Such an individual would not even be able to see straight. Even so, with this illustration our Lord taught that we ourselves have no place at all to be criticizing the smaller faults in others' lives while we ourselves are completely overlooking the large, glaring faults in our own lives.

Now, with this warning our Lord moved to the second part of His two-fold command – to that which we should do. We should not be judgmental against one another. Yet what should we do? In Matthew 7:5 our Lord gives answer, saying, *"Thou hypocrite, first cast out the beam out of thine own eye; and then shalt thou see clearly to cast out the mote out of thy brother's eye."* Before we go about to deal with the faults and failures of others, we must deal with our own faults and failures. We cannot actually be of any help unto others in sin if our spiritual sight is distorted and damaged by our own sin. Thus before we go forth to deal with the faults and failures of others, we must have clear spiritual sight ourselves.

Even so, Galatians 6:1 declares, *"Brethren, if a man be overtaken in a fault, ye which are spiritual, restore such an one in the spirit of meekness; considering thyself, lest thou also be tempted."* The instruction of God's Holy Word is very precise. Not just any of us is to restore the one who is "overtaken in a fault." Rather, only those who can be Biblically defined as the spiritual are to restore one who is "overtaken in a fault." If we ourselves are not walking in the Spirit, then it is not our place to deal with the faults and failures of others. We must first deal with the faults and failures of our own hearts and lives, and then we may "see clearly" to deal with the faults and failures of another. Furthermore, when we are in the place to go forth and "cast out the mote that is in [our] brother's eye," we must do so "in the spirit of meekness." Yea, we must approach the other with a spirit of godly humility and love. Such an approach cannot be about looking down upon another, but must be about helping another to get up and to be restored unto a healthy, godly walk with the Lord.

(Note: The characteristics of the judgmental are as follows: (1) They "blow out of proportion" the smaller faults and failures of others. (2) They overlook and ignore their own larger and glaring faults and failures. (3) They poke their fingers into situations where they do not belong. (4) They lack godly humility and love in their approach. (5) They devour and destroy, rather than restore and build up.)

20. We must not give that which is holy and precious unto those who fiercely oppose it.

Matthew 7:6 – "***Give not that which is holy unto the dogs, neither cast ye your pearls before swine***, *lest they trample them under their feet, and turn again and rend you.*"

In the context of Matthew 7:1-5, the holy things and precious pearls about which our Lord speaks are the corrective truths of God's Holy Word that might be humbly and lovingly delivered to those who are "overtaken in a fault." Even so, in Matthew 7:6 our Lord commands us not to give such holy and precious things unto those who might be described as "the dogs" and as "swine." So then, to whom is our Lord referring with this mention of dogs and swine? At that time the majority of dogs in the land of Israel were half-wild, mongrel dogs that ran in packs and foraged for food in the refuse pile. The swine in the land of Israel at that time were of a similar character, running wild and foraging in the refuse pile. These dogs and swine were not lovable pets. Rather, they were mean-spirited animals. Thus our Lord is instructing us not to deliver the corrective truths of God's holy and precious Word unto those who stand stubbornly and fiercely opposed to it. There is a time when we must walk away and shake the dust off our feet. There is a time when we must move on to deliver the holy and precious truths of God's Word to those who will hear and receive it, and must leave those who fiercely oppose such holy and precious things to the judgment of God's hand.

21. We must continue in a fervent and faith-filled prayer life.

Matthew 7:7-11 – "***Ask***, *and it shall be given you;* ***seek***, *and ye shall find;* ***knock***, *and it shall be opened unto you: for every one that asketh receiveth; and he that seeketh findeth; and to him that knocketh it shall be opened. Or what man is there of you, whom if his son ask bread, will he give him a stone? Or if he ask a fish, will he give him a serpent? If ye then, being evil, know how to give good gifts unto your children, how much more shall your Father which is in heaven give good things to them that ask him?*"

Luke 11:5-13 – "*And he said unto them, Which of you shall have a friend, and shall go unto him at midnight, and say unto him, Friend, lend me three loaves; for a friend of mine in his journey is come to me, and I have nothing to set before him? And he from within shall answer and say, Trouble me not: the door is now shut, and my children are with me in bed; I cannot rise and give thee. I say unto you, Though he will not rise and give him, because he is his friend, yet because of his importunity he will rise and give him as many as he needeth. And I say unto you, **Ask**, and it shall be given you; **seek**, and ye shall find; **knock**, and it shall be opened unto you. For every one that asketh receiveth; and he that seeketh findeth; and to him that knocketh it shall be opened. If a son shall ask bread of any of you that is a father, will he give him a stone? Or if he ask a fish, will he for a fish give him a serpent? Or if he shall ask an egg, will he offer him a scorpion? If ye then, being evil, know how to give good gifts unto your children: how much more shall your heavenly Father give the Holy Spirit to them that ask him?*"

Luke 18:1-7 – "*And he spake a parable unto them to this end, **that men ought always to pray, and not to faint**; Saying, There was in a city a judge, which feared not God, neither regarded man: and there was a widow in that city; and she came unto him, saying, Avenge me of mine adversary. And he would not for a while: but afterward he said within himself, Though I fear not God, nor regard man; yet because this widow troubleth me, I will avenge her, lest by her continual coming she weary me. And the Lord said, Hear what the unjust judge saith. And shall not God avenge his own elect, which cry day and night unto him, though he bear long with them?*"

Romans 12:12 – "*Rejoicing in hope; patient in tribulation; **continuing instant in prayer**.*"

Ephesians 6:18 – "***Praying always with all prayer and supplication in the Spirit,** and watching thereunto with all perseverance and supplication for all saints.*"

Philippians 4:6 – "*Be careful for nothing; **but in every thing by prayer and supplication with thanksgiving let your requests be made known unto God**.*"

Colossians 4:2 – "***Continue in prayer***, *and watch in the same with thanksgiving.*"

1 Thessalonians 5:17 – "***Pray without ceasing***."

James 1:6-8 – "***But let him ask in faith, nothing wavering***. *For he that wavereth is like a wave of the sea driven with the wind and tossed. For let not that man think that he shall receive any thing of the Lord. A double minded man is unstable in all his ways.*"

Jude 1:20 – "*But ye, beloved, building up yourselves on your most holy faith,* ***praying in the Holy Ghost***."

In Matthew 7:7-11 (see also Luke 11:5-13) our Lord Jesus Christ gave the three-fold command to ask, seek, knock in prayer. Now, there are different perspectives that may be taken as we consider the three elements of this command. We may view these three elements simply as parallel elements. Thus the asking, seeking, and knocking all direct our attention unto the same thing, that is – our prayer lives. From another perspective we may view these three elements as those that grow in intensity. Thus we may view the seeking as somewhat more intensive than the asking, and the knocking as somewhat more intensive even than the seeking. With this perspective we are brought to consider the growing fervency of our prayer lives.

Yet from another perspective we may view these three elements as each having a different focus for our prayer lives. Thus the asking would be a focus upon our daily needs, that we should be asking our Lord to meet our basic, daily needs. Furthermore, the seeking would be a focus upon a desire for guidance, that we should be fervently seeking for our Lord's guidance and direction in our daily living. Finally, the knocking would be a focus upon a hunger and thirst for our Lord's fellowship, that we should be even more fervently knocking in prayer that our Lord might draw nigh unto us in fellowship with Him.

However, no matter what perspective we may take there are some matters that are certain. All three of the elements in this three-fold command of our Lord are given in the present tense. Thus we are to be presently asking, presently seeking, and presently knocking in prayer. Indeed, we are to be continuing in such asking, seeking, and knocking throughout our daily walk. We are to be continuing in a fervent prayer life.

Even so, in Matthew 7:7-11 (see also Luke 11:5-13) our Lord presented two truths in order to encourage such a continuing, fervent prayer life. These two truths are the promise of our heavenly Father and the character of our heavenly Father. In verses 7-8 we find the certain promise of our heavenly Father – "*Ask, and it shall be given you; seek, and ye shall find; knock, and it shall be opened unto you: for every one that asketh receiveth; and he that seeketh findeth; and to him that knocketh it shall be opened.*" Every one of us who will continue in asking shall be receiving from the hand of our heavenly Father. Each one of us who will continue in seeking shall be finding from the hand of our heavenly Father. Each and every one of us who will continue in knocking shall be having the door of our heavenly Father's fellowship opened unto him or her. This is the promise of our Lord and heavenly Father. Let us then maintain a continuing, fervent prayer life!

Furthermore, in verses 9-11 we find the loving character of our heavenly Father – "*Or what man is there of you, whom if his son ask bread, will he give him a stone? Or if he ask a fish, will he give him a serpent? If ye then, being evil, know how to give good gifts unto your children, how much more shall your Father which is in heaven give good things to them that ask him?*" We are sinful and selfish by nature; yet we still "know how to give good gifts unto [our] children." When our children ask us for something that they genuinely need, we do not respond by giving them something harmful. Rather, we do what we can to meet their need in a genuine, and even generous, fashion. Yea, we are even willing to give gifts unto our children, to give them things that they have not earned or do not even deserve.

"How much more" then shall our heavenly Father, who is righteous and loving by nature, "give good things unto them that ask Him?" Indeed, our heavenly Father is multiplied times more gracious and generous unto us who are His own dear children than we will or could ever be unto our own dear children! Furthermore, let us take notice that our heavenly Father will only ever give "good things" unto us His own dear children. He will only ever give things that are good for and not harmful to our Christian lives. Let us then ever continue in fervent prayer unto Him. Yea, let us ever continue in fervent prayer with the encouragement and expectation that He shall, according to His own certain promise and loving nature, "give good things unto them that ask Him." As James 1:6 teaches us, let us "ask in faith, nothing wavering." Let us ever continue in both fervent and faith-filled prayer lives.

Even so, in the opening portion of Ephesians 6:18, we find four elements that our Lord requires of us in our prayer lives – "*Praying always with all prayer and supplication in the Spirit.*" First, we are required to be faithful in prayer, to be "praying always." In like manner, Romans 12:12 instructs us to be "*continuing instant in prayer;*" and Colossians 4:2 instructs us to "*continue in prayer.*" Again 1 Thessalonians 5:17 instructs us to "*pray without ceasing.*" Yet again Philippians 4:6 instructs us, "*Be careful for nothing; but in everything by prayer and supplication with thanksgiving let your requests be made known unto God.*" Finally, in Luke 18:1-7 our Lord Jesus Christ presented the parable of the widow and the unjust judge to teach us that we "*ought always to pray, and not to faint.*"

Second, we are required to have faith in prayer, to be praying "with all prayer." The word "prayer" here carries the idea of asking or requesting for something desired. The focus of this word is upon the matter of faith. In true, Biblical prayer we are setting our trust and hope in the Lord our God to meet our needs and to provide our request. We are not relying on any other source; we are placing our faith in the Lord. Even so, in Matthew 21:22 our Lord Jesus Christ gave the promise, "*And all things, whatsoever ye shall ask in prayer, believing, ye shall receive.*" Furthermore, in James 1:6-7 the warning is given, "*But let him ask in faith, nothing wavering. For he that wavereth is like a wave of the sea driven with the wind and tossed. For let not that man think that he shall receive any thing of the Lord.*"

Third, we are required to be fervent in prayer, to be praying "with all . . . supplication." The word "supplication" here carries the idea of entreating and even pleading out of a sense of desperate need. The focus of this word is upon the matter of fervency and earnestness. Even so, in the closing phrase of James 5:16, the promise is given, *"The effectual fervent prayer of a righteous man availeth much."* Furthermore, as we have previously noted, in Matthew 7:7-8 our Lord Jesus Christ gave the instruction and promise, *"Ask, and it shall be given you; seek, and ye shall find; knock, and it shall be opened unto you: for every one that asketh receiveth; and he that seeketh findeth; and to him that knocketh it shall be opened."* (See also Luke 11:910)

Fourth, we are required to be Spirit-filled in prayer, to be praying "in the Spirit." This means that we must be walking and praying in submission unto the righteous guidance of the indwelling Holy Spirit. Even so, in Romans 8:26-27 the assurance is given, *"Likewise the Spirit also helpeth our infirmities: for we know not what we should pray for as we ought: but the Spirit itself maketh intercession for us with groanings which cannot be uttered. And he that searcheth the hearts knoweth what is the mind of the Spirit, because he maketh intercession for the saints according to the will of God."* Again in Jude 1:20-21 the instruction is given, *"But ye, beloved, building up yourselves on your most holy faith, praying in the Holy Ghost, keep yourselves in the love of God, looking for the mercy of our Lord Jesus Christ unto eternal life."* Yet again in the closing portion of James 5:16 the promise is given, *"The effectual fervent prayer of a righteous man availeth much."* Finally, in 1 John 3:22 the promise is given, *"And whatsoever we ask, we receive of him, because we keep his commandments, and do those things that are pleasing in his sight."*

In addition, Philippians 4:6 reveals two further elements that our Lord requires of us in our prayer lives – *"Be careful for nothing; but in every thing by prayer and supplication with thanksgiving let your requests be made known unto God."* Fifth, we are required to be universal in prayer, to be praying "in every thing." Indeed, we are to be full of care (that is – of anxiety and worry) "for nothing." On the other hand, "in every thing" we are to let our "requests be made known unto God." We are to take every matter, every care, every problem, every conflict, every situation, every need, every issue, every decision, everything, no matter how small or big, no matter of what sort, unto the Lord our God "by prayer and supplication." We are to make our requests known unto God our heavenly Father by the heart-expression of prayer and with the heart-fervency of supplication.

Sixth, we are required to be thankful in prayer, to be praying "with thanksgiving." We are to make our requests known unto God our heavenly Father, not only by the heart-expression of prayer and with the heart-fervency of supplication, but also with the heart-gratitude of thanksgiving. We are to give thanks that God our heavenly Father graciously cares for us so as to hear and answer our prayers according to His righteous will and perfect wisdom. Then the anxieties and worries of our hearts will be replaced with the perfect peace of God. Thus Philippians 4:7 delivers the promise, "*And the peace of God, which passeth all understanding, shall keep your hearts and minds through Christ Jesus.*"

22. We must do unto others what we would want them to do unto us.

Matthew 7:12 – "***Therefore all things whatsoever ye would that men should do to you, do ye even so to them***: *for this is the law and the prophets.*"

Luke 6:31 – "***And as ye would that men should do to you, do ye also to them likewise.***"

First, we must take notice that the focus of this command is not upon what others have done, are doing, or will do to us. Rather, the focus of this command is upon what we ourselves should be doing unto others. Second, we must take notice that we are to do unto others, not what they have done unto us, or what we expect they will do unto us, but what we would want them to do unto us. How do you want others to treat you? This is how you are to treat them. Indeed, this you are to do whether or not they ever treat you this way. Finally, we must take notice that we are to do this in all things. The command begins, "Therefore all things whatsoever ye would . . . ."

23. We must examine ourselves and be certain that we have entered in at the narrow gate through faith and are truly saved in Christ.

Matthew 7:13-14 – "***Enter ye in at the strait gate****: for wide is the gate, and broad is the way, that leadeth to destruction, and many there be which go in thereat: because strait is the gate, and narrow is the way, which leadeth unto life, and few there be that find it.*"

Luke 13:23-30 – "*Then said one unto him, Lord, are there few that be saved? And he said unto them, **Strive to enter in at the strait gate***: *for many, I say unto you, will seek to enter in, and shall not be able. When once the master of the house is risen up, and hath shut to the door, and ye begin to stand without, and to knock at the door, saying, Lord, Lord, open unto us; and he shall answer and say unto you, I know you not whence ye are: then shall ye begin to say, We have eaten and drunk in thy presence, and thou hast taught in our streets. But he shall say, I tell you, I know you not whence ye are; depart from me, all ye workers of iniquity. There shall be weeping and gnashing of teeth, when ye shall see Abraham, and Isaac, and Jacob, and all the prophets, in the kingdom of God, and you yourselves thrust out. And they shall come from the east, and from the west, and from the north, and from the south, and shall sit down in the kingdom of God. And, behold, there are last which shall be first, and there are first which shall be last.*"

2 Corinthians 13:5 – "***Examine yourselves, whether ye be in the faith; prove your own selves. Know ye not your own selves, how that Jesus Christ is in you***, *except ye be reprobates?*"

In Matthew 7:13 and Luke 13:24 our Lord's command is centered upon our entering in by the right gate and the right way. From the further details of Matthew 7:13-14 and Luke 13:23-30, we learn that this "entering in" pertains to eternal salvation, to eternal life, and to an eternal home with the Lord. So then, these passages are a warning from our Lord in order that we might examine ourselves and be certain that we have entered into eternal salvation by the right gate and the right way. In like manner, 2 Corinthians provides the warning to examine ourselves, to know our own selves and find evidence within ourselves, that the Lord Jesus Christ truly is within us as our eternal Savior from sin.

In our day there are many who believe that we may all be going by a different way, but that we will all finally get to heaven in the end. Yet this is not so. According to our Lord's warning, the wide gate and broad way by which "the many" are "entering in" will lead only to destruction in the eternal torments of hell, where "there shall be weeping and gnashing of teeth." Rather, the gate and way that leads to life eternal with the Lord is narrow, "and few there be that find it." Now, it is not that only few find this narrow gate and way because our Lord has hidden it from them. Rather, it is that only few find this narrow gate and way because only few are willing to choose this gate and way.

The majority want to obtain eternal life through their own way. However, the narrow gate and way that actually leads to eternal life is not of our own choosing. It is the way of our Lord's choosing. So then, what is that way? Our Lord Jesus Christ Himself gives answer in John 14:6, saying, "*I am the way, the truth, and the life: no man cometh unto the Father, but by me.*" Again the Word of God gives answer in Acts 4:12, "*Neither is there salvation in any other: for there is none other name under heaven given among men, whereby we must be saved.*" Yet again the Word of God declares in 1 John 5:11-13, "*And this is the record, that God hath given to us eternal life, and this life is in his Son. He that hath the Son hath life; and he that hath not the Son of God hath not life. These things have I written unto that believe on the name of the Son of God; that ye might know that ye have eternal life, and that ye might believe on the name of the Son of God.*"

Even so, this leads us to another element of our Lord's warning in these passages. Not only must we generally understand that the right gate and way to eternal life is not of our choosing, but also we must specifically understand that the right gate and way to eternal life is "*not by works of righteousness which we have done.*" (See Titus 3:5) Thus our Lord Jesus Christ gave warning in Matthew 7:21-23, "*Not every one that saith unto me, Lord, Lord, shall enter into the kingdom of heaven; but he that doeth the will of my Father* which is in heaven. *Many will say to me in that day, Lord, Lord, have we not prophesied in thy name? And in thy name have cast out devils? And in thy name done many wonderful works? And then will I profess unto them, I never knew you: depart from me, ye that work iniquity.*" The Lord did not deny the claim that these individuals made. He did not deny that they had done these many works. Rather, He declared that He never knew them, and that in all of their works they were still those who worked iniquity. What was the problem? Romans 4:4-5 gives answer, "*Now to him that worketh is the reward not reckoned of grace, but of debt. But to him that worketh not, but believeth on him that justifieth the ungodly, his faith is counted for righteousness.*" Therefore, we must examine ourselves and be certain that we have entered in by the right gate, by the narrow gate and way, by the gate and way of "*grace . . . through faith*" and "*not of works.*" (See Ephesians 2:8-9)

24. We must beware of false prophets, who will appear good outwardly, but who will inwardly be as "ravening wolves."

Matthew 7:15-20 – "***Beware of false prophets***, *which come to you in sheep's clothing, but inwardly they are ravening wolves. Ye shall know them by their fruits. Do men gather grapes of thorns, or figs of thistles? Even so every good tree bringeth forth good fruit; but a corrupt tree bringeth forth evil fruit. A good tree cannot bring forth evil fruit, neither can a corrupt tree bring forth good fruit. Every tree that bringeth not forth good fruit is hewn down, and cast into the fire. Wherefore by their fruits ye shall know them.*"

Jude 1:17-18 – "*But, beloved,* ***remember ye*** *the words which were spoken before of the apostles of our Lord Jesus Christ;* ***how that they told you there should be mockers in the last time***, *who should walk after their own ungodly lusts.*"

In Matthew 24:11 our Lord Jesus Christ warned us, "*And many false prophets shall arise, and shall deceive many.*" Yea, in 2 Timothy 3:13 the warning is given, "*But evil men and seducers shall wax worse and worse, deceiving, and being deceived.*" In our own time there are many false prophets and false teachers out and about teaching what God's Holy Word calls "*damnable heresies*" and "*doctrines of devils.*" (See 2 Peter 2:1 & 1 Timothy 4:1) Even so, our Lord's command and counsel to us is that we beware of such. We are to be on our guard, lest we be "*tossed to and fro, and carried about with every wind of doctrine*" by which such deceivers seek to deceive us, devour us, and destroy us. (See Ephesians 4:14) Indeed, we must beware because, as our Lord revealed in Matthew 7:15, false prophets and false teachers will come "*in sheep's clothing,*" looking smooth and good outwardly, "*but inwardly they are ravening wolves.*"

So then, how shall we know if an individual is a false prophet and false teacher? In Matthew 7:20 our Lord proclaimed, "*Wherefore by their fruits ye shall know them.*" So then, what is this "fruit" by which we shall know these false prophets and false teachers? In Matthew 12:33-37 our Lord revealed the answer, saying, "*Either make the tree good, and his fruit good; or else make the tree corrupt, and his fruit corrupt: for the tree is known by his fruit. O generation of vipers, how can ye, being evil, speak good things? For out of the abundance of the heart the mouth speaketh. A good man out of the good treasure of the heart bringeth forth good things: and an evil man out of the evil treasure bringeth forth evil things. But I say unto you, That every idle word that men shall speak, they shall give account thereof in the day of judgment. For by thy words thou shalt be justified, and by thy words thou shalt be condemned.*"

It is by the fruit of their lips that we shall know them. It is by the message that they bring. Even so, Isaiah 8:20 proclaims, "*To the law and to the testimony: if they speak not according to this word, it is because there is no light in them.*" If their message and teaching is not according to the truth of God's Holy Word, then they are false and to be avoided. Even so, 1 Timothy 6:3-5 gives the command, "*If any man teach otherwise, and consent not to wholesome words, even the words of our Lord Jesus Christ, and to the doctrine which is according to godliness; he is proud, knowing nothing, but doting about questions and strifes of words, whereof cometh envy, strife, railings, evil surmisings, perverse disputings of men of corrupt minds, and destitute of the truth, supposing that gain is godliness: from such withdraw thyself.*"

103

Furthermore, in the surrounding context of Jude 1:17-18, we find a Biblical description of such false prophets and false teachers. In Jude 1:19 the description is given, *"These be they who separate themselves, sensual, having not the Spirit."* Even more, in Jude 1:11-16 the description is given, *"Woe unto them! For they have gone in the way of Cain, and ran greedily after the error of Balaam for reward, and perished in the gainsaying of Core. These are spots in your feasts of charity, when they feast with you, feeding themselves without fear: clouds they are without water, carried about of winds; trees whose fruit withereth, without fruit, twice dead, plucked up by the roots; raging waves of the sea, foaming out their own shame; wandering stars, to whom is reserved the blackness of darkness for ever. And Enoch also, the seventh from Adam, prophesied of these, saying, Behold, the Lord cometh with ten thousands of his saints, to execute judgment upon all, and to convince all that are ungodly among them of all their ungodly deeds which they have ungodly committed, and of all their hard speeches which ungodly sinners have spoken against him. These are murmurers, complainers, walking after their own lusts; and their mouth speaketh great swelling words, having men's persons in admiration because of advantage."*

25. We must learn the heart of our Lord to show compassion and mercy toward those in sin.

Matthew 9:9-13 – *"And as Jesus passed forth from thence, he saw a man, named Matthew, sitting at the receipt of custom: and he saith unto him, Follow me. And he arose, and followed him. And it came to pass, as Jesus sat at meat in the house, behold, many publicans and sinners came and sat down with him and his disciples. And when the Pharisees saw it, they said unto his disciples, Why eateth your Master with publicans and sinners? But when Jesus heard that, he said unto them, They that be whole need not a physician, but they that are sick.* **But go ye and learn what that meaneth, I will have mercy, and not sacrifice: for I am not come to call the righteous, but sinners to repentance.***"*

Jude 1:22 – "***And of some have compassion, making a difference.***"

The issue of controversy on the occasion of Matthew 9:9-13 concerned our Lord Jesus' dealings with publicans and sinners. It all began when Jesus saw a publican (a tax-collector) by the name of Matthew "sitting at the receipt of custom" and said unto him, "Follow Me." Now, a publican (tax-collector) in Israel at that time was often an Israelite who had been hired by the Romans to tax their own people. Such publicans were often a part of the criminal element of that day, and they were despised by other Israelites as a traitor to their people. Yet when our Lord Jesus Christ called this publican Matthew to follow Him, Matthew immediately responded by leaving all of his old life behind and by following after the Lord. In addition, we learn from Luke 5:29 that Matthew made a great feast for Jesus in his own house. "*And,*" Matthew 9:10 reveals, "*it came to pass, as Jesus sat at meat in the house, behold, many publicans and sinners came and sat down with Him and His disciples.*"

Now, this group of publicans and sinners would have included such individuals as criminals of various sorts, thieves, murderers, fornicators, harlots, and other types of public sinners. Even so, the fact that Jesus would sit at the same meal with such publicly sinful individuals was a great offense to the self-righteous, religious leaders of that day. Thus Matthew 9:11 states, "*And when the Pharisees saw it, they said unto His disciples, Why eateth your Master with publicans and sinners?*" These self-righteous Pharisees viewed such individuals as desperately wicked without any hope for salvation and reconciliation. Therefore, the Pharisees in their self-righteous arrogance continually looked down upon these public sinners and avoided any contact with them, thinking that any contact with such public sinners would corrupt them and make them dirty. Yet the Pharisees did not understand that their own self-righteous arrogance and pride made them just as corrupt, filthy, and desperately wicked in the sight of the Lord as were the public sinners upon whom they were looking down their haughty noses.

Even so, in Matthew 9:12-13 our Lord delivered His answer to the Pharisees' question – "*But when Jesus heard that, He said unto them, They that be whole need not a physician, but they that are sick.*"

But go ye and learn what that meaneth, I will have mercy, and not sacrifice: for I am not come to call the righteous, but sinners to repentance." The command herein is at the beginning of verse 13. Lest we become self-righteous and arrogant like the Pharisees of that day, we must learn the truth of our Lord's heart – He will have mercy, and not sacrifice. Here our Lord was quoting from the Old Testament passage of Hosea 6:6 where the Lord our God declared, *"For I desired mercy, and not sacrifice; and the knowledge of God more than burnt offerings."* Before our Lord will accept our religious activities as pleasing in His sight, He requires from us a heart of compassionate mercy toward those who are caught in the miry clay and horrible pit of sin.

Even so, the prophet Micah proclaimed in Micah 6:6-8, *"Wherewith shall I come before the LORD, and bow myself before the high God? Shall I come before him with burnt offerings, with calves of a year old? Will the LORD be pleased with thousands of rams, or with ten thousands of rivers of oil? Shall I give my firstborn for my transgression, the fruit of my body for the sin of my soul? He hath shewed thee, O man, what is good; and what doth the LORD require of thee, but to do justly, and to love mercy, and to walk humbly with thy God?"* Thus our Lord rebuked the self-righteous Pharisees of that day in Matthew 23:23, saying, *"Woe unto you, scribes and Pharisees, hypocrites! For ye pay tithe of mint and anise and cumin, and have omitted the weightier matters of the law, judgment, mercy, and faith: these ought ye to have done, and not to leave the other undone."*

When we encounter those who are in the midst of sin, we are not to look down upon them with a self-righteous attitude. Rather, we are to be moved with a compassionate spirit toward them. We should not avoid all contact with such individuals. Rather, we should seek to show spiritual mercy unto them. Yea, we should seek to show them the mercy of the Lord in being used of the Lord to help them out of the pit of their sin. As Jude 1:22 instructs, we must have godly compassion toward them, seeking to make a difference in their lives.

We must learn the compassionate and merciful heart of our Lord and must walk in unity with it. We must remember that our Lord did not come into the world in order to call the righteous unto Himself, for in truth *"there is none righteous, no, not one."* (See Romans 3:10) Rather, our Lord came into the world *"to seek and to save that which was lost"* in sin. (See Luke 19:10) He came into the world to call sinners unto repentance. He came into the world to save us sinners. Yea, *"while we were yet sinners, Christ died for us."* (See Romans 5:8) He did not avoid all contact with us wretched sinners. Rather, He came into this world of sin in order to show us mercy and to deliver us from the horrible pit of our sin. Even so, now our Lord and Savior Jesus Christ calls us to walk in His steps – to show our fellow sinners mercy by loving them and by leading them to the Lord Jesus Christ for deliverance. *"But go ye and learn what that meaneth, I will have mercy, and not sacrifice."*

26. We must be praying that our Lord will send forth more laborers into His harvest.

Matthew 9:37-38 – *"Then saith he unto his disciples, The harvest truly is plenteous, but the labourers are few;* **pray ye therefore the Lord of the harvest, that he will send forth labourers into his harvest.**"

Luke 10:1-2 – *"After these things the Lord appointed other seventy also, and sent them two and two before his face into every city and place, whither he himself would come. Therefore said he unto them, The harvest truly is great, but the labourers are few:* **pray ye therefore the Lord of the harvest, that he would send forth labourers into his harvest.**"

There is a great spiritual need before us. The field of this world is wide, and the lost souls in this world are many. Furthermore, the harvest of souls is truly plenteous. There are many souls around us whom our Lord has been drawing and preparing unto faith in Christ for salvation. There is no lack in the harvest. Yet there is a lack of laborers. There is a lack of harvesters. Therefore, our Lord gives instruction that with a heart of compassion and mercy toward those who are lost in sin, we are to be praying for more and more laborers to enter our Lord's harvest field and to bring in the harvest of souls.

We are to pray that our church leadership will labor faithfully in our Lord's harvest field. We are to pray that our missionaries will be faithful laborers in our Lord's harvest field. We are to pray that our fellow believers will be faithful laborers in our Lord's harvest field. Yea, we are to pray that our own children will rise up to labor faithfully in our Lord's harvest field.

27. We ourselves must go forth as laborers into our Lord's harvest, preaching the gospel unto the lost.

Matthew 10:6-7 – "*But go rather to the lost sheep of the house of Israel. **And as ye go, preach, saying, The kingdom of heaven is at hand**.*"

Mark 16:15 – "*And he said unto them, **Go ye into all the world, and preach the gospel to every creature**.*"

Luke 24:47-48 – "***And that repentance and remission of sins should be preached in his name among all nations**, beginning at Jerusalem. And ye are witnesses of these things.*"

Jude 1:23 – "***And others save with fear, pulling them out of the fire***; *hating even the garment spotted by the flesh.*"

Immediately after instructing the disciples in Matthew 9:37-38 to pray unto the Lord for more laborers to be sent forth into the Lord's harvest, our Lord sent forth these very disciples into His harvest. Thus we learn, not only that we are to pray unto the Lord for more laborers to be sent forth, but that we ourselves are to go forth as a part of those very laborers. We are not only to pray that others be sent forth. Rather, we are to pray for laborers and then to go forth as laborers ourselves.

Just as our Lord commanded the twelve to go forth unto the lost sheep of Israel and to preach the gospel unto them, even so our Lord has commanded us to go forth unto the lost around us and to preach the gospel unto them. Now, in the particular historical context of the account in Matthew 10:1-6, our Lord instructed the twelve not to go "*into the way of the Gentiles*" and not to go "*into any city of the Samaritans,*" but only to go "*to the lost sheep of the house of Israel.*" However, these particular restrictions only applied to the twelve at that particular time, and do not apply to us in this particular time. In fact, in Mark 16:18 after His death, burial, and resurrection, our Lord Jesus Christ commanded His disciples and all of His people throughout the time of the New Testament, saying, "*Go ye into all the world, and preach the gospel to every creature.*" Our Lord and Savior Jesus Christ has commanded us to go unto the lost world and to preach the gospel unto them.

Furthermore, in relation to the entire time of the New Testament, our Lord and Savior Jesus Christ declared in Acts 1:8, "*But ye shall receive power, after that the Holy Ghost is come upon you: and ye shall be witnesses unto Me both in Jerusalem, and in all Judaea, and in Samaria, and unto the uttermost part of the earth.*" Therefore, we ourselves are to go forth as a laborer in our Lord's harvest, preaching the gospel of "repentance and remission of sins" in our Lord's name "among all nations." We ourselves are to go forth in the fear of our Lord, seeking the salvation of lost souls through faith in Christ, in order that we might pull them out of the fire of God's wrath.

28. As we go forth with the gospel, we must be "wise as serpents," but "harmless as doves."

Matthew 10:16 – "*Behold, I send you forth as sheep in the midst of wolves:* **be ye therefore wise as serpents, and harmless as doves.**"

In the opening portion of Matthew 10:16, our Lord warned that He is sending us forth as helpless sheep into the midst of a pack of fierce wolves. As such, our Lord warned us that in sending us forth with His gospel, He is sending us forth to face fierce opposition. Indeed, there are many in this world who will fiercely oppose us as we go forth to preach the gospel of Christ. This they will do because they fiercely oppose our Lord Himself and anything that has to do with

109

Him. Thus they will fiercely oppose His gospel and the messengers of His gospel.

Even so, in light of this fierce opposition that we will face as we go forth with His gospel, our Lord gives us a two-fold command. First, our Lord used the picture of a serpent and instructed us to be "wise as serpents." As we go forth to preach the gospel unto the lost around us, we are to go forth with a Spirit-filled discernment and prudence. In our approach, our words, and our actions, we are to be spiritually discerning and prudent as we go forth with the gospel. We are to walk in wisdom toward the lost around us.

Second, our Lord used the picture of a dove and instructed us to be "harmless as doves." Herein the word "harmless" indicates a pure motive without deceit. Although we are to be "wise as serpents," we are not to be harmful as serpents. We are not to have the "forked tongue" of the serpent. With our tongue we are not to use deceit. In addition, we are not to be poisonous like a serpent. The poison of asps is not to be under our lips. Rather, we are to be "harmless as doves." As we go forth to preach the gospel unto the lost around us, we are to have the pure motive of Spirit-filled compassion and love. In our approach, our words, and our actions, we are to be blameless and harmless among the lost; for we are to shine as spiritual lights among them. As we go forth with the gospel, we are to be "wise as serpents," to be spiritually discerning and prudent, but to be "harmless as doves," to be spiritually compassionate and loving.

29. As we go forth with the gospel, we must beware the persecutions of men, fleeing these persecutions and preaching the gospel in the new places into which we flee.

Matthew 10:17-18 – "***But beware of men****: for they will deliver you up to the councils, and they will scourge you in their synagogues; and ye shall be brought before governors and kings for my sake, for a testimony against them and the Gentiles.*"

Matthew 10:21-25 – "*And the brother shall deliver up the brother to death, and the father the child: and the children shall rise up against their parents, and cause them to be put to death. And ye shall be hated of all men for my name's sake: but he that endureth to the end shall be saved. **But when they persecute you in this city, flee ye into another**: for verily I say unto you, Ye shall not have gone over the cities of Israel, till the Son of man be come. The disciple is not above his master, nor the servant above his lord. It is enough for the disciple that he be as his master, and the servant as his lord. If they have called the master of the house Beelzebub, how much more shall they call them of his household?*"

It is our Lord's desire that we be aware of the fact that as we go forth with the gospel, we will "be hated of all men" and will suffer persecution for His name's sake. Just as this spiritually dark world hated and persecuted our Lord Himself, even so they will hate and persecute us who are His faithful servants and witnesses. As we go forth with the gospel, such hatred and persecution should not surprise us. Yea, our Lord commands us to be fully aware and fully expecting that such hatred and persecution will come upon us. So then, what are we to do when this hatred and persecution actually does come upon us? In the opening portion of Matthew 10:23, our Lord gave answer, saying, "*But when they persecute you in this city, flee ye into another.*" Are we to give up and to cease going forth in preaching the gospel unto the lost? God forbid! Rather, we are to flee forth into another place, preaching the gospel in that new place. Then when persecution might come upon us in that place, we are to flee forth into yet another place, preaching the gospel in that new place.

<hr />

30. As we go forth with the gospel, we must trust the Holy Spirit to guide our words when we are delivered up before governing officials.

Matthew 10:19-20 – "***But when they deliver you up, take no thought how or what ye shall speak***: *for it shall be given you in that same hour what ye shall speak. For it is not ye that speak, but the Spirit of your Father which speaketh in you.*"

Mark 13:11 – "***But when they shall lead you, and deliver you up, take no thought beforehand what ye shall speak, neither do ye premeditate: but whatsoever shall be given you in that hour, that speak ye***: *for it is not ye that speak, but the Holy Ghost.*"

Luke 12:11-12 – "***And when they bring you unto the synagogues, and unto magistrates, and powers, take ye no thought how or what thing ye shall answer, or what ye shall say***: *for the Holy Ghost shall teach you in the same hour what ye ought to say.*"

Luke 21:10-15 – "*Then said he unto them, Nation shall rise against nation, and kingdom against kingdom: and great earthquakes shall be in divers places, and famines, and pestilences; and fearful sights and great signs shall there be from heaven. But before all these, they shall lay their hands on you, and persecute you, delivering you up to the synagogues, and into prisons, being brought before kings and rulers for my name's sake. And it shall turn to you for a testimony. **Settle it therefore in your hearts, not to meditate before what ye shall answer**: for I will give you a mouth and wisdom, which all your adversaries shall not be able to gainsay nor resist.*"

In times of persecution for the sake of our Lord's name and gospel, when it becomes a political and criminal offense to preach the gospel of Christ, we are not to plan ahead of time the defense that we will present for ourselves. Rather, we are rely upon God the Holy Spirit to fill us and to guide us "in that same hour" in the things that we are to speak. This we are to do in order that our words may find their source, not in the thoughts and emotions of our own human hearts, but in the pure truth and infinite wisdom of the Lord our God Himself.

Even so, we read concerning the apostles Peter and John in Acts 4. In Acts 4:1-3 we read, "*And as they* [that is – Peter and John] *spake unto the people, the priests, and the captain of the temple, and the Sadducees, came upon them, being grieved that they taught the people, and preached through Jesus the resurrection from the dead. And they laid hands on them, and put them in hold unto the next day: for it was now eventide.*" Then in Acts 4:5-7 we read, "*And it came to pass on the morrow, that their rulers, and elders, and scribes, and Annas the high priest, and Caiaphas, and John, and Alexander, and as many as were of the kindred of the high priest, were gathered together at Jerusalem. And when they* [that is – the rulers] *had set them* [that is – Peter and John] *in the midst, they asked, By what power, or by what name, have ye done this?"*

Even so, the opening portion of Acts 4:8 reveals the guidance by which the apostle Peter gave answer – *"Then Peter, filled with the Holy Ghost, said unto them . . . ."* So then, what was the result of this Spirit-filled defense? In Acts 4:13 we read, *"Now when they saw the boldness of Peter and John, and perceived that they were unlearned and ignorant men, they marvelled; and they took knowledge of them, that they had been with Jesus."* In like manner, we read in Acts 6:9-10 concerning the man of God Stephen, a man who was "full of faith and of the Holy Ghost" – *"Then there arose certain of the synagogue, which is called the synagogue of the Libertines, and Cyrenians, and Alexandrians, and of them of Cilicia and of Asia, disputing with Stephen. And they were not able to resist the wisdom and the spirit by which he spake."*

～～～

31. As we go forth with the gospel, we must be on our guard over our hearts and behavior that we might not walk in fear of the oppositions and persecutions of men.

Matthew 10:26 – *"**Fear them not therefore**: for there is nothing covered, that shall not be revealed; and hid, that shall not be known."*

Matthew 10:28-31 – *"**And fear not them which kill the body, but are not able to kill the soul**: but rather fear him which is able to destroy both soul and body in hell. Are not two sparrows sold for a farthing? And one of them shall not fall on the ground without your Father. But the very hairs of your head are all numbered. **Fear ye not therefore**, ye are of more value than many sparrows."*

Mark 13:9-10 – *"**But take heed to yourselves**: for they shall deliver you up to councils; and in the synagogues ye shall be beaten: and ye shall be brought before rulers and kings for my sake, for a testimony* *against them. And the gospel must first be published among all nations."*

Luke 12:4-9 – *"And I say unto you my friends,* **Be not afraid of them that kill the body, and after that have no more that they can do.** *But I will forewarn you whom ye shall fear: Fear him, which after he hath killed hath power to cast into hell; yea, I say unto you, Fear him. Are not five sparrows sold for two farthings, and not one of them is forgotten before God? But even the very hairs of your head are all numbered.* **Fear not therefore**: *ye are of more value than many sparrows. Also I say unto you, Whosoever shall confess me before men, him shall the Son of man also confess before the angels of God: but he that denieth me before men shall be denied before the angels of God."*

Luke 21:16-19 – *"And ye shall be betrayed both by parents, and brethren, and kinsfolks, and friends; and some of you shall they cause to be put to death. And ye shall be hated of all men for my name's sake. But there shall not an hair of your head perish.* **In your patience possess ye your souls**.*"*

Philippians 1:28 – *"**And in nothing terrified by your adversaries**: which is to them an evident token of perdition, but to you of salvation, and that of God."*

Revelation 2:9-10 – *"I know thy works, and tribulation, and poverty, (but thou art rich) and I know the blasphemy of them which say they are Jews, and are not, but are the synagogue of Satan.* **Fear none of those things which thou shalt suffer**: *behold, the devil shall cast some of you into prison, that ye may be tried; and ye shall have tribulation ten days: be thou faithful unto death, and I will give thee a crown of life."*

Although it is our Lord's desires that we be fully aware of the fierce opposition and hateful persecution which shall come against us as we go forth with the gospel, yet He does not want us to walk in fear of this opposition and persecution. In the opening portion of Mark 13:9, our Lord warns us to take heed unto ourselves, that is – unto the spirit and attitude of our hearts. Our Lord's focus here is not simply upon the emotion of fear. Rather, His focus is upon how that fear might control our hearts and our behavior. Even so, when times of opposition and persecution should rise against us, we must be on our guard over our own hearts, lest our hearts might be filled with fear, rather than faith, and lest our fearful hearts turn us aside from the path of faithfulness.

Rather, we are to walk in fullness of faith in the love and care of God our heavenly Father for us. Indeed, even if God our heavenly Father allows us to be cast down unto the ground in persecution, we must trust that He Himself is with us, that His own hand of love is holding us, and that He Himself will pour out upon us the grace that we need to continue faithful through such persecution and affliction. Yea, this we must do even if God our heavenly Father allows us to be cast down in death for His name's sake. We are to fear none of those things that we might suffer. Rather, with full assurance of faith in God our heavenly Father, we are to remain faithful even unto death in order that our Lord might reward us "a crown of life."

Even so, we read in Acts 7:54-60 concerning the man of God Stephen, *"When they heard these things, they were cut to the heart, and they gnashed on him with their teeth. But he, being full of the Holy Ghost, looked up stedfastly into heaven, and saw the glory of God, and Jesus standing on the right hand of God, and said, Behold, I see the heavens opened, and the Son of man standing on the right hand of God. Then they cried out with a loud voice, and stopped their ears, and ran upon him with one accord, and cast him out of the city, and stoned him: and the witnesses laid down their clothes at a young man's feet, whose name was Saul. And they stoned Stephen, calling upon God, and saying, Lord Jesus, receive my spirit. And he kneeled down, and cried with a loud voice, Lord, lay not this sin to their charge. And when he had said this, he fell asleep."*

Yet we cannot actually overcome the fear of such persecution and afflication through our own strength of determination. Rather, we must overcome this fear through the grace and power of the Lord our God. Even so, the apostle Paul gave testimony in 1 Thessalonians 2:1-2, saying, *"For yourselves, brethren, know our entrance in unto you, that it was not in vain: but even after that we had suffered before,* and were shamefully entreated, as ye know, at Philippi, we were bold in our God to speak unto you the gospel of God with much contention." The apostle's boldness for the gospel in the face of suffering and persecution was not found in himself. Rather, he found such boldness in the Lord his God. *"For God hath not given us the spirit of fear; but of power, and of love, and of a sound mind."* (2 Timothy 1:7) Therefore, we must not be *"ashamed of the testimony of our Lord;"* but we must willingly and boldly partake *"of the afflictions of the gospel according to the power of God."* (See 2 Timothy 1:8)

32. As we go forth with the gospel, we must boldly preach the truth of the Lord our God and Savior.

Matthew 10:27 – *"**What I tell you in darkness, that speak ye in light: and what ye hear in the ear, that preach ye upon the housetops.**"*

Indeed, we are not to walk in fear of the oppositions and persecutions of men. Rather, we are boldly to speak the truth of our Lord in public places and boldly to preach the truth of our Lord from the housetops. We are not to be shy and private in preaching the gospel to the lost. Rather, we are to go forth with Spirit-filled boldness in preaching the glorious gospel of our Lord Jesus Christ unto this lost world. We are to join with the apostle Paul from Romans 1:16 in saying, *"I am not ashamed of the gospel of Christ: for it is the power of God unto salvation to every one that believeth; to the Jew first, and also to the Greek."* Yea, we are to join with the persecuted church of Jerusalem from Acts 4:29 in praying, *"And now, Lord, behold their threatenings: and grant unto Thy servants, that with all boldness they may speak Thy Word."* Then we shall find the same answer that our Lord delivered unto them: for in Acts 4:31 we read, *"And when they had prayed, the place was shaken where they were assembled together; and they were all filled with the Holy Ghost, and they spake the word of God with boldness."*

33. As we go forth with the gospel, we must walk in the fear of the Lord our God and heavenly Father.

Matthew 10:28-31 – "*And fear not them which kill the body, but are not able to kill the soul: **but rather fear him which is able to destroy both soul and body in hell**. Are not two sparrows sold for a farthing? And one of them shall not fall on the ground without your Father. But the very hairs of your head are all numbered. Fear ye not therefore, ye are of more value than many sparrows.*"

Luke 12:5 – "***But I will forewarn you whom ye shall fear: Fear him, which after he hath killed hath power to cast into hell; yea, I say unto you, Fear him.***"

We are not to walk in the fear of men, who can only touch us in physical things. Rather, we are to walk in the fear of the Lord, who can touch us both in physical and in spiritual things. Yet walking in the fear of the Lord is not simply a matter of fear and trembling. It is also a matter of faith and trusting. Certainly if we are walking contrary to our Lord's will, then the fear of the Lord is a matter of fear and trembling; for then our Lord would be contrary to us. However, if we are walking in obedience to our Lord's will, then the fear of the Lord is a matter of faith and trusting; for then our Lord would be caring for us. Even so, Psalm 33:18-19 declares, "*Behold, the eye of the LORD is upon them that fear Him, upon them that hope in His mercy; to deliver their soul from death, and to keep them alive in famine.*" Even so also, our Lord Jesus Christ gives encouragement in Matthew 10:29-31, saying, "*Are not two sparrows sold for a farthing? And one of them shall not fall on the ground without your Father. But the very hairs of your head are all numbered. Fear ye not therefore, ye are of more value than many sparrows.*"

Yet walking in the fear of the Lord is also a third thing, for it is also a matter of faithfulness and serving. Even so, Psalm 128:1 declares, "*Blessed is every one that feareth the LORD; that walketh in His ways.*" Even so also, our Lord Jesus Christ gave warning in Matthew 10:32-33, saying, "*Whosoever therefore shall confess me before men, him will I confess also before my Father which is in heaven. But whosoever shall deny me before men, him will I also* deny before my Father which is in heaven." In like manner also, our Lord gave warning in verses 38-39, saying, "*And he that taketh not his cross, and followeth after me, is not worthy of me. He that findeth his life shall lose it: and he that loseth his life for my sake shall find it.*"

❧

34. We must come unto the Lord Jesus Christ in faith as our only spiritual Help and Hope.

Matthew 11:28 – "***Come unto me, all ye that labour and are heavy laden****, and I will give you rest.*"

In Matthew 11:20-27 we read concerning our Lord Jesus Christ, "*Then began he to upbraid the cities wherein most of his mighty works were done, because they repented not: Woe unto thee, Chorazin! Woe unto thee, Bethsaida! For if the mighty works, which were done in you, had been done in Tyre and Sidon, they would have repented long ago in sackcloth and ashes. But I say unto you, It shall be more tolerable for Tyre and Sidon at the day of judgment, than for you. And thou, Capernaum, which art exalted unto heaven, shalt be brought down to hell: for if the mighty works, which have been done in thee, had been done in Sodom, it would have remained until this day. But I say unto you, That it shall be more tolerable for the land of Sodom in the day of judgment, than for thee. At that time Jesus answered and said, I thank thee, O Father, Lord of heaven and earth, because thou hast hid these things from the wise and prudent, and hast revealed them unto babes. Even so, Father: for so it seemed good in thy sight. All things are delivered unto me of my Father: and no man knoweth the Son, but the Father; neither knoweth any man the Father, save the Son, and he to whomsoever the Son will reveal him.*"

Then, having upbraided the cities of Chorazin, Bethsaida, and Capernaum for their refusal to repent, and having thanked the Father for His gracious revelation of the gospel, and having declared that no man can know the Father except He Himself, the Son of God, reveal the Father to him, our Lord Jesus Christ proclaimed His call

118

and command in Matthew 11:28, saying, *"Come unto me, all ye that labour and are heavy laden, and I will give you rest."* This was just the message that the cities of Chorazin, Bethsaida, and Capernaum needed to hear and to heed. They needed to repent of their sin and of their self-righteousness, and they needed to come unto the Lord Jesus Christ in faith for salvation. This was the way that an individual could come to know the Father as his own heavenly Father. He needed to come unto God the Son, the Lord Jesus Christ, as his one and only way of new birth and entrance into the family of God.

Even so, the same holds true today. Those who are heavy laden under the burden and guilt of their sin need to come unto the Lord Jesus Christ in faith as their one and only Help and Hope of eternal salvation. Those who are laboring and toiling to save themselves from their sin through their own efforts need to come unto the Lord Jesus Christ in faith as their one and only Help and Hope of eternal salvation. Indeed, Acts 4:12 declares, *"Neither is there salvation in any other: for there is none other name under heaven given among men, whereby we must be saved."* Indeed, the Lord Jesus Christ Himself declared in John 14:6, *"I am the way, the truth, and the life: no man cometh unto the Father, but by me."* Therefore, we must come unto the Lord Jesus Christ as our one and only Way of eternal salvation from sin and of entrance into God's family.

35. We must actively and purposefully take our Lord's yoke upon us and learn of Him in our daily Christian walk.

Matthew 11:29-30 – *"**Take my yoke upon you, and learn of me**; for I am meek and lowly in heart: and ye shall find rest unto your souls. For my yoke is easy, and my burden is light."*

A yoke is placed upon an animal, such as an ox, in order that it may serve its master in the field according to his direction. Thus a yoke is a symbol of service. It is a symbol of being under the direction and control of another. Even so, our Lord and Savior Jesus Christ here commanded us who have come unto Him as Savior to take His yoke upon us and to learn of Him. He does not force His yoke of service upon us. Rather, He instructs us to actively and purposefully take His yoke of service upon ourselves and to learn through His direction and by His leading the way that we should go.

Having come to our Lord Jesus Christ in faith for eternal salvation, we must now actively and purposefully choose to submit ourselves under our Lord's direction and leading in our daily walk. We must actively and purposefully present ourselves as a living sacrifice unto Him. (See Romans 12:1) We must actively and purposefully deny ourselves, take up our cross daily, and follow Him. (See Luke 9:23) We must actively and purposefully abide in Him and allow Him to abide in us. (See John 15:4-5) We must actively and purposefully live unto Him who died for us. (See 2 Corinthians 5:15) We must actively and purposefully live according to the principle of Philippians 1:21 – *"For to me to live is Christ."* We must actively and purposefully acknowledge Him in all of our ways in order that He might direct our paths. (See Proverbs 3:6) We must actively and purposefully seek for Him to teach us His statutes and His standards for our lives. We must actively and purposefully walk in daily fellowship with Him, learning of Him and walking even as He walked.

Even so, one of the greatest lessons that we shall learn of Him is to be "meek and lowly in heart." Thus our Lord Jesus Christ declared in the opening portion of Matthew 11:29, saying, *"Take my yoke upon you, and learn of me; for I am meek and lowly in heart."* We will learn of Him to humble ourselves under the mighty hand of God our heavenly Father that He may pour out His grace upon us, lift us up, and exalt us in His due time. (See James 4:10; 1 Peter 5:6) We will learn to walk according to the same mindset that was in Christ Jesus, making ourselves of no reputation, taking upon ourselves the form of a servant, humbling ourselves in the sight of the Lord our God, obeying the will our Lord faithfully unto death, and sacrificing ourselves for His name's sake. (See Philippians 2:5-8) We will learn of Him the way of victory over the selfishness of our sinful flesh. We will learn of Him to walk well-pleasing unto God our heavenly Father, even as He ever walked well-pleasing unto the Father. We will learn of Him to bring forth much fruit unto the glory and praise of the Father.

Then as we follow our Lord's direction and learn of His ways, we shall find the great blessing of rest unto our souls. This our Lord promised in Matthew 11:29-30, saying, *"Take my yoke upon you, and learn of me; for I am meek and lowly of heart: and ye shall find rest unto your souls. For my yoke is easy and my burden is light."* Now, this does not mean that we shall find rest from all of the circumstantial problems in life. Nor does it mean that we shall find a life of circumstantial ease and comfort. Rather, this means that we shall find a spiritual rest within our hearts regardless of the circumstantial problems in life.

It means that we shall find a spiritual strengthening of our inner man by the Holy Spirit, according to the riches of our heavenly Father's glory, unto all patience and longsuffering with joyfulness. (See Ephesians 3:16; Colossians 1:11) It means that we shall find the peace of God that passeth all understanding, which shall keep our hearts and minds through Christ Jesus. (See Philippians 4:6-7) It means that we shall find the joy of our Lord, a joy unspeakable and full of glory, that we may rejoice and be exceeding glad even as we suffer for our Lord's sake. (See 1 Peter 1:7-8) It means that we shall find the abundant life of our Lord's fellowship and of the excellency of the knowledge of Christ Jesus our Lord. It means that we shall find our Lord Jesus Christ Himself ever living out His own life through us. (See Galatians 2:20) It means that we shall find the power of Christ resting upon us so that we can walk pleasing unto the Father and be filled with the fruits of righteousness through Him. (See Colossians 1:10; Philippians 1:11)

36. We must understand that what comes out of our hearts and mouths is that which defiles us.

Matthew 15:10-20 – *"And he called the multitude, and said unto them,* **Hear, and understand: not that which goeth into the mouth defileth a man; but that which cometh out of the mouth, this defileth a man.** *Then came his disciples, and said unto him, Knowest thou that the Pharisees were offended, after they heard this saying? But* *he answered and said, Every plant, which my heavenly Father hath not planted, shall be rooted up. Let them alone: they be blind leaders of the blind. And if the blind lead the blind, both shall fall into the ditch. Then answered Peter and said unto him, Declare unto us this parable. And Jesus said, Are ye also yet without understanding? Do not ye yet understand, that whatsoever entereth in at the mouth goeth into the belly, and is cast out into the draught? But those things which proceed out of the mouth come forth from the heart; and they defile the man. For out of the heart proceed evil thoughts, murders, adulteries, fornications, thefts, false witness, blasphemies: these are the things which defile a man: but to eat with unwashen hands defileth not a man.*"

Mark 7:14-23 – "*And when he had called all the people unto him, he said unto them, **Hearken unto me every one of you, and understand: there is nothing from without a man, that entering into him can defile him: but the things which come out of him, those are they that defile the man. If any man have ears to hear, let him hear**. And when he was entered into the house from the people, his disciples asked him concerning the parable. And he saith unto them, Are ye so without understanding also? Do ye not perceive, that whatsoever thing from without entereth into the man, it cannot defile him; because it entereth not into his heart, but into the belly, and goeth out into the draught, purging all meats? And he said, That which cometh out of the man, that defileth the man. For from within, out of the heart of men, proceed evil thoughts, adulteries, fornications, murders, Thefts, covetousness, wickedness, deceit, lasciviousness, an evil eye, blasphemy, pride, foolishness: all these evil things come from within, and defile the man.*"

In Matthew 15:1-9 (see also Mark 7:1-13) we find an account of a rebuke by the scribes and Pharisees against Jesus' disciples and of the response by our Lord Jesus unto them. There we read, "*Then came to Jesus scribes and Pharisees, which were of Jerusalem, saying, Why do thy disciples transgress the tradition of the elders? For they wash not their hands when they eat bread. But he answered and said unto them, Why do ye also transgress the commandment of God by your tradition? For God commanded, saying, Honour thy father and mother: and, He that curseth father or mother, let him die the death. But ye say, Whosoever shall say to his father or his mother, It is a gift, by whatsoever thou mightest be profited by me; and honour not his father or his mother, he shall be free. Thus have ye made the commandment of God of none effect by your tradition. Ye hypocrites, well did Esaias prophesy of you, saying, This people draweth nigh unto me with their mouth, and honoureth me with their lips; but their heart is far from me. But in vain they do worship me, teaching for doctrines the commandments of men."*

The scribes and Pharisees rebuked Jesus' disciples for breaking the traditions of the religious elders in the time. In turn, our Lord Jesus Christ rebuked the scribes and Pharisees for breaking the commandment of God through their traditions. The Lord their God had commanded children to honor their father and mother. Yet the religious leaders of that day had set up a system whereby one could dishonor his father or his mother and still be viewed as acceptable within the religious system. Thus our Lord concluded that although their words were religious words of honor toward God, yet their hearts were spiritually and actually far from God.

Then in this context our Lord delivered the command of Matthew 15:10 unto the multitude, saying, *"Hear and understand."* What is the truth that He commanded us to hear and to understand? In verse 11 He revealed that truth, saying, *"Not that which goeth into the mouth defileth a man; but that which cometh out of the mouth, this defileth a man."* Even so, our Lord Jesus Christ declared in verse 18, *"But those things which proceed out of the mouth come forth from the heart; and they defile the man. For out of the heart proceed evil thoughts, murders, adulteries, fornications, thefts, false witness, blasphemies."* This truth and principle we are commanded to hear and to understand. Indeed, with understanding we are also brought to a place of self-examination. We are brought to a place of asking ourselves – What are the attitudes, thoughts, desires, and motivations of our hearts; and what is the character of the words that come out of our mouths? Are we defiled in the sight of our Lord thereby? Oh, brethren, how we need to come to a broken and a contrite heart over the defilement of our hearts and mouths! Oh, how we need to mourn and repent of our unclean lips and of our unclean heart attitudes!

37. We must take heed and beware of the doctrine of the Pharisees and Sadducees, that is – the doctrine of hypocrisy.

Matthew 16:5-12 – "*And when his disciples were come to the other side, they had forgotten to take bread. Then Jesus said unto them,* **Take heed and beware of the leaven of the Pharisees and of the Sadducees***. And they reasoned among themselves, saying, It is because we have taken no bread. Which when Jesus perceived, he said unto them, O ye of little faith, why reason ye among yourselves, because ye have brought no bread? Do ye not yet understand, neither remember the five loaves of the five thousand, and how many baskets ye took up? Neither the seven loaves of the four thousand, and how many baskets ye took up? How is it that ye do not understand that I spake it not to you concerning bread, that ye should beware of the leaven of the Pharisees and of the Sadducees?* **Then understood they how that he bade them not beware of the leaven of bread, but of the doctrine of the Pharisees and of the Sadducees***.*"

Mark 8:11-15 – "*And the Pharisees came forth, and began to question with him, seeking of him a sign from heaven, tempting him. And he sighed deeply in his spirit, and saith, Why doth this generation seek after a sign? Verily I say unto you, There shall no sign be given unto this generation. And he left them, and entering into the ship again departed to the other side. Now the disciples had forgotten to take bread, neither had they in the ship with them more than one loaf. And he charged them, saying,* **Take heed, beware of the leaven of the Pharisees, and of the leaven of Herod***.*"

Luke 12:1 – "*In the mean time, when there were gathered together an innumerable multitude of people, insomuch that they trode one upon another, he began to say unto his disciples first of all,* **Beware ye of the leaven of the Pharisees, which is hypocrisy***.*"

In Matthew 16:6 (see also Mark 8:15 & Luke 12:1) our Lord Jesus Christ warned His disciples to "*take heed and beware of the leaven of the Pharisees and of the Sadducees*." Through further explanation the disciples came to the understanding in Matthew 16:12 that the Lord was warning them to beware "*of the doctrine of the Pharisees and of the Sadducees*." Yet what is this doctrine of the Pharisees and Sadducees of which we are to take heed and beware? In Luke 12:1 the answer is revealed; for therein our Lord gave the warning and explanation, *"Beware ye of the leaven of the Pharisees, which is hypocrisy."* The Pharisees and Sadducees were the very religious of their day. Now, although these two religious sects held to a number of different positions in their doctrine, they both held that outward religious activity was the way to be right with God. Thus they rigidly followed their religious practices and traditions while their hearts continued to be far from the Lord their God. This is hypocrisy.

Even so, such leaven of hypocrisy can also be found today. It can be found in any teaching that employs works of righteousness as the way to salvation. Such teaching is contrary to God's Holy Word, which teaches us that the only way of salvation is through faith in our Lord and Savior Jesus Christ. Yea, such teaching is false doctrine and hypocrisy. Furthermore, the leaven of hypocrisy can be found in any teaching that employs external works of righteousness (apart from the inner attitude of the heart) as the essential definition of true spirituality. Such teaching is also contrary to God's Holy Word, which teaches that our external works of righteousness are completely worthless if they do not issue forth from a heart that is right with the Lord our God. Such teaching is also false doctrine and hypocrisy. We must take heed and beware of the leaven of hypocrisy, both in our own behavior and in the teachings of others that would lead to it. Yea, we must take heed, beware, and flee from it.

38. We must deny ourselves, take up our cross daily, and follow our Lord.

Matthew 16:21-27 – *"From that time forth began Jesus to shew unto his disciples, how that he must go unto Jerusalem, and suffer many things of the elders and chief priests and scribes, and be killed, and be raised again the third day. Then Peter took him, and began to rebuke him, saying, Be it far from thee, Lord: this shall not be unto thee. But he turned, and said unto Peter, Get thee behind me, Satan: thou art an offence unto me: for thou savourest not the things that be of God, but those that be of men. Then said Jesus unto his disciples,* **If any man will come after me, let him deny himself, and take up his cross, and follow me.** *For whosoever will save his life shall lose it: and whosoever will lose his life for my sake shall find it. For what is a man profited, if he shall gain the whole world, and lose his own soul? Or what shall a man give in exchange for his soul? For the Son of man shall come in the glory of his Father with his angels; and then he shall reward every man according to his works."*

Mark 8:31-38 – *"And he began to teach them, that the Son of man must suffer many things, and be rejected of the elders, and of the chief priests, and scribes, and be killed, and after three days rise again. And he spake that saying openly. And Peter took him, and began to rebuke him. But when he had turned about and looked on his disciples, he rebuked Peter, saying, Get thee behind me, Satan: for thou savourest not the things that be of God, but the things that be of men. And when he had called the people unto him with his disciples also, he said unto them,* **Whosoever will come after me, let him deny himself, and take up his cross, and follow me.** *For whosoever will save his life shall lose it; but whosoever shall lose his life for my sake and the gospel's, the same shall save it. For what shall it profit a man, if he shall gain the whole world, and lose his own soul? Or what shall a man give in exchange for his soul? Whosoever therefore shall be ashamed of me and of my words in this adulterous and sinful generation; of him also shall the Son of man be ashamed, when he cometh in the glory of his Father with the holy angels."*

Luke 9:23-26 – *"And he said to them all,* **If any man will come after me, let him deny himself, and take up his cross daily, and follow me.** *For whosoever will save his life shall lose it: but whosoever will lose his life for my sake, the same shall save it. For what is a man advantaged, if he gain the whole world, and lose himself, or be cast away? For whosoever shall be ashamed of me and of my words, of him shall the Son of man be ashamed, when he shall come in his own glory, and in his Father's, and of the holy angels."*

126

John 12:23-26 – *"And Jesus answered them, saying, The hour is come, that the Son of man should be glorified. Verily, verily, I say unto you, Except a corn of wheat fall into the ground and die, it abideth alone: but if it die, it bringeth forth much fruit. He that loveth his life shall lose it; and he that hateth his life in this world shall keep it unto life eternal. **If any man serve me, let him follow me**; and where I am, there shall also my servant be: if any man serve me, him will my Father honour."*

In Matthew 16:24 (see also Mark 8:34; Luke 9:23) our Lord Jesus Christ delivered a three-fold instruction for our Christian lives. In the first place, we must deny ourselves. We must deny our own will for our lives. We must deny our own way for our lives. We must deny our own wants for our lives. We must deny our own preferences, pleasures, plans, purposes, prospects, pursuits, etc. for our lives. As the redeemed of the Lord, we must no longer live our lives as if they were our own. As the children of God, we must stop holding back our lives from our Lord in order to live them unto ourselves. As the people of God, we must cease trying to save our lives for our own interests. *"For,"* as our Lord declared in Mark 8:35 (see also Matthew 16:25; Luke 9:24), *"whosoever will save his life shall lose it; but whosoever shall lose his life for my sake and the gospel's, the same shall save it."*

If we try to save our Christian lives to live them unto ourselves for our own sake, in the end we will find that our Christian lives were lost to spiritual emptiness. Yea, we will find our Christian lives to be a withered, worthless waste. Yet if we will deny ourselves and will lose our Christian lives to live them unto our Lord for His sake and for His gospel's sake, then we will find that our Christian lives were truly saved unto spiritual fruitfulness. Yea, then we will find our Christian lives to be *"unto praise and honour and glory at the appearing of Jesus Christ."* (See 1 Peter 1:7)

On the one hand, we will have laid up our treasures on this earth where all will be lost in the end. On the other hand, we will have laid up our treasures in heaven where all will last for eternity. Our Lord's question from Matthew 16:26 (see also Mark 8:36-37; Luke 9:25) still rings forth today – *"For what is a man profited, if he shall* gain the whole world, and lose his own soul? Or what shall a man give in exchange for his soul?"* What does it profit us believers to gain all of the treasures of this present world only to lose the one thing that we can invest in eternity – our own present Christian lives? We only get this one Christian life to live, and what we do with it will be either to our eternal reward or to our eternal shame.

Even so, in Matthew 16:27 our Lord Jesus Christ proclaimed, *"For the Son of man shall come in the glory of his Father with his angels; and then he shall reward every man according to his works."* Furthermore, in the parallel account of Mark 8:38 (see also Luke 9:26) our Lord proclaimed, *"Whosoever therefore shall be ashamed of me and of my words in this adulterous and sinful generation; of him also shall the Son of man be ashamed, when he cometh in the glory of his Father with the holy angels."* Finally, in the closing portion of John 12:26, our Lord proclaimed, *"If any man serve me, him will my Father honour."*

In the second place, from our Lord's three-fold instruction in Matthew 16:24, we find that we must take up our cross. In fact, from the parallel account of Luke 9:23, we learn that we are to take up our cross daily. Yet what does it mean to take up one's cross daily? It means to take up the will of the Lord our God for each day of our lives. First, we are to deny ourselves, that is – to deny our own will for our lives. Then second, we are to take up our cross, that is – to take up our Lord's will for our lives. Not our will, but His will is to be done. We are to acknowledge Him and His will in all of our ways. (See Proverbs 3:6) Yea, we are to observe to do according to all His will in all our ways. This should be the very governing principle of our lives – to do the will of our Lord each day and to fulfill the work that He Himself has given us to do. Each day we are to present ourselves as a living sacrifice unto the Lord our God. (See Romans 12:1) We are to sacrifice ourselves to live wholly unto Him. We are not to seek our own will, but to seek our Lord's will in our daily living.

Indeed, this was the very conflict that had arisen between the Lord Jesus and Simon Peter in Matthew 16:21-23. Our Lord Jesus Christ had come, not to do His own will, but to do the will of the Father who had sent Him. (See John 6:38) He had come as the Lamb of God to take away the sin of the world. He had come according to the Father's will to give Himself in the suffering and sacrifice of the cross for our sins. Yet as our Lord began to explain unto His disciples the need for His suffering, His sacrificial death, and His resurrection, Peter began to rebuke Him and oppose these things.

Thus in Matthew 16:23 (see also Mark 8:33) our Lord Jesus Christ responded to Peter, saying, "*Get thee behind me, Satan: thou art an offence unto me: for thou savourest not the things that be of God, but those that be of men.*" Our Lord had come to do and to obey the will of the Father unto death, even unto the death of the cross. (See Philippians 2:8) Yet Peter was standing in opposition to that will of the Father. Yea, Peter was not savoring "the things that be of God," but was savoring "the things that be of men." Therefore, our Lord declared that Peter was an offense unto Him and referred to Peter as one who was at that moment yielded unto the will of Satan. Even so, when we ourselves choose our own will over our Lord's will in our daily living, we also are not savoring "the things that be of God," but are savoring "the thing that be of men." Yea, we are not savoring "the things that be of God," but are savoring "the things that be of ourselves." Indeed, when we do this, we also are an offense unto our Lord and are walking in the ways of Satan in opposition to our Lord.

In the third place, from our Lord's three-fold instruction in Matthew 16:24, we find that we must follow our Lord wherever He leads. No matter what the will of our Lord may be, no matter where He may lead us in our daily living, no matter what it may cost us to follow, nevertheless we are to follow Him. We are to trust Him and His will with all of our hearts. Then in full assurance of faith, we are to "run with patience" the course that He has set before us. (See Hebrews 12:1) Indeed, we are to deny ourselves, take up our cross daily, and follow Him.

If we would come after our Lord and follow Him, we must walk even as He walked. Just as He denied Himself for our sake, even so we also must deny ourselves for His sake. Just as He sacrificed Himself and laid down His own life for us, even so we also must cease to hold our own lives dear unto ourselves, but must lay down our lives as a living sacrifice unto Him. This is the manner by which our Lord and Savior Jesus Christ brought forth much fruit unto the glory of God the Father. Even so, this is the manner by which we also may bring forth much fruit unto the glory of God the Father. Thus our Lord declared in John 12:24, *"Verily, verily, I say unto you, Except a corn of wheat fall into the ground and die, it abideth alone: but if it die, it bringeth forth much fruit."* If we would serve our Lord, then we must walk after Him, denying ourselves even as He denied Himself, taking up our cross daily even as He took up His cross, and following Him. This alone is the way of spiritual fruit bearing. This alone is the way of abundant Christian living. This alone is the way of faithful service to our Lord. This alone is the way of fellowship with our Lord and of honor before our Lord.

---

39. We must sever and cast away anything in our lives that would cause a little child to stumble spiritually.

Matthew 18:1-9 – *"At the same time came the disciples unto Jesus, saying, Who is the greatest in the kingdom of heaven? And Jesus called a little child unto him, and set him in the midst of them, and said, Verily I say unto you, Except ye be converted, and become as little children, ye shall not enter into the kingdom of heaven. Whosoever therefore shall humble himself as this little child, the same is greatest in the kingdom of heaven. And whoso shall receive one such little child in my name receiveth me. But whoso shall offend one of these little ones which believe in me, it were better for him that a millstone were hanged about his neck, and that he were drowned in the depth of the sea. Woe unto the world because of offences! For it must needs be that offences come; but woe to that man by whom the offence cometh!* **Wherefore if thy hand or thy foot offend thee, cut them off, and cast them from thee***: it is better for thee to enter into life halt or maimed, rather than having two hands or two feet to be cast into everlasting fire.* **And if thine eye offend thee, pluck it out, and cast it from thee***: it is better for thee to enter into life with one eye, rather than having two eyes to be cast into hell fire."*

Mark 9:42-48 – "*And whosoever shall offend one of these little ones that believe in me, it is better for him that a millstone were hanged about his neck, and he were cast into the sea.* **And if thy hand offend thee, cut it off**: *it is better for thee to enter into life maimed, than having two hands to go into hell, into the fire that never shall be quenched: where their worm dieth not, and the fire is not quenched.* **And if thy foot offend thee, cut it off**: *it is better for thee to enter halt into life, than having two feet to be cast into hell, into the fire that never shall be quenched: where their worm dieth not, and the fire is not quenched.* **And if thine eye offend thee, pluck it out**: *it is better for thee to enter into the kingdom of God with one eye, than having two eyes to be cast into hell fire: where their worm dieth not, and the fire is not quenched.*"

As the disciples followed Jesus before His death, resurrection, and ascension, one of their continuing concerns was the matter of who would be the greatest in the kingdom of heaven. On the particular occasion of Matthew 18:1-9, our Lord Jesus Christ responded to their question by calling a little child into their midst and using that little child to illustrate the truth of the matter. First, our Lord declared unto them that an individual would not even enter the kingdom of God except he become as a little child in child-like faith upon Him as eternal Savior. Second, our Lord declared unto them that those believers who would faithfully humble themselves to the place of a little child in complete dependence and surrender of heart before their heavenly Father would be the very ones who will be greatest in the kingdom of heaven.

Then, having used this little child as an illustration for these two truths, our Lord began to speak concerning our relationship toward the little children themselves. First, our Lord raised up the work of ministering to little children unto the highest level, proclaiming in Matthew 18:5, "*And whoso shall receive one such little child in my name receiveth me.*" Second, our Lord gave a serious and solemn warning concerning our relationship toward these little children, proclaiming in Matthew 18:6-7 (see also Mark 9:42), "*But whoso shall offend one of these little ones which believe in me, it were better for him that a millstone were hanged about his neck, and that he were drowned in the depth of the sea. Woe unto the world because of offences! For it must needs be that offences come; but woe to that man by whom the offence cometh!"* Now, it is worthy of our notice that with these three verses our Lord has placed the receiving of a little child in His name in direct contrast to the offending of one of these little ones. The matter of concern herein is that matter of leading these little children in spiritual things. The word "offend" here means to cause one to stumble and be scandalized spiritually.

This then is our Lord's warning – It would be better that a millstone be hung about our neck and that we be drowned in the depths of the sea, than that we should cause one of these little ones who believe in Christ to stumble and be scandalized spiritually. Certainly this would include those who sexually molest children or who physically abuse children. Yet it would also include those who lead children astray spiritually through word or behavior. It would include those who selfishly ignore the spiritual needs of these little ones. It would include those who speak unto these little ones with grievous words, and thereby provoke them unto wrath. It would include those who would overthrow the faith of these little ones through false teaching. It would include those whose example of carnality and worldliness would lead these little ones toward a similar path of carnality and worldliness. It would include those who would walk before these little ones in hypocrisy, and thereby lead them by example into such hypocritical ways.

Even so, in Matthew 18:8-9 (see also Mark 9:43-48) our Lord delivered His instruction, saying, *"Wherefore* [for this reason] *if thy hand or thy foot offend thee, cut them off, and cast them from thee: it is better for thee to enter into life halt or maimed, rather than having two hands or two feet to be cast into everlasting fire. And if thine eye offend thee, pluck it out, and cast it from thee: it is better for thee to enter into life with one eye, rather than having two eyes to be cast into hell fire."* Let us remember that the immediate context of this instruction concerns the matter of our relationship to these little children, and even more so concerns the matter of our causing one of these little ones to stumble spiritually. Therefore, in this particular context our Lord has instructed us to sever and cast away anything in our lives that would cause a little child to stumble spiritually. We must sever and cast aside any example of hypocrisy or worldliness out of our lives lest it cause one of these little ones to stumble spiritually. We must sever and cast aside any grievous or unedifying words out of our mouths lest they cause one of these little ones to stumble spiritually. We must sever and cast aside any selfish or proud attitude out of our hearts lest it cause one of these little ones to stumble spiritually.

40. We must take heed that we not despise one of these little ones.

Matthew 18:10-14 – "***Take heed that ye despise not one of these little ones***; *for I say unto you, that in heaven their angels do always behold the face of my Father which is in heaven. For the Son of man is come to save that which was lost. How think ye? If a man have an hundred sheep, and one of them be gone astray, doth he not leave the ninety and nine, and goeth into the mountains, and seeketh that which is gone astray? And if so be that he find it, verily I say unto you, he rejoiceth more of that sheep, than of the ninety and nine which went not astray. Even so it is not the will of your Father which is in heaven, that one of these little ones should perish.*"

The souls of these little ones are precious in our Lord's sight. Our heavenly Father has assigned angels to them for their behalf. Our Lord and Savior Jesus Christ has come to seek and to save their lost souls. Indeed, our Father which is in heaven is not willing that even one of these little ones should perish in hell. Thus our Lord has commanded us to take heed that we not despise even one of these little ones. We are not to think that these little ones are spiritually unimportant. We are not to think that the ministry unto these little ones is spiritually unimportant. We are not to treat these little ones as if they are spiritually unimportant. Rather, we are to remember our Lord's declaration from Matthew 18:5, "*And whoso shall receive one such little child in my name receiveth me.*" Our Lord takes our treatment of these little ones quite personally. So then, let us receive them in His name accordingly.

133

41. We must follow our Lord's proscribed pattern for reconciliation when a fellow believer has trespassed against us.

Matthew 18:15-17 – "*Moreover if thy brother shall trespass against thee, go and tell him his fault between thee and him alone: if he shall hear thee, thou hast gained thy brother. But if he will not hear thee, then take with thee one or two more, that in the mouth of two or three witnesses every word may be established. And if he shall neglect to hear them, tell it unto the church: but if he neglect to hear the church, let him be unto thee as an heathen man and a publican.*"

First, we must take notice that this is our Lord's proscribed pattern to deal with a fellow believer that has trespassed against us. Our Lord's opening words in Matthew 18:15 were just this, "*Moreover if thy brother* [a fellow believer] *shall trespass* [commit a sin] *against thee.*" This is not the proscribed pattern specifically for dealing with false teachers. Nor is this the proscribed pattern specifically for dealing with a fellow believer who is living in such immorality as fornication, drunkenness, extortion, etc. Rather, this is our Lord's proscribed pattern specifically for dealing with a believer who has committed sin personally against another believer.

Second, we must take notice of the opening step in this proscribed pattern from our Lord. When a fellow believer commits a sin against us, what is the first step that we are to take? In the opening portion of Matthew 18:15, our Lord gave answer, saying, "*Moreover if thy brother shall trespass against thee, go and tell him his fault between thee and him alone.*" We are not to dwell upon the matter in our hearts, growing ever more embittered at this fellow believer. Nor are we to go and complain about this fellow believer unto others. Nor are we to gather an army of allies to stand against this fellow believer. Rather, the matter is to remain between that fellow believer and us alone. We are to go alone unto this fellow believer himself or herself and to tell him or her the fault (the trespass; the sin; the wrong doing) that he or she has committed against us.

Third, we must take notice of our Lord's purpose for which we are to approach this fellow believer who has sinned against us. In the closing portion of Matthew 18:15, our Lord revealed this purpose when He said, "*If he shall hear thee, thou hast gained thy brother.*" This is our Lord proscribed purpose – the purpose of reconciliation. In our approach unto this fellow believer, our purpose should not be to strive and to tear apart. We should not go looking for a fight. Rather, in our approach unto this fellow believer, our purpose should be to gain our brother or sister in Christ. Our purpose should be to reconcile the relationship and to restore it unto loving fellowship.

Yet what if this fellow believer who has sinned against us will not hear us when we make this first, private approach? In Matthew 18:16, our Lord gave answer, "*But if he will not hear thee, then take with thee one or two more, that in the mouth of two or three witnesses every word may be established.*" This then is the second step in our Lord's proscribed pattern for dealing with a believer who has committed sin against us. Again we are not to dwell upon the matter in our hearts, growing ever more embittered at this fellow believer. Nor are we to go and complain about this fellow believer unto others. Nor are we to gather an army of allies to stand against this fellow believer. Rather, we are to go a second time unto this fellow believer, this time taking one or two more as witnesses of our approach and of this fellow believer's response. Indeed, this we are to do in order that these witnesses might aid the process of reconciliation.

Yet what if this fellow believer continues to refuse the pathway of reconciliation? In the opening portion of Matthew 18:17, our Lord gave the answer, "*And if he shall neglect to hear them, tell it unto the church.*" Now, this is not a matter of false teaching or immoral behavior that is being brought before the church. Rather, this is a matter of a believer who has sinned against another believer and who has refused the path of reconciliation with that fellow believer. According to our Lord's proscribed pattern, such behavior is to be brought before the church for the disciplinary measures of the church. Even so, in the closing portion of Matthew 18:17, our Lord added, "*But if he neglect to hear the church, let him be unto thee as an heathen man and a publican.*"

135

In conclusion then, let us take note that each step in this pattern is directly proscribed and commanded by our Lord. Here our Lord commands the first step to go and tell him his fault alone. Here our Lord commands the second step to take with us one or two witnesses. Here our Lord commands the third step to tell it unto the church. Here our Lord commands the forth step of letting this one be unto us "as an heathen man and a publican." These things are not for us to take or leave as we will. They are not suggestions. They are commands.

42. We must ever be willing to forgive our fellow believers who sin against us.

Matthew 18:21-35 – *"Then came Peter to him, and said, Lord, how oft shall my brother sin against me, and I forgive him? Till seven times? Jesus saith unto him, **I say not unto thee, Until seven times: but, Until seventy times seven.** Therefore is the kingdom of heaven likened unto a certain king, which would take account of his servants. And when he had begun to reckon, one was brought unto him, which owed him ten thousand talents. But forasmuch as he had not to pay, his lord commanded him to be sold, and his wife, and children, and all that he had, and payment to be made. The servant therefore fell down, and worshipped him, saying, Lord, have patience with me, and I will pay thee all. Then the lord of that servant was moved with compassion, and loosed him, and forgave him the debt. But the same servant went out, and found one of his fellowservants, which owed him an hundred pence: and he laid hands on him, and took him by the throat, saying, Pay me that thou owest. And his fellowservant fell down at his feet, and besought him, saying, Have patience with me, and I will pay thee all. And he would not: but went and cast him into prison, till he should pay the debt. So when his fellowservants saw what was done, they were very sorry, and came and told unto their lord all that was done. Then his lord, after that he had called him, said unto him, O thou wicked servant, I forgave thee all that debt, because thou desiredst me: shouldest not thou also have had compassion on thy fellowservant, even as I had pity on thee? And* his lord was wroth, and delivered him to the tormentors, till he should pay all that was due unto him. So likewise shall my heavenly Father do also unto you, if ye from your hearts forgive not every one his brother their trespasses."

Luke 17:3-4 – "*Take heed to yourselves: If thy brother trespass against thee, rebuke him;* **and if he repent, forgive him. And if he trespass against thee seven times in a day, and seven times in a day turn again to thee, saying, I repent; thou shalt forgive him.**"

Ephesians 4:32 – "*And be ye kind one to another, tenderhearted,* **forgiving one another, even as God for Christ's sake hath forgiven you.**"

Colossians 3:13 – "*Forbearing one another,* **and forgiving one another, if any man have a quarrel against any: even as Christ forgave you, so also do ye.**"

In Matthew 18:21 Peter asked the Lord a question concerning the matter of forgiveness – "*Then came Peter to him, and said, Lord, how oft shall my brother sin against me, and I forgive him? Till seven times?*" In verse 22 we find our Lord's answer – "*Jesus saith unto him, I say not unto thee, Until seven times: but, Until seventy times seven.*" Even so, in verses 23-35 our Lord presented a parable in order to make His point. In this parable the king represents the Lord our God Himself. Furthermore, the servant who owed the king such a large sum of money that he could never pay it represents us ourselves in our debt of sinfulness against the Lord our God, which debt our Lord has forgiven us in our salvation. Finally, the fellow servant who owed the forgiven servant a significantly smaller sum represents a fellow believer who has sinned against us.

So then, the king of the parable indicated that the forgiven servant should have forgiven his fellow servant specifically because the king had forgiven him. Even so, Ephesians 4:32 indicates that we are to be "kind one to another, tenderhearted, forgiving one another, even as God for Christ's sake hath forgiven [us]." Yet because in the parable the forgiven servant did not forgive his fellow servant, the king became angry with him and sent him to be tormented with chastening. Even so, if we will not forgive our fellow believers who sin against us, our heavenly Father's anger will be kindled against us. Indeed, in His anger He will not forgive us of our daily sins against Him when we ask for forgiveness, but will bring down His hand of chastening heavy against us.

43. We must not allow anything of this world to divide our marriage relationships.

Matthew 19:4-6 – "*And he answered and said unto them, Have ye not read, that he which made them at the beginning made them male and female, and said, For this cause shall a man leave father and mother, and shall cleave to his wife: and they twain shall be one flesh? Wherefore they are no more twain, but one flesh.* **What therefore God hath joined together, let not man put asunder.*"

During our Lord's earthly ministry, the religious leaders of Israel would often ask questions of Him concerning religious matters, seeking to trip Him up in His answers. Thus in Matthew 19:3 we read, "*The Pharisees also came unto him, tempting him, and saying unto him, Is it lawful for a man to put away* [that is – divorce] *his wife for every cause?*" To this question our Lord Jesus Christ gave answer in Matthew 19:4-6. The matter about which the Pharisees approached our Lord was that of divorce and of the justifiable causes for a divorce. In response, our Lord immediately turned their attention unto God's institution of the marriage relationship at the creation and unto God's original purpose and principles for that marriage relationship. At the creation of mankind, even before the entrance of sin, the Lord our God instituted the marriage relationship.

In Genesis 2:7 we read concerning the creation of the first man Adam – "*And the LORD God formed man of the dust of the ground, and breathed into his nostrils the breath of life; and man became a living soul.*" Then in Genesis 2:18 we read, "*And the LORD God said, It is not good that the man should be alone; I will make him an help meet for him.*" Thus we read in Genesis 2:21-23, "*And the LORD God caused a deep sleep to fall upon Adam, and he slept: and*

He took one of his ribs, and closed up the flesh instead thereof; and the rib, which the LORD *God had taken from man, made he a woman, and brought her unto the man. And Adam said, This is now bone of my bones, and flesh of my flesh: she shall be called Woman, because she was taken out of Man.*" Yea, we might even consider this account to be the first wedding ceremony. In Genesis 2:22 we find that the Lord God brought the woman unto the man and gave her away unto the man to be his wife. Then in Genesis 2:23 we find that the man received the woman to be his wife. The Lord our God and Creator did not simply make them male and female, but also made them "the man and his wife."

Finally, in Genesis 2:24 the Lord God confirmed this marriage by proclaiming the three foundational principles for a good marriage relationship. There He declared, *"Therefore shall a man leave his father and his mother, and shall cleave unto his wife: and they shall be one flesh."* First, the husband is to leave his original priority relationship to his father and his mother. Second, the husband is to cleave unto his wife as his new priority relationship, that is – He is to hold his wife dearly in his heart and through his behavior. Third, the husband and the wife are actively to pursue a one-flesh unity with one another. In fact, in Matthew 19:5-6 our Lord Jesus Christ referred to this declaration of God our heavenly Father and indicated thereby that at the moment of marriage, God Himself puts a man and a woman together into the one-flesh relationship of marriage. Yea, in the opening portion of verse 6 our Lord declared, *"Wherefore they are no more twain, but one flesh."*

Even so, in the closing portion of Matthew 19:6, our Lord delivered the command, *"What therefore God hath put together, let not man put asunder."* Now, the phrase "put asunder" means "to separate, to divide." In every marriage the Lord our God Himself has put the husband and his wife together into a one-flesh marriage relationship. Furthermore, in our marriages we must actively and daily pursue the development and the maintenance of that one-flesh relationship. Therefore, we must not allow anything into our marriage relationships that would create division and separation in that one-flesh relationship. The principle here is not only that the Lord our God is against divorce, but also that He is against any sinfulness and selfishness of man that would work contrary to the one-flesh unity of our marriages. "*What God hath joined together, let not man put asunder.*" We must allow not anything of this world to divide the one-flesh unity of our marriage relationships.

44. We must ever help the little children to come unto Christ and never hinder them from coming unto Him.

Matthew 19:13-15 – "*Then were there brought unto him little children, that he should put his hands on them, and pray: and the disciples rebuked them. But Jesus said, **Suffer little children, and forbid them not, to come unto me**: for of such is the kingdom of heaven. And he laid his hands on them, and departed thence.*"

Luke 18:15-17 – "*And they brought unto him also infants, that he would touch them: but when his disciples saw it, they rebuked them. But Jesus called them unto him, and said, **Suffer little children to come unto me, and forbid them not**: for of such is the kingdom of God. Verily I say unto you, Whosoever shall not receive the kingdom of God as a little child shall in no wise enter therein.*"

Just as we have already learned from Matthew 18:10-14 that we are not to despise the little children, especially in spiritual matters, even so from Matthew 19:13-15 (see also Luke 18:15-17) we learn that we must not hinder the little children, but must ever help them in their spiritual walk with Christ. Now, it is important to note that our Lord spoke specifically concerning the children's relationship unto Him. He was not speaking concerning their relationship unto a religion or unto a church organization. Rather, He was speaking concerning their personal relationship unto Him and concerning their spiritual walk with Him. In all things we must help the little ones to develop and maintain a spiritual walk with and service to our Lord and Savior Jesus Christ. Indeed, in no way are we to hinder them or forbid them from such a spiritual walk and service.

45. When we are in a leadership role, we must lead by being the minister and servant of others.

Matthew 20:20-28 – *"Then came to him the mother of Zebedee's children with her sons, worshipping him, and desiring a certain thing of him. And he said unto her, What wilt thou? She saith unto him, Grant that these my two sons may sit, the one on thy right hand, and the other on the left, in thy kingdom. But Jesus answered and said, Ye know not what ye ask. Are ye able to drink of the cup that I shall drink of, and to be baptized with the baptism that I am baptized with? They say unto him, We are able. And he saith unto them, Ye shall drink indeed of my cup, and be baptized with the baptism that I am baptized with: but to sit on my right hand, and on my left, is not mine to give, but it shall be given to them for whom it is prepared of my Father. And when the ten heard it, they were moved with indignation against the two brethren. But Jesus called them unto him, and said, Ye know that the princes of the Gentiles exercise dominion over them, and they that are great exercise authority upon them. But it shall not be so among you: but whosoever will be great among you, let him be your minister; and whosoever will be chief among you, let him be your servant: even as the Son of man came not to be ministered unto, but to minister, and to give his life a ransom for many."*

Mark 9:33-37 – *"And he came to Capernaum: and being in the house he asked them, What was it that ye disputed among yourselves by the way? But they held their peace: for by the way they had disputed among themselves, who should be the greatest. And he sat down, and called the twelve, and saith unto them, If any man desire to be first, the same shall be last of all, and servant of all. And he took a child, and set him in the midst of them: and when he had taken him in his arms, he said unto them, Whosoever shall receive one of such children in my name, receiveth me: and whosoever shall receive me, receiveth not me, but him that sent me."*

Mark 10:35-45 – *"And James and John, the sons of Zebedee, come unto him, saying, Master, we would that thou shouldest do for us whatsoever we shall desire. And he said unto them, What would ye that I should do for you? They said unto him, Grant unto us that we may sit, one on thy right hand, and the other on thy left hand, in thy* *glory. But Jesus said unto them, Ye know not what ye ask: can ye drink of the cup that I drink of? And be baptized with the baptism that I am baptized with? And they said unto him, We can. And Jesus said unto them, Ye shall indeed drink of the cup that I drink of; and with the baptism that I am baptized withal shall ye be baptized: but to sit on my right hand and on my left hand is not mine to give; but it shall be given to them for whom it is prepared. And when the ten heard it, they began to be much displeased with James and John. But Jesus called them to him, and saith unto them, Ye know that they which are accounted to rule over the Gentiles exercise lordship over them; and their great ones exercise authority upon them. **But so shall it not be among you: but whosoever will be great among you, shall be your minister: and whosoever of you will be the chiefest, shall be servant of all.** For even the Son of man came not to be ministered unto, but to minister, and to give his life a ransom for many.*"

Luke 22:24-27 – "*And there was also a strife among them, which of them should be accounted the greatest. And he said unto them, The kings of the Gentiles exercise lordship over them; and they that exercise authority upon them are called benefactors. **But ye shall not be so: but he that is greatest among you, let him be as the younger; and he that is chief, as he that doth serve.** For whether is greater, he that sitteth at meat, or he that serveth? Is not he that sitteth at meat? But I am among you as he that serveth.*"

In Mark 9:33-37 & Luke 22:24-27 we read about a dispute and strife among the disciples over "*which of them should be accounted the greatest.*" Then just a short time later in Mark 10:35-45 & Matthew 20:20-28 we find that the controversy was stirred up yet again over this matter, as James and John, through the request of their mother, sought the highest place of honor in our Lord's coming kingdom. Although the Lord did not grant them such a position, the other ten disciples were moved with anger and indignation against James and John for the very fact that they would make such a request.

Even so, within the context of these disputes and controversies among the disciples, our Lord Jesus Christ took opportunity to instruct His disciples concerning the relationship of leadership and servanthood according to His will. First, our Lord mentioned a general practice that is clearly observable within the world around us. It is the reality that those of this world who are in higher places exercise dominion and authority over those below them. They rule over and lord it over those who are on a lower social level than they are. They require that those beneath them should minister and do service unto them. However, this is not how our Lord would have it to be among His people. Rather, it is the will of our Lord that those who would be great and chief among His people should be the minister and servant of those under them. Furthermore, our Lord presented Himself as the perfect example of this principle of servanthood. Our Lord Himself, who certainly is the greatest and chiefest above all, came to this earth "*not to be ministered unto, but to minister, and to give His life a ransom for many.*"

Our Lord and Savior Jesus Christ did not come in order that we should minister unto Him, but in order that He Himself might minister unto us. Yea, He came in order that He Himself, the Lord of all, might give His very own life as a ransom for us. Even so, we should walk in our Lord's steps. We who are in higher roles of authority and influence should give ourselves to serve and minister unto those under our authority and influence. The way of God's people is not to be about selfishly getting for one's self. Rather, it is to be about lovingly serving the other; even as the latter portion of Galatians 5:13 declares, "*But by love serve one another.*"

46. We must pay our taxes.

Matthew 22:15-22 – "*Then went the Pharisees, and took counsel how they might entangle him in his talk. And they sent out unto him their disciples with the Herodians, saying, Master, we know that thou art true, and teachest the way of God in truth, neither carest thou for any man: for thou regardest not the person of men. Tell us therefore, What thinkest thou? Is it lawful to give tribute unto Caesar, or not? But Jesus perceived their wickedness, and said, Why tempt ye me, ye hypocrites? Shew me the tribute money. And they brought unto him a penny. And he saith unto them, Whose is this image and* superscription? *They say unto him, Caesar's. Then saith he unto them,* **Render therefore unto Caesar the things which are Caesar's; and unto God the things that are God's.** *When they had heard these words, they marvelled, and left him, and went their way."*

Mark 12:13-17 – *"And they send unto him certain of the Pharisees and of the Herodians, to catch him in his words. And when they were come, they say unto him, Master, we know that thou art true, and carest for no man: for thou regardest not the person of men, but teachest the way of God in truth: Is it lawful to give tribute to Caesar, or not? Shall we give, or shall we not give? But he, knowing their hypocrisy, said unto them, Why tempt ye me? Bring me a penny, that I may see it. And they brought it. And he saith unto them, Whose is this image and superscription? And they said unto him, Caesar's. And Jesus answering said unto them,* **Render to Caesar the things that are Caesar's, and to God the things that are God's.** *And they marvelled at him."*

Luke 20:20-26 – *"And they watched him, and sent forth spies, which should feign themselves just men, that they might take hold of his words, that so they might deliver him unto the power and authority of the governor. And they asked him, saying, Master, we know that thou sayest and teachest rightly, neither acceptest thou the person of any, but teachest the way of God truly: Is it lawful for us to give tribute unto Caesar, or no? But he perceived their craftiness, and said unto them, Why tempt ye me? Shew me a penny. Whose image and superscription hath it? They answered and said, Caesar's. And he said unto them,* **Render therefore unto Caesar the things which be Caesar's, and unto God the things which be God's.** *And they could not take hold of his words before the people: and they marvelled at his answer, and held their peace."*

As we have previously noted, throughout our Lord's earthly ministry the religious leaders of Israel would often ask questions of our Lord Jesus Christ concerning religious matters, seeking to trip Him up in His answers. In Matthew 22:15-22 (see also Mark 12:13-17; Luke 20:20-26) we come to such a case, wherein they ask Him concerning the matter of taxes. It is interesting in this case that the Pharisees' disciples, who would have been much against paying taxes to the Roman power, and the Herodians, who would have been in favor of paying such taxes, came together on this matter. It is also interesting that this group began in their approach unto the Lord by commending His impartiality toward any person or group. Yet all of this was intended to set Jesus up for a fall, "to entangle Him in His talk."

However, God the Son, the Lord Jesus Christ, is not so easily entangled. Thus our Lord handled the matter in a marvelous way. Furthermore, in so doing He delivered this command for us all – "*Render therefore unto Caesar the things which are Caesar's; and unto God the things that are God's.*" To the Lord our God we owe our love, our submission, our trust, our praise, our thanksgiving, our adoration, our worship, our obedience, our lives. Let us then render unto God the things that are God's. Yet unto the government we owe our taxes. Indeed, what inscription is printed on our money? It is the inscription, "The United States of America." Let us then render unto our government the things that are our government's. Yea, let us then honestly pay our taxes.

47. We must love the Lord our God with all our heart, soul, mind, and strength.

Matthew 22:37-38 – "*Jesus said unto him, **Thou shalt love the Lord thy God with all thy heart, and with all thy soul, and with all thy mind.** This is the first and great commandment.*"

Mark 12:29-30 – "*And Jesus answered him, The first of all the commandments is, Hear, O Israel; The Lord our God is one Lord: **and thou shalt love the Lord thy God with all thy heart, and with all thy soul, and with all thy mind, and with all thy strength**: this is the first commandment.*"

In Matthew 22:34-36 (see also Mark 12:28) we read concerning a lawyer (that is – a so-called expert in the Law of Moses) who asked the Lord a question. Yet we learn that this lawyer of the Pharisee did not approach our Lord with a sincere desire to learn. Rather, he approached our Lord with a desire to tempt the Lord and to entangle Him in His words. Yet in the answer that our Lord delivered, we find two great precepts and principles by which to govern our lives. First, in Matthew 22:37-38 & Mark 12:29-30 our Lord presented a precept and principle to govern all of our relationship with the Lord our God. Second, in Matthew 22:39 & Mark 12:31 our Lord presented a precept and principle to govern all of our relationships with other people. Finally, our Lord indicated that these are the two essential commandments for all godliness and righteous living. *"On these two commandments hang all the law and the prophets."* (Matthew 22:40) On these two commandments hang everything that the Lord our God desires for us to do in our Christian lives.

In the first place, we consider the first of these two great commands, which is quoted from Deuteronomy 6:4-5. We are to love the Lord our God with all of our heart, soul, mind, and strength. Indeed, we are to love the Lord our God with all of our being. This love for the Lord our God and Savior is not simply an external show. It is not a matter of drawing nigh unto the Lord with the words of our mouths and honouring the Lord with our lips, while our hearts are far from Him. No! This is a love for our Lord with our entire being. This is a love for our Lord that encompasses both our inner man and our external behavior. In fact, this is a love for our Lord that begins in our hearts and then flows outward from our hearts through our soul, mind, and strength. Obedience to this command does not allow for any form of hypocrisy in our relationship with our Lord. Our inner man of the heart is the center and foundation of true, godly love for our Lord.

Even so, this love for the Lord our God and Savior is the opposite of any selfish, self-centered, self-serving way. In 1 John 2:15 God's Holy Word gives the instruction, *"Love not the world, neither the things that are in the world. If any man love the world, the love of the Father is not in him."* Herein we learn that a love for this world and for the things of this world is the opposite of love for the Lord our God. So then, what is the nature of this world and the things of this world? 1 John 2:16 gives answer, saying, *"For all that is in the world, the lust of the flesh, and the lust of the eyes, and the pride of life, is not of the Father, but is of the world."* Indeed, the very essence of that which is the opposite of love for our Lord is "the lust of the flesh, and the lust of the eyes, and the pride of life." Or, to put it in other words – The very essence of that which is the opposite of love for our Lord is self, self, self. Therefore, any time that we walk in a selfish, self-centered, self-serving way we are not walking in love for our Lord.

On the other hand, this love for the Lord our God and Savior requires faithful obedience and service unto our Lord. In the opening portion of John 15:21, our Lord Jesus Christ declared, *"He that hath my commandments and keepeth them, he it is that loveth me."* In Deuteronomy 11:1 the instruction is given, *"Therefore thou shalt love the* LORD *thy God, and keep his charge, and his statutes, and his judgments, and his commandments, alway."* Again in Deuteronomy 11:13 the prerequisite to blessing is revealed – *"And it shall come to pass, if ye shall hearken diligently unto my commandments which I command you this day, to love the* LORD *your God, and to serve him with all your heart and with all your soul . . . ."* Yet again in verse 22 the prerequisite is revealed – *"For if ye shall diligently keep all these commandments which I command you, to do them, to love the* LORD *your God, to walk in all his ways, and to cleave unto him . . . ."* Loving our Lord, obeying our Lord, and serving our Lord are all interconnected. Thus we are to love Him, yea to serve and obey Him, with all our heart, soul, mind, and strength. This is the first great commandment, the one concerning our relationship with the Lord our God.

48. We must love our neighbor as ourselves without hypocrisy, working no ill whatsoever to our neighbor.

Matthew 22:39-40 – *"And the second is like unto it,* **Thou shalt love thy neighbour as thyself.** *On these two commandments hang all the law and the prophets."*

Mark 12:31 – *"And the second is like, namely this,* **Thou shalt love thy neighbour as thyself.** *There is none other commandment greater than these."*

Romans 12:9 – "***Let love be without dissimulation.*** *Abhor that which is evil; cleave to that which is good.*"

Romans 13:8-10 – "***Owe no man any thing, but to love one another:*** *for he that loveth another hath fulfilled the law. For this, Thou shalt not commit adultery, Thou shalt not kill, Thou shalt not steal, Thou shalt not bear false witness, Thou shalt not covet; and if there be any other commandment, it is briefly comprehended in this saying, namely,* **Thou shalt love thy neighbour as thyself.** *Love worketh no ill to his neighbour: therefore love is the fulfilling of the law.*"

1 Timothy 1:5 – "***Now the end of the commandment is charity out of a pure heart, and of a good conscience, and of faith unfeigned.***"

In the second place, we consider the second of the two greatest commands, which is quoted from Leviticus 19:18. We are to love our neighbor as we naturally love ourselves. This love for our neighbor is a matter of serving and honoring the other as we would naturally serve and honor ourselves. In Romans 12:10 the instruction is given, "*Be kindly affectioned one to another with brotherly love; in honour preferring one another.*" Again in Galatians 5:13-14 the truth is given, "*For, brethren, ye have been called unto liberty; only use not liberty for an occasion to the flesh, but by love serve one another. For all the Law is fulfilled in one word, even in this; Thou shalt love thy neighbor as thyself.*"

Even so, this love for our neighbor is the opposite of any selfish, self-centered, self-serving way. In the opening portion of Romans 12:9 the instruction is given, "*Let love be without dissimulation.*" Now, a simple understanding for the word "dissimulation" might be "selfish motivation." Our love for our neighbor is to be without any form of selfish motivation. Also in 1 Corinthians 13:4-5 the truth is given, "*Charity suffereth long, and is kind; charity envieth not; charity vaunteth not itself, is not puffed up, doth not behave itself unseemly, seeketh not her own, is not easily provoked, thinketh no evil.*" Now, in the New Testament the word "charity" may be defined as godly love in our behavior toward others. Even so, godly love toward our neighbor is the opposite of vaunting self, of puffing up self, and of seeking for self. Yea, it is the opposite of self, self, self.

148

Furthermore, this love for our neighbor must be without hypocrisy. A more full understanding for the word "dissimulation" in Romans 12:9 would be "the practice of concealing something under a false appearance, of making a false show of something." It is possible to speak words that sound loving and to perform actions that appear loving while being without love in our heart toward another. Yea, it is possible to speak such words that sound loving and to perform such actions that appear loving with selfish motivation in order to manipulate another for our own advantage. Such "loving" words and actions are employed only to conceal the selfish motivation of our heart. Such "loving" words and actions are a false, outward show without any true, inward reality. They are feigned. They are a fake. They are pretending. They are hypocritical. Yet our Lord looks upon our hearts. He tries the reality of our hearts, and He requires that we love our neighbor as ourselves in truth from our hearts without the false shows and appearances of hypocrisy and selfish manipulation. Thus the command is revealed in 1 Timothy 1:5 that we are to have charity (godly love toward others) "out of a pure heart."

Finally, from Romans 13:10 we learn that this love for our neighbor will work no ill whatsoever at all toward our neighbor. Indeed, that which works ill to another is not love at all and that which is done for selfish advantage at the expense of another is not love at all. Rather, according to 1 Timothy 1:5 our love toward others is to be out of "a good conscience" and out of "faith unfeigned." It is to be a godly love that is produced by the filling influence of God the Holy Spirit. As such, it is to be a love that possesses a giving heart and a giving hand. Even so, in 1 John 3:16-18 the truth and warning is revealed, "*Hereby perceive we the love of God, because He laid down his life for us: and we ought to lay down our lives for the brethren. But whoso hath this world's good, and seeth his brother have need, and shutteth up his bowels of compassion from him, how dwelleth the love of God in him? My little children, let us not love in word, neither in tongue; but in deed and in truth.*" Yea, this is the type of love that we owe unto others, according to Romans 13:8; and thereby we shall fulfill the law of Christ in relation to others.

49. We must keep the religious standards that are set before us, but must not be hypocrites in so doing.

Matthew 23:1-7 – "*Then spake Jesus to the multitude, and to his disciples, saying, The scribes and the Pharisees sit in Moses' seat:* **all therefore whatsoever they bid you observe, that observe and do; but do not ye after their works**: *for they say, and do not. For they bind heavy burdens and grievous to be borne, and lay them on men's shoulders; but they themselves will not move them with one of their fingers. But all their works they do for to be seen of men: they make broad their phylacteries, and enlarge the borders of their garments, and love the uppermost rooms at feasts, and the chief seats in the synagogues, And greetings in the markets, and to be called of men, Rabbi, Rabbi.*"

Seven times throughout the latter portion of this Matthew 23 our Lord pronounced a woe upon the scribes and Pharisees, calling them hypocrites. We find these at the beginning of verses 13, 14, 15, 23, 25, 27, & 29, where we hear our Lord's proclamation – "*Woe unto you, scribes and Pharisees, hypocrites!*" In addition, at the beginning of verse 16, our Lord proclaimed against them, saying, "*Woe unto you, ye blind guides!*" At the beginning of both verses 17 & 19, our Lord called them "*fools and blind.*" Again at the beginning of verse 24, He called them "*blind guides.*" Yet again at the beginning of verse 26, He referred to each of them as a "*blind Pharisee.*" Finally, in verse 33 our Lord rebuked them, saying, "*Ye serpents, ye generation of vipers, how can ye escape the damnation of hell?*" Certainly these scribes and Pharisees of Jesus day were not right with the Lord their God. In fact, they were not even saved from their sin.

Yet in Matthew 23:2-3 our Lord Jesus Christ gave instruction unto the multitudes and unto His disciples, saying, "The scribes and the Pharisees sit in Moses' seat: all therefore whatsoever they bid you observe, that observe and do; but do not yea after their works: for they say, and do not." These scribes and Pharisees were the religious leaders over Israel in that day. They sat in the place of Moses' seat, that is – they were in the place of religious authority. Therefore, our Lord instructed the multitudes and His disciples to respect that place of authority by keeping the standards that these religious leaders placed over them. Although these religious leaders themselves were hypocrites, nevertheless their proscribed standards were to be followed. The hypocrisy of these scribes and Pharisees did not grant a complete rejection of their religious authority or a complete rejection of the religious standards that they had set therein.

On the other hand, our Lord Jesus Christ instructed the multitudes and His disciples not to follow the actual works and ways of these hypocritical religious leaders. In the closing portion of verse 3, our Lord declared, *"But do not ye after their works: for they say, and do not."* Do after their religious standards – Yes. Do after their hypocritical works and ways – No. So then, what is the essence of such hypocritical works and ways? In Matthew 23:4-7 our Lord Jesus Christ revealed the answer. The essence of such hypocritical works and ways involves three primary characteristics. First, there is a heavy-handed spirit of controlling others. Second, there is no willingness to serve others. There is no willingness to lift even a single finger in order to help those who are spiritually burdened and in order to minister unto their need. Third, there is a driving desire for the praise of others. There is a hunger and thirst for public recognition and honor. In all, the essence of such hypocritical works and ways is all about self and not at all about serving. Thus our Lord commands us not to walk with such works and ways.

~~~~~~

50. We must not seek to be exalted before others, but must humble ourselves to serve others.

Matthew 23:8-12 – *"**But be not ye called Rabbi: for one is your Master, even Christ; and all ye are brethren. And call no man your father upon the earth: for one is your Father, which is in heaven. Neither be ye called masters: for one is your Master, even Christ. But he that is greatest among you shall be your servant.** And whosoever shall exalt himself shall be abased; and he that shall humble himself shall be exalted."*

Luke 14:7-14 – *"And he put forth a parable to those which were bidden, when he marked how they chose out the chief rooms; saying*

151

unto them, *When thou art bidden of any man to a wedding, **sit not down in the highest room**; lest a more honourable man than thou be bidden of him; and he that bade thee and him come and say to thee, Give this man place; and thou begin with shame to take the lowest room. But when thou art bidden, **go and sit down in the lowest room**; that when he that bade thee cometh, he may say unto thee, Friend, go up higher: then shalt thou have worship in the presence of them that sit at meat with thee. For whosoever exalteth himself shall be abased; and he that humbleth himself shall be exalted. Then said he also to him that bade him, **When thou makest a dinner or a supper, call not thy friends, nor thy brethren, neither thy kinsmen, nor thy rich neighbours; lest they also bid thee again, and a recompence be made thee. But when thou makest a feast, call the poor, the maimed, the lame, the blind: and thou shalt be blessed; for they cannot recompense thee**: for thou shalt be recompensed at the resurrection of the just.*"

John 13:12-17 – *"So after he had washed their feet, and had taken his garments, and was set down again, he said unto them, Know ye what I have done to you? Ye call me Master and Lord: and ye say well; for so I am. If I then, your Lord and Master, have washed your feet; **ye also ought to wash one another's feet. For I have given you an example, that ye should do as I have done to you.** Verily, verily, I say unto you, The servant is not greater than his lord; neither he that is sent greater than he that sent him. If ye know these things, happy are ye if ye do them.*"

The hypocritical scribes and Pharisees of Jesus' day sought after titles of recognition and positions of honor. They sought to be exalted by others and to exalt themselves before others. Yet such is not to be the way of our Lord's people. We are not to seek after titles of recognition and positions of honor before men. We are not to seek to be exalted and to exalt ourselves before men. Rather, we are to humble ourselves before the Lord our God and to serve others in humility. In Matthew 23:11 our Lord repeated unto the multitude and His disciples that instruction which had privately delivered unto His disciples in Matthew 20:26-27, *"But He that is greatest among you shall be your servant."* Just our Lord and Master Jesus Christ humbled Himself to serve us, even so we are to humble ourselves in order to serve others. Pleasing our friends in order to obtain a return should not be our focus. Rather, serving the needy who cannot repay us in any way should be our focus. In addition, our Lord delivered the warning and the promise in Matthew 23:12 (see also Luke 14:11), "*And whosoever shall exalt himself shall be abased* [that is – at the hand of the Lord our God]; *and he that shall humble himself shall be exalted* [that is – by the hand of the Lord our God]." Even so, we must not seek after exalted recognition, but after humble service.

51. We must repent of our hypocrisy and must seek to be cleansed from the heart out.

Matthew 23:25-26 – "*Woe unto you, scribes and Pharisees, hypocrites! For ye make clean the outside of the cup and of the platter, but within they are full of extortion and excess.* **Thou blind Pharisee, cleanse first that which is within the cup and platter, that the outside of them may be clean also.**"

Here our Lord made reference to "the cup and the platter" as an illustration for the hearts of these hypocrites. He indicated that they were careful and particular about keeping the outside of "the cup and platter" clean, while they allowed the inside to be filled with all forms of filth and uncleanness. Why did they do this? They did so because they did their works to be seen of men and because the outside of "the cup and platter" (that is – the outward appearance of their lives) was that which was seen by others.

Yet our Lord looks upon the inside of "the cup and platter," that is – Our Lord looks upon our hearts. If our hearts are not clean in His sight, that is – if our hearts are full of unrighteousness and iniquity in His sight, then our lives will not be acceptable before Him no matter how righteous and clean they may appear unto men. Thus our Lord gave the instruction that we should first cleanse the unrighteousness and iniquity of our inner man in order that the outward life may also be truly clean and acceptable in His sight. So then, how do we so cleanse our inner man? We do so through the humble repentance of a broken and contrite heart before our Lord over the unrighteousness and iniquity of our inner man. We must acknowledge the "inner-man" iniquity. We must confess and repent of that "inner-man" iniquity. We must seek our Lord's grace to turn from and to cast away that "inner-man" iniquity. Then shall we cease the works and ways of hypocrisy and shall find cleansing from the heart out.

52. We must not be deceived by anyone into following a false Christ.

Matthew 24:4-5 – "*And Jesus answered and said unto them,* **Take heed that no man deceive you**. *For many shall come in my name, saying, I am Christ; and shall deceive many.*"

Mark 13:5-6 – "*And Jesus answering them began to say,* **Take heed lest any man deceive you**: *for many shall come in my name, saying, I am Christ; and shall deceive many.*"

Luke 21:8 – "*And he said,* **Take heed that ye be not deceived**: *for many shall come in my name, saying, I am Christ; and the time draweth near: go ye not therefore after them.*"

In Matthew 24:1-2 (see also Mark 13:1-2; Luke 21:5-6) we find a prophecy that our Lord Jesus Christ delivered concerning the destruction of the temple in Jerusalem – "*And Jesus went out, and departed from the temple: and his disciples came to him for to shew him the buildings of the temple. And Jesus said unto them, See ye not all these things? Verily I say unto you, There shall not be left here one stone upon another, that shall not be thrown down.*" Now, this prophetic utterance brought forth some questions into the minds of the disciples concerning things to come and the end of the world. Thus we read in Matthew 24:3 (see also Mark 13:3-4; Luke 21:7), "*And as he sat upon the mount of Olives, the disciples came unto Him privately, saying, Tell us, when shall these things be? And what shall be the sign of thy coming, and of the end of the world?*" Our Lord's response to these questions is then recorded in Matthew 24-25; Mark 13; & Luke 21.

Involved in our Lord's response, He also delivered some commands and instructions. In their context some of these instructions apply specifically unto the children of Israel during the time of the Great Tribulation. However, others of these instructions are more generally applied unto all of God's people. In Matthew 24:4-5 (see also Mark 13:5-6; Luke 21:8) we find one of these more general instructions. Throughout this time of the church, and especially as we draw closer unto the time of the end, false teachers and false prophets will be in the world, seeking to deceive us and to turn us away from our one, true Lord and Savior Jesus the Christ. Yea, many will even go about in our Lord's name, claiming to be Christ. They will claim that they are directly sent from God. They will claim that they are special prophets from God. They will claim that they are anointed in a special way with the power of God. Yea, they will even claim to be the divine Son of God Himself. Even so, 1 John 4:1 gives us the warning, saying, *"Beloved, believe not every spirit, but try the spirits whether they are of God: because many false prophets are gone out into the world."* Again 2 Timothy 3:13 gives the warning, saying, *"But evil men and seducers shall wax worse and worse, deceiving, and being deceived."*

Indeed, we must take heed that we not be deceived by these false teachers, by these evil men and seducers, and that we do not follow after them and their false teachings. Yet how shall we be able to discern whether a particular teacher and his particular teaching is true or false? To this question Isaiah 8:20 gives answer, saying, *"To the law and to the testimony: if they speak not according to this word, it is because there is no light in them."* If they speak not according to the true and holy Word of God, they are teaching falsehood and deception. We must not listen to them, and we must not follow after them.

53. We must not be troubled in heart at the signs of the times.

Matthew 24:6-8 – "*And ye shall hear of wars and rumours of wars: see that ye be not troubled: for all these things must come to pass, but the end is not yet. For nation shall rise against nation, and kingdom against kingdom: and there shall be famines, and pestilences, and earthquakes, in divers places. All these are the beginning of sorrows.*"

Mark 13:7-8 – "*And when ye shall hear of wars and rumours of wars, be ye not troubled: for such things must needs be; but the end shall not be yet. For nation shall rise against nation, and kingdom against kingdom: and there shall be earthquakes in divers places, and there shall be famines and troubles: these are the beginnings of sorrows.*"

Luke 21:9 – "*But when ye shall hear of wars and commotions, be not terrified: for these things must first come to pass; but the end is not by and by.*"

There are many today who have set their focus upon the subject of prophecy and upon the "signs of the times." They point to the "wars and rumours of wars." They point to the turmoil among the nations. They point to the "famines, and pestilences, and earthquakes, in divers places." However, it is common for such individuals to focus upon such things in a wrong fashion. Many who focus upon such things become worried and troubled in heart over these things. Yet that is just what our Lord Jesus Christ commanded us not to do. Yes, our Lord warned us in advance that such things would come. Yes, we can clearly see such things all around us in the world today. Yet our Lord directly commanded and instructed us with these words – "*See that ye be not troubled.*" For us to be aware and to be warned concerning such things is in accord with our Lord's will for us. However, for our hearts to be full of worries and fears over such things is directly contrary to our Lord's will for us.

54. We must watch and be ready for our Lord's coming through faithful obedience to His will.

Matthew 24:42-46 – "***Watch therefore: for ye know not what hour your Lord doth come***. *But know this, that if the goodman of the house had known in what watch the thief would come, he would have watched, and would not have suffered his house to be broken up.* ***Therefore be ye also ready: for in such an hour as ye think not the Son of man cometh***. *Who then is a faithful and wise servant, whom his lord hath made ruler over his household, to give them meat in due season? Blessed is that servant, whom his lord when he cometh shall find so doing.*"

Luke 12:35-40 – "***Let your loins be girded about, and your lights burning; and ye yourselves like unto men that wait for their lord, when he will return from the wedding; that when he cometh and knocketh, they may open unto him immediately***. *Blessed are those servants, whom the lord when he cometh shall find watching: verily I say unto you, that he shall gird himself, and make them to sit down to meat, and will come forth and serve them. And if he shall come in the second watch, or come in the third watch, and find them so, blessed are those servants. And this know, that if the goodman of the house had known what hour the thief would come, he would have watched, and not have suffered his house to be broken through.* ***Be ye therefore ready also: for the Son of man cometh at an hour when ye think not***.*"

Luke 21:34-36 – "***And take heed to yourselves, lest at any time your hearts be overcharged with surfeiting, and drunkenness, and cares of this life, and so that day come upon you unawares***. *For as a snare shall it come on all them that dwell on the face of the whole earth.* ***Watch ye therefore, and pray always***, *that ye may be accounted worthy to escape all these things that shall come to pass, and to stand before the Son of man.*"

1 Thessalonians 5:1-6 – "*But of the times and the seasons, brethren, ye have no need that I write unto you. For yourselves know perfectly that the day of the Lord so cometh as a thief in the night. For when they shall say, Peace and safety; then sudden destruction cometh*

upon them, as travail upon a woman with child; and they shall not escape. But ye, brethren, are not in darkness, that that day should overtake you as a thief. Ye are all the children of light, and the children of the day: we are not of the night, nor of darkness. ***Therefore let us not sleep, as do others; but let us watch and be sober****."*

Titus 2:11-13 – "*For the grace of God that bringeth salvation hath appeared to all men,* ***teaching us that, denying ungodliness and worldly lusts, we should live soberly, righteously, and godly, in this present world; looking for that blessed hope, and the glorious appearing of the great God and our Saviour Jesus Christ****."*

Jude 1:21 – "*Keep yourselves in the love of God,* ***looking for the mercy of our Lord Jesus Christ unto eternal life****."*

No, we do not know in what hour our Lord will come; for He has not revealed this unto us. In fact, He has revealed that His coming will be in an hour that we do not expect. Yet we have full knowledge and full assurance of faith that He shall indeed come again. We know that the day of the Lord shall come "as a thief in the night" upon this world of spiritual darkness. We know that when this world of spiritual darkness claims peace and safety for itself, the day of the Lord shall come suddenly upon it with the destruction of the Lord's judgment. We know that when that sudden destruction comes from the hand of our Lord, the wicked of this world shall not escape.

Yet we also have full knowledge and full assurance of faith that we believers are not the children of spiritual darkness. We know that as the children of God, we are the children of light. We know that the day of our Lord's judgment and destruction upon this spiritually dark world will not overtake us as a thief in the night. Therefore, we should maintain a daily walk that is befitting the children of light who shall escape that coming day of judgment and destruction. We should not become lethargic and "sleepy" in our daily Christian walk. Rather, we should be alert and watching for that coming day. Indeed, our Lord has instructed us to watch and to be ready at all times for His coming.

Yet what does it mean to watch and be ready for His coming? Does it mean that we should stand gazing up into the sky, looking for the sign of His coming? In Matthew 24:45-46 our Lord revealed the answer, saying, "*Who then is a faithful and wise servant, whom his lord hath made ruler over his household, to give them meat in due season? Blessed is that servant, whom his lord when he cometh shall find so doing.*" A faithful and wise servant remains ready for his lord's return by faithfully doing that which his lord has called him to do. Even so, we ourselves remain ready for our Lord's coming by faithfully doing that which our Lord has called us to do, by faithfully doing His will. We remain ready by taking heed unto ourselves that we not become focused upon the desires and cares of this life. We remain ready by remaining focused upon our Lord through daily fellowship and prayer. We remain ready by "denying ungodliness and worldly lusts" and by "living soberly, righteously, and godly in this present world." Knowing that our Lord could come at any time, we remain watchful and ready by maintaining a faithful walk of love for and service to Him.

55. We must regularly practice the Lord's Supper in remembrance of His death until He come.

Matthew 26:26-28 – "*And as they were eating, Jesus took bread, and blessed it, and brake it, and gave it to the disciples, and said, **Take, eat; this is my body**. And he took the cup, and gave thanks, and gave it to them, saying, **Drink ye all of it; for this is my blood of the new testament, which is shed for many for the remission of sins**.*"

Mark 14:22-24 – "*And as they did eat, Jesus took bread, and blessed, and brake it, and gave to them, and said, **Take, eat: this is my body**. And he took the cup, and when he had given thanks, he gave it to them: and they all drank of it. And he said unto them, This is my blood of the new testament, which is shed for many.*"

Luke 22:19-20 – "*And he took bread, and gave thanks, and brake it, and gave unto them, saying, This is my body which is given for*

159

you: **this do in remembrance of me**. *Likewise also the cup after supper, saying, This cup is the new testament in my blood, which is shed for you.*"

1 Corinthians 11:23-26 – "**For I have received of the Lord that which also I delivered unto you,** *that the Lord Jesus the same night in which he was betrayed took bread: and when he had given thanks, he brake it, and said,* **Take, eat: this is my body, which is broken for you: this do in remembrance of me.** *After the same manner also he took the cup, when he had supped, saying, This cup is the new testament in my blood:* **this do ye, as oft as ye drink it, in remembrance of me.** *For as often as ye eat this bread, and drink this cup, ye do shew the Lord's death till he come.*"

The celebration of the Lord's Supper is an ordinance that has been divinely delivered for each local body of believers (each local church) to obey. The apostle Paul received this ordinance from the Lord and delivered it to the local church at Corinth. Even so, through the inspiration of God's Word, it is also delivered unto us. Furthermore, in this divine ordinance we find a three-fold command. We are to eat of the bread. We are to drink of the cup. We are to do this as a memorial in remembrance of our Lord and of His sacrificial death for us.

Finally, we learn that the broken bread and the cup of juice are a representation of our Lord's broken body and shed blood upon the cross. In this memorial we do show (or, do represent) our Lord's death until He return in the second coming. The broken bread represents our Lord's broken body upon the cruel cross, which was given up as a sin offering for us sinners. The cup of juice represents our Lord's shed blood upon the cross, which was shed for the remission (or, forgiveness) of our sins. In addition, the cup of juice represents the new testament (or, new covenant) that is provided in our Lord Jesus Christ's shed blood upon the cross. What is that new testament (or, new covenant)? It is that by faith in Christ we should be made a new creation in Christ, that by faith in Christ we should be born again spiritually as the very children of God, that by faith in Christ our old man should be crucified with Him, and we should be spiritually raised with Him unto newness of life. Even so, we are to continue regularly (often) in the celebration and memorial of the Lord's Supper with an anticipation of our Lord's return for us "until He come."

56. We must faithfully watch and pray so that we do not fail in the time of temptation.

Matthew 26:41 – *"**Watch and pray, that ye enter not into temptation**: the spirit indeed is willing, but the flesh is weak."*

Mark 14:38 – *"**Watch ye and pray, lest ye enter into temptation**. The spirit truly is ready, but the flesh is weak."*

Luke 22:40 – *"And when he was at the place, he said unto them, **Pray that ye enter not into temptation**."*

Luke 22:46 – *"And said unto them, Why sleep ye? **Rise and pray, lest ye enter into temptation**."*

Our Lord Jesus had informed His disciples that He would be taken that night and that they would be scattered abroad. In response Peter declared that he would never be offended in Jesus, not even if all others were. Yet the Lord informed Peter that even that very night, before the cock would crow, he would deny Him three times. Again in response Peter declared that it would never be so, not even if he were required to die for the Lord Jesus. Then our Lord Jesus and the disciples came unto the Garden of Gethsemane; and Jesus called aside three of His disciples, Peter, James, and John, to pray with Him for a time. Yet while the Lord went aside in prayer, these disciples fell asleep. Three times the Lord went aside in prayer, and three times He found the disciples sleeping instead of praying.

Now, before the first time wherein our Lord went aside in prayer, He instructed His disciples according to Luke 22:40, saying, *"Pray that ye enter not into temptation."* Furthermore, after His first hour of prayer, Jesus confronted Peter in the closing portion of Matthew 26:40 (see also Mark 14:37) for falling asleep, saying, *"What, could*

161

ye not watch with me one hour?" Then our Lord Jesus Christ added the instruction of Matthew 26:41 (see also Mark 14:38; Luke 22:46), *"Watch and pray, that ye enter not into temptation: the spirit indeed is willing, but the flesh is weak."* Certainly Peter's spirit was willing to stand with the Lord Jesus through it all. Yet his flesh was weak, and in the hour of temptation that weakness of his flesh would bring defeat. However, there was a defense against spiritual weakness and defeat. Through faithful watching in praying, Peter might stand, not in the spiritual weakness of his own flesh, but in the spiritual strength of God Himself. Yet Peter and the other disciples did not take up this provision for victory. Thus when the hour of temptation came upon them, they failed and were scattered abroad. They were offended in the Lord Jesus. Indeed, Peter did deny Him thrice.

Even so, we must face the evil day of temptation time and again throughout our Christian walk upon this earth. Thus time and again our Lord delivers His instruction unto us, *"Watch and pray, that ye enter not into temptation."* Certainly our spirit may be willing, but our flesh is spiritually weak. As such, if we attempt to stand against temptation in our own strength, we will fail in our own weakness. However, if we stand in our Lord's strength, we will be able to withstand unto victory. Thus Ephesians 6:10 proclaims, *"Finally, my brethren, be strong in the Lord, and in the power of his might;"* and the opening portion of verse 18 gives the instruction, *"Praying always with all prayer and supplication in the Spirit."*

57. We must go forth as laborers into our Lord's harvest, teaching others to follow our Lord Jesus Christ from conversion to spiritual maturity.

Matthew 28:18-20 – *"And Jesus came and spake unto them, saying, All power is given unto me in heaven and in earth. **Go ye therefore, and teach all nations, baptizing them in the name of the Father, and of the Son, and of the Holy Ghost: teaching them to observe all things whatsoever I have commanded you**: and, lo, I am with you alway, even unto the end of the world. Amen."*

Already in this study we have learned from Matthew 9:37-38 that we are to be praying for our Lord to send forth more laborers into His harvest. Furthermore, we have already learned from Matthew 10:6-7 that we ourselves are to be going forth as laborers into our Lord's harvest, preaching the gospel unto the lost. Here in Matthew 28:19-20 our Lord extends this responsibility a bit further. Yes, we are to be praying for more laborers to be sent forth. Yes, we are to go forth ourselves, preaching the gospel unto the lost. Yet we are also to go forth, seeking to teach others the whole truth of our Lord and Savior Jesus Christ. In Matthew 28:19-20 our responsibility extends further than preaching the gospel unto the lost. It extends also unto baptizing the new converts and unto teaching and training them in obedience to all that our Lord has commanded us. So then, let us consider all that is involved in this command and commission from our Lord to us.

In the first place, we find that we must be going forth with purpose. The opening three words of our Lord's instruction to us are, "*Go ye therefore.*" As the children of God and the servants of Christ, we are not in this world just to "get by." Rather, we are in this spiritually dark world of sin to go forth. Our Lord has sent us forth with a message and a ministry unto this lost world. We are the ambassadors of our Lord Jesus Christ to the lost souls of this world. We are to bear witness unto Him. We are to proclaim His name and His truth in His stead. His gospel message of repentance and remission of sins is to be preached in His name among all people. Even so, we are those who are to go forth and preach that gospel message. Yes indeed, we are to go forth with purpose! Our Lord has sent us forth with purpose; and we are to go forth with purpose. At all times that we are out in this world, we should be burdened with the purpose that our Lord has given us – to proclaim His name and His truth unto all people. Yea, this purpose should so govern our hearts and lives that we are ever looking for opportunities to proclaim our Lord's name and truth unto those who will hear.

Thus, in the second place, we find that as we are going forth, we must be preaching the gospel unto the lost. Our Lord's instruction to us continues, "*Go ye therefore, and teach all nations.*" Now, this command to "teach all nations" is the central command of the passage. It actually encompasses all that is given to us in the passage. Therefore, this teaching responsibility includes the baptizing and the training of converts. However, before we can baptize and train converts, they must first be converts, that is – they must first come unto salvation through faith in Jesus Christ as Savior. Thus, as we go forth, our first responsibility is to preach the gospel to lost souls that they might believe on the Lord Jesus Christ for eternal salvation. Even so, our Lord commanded us in Mark 16:15, *"Go ye into all the world, and preach the gospel to every creature."* We are to go forth into the world with purpose; and that purpose is to preach the gospel of Jesus Christ unto lost souls.

Then in the third place, we find that we must baptize new converts, that is – those who place their faith in the Lord Jesus Christ as Savior. Again our Lord's instruction to us continues, *"Go ye therefore, and teach all nations, baptizing them in the name of the Father, and of the Son, and of the Holy Ghost."* We are required to preach the gospel unto the lost. Yet we cannot force them to believe in Christ for salvation. That is a choice that they must make from their own hearts. Some of those to whom we preach the gospel will reject our message, whereas others will receive it and believe on Christ. It is then our responsibility to teach and encourage the new converts to take the first public step of obedience in believer's baptism, that is – to be baptized by immersion after salvation in the name of the Father, the Son, and the Holy Ghost into a Biblically faithful church.

Then in the fourth place, we find that we must train up these new converts unto spiritual maturity. Our Lord's instruction continues, *"Go ye therefore, and teach all nations, baptizing them in the name of the Father, and of the Son, and of the Holy Ghost: teaching them to observe all things whatsoever I have commanded you."* Again, we are responsible to direct new converts to take the step of obedience in believer's baptism. Yet again we cannot force them to obey. Some of the new converts will continue forward in obedience, whereas others will turn aside. It is then our responsibility to teach and train up these newly baptized converts to walk in faithful obedience unto all that our Lord has commanded us. Yea, we are to teach and train them up to be faithful servants of the Lord themselves, who may be able in turn to teach others also.

In the fifth and final place, we find that we must trust in our Lord for His grace and help in this process. Our Lord's opening declaration to this instruction is just this, "*All power is given unto Me in heaven and in earth.*" Our Lord and Savior Jesus Christ is the sovereign and almighty Lord of heaven and earth. Even so, in all of His power and authority, He stands with us and goes before us as we go forth in obedience unto His command and commission. Yea, in the closing portion of this instruction, He gives us the promise, "*And, lo, I am with you always, even unto the end of the world. Amen.*" Yea, amen and AMEN!

58. We must take heed that we hear the message of God's Word with honest and good hearts.

Mark 4:1-25 – "*And he began again to teach by the sea side: and there was gathered unto him a great multitude, so that he entered into a ship, and sat in the sea; and the whole multitude was by the sea on the land. And he taught them many things by parables, and said unto them in his doctrine,* **Hearken**; *behold, there went out a sower to sow: and it came to pass, as he sowed, some fell by the way side, and the fowls of the air came and devoured it up. And some fell on stony ground, where it had not much earth; and immediately it sprang up, because it had no depth of earth: but when the sun was up, it was scorched; and because it had no root, it withered away. And some fell among thorns, and the thorns grew up, and choked it, and it yielded no fruit. And other fell on good ground, and did yield fruit that sprang up and increased; and brought forth, some thirty, and some sixty, and some an hundred. And he said unto them,* **He that hath ears to hear, let him hear**.

And when he was alone, they that were about him with the twelve asked of him the parable. And he said unto them, Unto you it is given to know the mystery of the kingdom of God: but unto them that are without, all these things are done in parables: that seeing they may see, and not perceive; and hearing they may hear, and not understand; lest at any time they should be converted, and their sins should be forgiven them. And he said unto them, Know ye not this parable? And how then will ye know all parables? The sower soweth the word. And these are they by the way side, where the word is sown; but when they have heard, Satan cometh immediately, and taketh away the word that was sown in their hearts. And these are they likewise which are sown on stony ground; who, when they have heard the word, immediately receive it with gladness; and have no root in themselves, and so endure but for a time: afterward, when affliction or persecution ariseth for the word's sake, immediately they are offended. And these are they which are sown among thorns; such as hear the word, and the cares of this world, and the deceitfulness of riches, and the lusts of other things entering in, choke the word, and it becometh unfruitful. And these are they which are sown on good ground; such as hear the word, and receive it, and bring forth fruit, some thirtyfold, some sixty, and some an hundred.

*And he said unto them, Is a candle brought to be put under a bushel, or under a bed? And not to be set on a candlestick? For there is nothing hid, which shall not be manifested; neither was any thing kept secret, but that it should come abroad. **If any man have ears to hear, let him hear**. And he said unto them, **Take heed what ye hear**: with what measure ye mete, it shall be measured to you: and unto you that hear shall more be given. For he that hath, to him shall be given: and he that hath not, from him shall be taken even that which he hath."*

Luke 8:4-18 – *"And when much people were gathered together, and were come to him out of every city, he spake by a parable: A sower went out to sow his seed: and as he sowed, some fell by the way side; and it was trodden down, and the fowls of the air devoured it. And some fell upon a rock; and as soon as it was sprung up, it withered away, because it lacked moisture. And some fell among thorns; and the thorns sprang up with it, and choked it. And other fell on good ground, and sprang up, and bare fruit an hundredfold. And when he had said these things, he cried, **He that hath ears to hear, let him hear**. And his disciples asked him, saying, What might this parable be? And he said, Unto you it is given to know the mysteries of the kingdom of God: but to others in parables; that seeing they might not see, and hearing they might not understand.*

*Now the parable is this: The seed is the word of God. Those by the way side are they that hear; then cometh the devil, and taketh away the word out of their hearts, lest they should believe and be saved. They on the rock are they, which, when they hear, receive the word with joy; and these have no root, which for a while believe, and in time of temptation fall away. And that which fell among thorns are they, which, when they have heard, go forth, and are choked with cares and riches and pleasures of this life, and bring no fruit to perfection. But that on the good ground are they, which in an honest and good heart, having heard the word, keep it, and bring forth fruit with patience. No man, when he hath lighted a candle, covereth it with a vessel, or putteth it under a bed; but setteth it on a candlestick, that they which enter in may see the light. For nothing is secret, that shall not be made manifest; neither any thing hid, that shall not be known and come abroad. **Take heed therefore how ye hear**: for whosoever hath, to him shall be given; and whosoever hath not, from him shall be taken even that which he seemeth to have."*

Revelation 2:7 – "***He that hath an ear, let him hear what the Spirit saith unto the churches****; To him that overcometh will I give to eat of the tree of life, which is in the midst of the paradise of God.*"

Revelation 2:11 – "***He that hath an ear, let him hear what the Spirit saith unto the churches****; He that overcometh shall not be hurt of the second death.*"

Revelation 2:17 – "***He that hath an ear, let him hear what the Spirit saith unto the churches****; To him that overcometh will I give to eat of the hidden manna, and will give him a white stone, and in the stone a new name written, which no man knoweth saving he that receiveth it.*"

Revelation 2:29 – "***He that hath an ear, let him hear what the Spirit saith unto the churches***."

Revelation 3:6 – "***He that hath an ear, let him hear what the Spirit saith unto the churches***."

Revelation 3:13 – "***He that hath an ear, let him hear what the Spirit saith unto the churches.***"

Revelation 3:22 – "***He that hath an ear, let him hear what the Spirit saith unto the churches.***

Let us take note of the number of times in Mark 4:1-25 that our Lord gave instruction concerning the matter of hearing. In verse 3 our Lord began His parable with one word of command, "*Hearken.*" Then in verse 9 (see also Luke 8:8) our Lord concluded His parable with the instruction, "*He that hath ears to hear, let him hear.*" Yet again in verse 23 He repeated that instruction, saying, "*If any man have ears to hear, let him hear.*" Finally, in verse 24 (see also Luke 8:18) our Lord delivered the counsel, "*Take heed what ye hear: with what measure ye mete, it shall be measured to you, and unto you that hear shall more be given.*"

Yet the matter of hearing about which our Lord spoke was not simply that of physical hearing. Rather, our Lord was speaking concerning the hearing and receiving of our hearts in relation to the message of His Word. In His interpretation of His parable, our Lord revealed that the seed which the sower was sowing represented the message of God's Word. Then our Lord spoke concerning four different groups of people and concerning how they heard and received that message into their hearts.

In the first place, He spoke concerning those who did not understand or receive that message. In their case, Satan immediately came and took away the message of God's Word out of their hearts. In the second place, our Lord spoke concerning those who did hear the message of God's Word and who immediately received it with gladness. Yet in their case, these individuals did not allow the truth of God's Word to take deep root in their hearts. Thus when the heat and fire of affliction or persecution arose for the sake of God's Word, these believers were quick to fall away unto a life of sin. In the third place, our Lord spoke concerning those who both heard and received the Word, but also who allowed the cares of this world, and the deceitfulness of riches, and the lusts of other things to enter into their hearts. Therefore, these worldly desires became as thorns to choke out the truth of God's Word from their hearts. Even so, these believers became spiritually unfruitful. Finally, our Lord spoke concerning those who heard the message of God's Word, received it with spiritual understanding, and (according to Luke 8:15) obeyed that truth with an honest and good heart. Such are those believers who bring forth spiritual fruit unto the glory of the Father.

Then our Lord gave us the command and instruction in Mark 4:24 (see also Luke 8:18) to take heed how we hear, receive, and respond unto the message of God's Word from our hearts. Yea, His counsel was that we might be those of an honest, good, and obedient heart toward His Word, and not those of a hard heart, or those of a shallow heart, or those of a worldly heart. Furthermore, He gave the warning and the promise in Mark 4:24-25 (see also Luke 8:18), saying, *"Take heed what ye hear: with what measure ye mete, it shall be measured unto you: and unto you that hear shall more be given. For he that hath, to him shall be given: and he that hath not, from him shall be taken even that which he hath."* The promise here is this – Those who hear, receive, and obey the truth of God's Word with an honest and good heart shall be taught even more. Yet the warning is this – Those who do not so hear, receive, and obey the truth of God's Word shall lose that truth which has already been made available unto them. Yea, the Lord our God Himself shall take it away from them. Let us then take heed how we hear! Yea, let us take heed that we hear the message of God's Word with an honest and good heart.

59. At times we must come apart from the ordeals of public ministry in order to rest.

Mark 6:30-32 – *"And the apostles gathered themselves together unto Jesus, and told him all things, both what they had done, and what they had taught. And he said unto them, **Come ye yourselves apart into a desert place, and rest a while**: for there were many coming and going, and they had no leisure so much as to eat. And they departed into a desert place by ship privately."*

Although our Lord most certainly is against laziness and apathy in the ministry, and although He most certainly desires fervency and faithful commitment in our labors for Him, yet there are times that we must come apart from the labors and ordeals of public ministry in order that we might get some rest. Our physical bodies do not have infinite energy, and our minds do not have infinite capacity. In the work and ministry of our Lord, there most certainly will come physical, mental, and emotional fatigue. Even so, because our Lord truly cares for us and truly understands our weaknesses, He instructs us to come apart at times for physical, mental, and emotional rest and refreshing. Furthermore, in love one for another we ought to consider this need, not only for our own selves, but also for our family members and for our fellows laborers in the ministry.

60. We must not forbid those who truly minister for Christ's sake, even though they may not directly join with us in ministry.

Mark 9:38-41 – *"And John answered him, saying, Master, we saw one casting out devils in thy name, and he followeth not us: and we forbad him, because he followeth not us. But Jesus said, **Forbid him not**: for there is no man which shall do a miracle in my name, that can lightly speak evil of me. For he that is not against us is on our part. For whosoever shall give you a cup of water to drink in my name, because ye belong to Christ, verily I say unto you, he shall not lose his reward."*

Luke 9:49-50 – *"And John answered and said, Master, we saw one casting out devils in thy name; and we forbad him, because he followeth not with us. And Jesus said unto him, **Forbid him not**: for he that is not against us is for us."*

We must come to understand that the ministry and work of our Lord is not about us and our own particular effort of ministry. Rather, the work and ministry of our Lord is about Him and about the exaltation of His name and His truth throughout the whole world. It is not about our gathering of a great following after ourselves. It is not that we might increase. Rather, it is that we might decrease, and that our Lord might increase. It is about a growing number of converts and disciples throughout the world who will follow after our Lord and Savior Jesus Christ. Therefore, our hearts should be filled with joy and rejoicing for any and all those who might stand true unto the truth of our Lord, for the name of our Lord, in the work of our Lord. We should not be upset that some might not work and minister with and for us. Rather, we should rejoice when they work and minister with and for our Lord. We should not forbid them. We should not hinder them. We should not speak against their faithful work and ministry. Rather, we should rejoice that they follow Christ and that Christ is preached.

61. We must maintain a spiritually pure and morally preserving character in the attitudes and motives of our hearts.

Mark 9:50 – *"Salt is good: but if the salt have lost his saltness, wherewith will ye season it?* **Have salt in yourselves***, and have peace one with another."*

In the closing portion of this verse, our Lord delivered the command that we are to "have salt" in ourselves. Now, in our day and time the primary purpose of salt appears to be for the use of flavoring. Yet that was not the case in the day and time in which our Lord was speaking. Rather, in that day and time the primary purpose of salt was for the use of purifying and preserving. They would salt their meat in order to cure (purify) it and preserve it. Thus in the context of that time, when our Lord commanded them to "have salt" in themselves, He was commanding them to have a character in themselves that was pure, that was thereby able to be a force of spiritual and moral purification and preservation within society. Even so, our Lord's command remains for us yet today. We ourselves must have and maintain a spiritually pure and preserving character in ourselves.

Yet there is something more for us to understand from this command. We must consider the specific place wherein our Lord instructs us to have this spiritually pure and morally preserving character. Indeed, our Lord instructed, "Have salt in yourselves." In this our Lord was not simply speaking of a spiritually pure and morally preserving character in our interactions with others, or in our outward actions and behavior, or in our words and communication. Although it is certainly true that a spiritually pure and morally preserving character within ourselves will affect these things, such is not the specific focus of our Lord's instruction. Rather, the specific focus of our Lord's instruction here is upon the inner attitudes and motives of our hearts.

It is important for us to recognize the context about which this conversation between the Lord and His disciples began. It began in Mark 9:33-34 with the disciples' disputing in the way over who among them should be the greatest. Such disputing demonstrated the impure selfishness of their inner attitudes and motivations. Yet in concluding His confrontation of this matter, our Lord instructed them to have spiritually pure attitudes and motives within their hearts. They were not to be filled with self-centered attitudes and motives of heart. Rather, they were to be filled with selfless, God-centered, and others-centered attitudes and motives of heart. Even so, we also are not to have hearts filled with self-centered attitudes and motives. Rather, in obedience to our Lord's command we are to have hearts filled with selfless, God-centered, and others-centered attitudes and motives. We are to "have salt" within ourselves.

62. We must have peace one with another as much as we are able.

Mark 9:50 – "*Salt is good: but if the salt have lost his saltness, wherewith will ye season it? Have salt in yourselves, **and have peace one with another**.*"

Romans 12:18 – "***If it be possible, as much as lieth in you, live peaceably with all men.***"

Romans 14:19 – "***Let us therefore follow after the things which make for peace***, *and things wherewith one may edify another*."

2 Corinthians 13:11 – "*Finally, brethren, farewell. Be perfect, be of good comfort, be of one mind,* **live in peace***; and the God of love and peace shall be with you*."

Colossians 3:15 – "***And let the peace of God rule in your hearts, to the which also ye are called in one body****; and be ye thankful*."

1 Thessalonians 5:13 – "*And to esteem them very highly in love for their work's sake.* ***And be at peace among yourselves***."

Hebrews 12:14 – "***Follow peace with all men****, and holiness, without which no man shall see the Lord*."

1 Peter 3:11 – "*Let him eschew evil, and do good;* ***let him seek peace, and ensue it***."

In Mark 9:50 our Lord Jesus Christ delivered a two-fold instruction, saying, "Have salt in yourselves [that is – maintian spiritually pure attitudes and motivations in your hearts], and have peace one with another." Herein our Lord connected the characteristics of purity and peaceableness. Even so, in James 3:17-18 the truth is revealed, "*But the wisdom that is from above is first pure, then peaceable, gentle, and easy to be intreated, full of mercy and good fruits, without partiality, and without hypocrisy. And the fruit of righteousness is sown in peace of them that make peace*." Indeed, the wisdom that is from above (that is – a heart attitude and motivation that is godly in nature) is "first pure, then peaceable."

So then, again we must remember how the conversation in Mark 9:50 began between our Lord and his disciples. It began with the disciples' disputing in the way over who among them should be greatest. The attitudes and motivations of their hearts were not spiritually pure, but were self-centered; and such self-centered attitudes and motivations did not lead unto peace between them, but led unto disputing among them. Even so, James 4:1 declares, "*From whence come wars and fightings among you? Come they not hence, even of your lusts* [that is – of your selfish desires] *that war in your members?"* Thus the first half of Proverbs 13:10 adds, *"Only by pride cometh contention."* Yet such is not that manner in which our Lord would have us to behave. Rather, He instructs us to *"have peace one with another,"* to *"live peaceably with all men,"* to *"follow after the things which make for peace,"* to *"let the peace of God rule in our hearts,"* to *"live in peace,"* to *"be at peace"* among ourselves, to *"seek peace"* and pursue it, *"to follow peace with all men."*

Now, certainly there are times, as Jude 1:3 instructs, that we must *"earnestly contend for the faith."* Indeed, certainly there are times, as 1 Timothy 6:12 instructs, that we must *"fight the good fight of faith."* However, most of our fightings and disputings are not a part of these things. Rather, most of our fightings and disputings are rooted in the self-centeredness of our hearts. Thus in the areas of personal opinion, personal preference, personal desire, personal advancement, etc., our Lord commands us, not to fight for our own way, but to *"have peace one with another."*

63. We must pray with fullness of faith in God our heavenly Father.

Mark 11:19-24 – *"And when even was come, he went out of the city. And in the morning, as they passed by, they saw the fig tree dried up from the roots. And Peter calling to remembrance saith unto him, Master, behold, the fig tree which thou cursedst is withered away. And Jesus answering saith unto them,* **Have faith in God.** *For verily I say unto you, That whosoever shall say unto this mountain, Be thou removed, and be thou cast into the sea; and shall not doubt in his heart, but shall believe that those things which he saith shall come to pass; he shall have whatsoever he saith. Therefore I say unto you,* **What things soever ye desire, when ye pray, believe that ye receive them, and ye shall have them.**"

Our Lord's instruction in this context deals directly with our prayer lives. As we pray, no matter for what we might pray, whether great or small, we are to pray with fullness of faith and without doubting.

Yet it is not our faith as an object that should fill our hearts with such confidence. Rather, it is the object of our faith that should fill our hearts with such confidence. It is not how great and glorious our faith is that matters. Rather, it is how great and glorious is the God in whom we place our faith that matters. In fact, faith by its very nature does not contribute any power at all. Rather, faith is trusting in another who does have the power to accomplish the task. Yea, faith in God is trusting in the One who is all-powerful to accomplish the task. The faith itself is not the power. Rather, the God Himself in who we have faith is the all-powerful One. Thus our Lord Jesus Christ did not simply instruct us to have faith when we pray. Rather, He instructed us to *"have faith in God"* when we pray. We must *"believe that he is, and that he is a rewarder of them that diligently seek him."* (See Hebrews 11:6) We must believe that the Lord our God and heavenly Father is both willing and able to answer our prayer. First, we must believe that in His goodness and graciousness He is willing to answer our prayer and to meet our need. Furthermore, we must believe that in His greatness and gloriousness He is able to answer our prayer and to meet our need. We must *"have faith in God"* and have no doubt in our hearts concerning the Lord our God, that is – concerning His greatness, His gloriousness, His goodness, and His graciousness.

64. We must have a heart of forgiveness toward others when we pray.

Mark 11:25-26 – *"**And when ye stand praying, forgive, if ye have ought against any**: that your Father also which is in heaven may forgive you your trespasses. But if ye do not forgive, neither will your Father which is in heaven forgive your trespasses."*

First, we must take notice how our Lord directly connected the matter of forgiveness to the matter of praying. Apparently our choice to forgive or not to forgive has a direct impact upon the success or hindrance of our prayer lives. Thus when we engage in prayer, we should examine our hearts to be certain that we have forgiven those who have done anything against us. Furthermore, we must take notice of the extent unto which our Lord has directed us to give this forgiveness. He instructed, "*Forgive, if ye have ought* [that is – anything] *against any* [that is – any one]." Any offense by any person should be forgiven from our hearts. Finally, we must take notice of our Lord's warning concerning this matter. Indeed, He revealed that if we refuse to forgive others their offenses against us, God our heavenly Father will refuse to forgive our sins and offenses against Him. Even so, our very prayers will be hindered; for our own unforgiven sin will separate between us and our God, so that He will not hear and answer our prayers.

65. We must beware of those who love the recognition and honor of others, who take advantage of others for selfish gain, and who are hypocritical in religious matters.

Mark 12:38-40 – "*And he said unto them in his doctrine, Beware of the scribes, which love to go in long clothing, and love salutations in the marketplaces, and the chief seats in the synagogues, and the uppermost rooms at feasts: which devour widows' houses, and for a pretence make long prayers: these shall receive greater damnation.*"

Luke 20:45-47 – "*Then in the audience of all the people he said unto his disciples, Beware of the scribes, which desire to walk in long robes, and love greetings in the markets, and the highest seats in the synagogues, and the chief rooms at feasts; which devour widows' houses, and for a shew make long prayers: the same shall receive greater damnation.*"

With this command our Lord Jesus Christ is instructing us to be on our guard against a certain kind of religious leader. Indeed, He is instructing us to have spiritual discernment concerning the unspiritual character of such religious leaders, in order that we might not follow after them. So then, against what kind of religious leader are we to be on our guard? What are those characteristics for which we must have the spiritual discernment to see and to beware?

Through confronting three elements of behavior among the religious leaders of that day, our Lord Jesus Christ revealed the three-fold answer. First, we must be on our guard concerning religious leaders who love the recognition and honor of others. In Mark 12:38-39 (see also Luke 20:46) our Lord described the religious leaders against whom we are to beware, saying, "*Beware of the scribes, which love to go in long clothing, and love salutations in the marketplace, and the chief seats in the synagogues, and the uppermost rooms at feasts.*" Such individuals love to be seen of men. They love to be recognized by men. They love to be honored among men. They love to receive rewards from men. They love to have their own name and person to be praised and exalted above others. They love to be treated above others as better than others. They esteem themselves as better than others. The way of humility is foreign to their thoughts and behavior. Rather, they employ religious things for self and for the glory of self. Concerning such individuals our Lord commands us – Beware!

Furthermore, we must be on our guard against religious leaders who take advantage of others, especially of the poor and needy, for selfish gain. In the opening portion of Mark 12:40 (see also Luke 20:47) our Lord continued His description of these religious leaders, saying, "*Which devour widows' houses.*" Such religious leaders will use their religious position and prestige as a tool to take advantage of those whom they ought to be serving. This they will do in order to gain more for themselves. They use their position and prestige to lord it over others and to manipulate others. The way of self-sacrifice and serving others is foreign to their thoughts and behavior. Rather, they employ their religious position and prestige for self and the benefit of self. Concerning such individuals our Lord commands us – Beware!

Finally, we must be on our guard against religious leaders who are hypocritical in religious things. Again in Mark 12:40 (see also Luke 20:47) our Lord continued His description of these religious leaders, saying, "*And for a pretence make long prayers.*" These long prayers are not rooted in a truly spiritual prayer life. Rather, they are delivered "for a pretence." They are delivered to "be seen of men." Certainly, such individuals outwardly involve themselves in religious activities, and that to an extensive amount. Yet such

177

religious activity is not rooted in a truly Spirit-filled heart. Rather, it is motivated for self and for the glory of self. Concerning such individuals our Lord commands us – Beware!

66. We must watch and be ready for our Lord's coming through a faithful and fervent prayer life.

Mark 13:32-37 – "***Take ye heed, watch and pray: for ye know not when the time is****. For the Son of man is as a man taking a far journey, who left his house, and gave authority to his servants, and to every man his work, and commanded the porter to watch. **Watch ye therefore***: for ye know not when the master of the house cometh, at even, or at midnight, or at the cockcrowing, or in the morning: lest coming suddenly he find you sleeping. And what I say unto you I say unto all, **Watch***."

Luke 21:34-36 – "*And take heed to yourselves, lest at any time your hearts be overcharged with surfeiting, and drunkenness, and cares of this life, and so that day come upon you unawares. For as a snare shall it come on all them that dwell on the face of the whole earth. **Watch ye therefore, and pray always***, that ye may be accounted worthy to escape all these things that shall come to pass, and to stand before the Son of man.*"

1 Peter 4:7 – "*But the end of all things is at hand: be ye therefore sober, **and watch unto prayer***."

Previously in our study, we learned from Matthew 24:42-46 that we must watch and be ready for our Lord's coming through faithful obedience to His will. Now, from Mark 13:32-37 (see also Luke 21:34-36) we learn of another important ingredient to our watching and being ready for our Lord's coming. Indeed, as we wait and watch for our Lord's coming, we must do so through faithful obedience unto His will for our lives. Yea, we must do so by faithfully fulfilling the responsibilities and work that our Lord has called us to do. Even so, in Mark 13:34 our Lord Jesus Christ described Himself as "*a man taking a far journey, who left his house, and gave authority*

178

[that is – a matter of responsibility], *and to every man his work.*"
Indeed, every one of us has been called by our Lord to a specific
responsibility and work for our Lord. Yet we will not be effective
in fulfilling that responsibility and work if we do not faithfully
continue in fervent prayer. Without our Lord we can do nothing.
Yet through Him and His strength in us, we can do all that He has
called us to do. So then, how shall we walk in His strength? How
shall we be "*strong in the Lord, and in the power of His might*"?
(See Ephesians 6:10) We shall do so by "*praying always with all
prayer and supplication in the Spirit.*" (See Ephesians 6:18) We
shall do so through a faithful and fervent prayer life. Thus our Lord
instructed us, "*Take ye heed, watch and pray;*" "*Watch ye therefore,
and pray always;*" and "*Watch unto prayer.*"

67. We must be merciful, even as our heavenly Father is merciful.

Luke 6:36 – "***Be ye therefore merciful, as your Father also is
merciful.***"

Luke 10:37 – "*And he said, He that shewed mercy on him. Then
said Jesus unto him, **Go, and do thou likewise**.*"

Colossians 3:12 – "***Put on therefore, as the elect of God, holy and
beloved, bowels of mercies**, kindness, humbleness of mind, meekness,
longsuffering.*"

The word "merciful" means "to help those who are in the midst of
trouble and need." Even so, as much as we are able, we are required
to help those around us who are in the midst of some trouble or
some need. Furthermore, our Lord delivered this command in the
context of the instructions to love our enemies, to do good unto them,
and to pray for them. Thus our Lord is not simply instructing us to
be merciful unto our family and friends, or unto those whom we
like, or unto nice people. Rather, he is instructing us also to be
merciful unto our enemies and our persecutors, yea unto those whom
we might not like or those who might mistreat us in some way.

179

Even so, in Luke 10 our Lord Jesus Christ delivered a parable to a certain lawyer in order to teach this same truth. In Luke 10:25-37 we read, *"And, behold, a certain lawyer stood up, and tempted him, saying, Master, what shall I do to inherit eternal life? He said unto him, What is written in the Law? How readest thou? And he answering said, Thou shalt love the Lord thy God with all thy heart, and with all thy soul, and with all thy strength, and with all thy mind; and thy neighbour as thyself. And he [that is – Jesus] said unto him [that is – unto the lawyer], Thou hast answered right: this do, and thou shalt live. But he, willing to justify himself, said unto Jesus, And who is my neighbour? And Jesus answering said, A certain man went down from Jerusalem to Jericho, and fell among thieves, which stripped him of his raiment, and wounded him, and departed, leaving him half dead. And by chance there came down a certain priest that way: and when he saw him, he passed by on the other side. And likewise a Levite, when he was at the place, came and looked on him, and passed by on the other side. But a certain Samaritan, as he journeyed, came where he was: and when he saw him, he had compassion on him, and went to him, and bound up his wounds, pouring in oil and wine, and set him on his own beast, and brought him to an inn, and took care of him. And on the morrow when he departed, he took out two pence, and gave them to the host, and said unto him, Take care of him; and whatsoever thou spendest more, when I come again, I will repay thee. Which now of these three, thinkest thou, was neighbour unto him that fell among the thieves? And he said, He that shewed mercy on him. Then said Jesus unto him, Go, and do thou likewise."*

In closing this parable our Lord asked the lawyer which of the three men, the priest, the Levite, or the Samaritan, had behaved as a neighbor to the man who had fallen among the thieves. In answer the lawyer indicated that it was the Samaritan who had shown mercy on the man who had fallen among the thieves. Then our Lord gave the command, *"Go, and do thou likewise."* As such, through the command of Luke 6:36, our Lord is instructing us to go and do likewise. Just as our heavenly Father is merciful by nature, even so we who are His children are to be merciful by nature. Even so, just as our heavenly Father demonstrates mercy unto those in need with abundance and tenderness, even so we who are His children are to demonstrate mercy unto those in need with abundance and tenderness. Indeed, just as our heavenly Father has shown great mercy unto us who were ungodly sinners against Him, even so we who are His children are to show great mercy unto those who are our enemies and persecutors against us.

68. We must have a forgiving heart toward those who sin against us.

Luke 6:37 – *"Judge not, and ye shall not be judged: condemn not, and ye shall not be condemned:* **forgive, and ye shall be forgiven.***"*

Again and again in God's Word we are instructed to have a heart of forgiveness and to forgive those who do us any wrong. In fact, our hearts must become forgiving hearts in character. As the children of God, our heart attitude should be full of forgiveness toward others. Furthermore, in God's Word the instruction to forgive others is connected again and again unto the forgiveness that we ourselves will receive. Just as much as we ourselves grant daily forgiveness unto others, even as much our Lord will grant daily forgiveness unto us. Yet at any time and on any occasion wherein we withhold forgiveness from another, from that time the Lord our God Himself will withhold daily forgiveness from us. So then, let us consider – How often are we sinned against in a day, in a week, in a month, in a year? Even so, then let us consider – How often do we ourselves grant forgiveness unto those who commit these sins against us?

69. We must have a giving heart toward those in need.

Luke 6:38 – *"**Give**, and it shall be given unto you; good measure, pressed down, and shaken together, and running over, shall men give into your bosom. For with the same measure that ye mete withal it shall be measured to you again."*

Romans 12:13 – "***Distributing to the necessity of saints****; given to hospitality.*"

2 Corinthians 8:1-15 – "*Moreover, brethren, we do you to wit of the grace of God bestowed on the churches of Macedonia; how that in a great trial of affliction the abundance of their joy and their deep poverty abounded unto the riches of their liberality. For to their power, I bear record, yea, and beyond their power they were willing of themselves; praying us with much intreaty that we would receive the gift, and take upon us the fellowship of the ministering to the saints. And this they did, not as we hoped, but first gave their own selves to the Lord, and unto us by the will of God. Insomuch that we desired Titus, that as he had begun, so he would also finish in you the same grace also. Therefore, as ye abound in every thing, in faith, and utterance, and knowledge, and in all diligence, and in your love to us, **see that ye abound in this grace also**. I speak not by commandment, but by occasion of the forwardness of others, and to prove the sincerity of your love. For ye know the grace of our Lord Jesus Christ, that, though he was rich, yet for your sakes he became poor, that ye through his poverty might be rich. And herein I give my advice: for this is expedient for you, who have begun before, not only to do, but also to be forward a year ago. **Now therefore perform the doing of it; that as there was a readiness to will, so there may be a performance also out of that which ye have**. For if there be first a willing mind, it is accepted according to that a man hath, and not according to that he hath not. For I mean not that other men be eased, and ye burdened: but by an equality, that now at this time your abundance may be a supply for their want, that their abundance also may be a supply for your want: that there may be equality: as it is written, He that had gathered much had nothing over; and he that had gathered little had no lack.*"

2 Corinthians 8:24 – "***Wherefore shew ye to them, and before the churches, the proof of your love***, *and of our boasting on your behalf.*"

2 Corinthians 9:6-11 – "*But this I say, He which soweth sparingly shall reap also sparingly; and he which soweth bountifully shall reap also bountifully. **Every man according as he purposeth in his***

heart, so let him give; not grudgingly, or of necessity: *for God loveth a cheerful giver. And God is able to make all grace abound toward you; that ye, always having all sufficiency in all things, may abound to every good work: (As it is written, He hath dispersed abroad; he hath given to the poor: his righteousness remaineth for ever. Now he that ministereth seed to the sower both minister bread for your food, and multiply your seed sown, and increase the fruits of your righteousness;) being enriched in every thing to all bountifulness, which causeth through us thanksgiving to God.*"

Hebrews 13:16 – "***But to do good and to communicate forget not****: for with such sacrifices God is well pleased.*"

Our Lord would not have us to be greedy and stingy people. Rather, He would have us to be generous and giving people. Our heart attitudes should not be full of the desire to get, get, get more for ourselves. Rather, our heart attitudes should be full of the willingness to give, give, give as we are able to help others in need. Even so, with the opening word of Luke 6:38 our Lord commands us, "*Give.*" Even so also, in Deuteronomy 15:7-8 the Lord our God instructed His people, saying, "*If there be among you a poor man of one of thy brethren within any of thy gates in thy land which the LORD thy God giveth thee, thou shalt not harden thine heart, nor shut thine hand from thy poor brother: but thou shalt open thine hand wide unto him, and shalt surely lend him sufficient for his need, in that which he wanteth.*" Also in Acts 20:35 the principle is revealed, "*I have shewed you all things, how that so labouring ye ought to support the weak, and to remember the words of the Lord Jesus, how he said, It is more blessed to give than to receive.*"

Yet our Lord also delivers a divine promise with His command, saying, "*Give, and it shall be given unto you.*" Yea, our Lord further reveals that the extent and abundance to which we ourselves are willing to give unto others is the same extent and abundance with which we ourselves will receive from the hand of others. Thus He declared, "*Good measure, pressed down, and shaken together, and running over, shall men give into your bosom. For with the same measure that ye mete withal it shall be measured to you again.*" Now, this does not mean that every individual toward which we display a giving heart and a giving hand will, in turn, have a giving heart and a giving hand back toward us. Rather, this means that the Lord our God Himself will so move to employ various and sundry of those around us as His own divine tools of giving unto us, even as we ourselves open our hearts and hands to give unto others.

Even so, Psalm 41:1-3 proclaims, "*Blessed is he that considereth the poor: the LORD will deliver him in time of trouble. The LORD will preserve him, and keep him alive; and he shall be blessed upon the earth: and thou wilt not deliver him unto the will of his enemies. The LORD will strengthen him upon the bed of languishing: thou wilt make all his bed in his sickness.*" Again Proverbs 19:17 declares, "*He that hath pity upon the poor lendeth unto the LORD; and that which he hath given will he* [the Lord] *pay him again.*" Yet again the principle is revealed in Proverbs 11:24-26, "*There is that scattereth, and yet increaseth; and there is that withholdeth more than is meet, but it tendeth to poverty. The liberal soul* [that is – the giving soul] *shall be made fat: and he that watereth shall be watered also himself. He that withholdeth corn, the people shall curse him: but blessing shall be upon the head of him that selleth it.*" Finally, the promise is given in Proverbs 22:9, "*He that hath a bountiful eye shall be blessed; for he giveth of his bread to the poor.*" Yet the warning is delivered in Proverbs 21:13, "*Whoso stoppeth his ears at the cry of the poor, he also shall cry himself, but shall not be heard.*" Yes, our Lord would have us to be a generous and giving people toward those in need. In this our Lord will be "well pleased."

Indeed, our Lord would have us especially to be a generous and giving people toward fellow believers and toward His ministry. He would have us to abound in the grace of giving toward such. Yea, He would have us so to abound in order that we might prove the sincerity of our love for Him and for one another. Yet He would have us so to abound, not grudgingly, but cheerfully out of sincere love. Even so, He has proclaimed His principle that if we sow sparingly in such giving, we "shall reap also sparingly," but if we sow bountifully in such giving, we "shall reap also bountifully."

70. We must rejoice above all else because our names are written in heaven.

Luke 10:17-20 – "*And the seventy returned again with joy, saying, Lord, even the devils are subject unto us through thy name. And he said unto them, I beheld Satan as lightning fall from heaven. Behold, I give unto you power to tread on serpents and scorpions, and over all the power of the enemy: and nothing shall by any means hurt you.* **Notwithstanding in this rejoice not, that the spirits are subject unto you; but rather rejoice, because your names are written in heaven.**"

As our Lord sent the seventy out, two-by-two, to preach the Word of truth, He granted them power over the forces of the devil and protection from anything that might hurt them. Even so, they rejoiced greatly over these blessings. Yet our Lord directed them not to rejoice so much for the blessings of power and protection that they might obtain in this life, but to rejoice far more for the blessing of having their names eternally written in heaven. Therefore, regardless of our circumstances in this life, we ourselves ought to be moved every day unto joy and rejoicing because of the blessings of our eternal salvation, eternal redemption, eternal adoption, and eternal life.

71. We must take heed to our heart attitude and beware that covetousness not enter therein.

Luke 12:13-21 – "*And one of the company said unto him, Master, speak to my brother, that he divide the inheritance with me. And he said unto him, Man, who made me a judge or a divider over you? And he said unto them,* **Take heed, and beware of covetousness**: *for a man's life consisteth not in the abundance of the things which he possesseth. And he spake a parable unto them, saying, The ground of a certain rich man brought forth plentifully: and he thought within himself, saying, What shall I do, because I have no room where to bestow my fruits? And he said, This will I do: I will pull down my barns, and build greater; and there will I bestow all my fruits and* my goods. *And I will say to my soul, Soul, thou hast much goods laid up for many years; take thine ease, eat, drink, and be merry. But God said unto him, Thou fool, this night thy soul shall be required of thee: then whose shall those things be, which thou hast provided? So is he that layeth up treasure for himself, and is not rich toward God."*

1 Timothy 6:9-11 – *"But they that will be rich fall into temptation and a snare, and into many foolish and hurtful lusts, which drown men in destruction and perdition. For the love of money is the root of all evil: which while some coveted after, they have erred from the faith, and pierced themselves through with many sorrows.* ***But thou, O man of God, flee these things****; and follow after righteousness, godliness, faith, love, patience, meekness."*

Hebrews 13:5 – ***"Let your conversation be without covetousness****; and be content with such things as ye have: for he hath said, I will never leave thee, nor forsake thee."*

There is a philosophy in this world that greatly rules and reigns within the hearts of so many, whether they are great or small. This philosophy, in one form or another, is that whoever possesses the most at the end of his life wins. Yet in Luke 12:15 our Lord Jesus Christ clearly revealed that this philosophy is false, for He declared that a person's life does not consist in the abundance of the things that he possesses. Possessing the most is not the essence of life. Possessing the most is not that which gives life real meaning and real worth. Thus our Lord commands us to take heed and beware against the attitude of covetousness. Yea, our Lord commands us to be consciously and actively on our guard over our hearts that we never allow the ungodly attitude of covetousness to enter into any part of our Christian walk. In fact, we are instructed in Ephesians 5:3, *"But fornication, and all uncleanness or covetousness, let it not be once named among you."*

Yet what is this ungodly attitude of covetousness? It is the motivating desire to grasp tightly onto what we already have and to get more so that what we have is greater. On the one hand, it is to be filled with the desire to be rich and to get more. On the other hand, it is to set one's hope and trust in uncertain riches. It is not to be content with the things that our Lord has graciously given to us. It is to set our affection upon the material things of this world. It is to set the priority of our hearts upon laying up treasures for ourselves, and not upon being rich toward the things of God. Indeed, this was the sinful attitude of the rich man in our Lord's parable of Luke 12:16-21.

What then are the reasons that we ought to actively and aggressively resist the ungodly attitude of covetousness from entering into our hearts? The first reason is that the covetous individual is abhorred of the Lord our God. Psalm 10:3 reveals the truth, saying, *"For the wicked boasteth of his heart's desire, and blesseth the covetous, whom the LORD abhorreth."* The second reason is that covetousness is idolatry in the sight of God. Colossians 3:5 reveals the truth, saying, *"Mortify therefore your members which are upon the earth; fornication, uncleanness, inordinate affection, evil concupiscence, and covetousness, which is idolatry."*

The third reason is that covetousness will turn us aside from the Word of God. Concerning the thorny ground in the parable of the sower, our Lord gave explanation in Mark 4:18-19, saying, *"And these are they which are sown among thorns; such as hear the word, and the cares of this world, and the deceitfulness of riches, and the lusts of other things entering in, choke the word, and it becometh unfruitful."* In like manner, 1 Timothy 6:10 reveals that those who love money and who covet after material things will err *"from the faith,"* that is – from a walk after the truth of God's Holy Word.

The fourth reason is that covetousness will turn us aside from the service of God. In Matthew 6:24 our Lord gave the warning, saying, *"No man can serve two masters: for either he will hate the one, and love the other; or else he will hold to the one, and despise the other. Ye cannot serve God and mammon* [material things]." It is spiritually impossible to mix the love and pursuit after material things with the love and pursuit after the Lord our God. It is spiritually impossible to serve both the Lord God and material things at the same time in our lives. At any given time that we are serving one of these masters, we cannot be serving the other of these masters. If we serving material things, then we will not be serving God.

The fifth reason is that the covetous heart is never truly satisfied. Ecclesiastes 5:10 declares, *"He that loveth silver shall not be satisfied with silver; nor he that loveth abundance with increase: this is also vanity."* The sixth reason is that covetousness brings sorrow and spiritual destruction. 1 Timothy 6:9-10 declares, *"But they that will be rich fall into temptation and a snare, and into many foolish and hurtful lusts, which drown men in destruction and perdition. For the love of money is the root of all evil: which while some coveted after, they have erred from the faith, and pierced themselves through with many sorrows."* To this the first half of Proverbs 15:27 adds, *"He that is greedy of gain troubleth his own house."* The seventh and final reason is that the covetous shall be chastened by the Lord our God. Even so, in the opening portion of Isaiah 57:17 the Lord our God proclaimed, *"For the iniquity of his covetousness was I wroth, and smote him."*

72. We must recognize that a life of obedient service to our Lord is nothing more than our duty.

Luke 17:7-10 – *"But which of you, having a servant plowing or feeding cattle, will say unto him by and by, when he is come from the field, Go and sit down to meat? And will not rather say unto him, Make ready wherewith I may sup, and gird thyself, and serve me, till I have eaten and drunken; and afterward thou shalt eat and drink? Doth he thank that servant because he did the things that were commanded him? I trow* [think] *not.* **So likewise ye, when ye shall have done all those things which are commanded you, say, We are unprofitable servants: we have done that which was our duty to do.***"*

We are the servants of our Lord and Savior Jesus Christ. We are not our own. We have been bought with the price of His own shed blood and sacrificial death. Thus we are to live, not unto ourselves, but unto Him who died for us. He sacrificed Himself for us to provide us with newness of life, and now we are to present ourselves as a living sacrifice to serve Him with our lives. We are to deny ourselves, take up our cross daily, and follow Him. Yea, now we are to yield ourselves unto our Lord as His servants of righteousness. Yet such yieldedness is not a service above and beyond the call of duty. Rather, such yieldedness is only our reasonable service. It is nothing more than our duty unto our Lord who died for us. When we give our lives in faithful obedience to our Lord's will, we must not think of ourselves more highly than we ought to think. We must not think of ourselves as someone special who is worthy of great reward. Rather, we must humbly acknowledge that we ourselves are unprofitable servants who have simply done that which was our duty to do.

73. We must not allow the place in which God's people assemble for worship to become a place for merchandizing.

John 2:15-17 – "*And when he had made a scourge of small cords, he drove them all out of the temple, and the sheep, and the oxen; and poured out the changers' money, and overthrew the tables; and said unto them that sold doves, **Take these things hence; make not my Father's house an house of merchandise**. And his disciples remembered that it was written, The zeal of thine house hath eaten me up.*"

In this time of the New Testament church, the Old Testament temple is no longer the established house of God and place of worship. Rather, in this time of the New Testament church, the house and habitation of God is no longer a physical building, but is the assembly of God's own people themselves. Even so, Ephesians 3:19-22 declares, "*Now therefore ye are no more strangers and foreigners, but fellowcitizens with the saints, and of the household of God; and are built upon the foundation of the apostles and prophets, Jesus Christ Himself being the chief corner stone; in whom all the building fitly framed together growth unto an holy temple in the Lord: in whom ye also are builded together for an habitation of God through the Spirit.*" Thus in this time of the New Testament church, our zeal for the house of God is no longer a zeal for a physical temple building. Now our zeal for the house of God is to be a zeal for the assembling together of God's people for worship, prayer, praise, and edification. Yea, it is to be a zeal that the things of God be the central focus of all things. It is to be a zeal that the name of Jesus Christ and the truth of God's Word be exalted.

Thus we must not allow this place and time of assembling together to be made into a place and time of marketing, merchandising, and moneymaking. We must remember that God our heavenly Father and the material things of this world are two separate masters that stand in opposition to one another. We cannot love both in our hearts at the same time. We cannot hold to both by our pursuits at the same time. We cannot serve both with our lives at the same time. We must choose between the one or the other. Therefore, when marketing, merchandising, and moneymaking become the focus of our assembling together, then the true, Biblical worship of the Lord our God from our hearts will be set aside. Therefore also, if we would have the true, Biblical worship of the Lord our God as the focus of our assembling together, then marketing, merchandising, and moneymaking must be cast aside.

74. We must decrease, while our Lord must increase.

John 3:27-30 – *"John answered and said, A man can receive nothing, except it be given him from heaven. Ye yourselves bear me witness, that I said, I am not the Christ, but that I am sent before him. He that hath the bride is the bridegroom: but the friend of the bridegroom, which standeth and heareth him, rejoiceth greatly because of the bridegroom's voice: this my joy therefore is fulfilled.* ***He must increase, but I must decrease.****"*

After Jesus was baptized by John the Baptist and had begun His own preaching ministry, some of John's disciples developed a bit of concern that Jesus was drawing a larger following than John was, and that many of John's own followers had turned aside to follow after Jesus. In fact, these disciples developed a bit of concern that Jesus had begun to undercut John's ministry. Thus we read in John

3:26, "*And they came unto John, and said unto him, Rabbi, he that was with thee beyond Jordan, to whom thou bearest witness, behold, the same baptizeth, and all men come to him.*" These disciples of John believed the John Himself ought to remain in the place of priority since he was the one who had initiated Jesus ministry by baptizing Him and bearing Him witness. Thus they became very concerned that Jesus' ministry had begun to eclipse John's ministry. Yea, it appears that they were even offended that Jesus, whom John had initiated into the ministry, had somehow done John wrong by taking the position of priority for Himself.

Yet John Himself had a completely different viewpoint concerning this matter. John understood his place in the ministry of the Lord. He understood that his ministry for the Lord had been given to him directly at the hand of God Himself and that it extended only as far as the Lord his God intended for it to extend. He understood that he could receive nothing more in his ministry than that which had been given to him from heaven. Furthermore, John understood and continually proclaimed that he himself was not the Christ, but was only a forerunner pointing unto Christ. He understood that the Lord Jesus Christ was the Bridegroom, and that he himself was only the friend of the Bridegroom. He understood that the Bridegroom, the Lord Jesus Christ, was the One who was to receive the bride, and that the friend of the Bridegroom, John himself, was to rejoice greatly as the bride followed after the Bridegroom. Thus John declared that as people followed after the Lord Jesus Christ, his own joy was fulfilled. Furthermore, he also declared the principle that governed his life and ministry – "*He must increase, but I must decrease.*"

Even so, brethren, this same principle and precept should govern all in our lives and ministries. In our daily Christian walk, we must deny ourselves and our own will and must follow our Lord and His will. Yea, we must put to death the thoughts, desires, and ways of our self and must put on our Lord Jesus Christ, abiding in Him and allowing Him to abide in us and to live out His life through us. We must walk according to the principle – "*For to me to live is Christ.*" (Philippians 1:21) We must no longer live unto ourselves, but must live unto our Lord Jesus Christ who died for us. (See 2 Corinthians

5:15) We must be willing to suffer the loss of all things and to count all of the accomplishments in our lives as dung for the one objective of the excellency of the knowledge of Christ Jesus our Lord – that we might know Him yet more and more. (See Philippians 3:8-11) Yes, He must increase; but we must decrease.

In our witness to a lost world, we must not preach ourselves, but must preach Christ Jesus the Lord and must bear witness unto Him. We must approach the lost, not with enticing words out of our own wisdom, but under the filling influence of the Holy Spirit of Christ, knowing nothing among them except Jesus Christ and Him crucified. Then when souls come unto Christ through faith for salvation, we must reject all self-glory and must give unto our Lord the glory due unto His name. We must view ourselves as nothing more than the servants of Christ and must attribute all of the credit and glory unto the Lord our God who has given the increase. Any glorying that we do must be glorying in the Lord and in those things that He Himself has brought forth through us. Oh yes, He must increase; but we must decrease.

In our efforts of ministry toward other believers, we must not minister for personal recognition, but must gladly spend and be spent, all that our fellow brothers and sisters in Christ might grow in the things of the Lord. We must not seek our own things, but only those things that are Christ's. We must not minister so as to please men, but only so as to serve our Lord Jesus Christ. Those in leadership roles are not to draw a following after themselves, but in all things to direct people to follow after Christ and to walk in His truth. We must labor and travail for one purpose – that Christ might be fully formed in those unto whom we minister. Those in teaching roles are not to teach those things that are after man's wisdom, but only to teach those things that are after Christ Himself. In everything the governing principle must be – "He must increase, but I must decrease."

75. We must worship the Lord our God "in spirit and in truth."

John 4:21-24 – "*Jesus saith unto her, Woman, believe me, the hour cometh, when ye shall neither in this mountain, nor yet at Jerusalem, worship the Father. Ye worship ye know not what: we know what we worship: for salvation is of the Jews. But the hour cometh, and now is,* **when the true worshippers shall worship the Father in spirit and in truth: for the Father seeketh such to worship him.** *God is a Spirit:* **and they that worship him must worship him in spirit and in truth**."

At the time of our Lord's earthly ministry, there was a significant dispute between the Jews and the Samaritans concerning the matter of worship. One of the specific matters of dispute concerned the correct place wherein worship was to be delivered unto the Lord God. Even so, when our Lord Jesus Christ met with the Samaritan woman at Jacob's well, she brought up this matter for discussion. Thus we read in John 4:19-20, "*The woman saith unto him, Sir, I perceive that thou art a prophet. Our fathers worshipped in this mountain; and ye* [that is – ye Jews] *say, that in Jerusalem is the place where men ought to worship.*" Then in verses 21-24 we find our Lord's response.

In this response unto the Samaritan woman, our Lord indicated that for the time of the Old Testament the Jews had it correct. For the time of the Old Testament the correct place for worship, yea the place and city where the Lord God Jehovah had set His name, was the city of Jerusalem. Yet in our Lord's response to the Samaritan woman, He also indicated that for the time of the New Testament the particular place of worship would no longer be a primary issue. Rather, our Lord indicated that for this time of the New Testament, the true worshippers would be defined, not by the place where they worshipped, but by the manner how they worshipped. He indicated that the true worshippers would now be defined as those who "*worship the Father in spirit and in truth.*" In addition, He indicated that such worshippers were the very kind of worshippers for which God our heavenly Father is seeking. Thus our Lord Jesus Christ declared in verse 24, "*God is a Spirit: and they that worship him must worship him in spirit and in truth.*"

Yet what does it mean to *"worship the Father in spirit and in truth"*? First, in considering the phrase, "in spirit and in truth," as a whole, it is clear that our Lord is defining true worship, not as a matter of external place or external activity, but as matter of the inner heart. Certainly a heart that is truly right with God our heavenly Father will demonstrate this in an external manner that is approved by God our heavenly Father. However, external activity itself, no matter how well it may appear to be right, is not the defining element of true worship. True worship is defined by the spiritual condition of the inner man. Yea, true worship is defined by whether or not our hearts are truly set aright toward God our heavenly Father.

Second, in considering the phrase, "in spirit and in truth," by its individual parts, we find two characteristics. The first concerns the depth of true worship, and the second concerns the direction of true worship. In its depth true worship must be rooted in the regenerated spirit of the believer in perfect union with the indwelling Holy Spirit of God. Worship "in spirit" is not simply emotional worship. Rather, it is spiritual worship. It is worship that flows out of our regenerated spirit as it is directed by the indwelling Holy Spirit. It is worshipping under the filling influence of God the Holy Spirit. It is worshipping with full surrender to the direction of the Holy Spirit. Then in its direction true worship must be rooted in the truth of God's Holy Word. Worship "in truth" is not simply sincere worship. Rather, it is Biblical worship. It is worship that flows directly out of the truth and teaching of God's Word. Yea, there is no true worship that is contrary to God's Word of truth.

Finally, in considering the phrase "in spirit and in truth" through its unity, we find that spiritual worship (that is – Spirit-filled worship) and Biblical worship are perfectly unified with one another. The Holy Spirit of God is the Spirit of truth. The Holy Word of God is the Word of the Spirit, for the Holy Spirit is the Person of the Godhead who moved the holy men of God to communicate the Holy Scriptures. (See 2 Peter 1:21) Even so, we must understand that there is no worship in and under the filling influence of the Holy Spirit that is contrary to the truth of God's Word. Even so also, we must understand that there is no worship in full accord with the truth of God's Word that is not in and under the filling influence of the Holy Spirit. It is not possible to have true worship without both. In fact, it is not truly possible to have the one without the other. It is not truly possible to be filled with the Spirit while rejecting the Word, nor is it truly possible to be filled with the Word while refusing the Spirit. They come together, or they come not at all. If we would worship the Lord our God with true worship, we must worship Him under the filling influence of the His Holy Spirit in accord with the truth of His Holy Word.

76. We must love one another as our Lord Jesus Christ has loved us, with purity and fervency of heart.

John 13:34-35 – "*A new commandment I give unto you, That ye love one another; as I have loved you, that ye also love one another. By this shall all men know that ye are my disciples, if ye have love one to another.*"

John 15:12-13 – "*This is my commandment, That ye love one another, as I have loved you. Greater love hath no man than this, that a man lay down his life for his friends.*"

John 15:17 – "*These things I command you, that ye love one another.*"

Ephesians 5:2 – "*And walk in love, as Christ also hath loved us, and hath given himself for us an offering and a sacrifice to God for a sweetsmelling savour.*"

Colossians 3:14 – "*And above all these things put on charity, which is the bond of perfectness.*"

1 Thessalonians 4:9-10 – "*But as touching brotherly love ye need not that I write unto you: for ye yourselves are taught of God to love one another. And indeed ye do it toward all the brethren which are in all Macedonia: but we beseech you, brethren, that ye increase more and more.*"

Hebrews 13:1 – "***Let brotherly love continue****.*"

1 Peter 1:22 – "*Seeing ye have purified your souls in obeying the truth through the Spirit unto unfeigned love of the brethren,* **see that ye love one another with a pure heart fervently***.*"

1 Peter 2:17 – "*Honour all men.* **Love the brotherhood***. Fear God. Honour the king.*"

1 Peter 4:8 – "***And above all things have fervent charity among yourselves****: for charity shall cover the multitude of sins.*"

1 John 3:10-18 – "*In this the children of God are manifest, and the children of the devil: whosoever doeth not righteousness is not of God, neither he that loveth not his brother. For this is the message that ye heard from the beginning,* **that we should love one another***. Not as Cain, who was of that wicked one, and slew his brother. And wherefore slew he him? Because his own works were evil, and his brother's righteous. Marvel not, my brethren, if the world hate you. We know that we have passed from death unto life, because we love the brethren. He that loveth not his brother abideth in death. Whosoever hateth his brother is a murderer: and ye know that no murderer hath eternal life abiding in him. Hereby perceive we the love of God, because he laid down his life for us:* **and we ought to lay down our lives for the brethren***. But whoso hath this world's good, and seeth his brother have need, and shutteth up his bowels of compassion from him, how dwelleth the love of God in him?* **My little children, let us not love in word, neither in tongue; but in deed and in truth***.*"

1 John 3:23 – "*And this is his commandment, That we should believe on the name of his Son Jesus Christ,* **and love one another, as he gave us commandment***.*"

1 John 4:7-11 – "***Beloved, let us love one another****: for love is of God; and every one that loveth is born of God, and knoweth God. He that loveth not knoweth not God; for God is love. In this was manifested the love of God toward us, because that God sent his only begotten Son into the world, that we might live through him.*

Herein is love, not that we loved God, but that he loved us, and sent his Son to be the propitiation for our sins. **Beloved, if God so loved us, we ought also to love one another**."

1 John 4:16-21 – "*And we have known and believed the love that God hath to us. God is love; and he that dwelleth in love dwelleth in God, and God in him. Herein is our love made perfect, that we may have boldness in the day of judgment: because as he is, so are we in this world. There is no fear in love; but perfect love casteth out fear: because fear hath torment. He that feareth is not made perfect in love. We love him, because he first loved us. If a man say, I love God, and hateth his brother, he is a liar: for he that loveth not his brother whom he hath seen, how can he love God whom he hath not seen?* **And this commandment have we from him, That he who loveth God love his brother also**."

2 John 1:5-6 – "*And now I beseech thee, lady, not as though I wrote a new commandment unto thee, but that which we had from the beginning,* **that we love one another**. *And this is love, that we walk after his commandments.* **This is the commandment, That, as ye have heard from the beginning, ye should walk in it**."

In John 13:34 our Lord Jesus Christ delivered a "*new commandment*" unto His disciples, the command that they should "*love one another*" even as He had loved them. Now, the command to love one another is not itself the new part of the command. Even in the time of the Old Testament, the Lord God had commanded His people to love one another as themselves. Yet in the time of the New Testament, we now have a new and higher example and standard for our love toward one another. Now we are commanded to love one another, not simply as ourselves, but as our Lord Jesus Christ Himself has loved us.

How then has our Lord loved us? He has loved us by giving up of Himself for us. He has loved us by laying down his very life for us. Even so, He now commands us to love one another in the same manner – to love one another by giving up our very selves and by laying down our very lives for one another. Yea, He commands us to love one another by sacrificing of ourselves one for another even as He sacrificed of Himself for us. Furthermore, it is by this very love of self-sacrifice that we shall demonstrate to all around us that we truly are the disciples of our Lord Jesus Christ. (See John 13:35) Yes, with the words of our mouth, we may proclaim that we are the followers of our Lord Jesus Christ. Yet with our love for one another, we prove that we truly are the followers of our Lord Jesus Christ.

Our Lord Jesus Christ loved us by giving Himself as a sacrifice for our sake. Thus we are to love one another as He has loved us – by giving up of ourselves in sacrifice for the sake of the others. Indeed, this self-sacrificing love is to be the very nature of our daily Christian walk. We are to walk in Christ-like love. (See Ephesians 5:2) We are not simply to demonstrate Christ-like love on scattered moments. Rather, we are to be characterized by Christ-like love in all of our behavior. Furthermore, we must understand that just such self-sacrificing love is well pleasing unto God our heavenly Father. Just as Christ's loving sacrifice for our sake was a sacrifice unto God the Father of a sweet-smelling savor, even so our loving sacrifice for one another is a sacrifice unto God of a sweet-smelling savor. Our love for one another rises up before God as a beautiful perfume. Yet this love must truly flow toward others with both purity of heart and fervency of heart. We must be certain to *"love one another with a pure heart fervently."* (See 1 Peter 1:22) We must not simply love in word and tongue, but must love one another in deeds (works) and in truth. (See 1 John 3:18) Yea, such love must increase more and more among us. (See 1 Thessalonians 4:10)

Through all of this we learn a number of truths. First, we learn the motive for our love toward one another – that the Lord our God first loved us. (See 1 John 4:9-11) Second, we learn the standard for our love toward one another – the self-sacrifice that our Lord Jesus Christ made for us in love. (See John 13:34; 15:12; Ephesians 5:2; 1 John 3:16) Third, we learn the reality of our love toward one another – with a pure and fervent heart, not simply in our words, but also in our deeds. (See 1 Peter 1:22; 4:8; 1 John 3:16-18) Fourth, we learn the spirituality of our love toward one another – that those who walk in the spirit of godly love give evidence thereby that they are walking in righteous fellowship with the Lord. (See John 13:35;

1 John 3:10-15; 4:7-8, 12, 16, 19-21) Finally, we learn the reward of our love toward one another – that we shall have "boldness in the day of judgment." (See 1 John 4:16-18)

77. We must not allow our hearts to become troubled, but must set our trust in our Lord.

John 14:1 – *"**Let not your heart be troubled: ye believe in God, believe also in me**."*

John 14:27 – *"Peace I leave with you, my peace I give unto you: not as the world giveth, give I unto you. **Let not your heart be troubled, neither let it be afraid**."*

John 16:33 – *"These things I have spoken unto you, that in me ye might have peace. In the world ye shall have tribulation: **but be of good cheer; I have overcome the world**."*

1 Pet. 3:14-15 – *"But and if ye suffer for righteousness' sake, happy are ye: **and be not afraid of their terror, neither be troubled**; but sanctify the Lord God in your hearts: and be ready always to give an answer to every man that asketh you a reason of the hope that is in you with meekness and fear:"*

In this world of spiritual darkness, our lives shall be full of much circumstantial trouble. Even so, the man of God Job declared in Job 14:1, *"Man that is born of a woman is of few days, and full of trouble."* Yet even as these circumstantial troubles may abound from without, it is not necessary that our hearts should be full of trouble within. Yea, even while these circumstantial troubles do abound from without, our Lord commands us not to allow our hearts to be troubled, but rather to be of good cheer. Twice in John 14 our Lord specifically commands us, *"Let not your heart be troubled."* This command indicates that we ourselves must purposefully decide not to allow our hearts to be troubled at the troubles of this life. Yea, it indicates that we ourselves are the ones who decide whether or not to allow our hearts to be so troubled. Whether or not our hearts become troubled is not determined by the circumstances that we face. Rather, it is determined by the decision that we ourselves make in the face of those circumstances. Furthermore, this is a direct command from our Lord. He commands us, *"Let not your heart be troubled."* He commands us, *"Neither let it be afraid."* He commands us, *"Be of good cheer."* Even so, disobedience is sin.

Yet how is it possible not to allow our hearts to be troubled while our lives are full of trouble? How is it possible to be good of cheer even while in the midst of the most troublesome times? It is possible because our Lord has given unto us His provision of peace. Yet this is not a provision of some theoretical element of peace. Rather, this is a provision of our Lord's own peace. In the opening portion of John 14:27, He declared, *"Peace I leave with you, my peace I give unto you: not as the world giveth, give I unto you."* This is not the empty peace of the world, that is circumstantially shallow and that passes quickly away with changing circumstances. Rather, this is the very peace of God Himself, that is deeply abiding and that surpasses all understanding even in the midst of the worst circumstances. Thus, having already provided us with the gift of His own divine peace, our Lord may command us, *"Let not your heart be troubled, neither let it be afraid."*

Yet how do we take hold upon this gift of peace that our Lord has so gracious provided unto us? We take hold upon this peace through abiding in our Lord Jesus Christ. In the opening portion of John 16:33, our Lord declared, *"These things have I spoken unto you, that in me ye might have peace."* Yes, in the world we shall have much trouble and tribulations. Yet even in the midst of the worst trouble and tribulation, we may be of good cheer. How? Our Lord has overcome the world; and as we abide in Him, in Him we also shall overcome the world. So then, how do we abide in Him that we might be filled with His peace? We do so by setting our trust in Him. In John 14:1 our Lord declared, *"Let not your heart be troubled: ye believe in God, believe also in me."* When facing the troubles of this life, these are our options – Either we set our trust in our Lord, and thus abide in Him and have His peace abiding in us in order that we may be of good cheer. Or, we our focus upon the troubles themselves, and thus allow our hearts to be troubled.

78. We must keep our Lord's commandments to demonstrate our love for Him.

John 14:15 – *"If ye love me, keep my commandments."*

John 14:21 – *"He that hath my commandments, and keepeth them, he it is that loveth me: and he that loveth me shall be loved of my Father, and I will love him, and will manifest myself to him."*

John 14:23 – *"Jesus answered and said unto him, If a man love me, he will keep my words: and my Father will love him, and we will come unto him, and make our abode with him."*

There are two great truths that we need to glean from these verses. The first of these great truths is that our love for our Lord is defined, not by our emotional feelings or by our verbal declarations, but by our faithful obedience. It is not how much we have feelings of love for our Lord that counts, but how much we walk in obedience to His commandments. It is not how much we claim to love our Lord that counts, but how much we walk in obedience to His commandments. If we desire to demonstrate our love for our Lord, then we must keep His commandments. The one who keeps His commandments is the one who truly loves the Lord. Yea, if we truly love our Lord, then we will indeed keep His words and His commandments.

Then the second of these great truths is that God our heavenly Father and Jesus Christ our Lord will abide in intimate, loving fellowship with those who walk in obedience unto their words and commands. The obedient ones are the ones unto whom our Lord will manifest Himself in the fullness of His blessed fellowship. The obedient ones are the ones with whom the Father and the Son will walk and abide in fellowship. Therefore, we must faithfully keep our Lord's commandments in order to demonstrate our true love for Him and in order to find the blessing of His fellowship with us.

201

79. We must be abiding in our Lord Jesus Christ through faith, and must allow Him to be abiding in us.

John 15:4-6 – "***Abide in me, and I in you.*** *As the branch cannot bear fruit of itself, except it abide in the vine; no more can ye, except ye abide in me. I am the vine, ye are the branches: he that abideth in me, and I in him, the same bringeth forth much fruit: for without me ye can do nothing. If a man abide not in me, he is cast forth as a branch, and is withered; and men gather them, and cast them into the fire, and they are burned.*"

Romans 13:14 – "***But put ye on the Lord Jesus Christ****, and make not provision for the flesh, to fulfil the lusts thereof.*"

Colossians 2:6 – "***As ye have therefore received Christ Jesus the Lord, so walk ye in him.***"

1 John 2:27-28 – "*But the anointing which ye have received of him abideth in you, and ye need not that any man teach you: but as the same anointing teacheth you of all things, and is truth, and is no lie, and even as it hath taught you, ye shall abide in him.* ***And now, little children, abide in him****; that, when he shall appear, we may have confidence, and not be ashamed before him at his coming.*"

We are required day-by-day and moment-by-moment to abide in Christ, and to allow Christ to abide in us. This is not a suggestion. This is a command. Furthermore, it is only those who do faithfully abide in Him and allow Him to abide in them who bring forth much fruit unto the glory of the Father. Yet those who do not abide in Him from moment to moment and from day to day are completely unable to bring forth any such fruit. Without abiding in Him and He in us, we can do nothing of any spiritual value in the sight of God our heavenly Father. Rather, those who do not abide in Him will develop withered Christian lives and will fall under the heavy hand of God's chastening. Faithfully abiding in Christ is no small matter to our Christian lives. Rather, it is the very foundation for any and all true growth and fruitfulness in our Christian lives. Let us then every day and every moment abide in Him and allow Him to abide in us.

Indeed, according to Romans 13:14 we are to be putting on our Lord Jesus Christ every day of our Christian lives. Indeed, according to Colossians 2:6 we are to be walking in our Lord Jesus Christ every step of our Christian lives. Yet Colossians 2:6 reveals something more in this matter. It not only reveals what we are required to do. It also reveals how we are required to do it; for it declares, *"As ye have therefore received Christ Jesus the Lord, so walk ye in him."* Herein the "how" is revealed through the "just as, even so" language of the instruction. Just as (that is – in the same manner as) we have received the Lord Jesus Christ for eternal salvation, even so we are to walk in Him for daily fellowship. So then, through what manner did we receive our Lord for eternal salvation? John 1:12 gives answer, saying, *"But as many as received him, to them gave he power to become the sons of God, even to them that believe on his name."* We received our Lord for eternal salvation through faith in Him; therefore, we also abide and walk in Him for daily fellowship through faith in Him. Even so, Ephesians 3:17 reveals that our Lord Jesus Christ dwells and abides in our hearts "by faith." *"For we walk by faith, not by sight."* (2 Corinthians 5:7).

Every step of our Christian walk we must set the focus of our faith upon our Lord Jesus Christ, in order that we might be putting Him on spiritually, abiding in Him spiritually, and walking in and with Him spiritually. Furthermore, 1 John 2:27-28 informs us that we are taught and are guided to be abiding in our Lord Jesus Christ through the indwelling Holy Spirit. He is the "Anointing" which we have received of Christ and which abides in us. Finally, 1 John 2:28 also informs us that through living a daily life of abiding in our Lord Jesus Christ, we shall have confidence of approval at our Lord's coming, and shall have no need to be ashamed.

80. We must abide in our Lord's loving fellowship by keeping His commandments.

John 15:9-10 – "*As the Father hath loved me, so have I loved you: **continue ye in my love. If ye keep my commandments, ye shall abide in my love;** even as I have kept my Father's commandments, and abide in his love.*"

Jude 1:21 – "***Keep yourselves in the love of God,*** *looking for the mercy of our Lord Jesus Christ unto eternal life.*"

As we have seen in the previous command, abiding in our Lord Jesus Christ is the very foundation to abundant, fruitful Christian living. Thus our Lord here commands us to continue (or, abide) in His love, that is – in His loving fellowship. Now, according to Romans 8:31-39 nothing can separate us from the saving love of God our heavenly Father and of Jesus Christ our Lord. Yet in our daily walk upon this earth, we must continue to abide in our Lord's loving fellowship. This we do by keeping His commandments. Just as He Himself continued in God the Father's loving fellowship by keeping His commandments, even so we continue in our Lord's loving fellowship by keeping His commandments.

81. When the world hates us who serve our Lord, we must not be surprised, but must remember that it first hated our Lord Himself.

John 15:18-25 – "*If the world hate you, ye know that it hated me before it hated you. If ye were of the world, the world would love his own: but because ye are not of the world, but I have chosen you out of the world, therefore the world hateth you. **Remember the word that I said unto you,** The servant is not greater than his lord. If they have persecuted me, they will also persecute you; if they have kept my saying, they will keep yours also. But all these things will they do unto you for my name's sake, because they know not him that sent me. If I had not come and spoken unto them, they had not had sin: but now they have no cloke for their sin. He that* *hateth me hateth my Father also. If I had not done among them the works which none other man did, they had not had sin: but now have they both seen and hated both me and my Father. But this cometh to pass, that the word might be fulfilled that is written in their law, They hated me without a cause.*"

1 Peter 4:12-14 – "***Beloved, think it not strange concerning the fiery trial which is to try you, as though some strange thing happened unto you****: but rejoice, inasmuch as ye are partakers of Christ's sufferings; that, when his glory shall be revealed, ye may be glad also with exceeding joy. **If ye be reproached for the name of Christ**, happy are ye; for the spirit of glory and of God resteth upon you: on their part he is evil spoken of, but on your part he is glorified.*"

1 John 3:13 – "***Marvel not, my brethren, if the world hate you.***"

Let it be clearly known and understood by every one of us – If we faithfully serve our Lord Jesus Christ in our lives, we will encounter the hatred of this sinful world. This is not just a possibility; this is a certainty. Our Lord Himself warned us that it shall be so. In the opening portion of Matthew 10:22, He declared, "*And ye shall be hated of all men for my name's sake.*" Again in Matthew 24:9 He declared, "*Then shall they deliver you up to be afflicted, and shall kill you: and ye shall be hated of all nations for my name's sake.*" Thus we are instructed in 1 John 3:13, "*Marvel not, my brethren, if the world hate you.*" Such hatred should not surprise us. Yea, God's Holy Word commands us not to marvel – not to be surprised.

Rather, our Lord instructs us to remember – to know and to remember that the world hated Him, our Lord and Master, before it hated us His servants. We who are the servants of the Lord are no longer of this world. Our Lord has chosen us out of this world and has sent us into this world as witnesses for His name's sake. Now, since this world first hates our Lord and His name, it will in turn hate us who bear witness unto His name. We must not be surprised at this hatred. Rather, we must know that it is a natural part of serving our Lord. Indeed, we must know that it is a natural part of following after Him and of walking even as He walked.

So then, we are not to think it strange or to be surprised when we experience the fiery trial of the world's reproach and hatred against us as the followers of Christ. The experience of such a fiery trial by a faithful servant of the Lord is not a strange thing at all, but is actually a normal part of the Christian life. Just as our Lord suffered the fiery trial of reproach and hatred from this world, even so we who are His servants shall be partakers of our Lord's sufferings by also experiencing the fiery trial of reproach and hatred from this world.

82. When we pray, we must ask of the Father in our Lord's name.

John 16:24-25 – "***Hitherto have ye asked nothing in my name: ask, and ye shall receive****, that your joy may be full. These things have I spoken unto you in proverbs: but the time cometh, when I shall no more speak unto you in proverbs, but I shall shew you plainly of the Father.*"

To that point the disciples were able to ask things directly of the Lord Jesus Christ as He physically walked with them upon the earth. However, He knew that He was shortly to depart from them. He knew that He would be crucified the next day, that He would arise again from the dead on the third day, and that He would ascend into heaven forty days thereafter. Thus He explained to His disciples that in that day they would no longer be able to ask things directly of Him. Thus also He explained to them that from that day forward they would be required to ask things of the Father through prayer. Yet He also granted them a great foundation for such praying; for He instructed them, not simply to ask of the Father, but to ask in His own name.

Now, to ask in Jesus name does not simply mean to add the phrase, "in Jesus name," at the end of our prayers. Rather, it means to ask in accord with our Lord Jesus Christ's own authority. His name is the name that is above every name, and to ask in that name is to ask according to the greatness and authority of that name. Yet it also means to ask in accord with our Lord Jesus Christ's own will. His name is His endorsement of our request. If our request is not in accord with His will, then He will not endorse it; and then we will have used His name in vain. Thus asking in our Lord's name should grant us boldness in coming before the Father in prayer, but it should also move us unto carefulness that our requests be in accord with our Lord's will. Yet if we do ask in our Lord's name, according to His authority and His will, then we shall receive of the Father; and then our joy shall be full.

83. The lost sinner must know and believe that Jesus Christ is the only Savior.

Acts 4:10-12 – "*Be it known unto you all, and to all the people of Israel*, *that by the name of Jesus Christ of Nazareth, whom ye crucified, whom God raised from the dead, even by him doth this man stand here before you whole. This is the stone which was set at nought of you builders, which is become the head of the corner. Neither is there salvation in any other: for there is none other name under heaven given among men, whereby we must be saved.*"

Acts 13:38-39 – "*Be it known unto you therefore, men and brethren, that through this man is preached unto you the forgiveness of sins: and by him all that believe are justified from all things*, *from which ye could not be justified by the law of Moses.*"

84. We must choose out Spirit-filled men of godly wisdom and integrity to serve as deacons.

Acts 6:3 – "*Wherefore, brethren, look ye out among you seven men of honest report, full of the Holy Ghost and wisdom, whom we may appoint over this business.*"

When seeking out from among ourselves those men who might serve as deacons in the church ministry, our standard is not to be that such men are successful in the things of this world. We are not simply to seek out men of financial skills or managerial skills. Rather, we are to seek out men of spiritual character. We are to seek out men who are filled with the Holy Spirit of God and who walk in the Spirit. We are to seek out men who have wisdom, not the wisdom of the world, but the wisdom of God. We are to seek out men, not according to their worldly successes, but according to their spiritual integrity.

85. We must repent of the wickedness of selfish thinking rather than spiritual thinking, and must seek God's forgiveness thereof.

Acts 8:14-24 – "*Now when the apostles which were at Jerusalem heard that Samaria had received the word of God, they sent unto them Peter and John: who, when they were come down, prayed for them, that they might receive the Holy Ghost: (for as yet he was fallen upon none of them: only they were baptized in the name of the Lord Jesus.) Then laid they their hands on them, and they received the Holy Ghost. And when Simon saw that through laying on of the apostles' hands the Holy Ghost was given, he offered them money, saying, Give me also this power, that on whomsoever I lay hands, he may receive the Holy Ghost. But Peter said unto him, Thy money perish with thee, because thou hast thought that the gift of God may be purchased with money. Thou hast neither part nor lot in this matter: for thy heart is not right in the sight of God. Repent therefore of this thy wickedness, and pray God, if perhaps the thought of thine heart may be forgiven thee. For I perceive that thou art in the gall of bitterness, and in the bond of iniquity. Then answered Simon, and said, Pray ye to the Lord for me, that none of these things which ye have spoken come upon me.*"

In Acts 8:14-24 we read about Simon's sinful thinking concerning the things of God from the materialistic perspective, rather than from the spiritual perspective. Because of this sinful thinking from the materialistic perspective, the apostle Peter instructed Simon to repent of his wickedness and to seek for God's forgiveness. Even so, when we allow our own hearts to develop such a materialistic attitude toward the things of God, rather than a spiritual attitude, we also must repent of our sinful attitude and must seek God's forgiveness. Yea, when we begin to think that the blessings of God may be earned through materialistic and physical means, then we must recognize that such thinking of heart is indeed wickedness in the sight of the Lord our God; and we must repent thereof.

86. As we go forth with the gospel, we must trust the Holy Spirit to guide us unto the right place and the right people.

Acts 8:26-29 – *"And the angel of the Lord spake unto Philip, saying,* **Arise, and go** *toward the south unto the way that goeth down from Jerusalem unto Gaza, which is desert. And he arose and went: and, behold, a man of Ethiopia, an eunuch of great authority under Candace queen of the Ethiopians, who had the charge of all her treasure, and had come to Jerusalem for to worship, was returning, and sitting in his chariot read Esaias the prophet. Then the Spirit said unto Philip,* **Go near, and join thyself to this chariot."**

Acts 10:19-20 – *"While Peter thought on the vision, the Spirit said unto him, Behold, three men seek thee.* **Arise therefore, and get thee down, and go with them,** *doubting nothing: for I have sent them."*

Acts 16:6-10 – *"Now when they had gone throughout Phrygia and the region of Galatia,* **and were forbidden of the Holy Ghost to preach the word in Asia,** *after they were come to Mysia, they assayed to go into Bithynia:* **but the Spirit suffered them not.** *And they passing by Mysia came down to Troas. And a vision appeared to Paul in the night;* **there stood a man of Macedonia, and prayed him, saying, Come over into Macedonia, and help us.** *And after he had seen the vision, immediately we endeavoured to go into Macedonia,* **assuredly gathering that the Lord had called us for to preach the gospel unto them."**

Now, we are not now to expect that the Holy Spirit will guide us through actual verbal statements or through visions and dreams. However, the indwelling Holy Spirit will indeed guide us through that still, small voice within our hearts and through the circumstances of our lives. Even so, in accord with that guidance, we must go where He would have us to go; and we must give the gospel unto whom He would have us to give it.

87. We must be willing to separate unto the ministry those whom the Holy Spirit calls.

Acts 13:1-3 – *"Now there were in the church that was at Antioch certain prophets and teachers; as Barnabas, and Simeon that was called Niger, and Lucius of Cyrene, and Manaen, which had been brought up with Herod the tetrarch, and Saul. As they ministered to the Lord, and fasted, **the Holy Ghost said, Separate me Barnabas and Saul for the work whereunto I have called them.** And when they had fasted and prayed, and laid their hands on them, they sent them away."*

Whether the Holy Spirit of God might set His call upon dear members within our church or upon our own dear sons and daughters, we must be willing to let them go for the work of the Lord. So then, just as the church at Antioch laid their hands upon Barnabas and Saul in order to demonstrate their blessing, even so we also should send away with our blessing those whom the Holy Spirit calls from among us. Furthermore, just as the church at Antioch sent away Barnabas and Saul with their prayers, even so we also should send away those whom the Holy Spirit calls from among us with our continuing prayers for them. Yes, such a sending away will require that they be separated from us in location and time; and such a separation may be difficult for us emotionally. Yet we must be willing for the sake of the Lord and His work. On the other hand, they need never be separate from us in our prayers and support.

88. Those who are called unto pastoral ministry must take heed to themselves and to the flock that they feed the flock according to the Word and will of God, taking the spiritual oversight thereof with a willingness of heart and with a burden to edify.

Acts 20:28-31 – "*Take heed therefore unto yourselves, and to all the flock, over the which the Holy Ghost hath made you overseers, to feed the church of God, which he hath purchased with his own blood. For I know this, that after my departing shall grievous wolves enter in among you, not sparing the flock. Also of your own selves shall men arise, speaking perverse things, to draw away disciples after them. Therefore watch, and remember, that by the space of three years I ceased not to warn every one night and day with tears.*"

Colossians 4:17 – "*And say to Archippus, Take heed to the ministry which thou hast received in the Lord, that thou fulfil it.*"

1 Peter 5:1-2 – "*The elders which are among you I exhort, who am also an elder, and a witness of the sufferings of Christ, and also a partaker of the glory that shall be revealed: Feed the flock of God which is among you, taking the oversight thereof, not by constraint, but willingly; not for filthy lucre, but of a ready mind.*"

In the first place, those who are called unto pastoral ministry must remember that they are servants and stewards of the Lord. They have been called by the Holy Spirit of God, and they are to minister to the church of God that the Lord Jesus Christ purchased with His own blood. They must ever remember that the Lord Jesus Christ is the true owner of the flock and that they are simply His stewards of His flock.

In the second place, those who are called unto pastoral ministry must take heed unto their own spiritual character, both in their personal walk and in their public ministry. This they must do, ever recognizing that they cannot minister aright unto the members of the Lord's flock if they are not personally right with the Lord.

In the third place, those who are called unto pastoral ministry must take heed unto the members of the flock to feed them and edify them spiritually. This they are to do for the purpose that the members of the flock might "walk worthy of the Lord unto all pleasing, being fruitful in every good work, and increasing in the knowledge of God." (See Colossians 1:10) God the Holy Spirit has made them spiritual overseers and leaders for the Lord's flock. Therefore, they must be faithful to take up that spiritual oversight for the members of the Lord's flock. As such, they must be motivated by personal willingness, not by human pressure, and by a burden ("ready mind") to edify others, not by a desire to obtain wealth.

Finally, those who are called unto pastoral ministry must watch over the members of the Lord's flock to protect them from the destruction of false teachers and their false teaching. Even so, the apostle Paul gave warning in Acts 20:29-30, "*For I know this, that after my departing shall grievous wolves enter in among you, not sparing the flock. Also of your own selves shall men arise, speaking perverse things, to draw away disciples after them.*" Therefore, in Acts 20:31 the apostle gave the instruction and example, saying, "*Therefore watch, and remember, that by the space of three years I ceased not to warn every one night and day with tears.*"

89. We must recognize that we are spiritually "dead indeed unto sin, but alive unto God through Jesus Christ our Lord."

Romans 6:11 – "*Likewise reckon ye also yourselves to be dead indeed unto sin, but alive unto God through Jesus Christ our Lord.*"

Now, the word "likewise" here reveals that there is a connection between the instruction of this verse and the truth of the previous verse. Even so, in Romans 6:10 we read, "*For in that he* [our Lord and Savior Jesus Christ] *died, he died unto sin once: but in that he liveth, he liveth unto God.*" So then, just as our Lord Jesus Christ died unto sin, even so we who have received Him through faith as our Savior have died unto sin. In addition, just as our Lord Jesus Christ is now alive unto God, even so we also are now alive unto

God. Yet how exactly are Christ's death unto sin and our death unto sin connected, and how exactly are Christ's living unto God and our living unto God connected?

The answer to this question is found in the earlier context of Romans 6:3-9. Concerning the connection between Christ's death unto sin and our death unto sin, verses 3-7 read, "*Know ye not, that so many of us as were baptized into Jesus Christ were **baptized into his death**? Therefore we are buried **with him** by baptism **into death**: that like as Christ was raised up from the dead by the glory of the Father, even so we also should walk in newness of life. For if we have been planted together **in the likeness of his death**, we shall be also in the likeness of his resurrection: knowing this, **that our old man is crucified with him**, that the body of sin might be destroyed, that henceforth we should not serve sin. **For he that is dead is freed from sin**.*"

In the first place, we learn that at the moment of our faith in Christ for salvation, we were spiritually joined with Him into death. In the opening line of 4, we read, "*Therefore we are buried **with him** by baptism **into death**.*" Yet, in the second place, we learn, not that we were simply joined with Him into death, but that we were specifically joined with Him into the likeness of ***His own*** death. Even so, in verse 3 we read, "*Know ye not, that so many of us as were baptized into Jesus Christ were baptized into **his** death.*" Again in the opening portion of verse 5, we read, "*For if we have been planted together **in the likeness of his death**.*" So then, what kind of death did our Lord Jesus Christ Himself die? In the opening portion of verse 10, we read, "*For in that he died, **he died unto sin** once.*" Thus, in the third place, we learn that at the moment of our faith in Christ for salvation we were spiritually joined with Him into His death, which was a death unto sin. He died unto sin once. Likewise, we died spiritually unto sin with Him.

Furthermore, concerning the connection between Christ's living unto God and our living unto God, verses 4-5 read, "*Therefore we are buried with him by baptism into death: that like as Christ was raised up from the dead by the glory of the Father, even so we also should walk **in newness of life**. For if we have been planted*"

213

*together in the likeness of his death, **we shall be also in the likeness of his resurrection**.*" Just as at the moment of our faith in Christ for salvation, we were spiritually joined with Him into His death, even so also at the moment of our faith in Christ for salvation, we were spiritually joined with Him into His resurrection. So then, what was the nature of Christ's resurrection life with which we have been spiritually joined? In verse 10 the answer is given – *"For in that he died, he died unto sin once: but in that he liveth, **he liveth unto God**.*" This is the nature of His resurrection life and the nature of our newness in life – living unto God. In His resurrection He was raised up to live unto God. In like manner, through being spiritually joined with His resurrection, we were given newness of life in order to live unto God.

Yet what does it mean that we are now dead unto sin, but alive unto God? Every human individual comes into this world as a living soul with a physical body and with an eternal spirit. Our living soul includes who we essentially are as a living person. It encompasses all of our personality – our intellect, mind, and thinking; our emotions, attitude, and affections; our will, purposes, and motivations; our heart, character, and priorities. Now, as a living soul we interact with this physical world through the five senses of our physical bodies. Also as a living soul we interact in spiritual fellowship with God through our eternal spirit. Furthermore, according to the teaching of God's Word, physical death is to be defined as the separation of the living soul and eternal spirit from the physical body. When this separation occurs, the physical body dies. This is physical death. In addition, according to the teaching of God's Word, spiritual death is also to be defined as a form of separation. It is to be defined as the spiritual separation of the eternal spirit from the life and fellowship of God.

Now, the Biblical truth is that we all came into this world as a living soul that was spiritually dead unto God and His fellowship. As Ephesians 2:12 reveals, we were *"without God in the world;"* and as Ephesians 4:18 reveals, we were *"alienated* [or, separated] *from the life of God."* Yea, as Ephesians 2:1 declares, we were spiritually *"dead in trespasses and sins."* Before the moment of our salvation, our eternal spirit was spiritually alive unto sin, but spiritually dead

214

unto God in sin. However, at the very moment of our faith in Christ, God re-created our eternal spirit. At that moment we were made new spiritual creatures in Christ Jesus. (See 2 Corinthians 5:17) Yea, at that moment two events occurred unto us spiritually.

The first of these events was that our old spirit, the one that was spiritually dead in sin unto the life and fellowship of God, was crucified with Christ and taken away from us. Even so, Romans 6:6 declares, *"Knowing this, that our old man is crucified with him, that the body of sin might be destroyed, that henceforth we should not serve sin."* Before our salvation we were spiritually dead in sin without Christ. Yet at the moment of our salvation, we were made spiritually dead unto sin in Christ. Thereby we were set free from the ownership and mastery of sin in order that we might no longer serve sin with our daily living. Before our salvation sin owned our eternal spirit, and we were spiritually powerless to deny the reign of sin over our daily living. Yet at the moment of our salvation, our old spirit was crucified with Christ and taken away. Now sin no longer owns our eternal spirit. Now the power of sin over our eternal spirit has been destroyed. Now we can say, "NO," to sin. Now we can live our daily lives without serving sin.

The second of these events was that God our heavenly Father put a new spirit within us. Even so, that new spirit which God has placed within us is created after God *"in righteousness and true holiness."* (See Ephesians 4:24) Before our salvation we were spiritually dead unto God in sin. Now we are spiritually alive unto God in Christ. Now we are partakers of God's own perfectly righteous nature, and thereby we are now able to serve the Lord our God faithfully in our daily living. Sin no longer owns our eternal spirit. Now the Lord our God and Savior owns our eternal spirit. Indeed, now we can cease to live in the old life of sin; and we can now live in newness of life unto God. Even so, this all we are commanded in Romans 6:11 to reckon (that is – to recognize and believe) as true concerning ourselves as believers.

90. We must not yield ourselves and our members to obey the lusts of sin in our daily living.

Romans 6:12-13 – *"**Let not sin therefore reign in your mortal body, that ye should obey it in the lusts thereof. Neither yield ye your members as instruments of unrighteousness unto sin**: but yield yourselves unto God, as those that are alive from the dead, and your members as instruments of righteousness unto God."*

1 Thessalonians 4:4-5 – *"That every one of you should know how to possess his vessel in sanctification and honour; **not in the lust of concupiscence**, even as the Gentiles which know not God."*

In Romans 6:11 we are commanded to "reckon" (to recognize and believe) that we as believers are *"dead indeed unto sin, but alive unto God through Jesus Christ our Lord."* Then in Romans 6:12-13 the two parts of the instruction from verse 11 are given application unto our daily living. As believers we are now spiritually dead unto sin in Christ. Thus we should no longer serve sin with our daily living. Furthermore, as believers we are now spiritually alive unto God in Christ. Thus we should walk in newness of life in our daily living. Basically in Romans 6:12-13 we find a two-fold instruction, the one concerning what we should not do and the other concerning what we should do, the one concerning that unto which we should not yield ourselves and our members and the other concerning the One unto whom we should yield ourselves and our members.

With this point let us consider the instruction concerning that unto which we should not yield ourselves and our members. This instruction is delivered in three phrases. First, we are instructed not to allow sin to reign in our mortal body, that is – in our daily living upon this earth. Second, we are instructed not to obey sin in its sinful lusts. Third, we are instructed not to yield our various members (such as – our mind, our heart, our mouth, our eyes, our hands, etc.) unto sin to be instruments of unrighteousness. We are spiritually dead indeed unto sin through Jesus Christ our Lord and Savior. Therefore, we now have the spiritual ability to say "No" unto sin and its lusts. Even so, now that we have this spiritual ability, we should actually use it. In our daily living we should actually say "No" unto sin and its lusts. We should actually say "No" when sin desires to reign in our daily living. We should actually say "No" when the lusts of sin call for our attention and our obedience. We should actually say "No" when sin seeks to use one of our members, whatever member it may be, for unrighteous behavior. We must not yield ourselves and our members to obey the lusts of sin in our daily living.

91. We must yield ourselves and our members to obey the will of God in our daily living.

Romans 6:13 – "*Neither yield ye your members as instruments of unrighteousness unto sin: **but yield yourselves unto God, as those that are alive from the dead, and your members as instruments of righteousness unto God**.*"

Romans 6:19 – "*I speak after the manner of men because of the infirmity of your flesh: for as ye have yielded your members servants to uncleanness and to iniquity unto iniquity; **even so now yield your members servants to righteousness unto holiness**.*"

Romans 12:1 – "*I beseech you therefore, brethren, by the mercies of God, **that ye present your bodies a living sacrifice, holy, acceptable unto God**, which is your reasonable service.*"

1 Thessalonians 4:4 – "***That every one of you should know how to possess his vessel in sanctification and honour***.*"

1 Peter 3:15 – "***But sanctify the Lord God in your hearts***: *and be ready always to give an answer to every man that asketh you a reason of the hope that is in you with meekness and fear.*"

With this point we now consider the instruction concerning the One unto whom we should yield ourselves and our members. Even so, we are instructed to yield ourselves as a living sacrifice, to live our lives holy and acceptable unto God. Furthermore, we are instructed to yield our various members (such as – our mind, our heart, our

217

mouth, our eyes, our hands, etc.) unto God to be instruments of righteousness. As believers we are spiritually alive indeed unto God through Jesus Christ our Lord and Savior. Therefore, we now have the spiritual ability to say "Yes" unto God and His will. Even so, now that we have this spiritual ability, we should actually use it. In our daily living we should actually say "Yes" unto God and His will. We should actually say "Yes" and actually yield ourselves when the Lord our God seeks to reign in our daily living. We should actually say "Yes" and actually yield ourselves when the Lord our God calls us to walk in our daily living, not at all unto ourselves, but wholly in a manner that is acceptable unto Him. We should actually say "Yes" and actually yield ourselves when the Lord our God seeks to use one of our members, whatever member it may be, for righteous and holy behavior. We must yield ourselves and our members to obey the will of God in our daily living.

This is what it means to sanctify the Lord God in our hearts. It means to set Him apart in our hearts as the priority and focus of our hearts. As such, it means to walk in close fellowship with the Lord our God and to submit ourselves in committed obedience and service unto Him. Furthermore, not only should we sanctify the Lord in our hearts, but also our physical bodies and their physical members should be possessed in sanctification unto the Lord our God. Our physical bodies and their physical members are to be set apart in consecration and submission unto Him. This alone is the means by which our physical bodies and their physical members can be possessed and employed in a manner that honors the Lord our God, and in a manner that will bring forth our Lord's honor upon us.

92. We Gentiles must not be high minded against the unbelieving nation of Israel.

Romans 11:18-25 – "***Boast not against the branches*** [the Israelites]. *But if thou* [as a Gentile] *boast, thou bearest not the root, but the root thee. Thou wilt say then, The branches were broken off, that I might be graffed in. Well; because of unbelief they were broken* *off, and thou standest by faith. **Be not highminded**, but fear: for if God spared not the natural branches, take heed lest he also spare not thee. Behold therefore the goodness and severity of God: on them which fell, severity; but toward thee, goodness, if thou continue in his goodness: otherwise thou also shalt be cut off. And they also, if they abide not still in unbelief, shall be graffed in: for God is able to graff them in again. For if thou wert cut out of the olive tree which is wild by nature, and wert graffed contrary to nature into a good olive tree: how much more shall these, which be the natural branches, be graffed into their own olive tree? For I would not, brethren, that ye should be ignorant of this mystery, **lest ye should be wise in your own conceits**; that blindness in part is happened to Israel, until the fulness of the Gentiles be come in."*

Yes, the unbelief of the Israelites as a nation has opened the way for the gift of salvation to be offered more fully unto us Gentiles. Yet this unbelief on the part of the Israelites should not cause us Gentiles to be highminded and conceited about our faith in Christ, nor to boast against their unbelief. Rather, like the apostle Paul we should be burdened that the Israelites might also come unto the Lord Jesus through faith as their Messiah and Savior.

93. We Gentiles must walk in the fear of the Lord our God, beholding His goodness and severity in relation to our salvation.

Romans 11:20-23 – *"Well; because of unbelief they were broken off, and thou standest by faith. Be not highminded, **but fear**: for if God spared not the natural branches, take heed lest he also spare not thee. **Behold therefore the goodness and severity of God**: on them which fell, severity; but toward thee, goodness, if thou continue in his goodness: otherwise thou also shalt be cut off. And they also, if they abide not still in unbelief, shall be graffed in: for God is able to graff them in again."*

Indeed, let us set our meditation upon the goodness of the Lord our God toward us Gentiles. Yes, He brought His severity down upon

His chosen people Israel because of their unbelief. Yet along with that severity upon them, He poured out His goodness upon us Gentiles in opening wide unto us the way of eternal salvation. Yet it is also true that the severity of the Lord our God will also fall upon any of us Gentiles who remain in unbelief. Thus we Gentiles should walk in the fear of the Lord our God, praising Him for His goodness toward us in providing the gift of salvation, and fleeing the wrath to come by receiving that gift of salvation through faith in the Lord Jesus Christ.

94. We must not be conformed unto this world.

Romans 12:2 – "***And be not conformed to this world****: but be ye transformed by the renewing of your mind, that ye may prove what is that good, and acceptable, and perfect, will of God."*

Ephesians 4:17-19 – "***This I say therefore, and testify in the Lord, that ye henceforth walk not as other Gentiles walk,*** *in the vanity of their mind, having the understanding darkened, being alienated from the life of God through the ignorance that is in them, because of the blindness of their heart: who being past feeling have given themselves over unto lasciviousness, to work all uncleanness with greediness."*

Ephesians 5:3-7 – *"But fornication, and all uncleanness, or covetousness, let it not be once named among you, as becometh saints; neither filthiness, nor foolish talking, nor jesting, which are not convenient: but rather giving of thanks. For this ye know, that no whoremonger, nor unclean person, nor covetous man, who is an idolater, hath any inheritance in the kingdom of Christ and of God. Let no man deceive you with vain words: for because of these things cometh the wrath of God upon the children of disobedience.* ***Be not ye therefore partakers with them.****"*

According to Galatians 1:4 our Lord Jesus Christ *"gave himself for our sins, that he might deliver us from this present evil world, according to the will of God and our Father."* This world's system is following after the course of that wicked one, the devil. It is a system of spiritual darkness and evil. Yet according to 1 Peter 2:9 God our heavenly Father hath called us *"out of darkness into His marvelous light."* Yes, before the moment of our faith in the Lord Jesus Christ for salvation, we ourselves were a part of this world's darkness. Yet now through faith in the Lord Jesus Christ for salvation, we are light in Him. Therefore, we are now to walk as children of light. (See Ephesians 5:8) We are no longer to walk as this world of darkness walks. We are no longer to be motivated by the same motivations. We are no longer to possess the same priorities or to pursue the same objectives.

The foundational priority of this world's system is centered upon self. As 1 John 2:16 reveals, it is all about *"the lust of the flesh, and the lust of the eyes, and the pride of life."* Yet the foundational priority of our hearts and lives as the children of light should be centered upon our Lord, upon Him who died for us in order to save us from our sins. Thus we are no longer to have fellowship at all with the *"unfruitful works of darkness"* that are so much a part of this world's system. We are no longer to be conformed unto this world, that is – to be formed after this world's image. Indeed, this instruction encompasses every area of our lives – our thoughts, our feelings, our motivations, our goals, our dreams, our desires, our priorities, our decisions, our communication, our marriage relationships, our home lives, our manner of working, our financial management, our appearance, our music, our entertainment, etc.

Each and every day we must decide that we will not follow the ways of this present evil world or have fellowship in their unrighteous behavior. Thus the young man is instructed in Proverbs 1:10-15, *"My son, if sinners entice thee, consent thou not. If they say, Come with us, let us lay wait for blood, let us lurk privily for the innocent without cause: let us swallow them up alive as the grave; and whole, as those that go down into the pit: we shall find all precious substance, we shall fill our houses with spoil: cast in thy lot among us; let us all have one purse: my son, walk not thou in the way with them; refrain thy foot from their path."*

95. We must be transformed by the renewing of our mind.

Romans 12:2 – "*And be not conformed to this world:* **but be ye transformed by the renewing of your mind**, *that ye may prove what is that good, and acceptable, and perfect, will of God.*"

Romans 12:2 begins with a negative instruction concerning that which we are not to do. Then it continues with a positive instruction concerning that which we are to do. Our hearts and lives are no longer to be formed after the image of this world's system. Rather, our hearts and lives are now to be formed after a new image. Yea, our hearts and lives are now to be transformed into a new image. What then is that new image? It is the very image of our Lord and Savior Jesus Christ Himself.

This is the purpose of God our heavenly Father, even as Romans 8:29 declares, "*For whom he did foreknow, he also did predestinate* **to be conformed to the image of his Son**, *that he might be the firstborn among many brethren.*" Yea, this is the great purpose of the indwelling Holy Spirit, even as 2 Corinthians 3:18 declares, "*But we all, with open face beholding as in a glass the glory of the Lord,* **are changed into the same image from glory to glory**, *even as by the Spirit of the Lord.*" Even so, this is the divinely ordained purpose for pastoral ministry, even as the apostle Paul expressed his burden for the Galatian believers in Galatians 4:19, saying, "*My little children, of whom I travail in birth again* **until Christ be formed in you**." Finally, this is also the divinely ordained purpose for our edification one of another in the ministry of the church. Thus Ephesians 4:11-13 declares, "*And he gave some, apostles; and some, prophets; and some, evangelists; and some, pastors and teachers; for the perfecting of the saints, for the work of the ministry, for the edifying of the body of Christ: till we all come in the unity of the faith, and of the knowledge of the Son of God, unto a perfect man,* **unto the measure of the stature of the fulness of Christ**."

Thus concerning our victory over our sinful flesh, we are instructed in Romans 13:14, "**But put ye on the Lord Jesus Christ**, *and make not provision for the flesh, to fulfil the lusts thereof.*" Again concerning the attitudes of our heart, we are instructed in Philippians 2:5, *"Let this mind be in you, **which was also in Christ Jesus**."* Yet again concerning the behavior of our daily walk, we are instructed in 1 John 2:6, *"He that saith he abideth in him **ought himself so to walk, even as he walked**."* Finally, concerning our response to suffering, we are instructed in 1 Peter 2:19-21, *"For this is thankworthy, if a man for conscience toward God endure grief, suffering wrongfully. For what glory is it, if, when ye be buffeted for your faults, ye shall take it patiently? But if, when ye do well, and suffer for it, ye take it patiently, this is acceptable with God. For even herunto were ye called: because Christ also suffered for us, **leaving us an example, that ye should follow his steps**."*

Yet there is one element more in the instruction of Romans 12:2, for therein we learn the way by which we are to be transformed into the image of Christ. We are to be transformed by the renewing of our minds. This transformation begins with the renewing of our inner man, with the renewing of our heart-focus and mindset. Out of our hearts issues forth the character of our behavior and life. Thus our transformation must begin from the inside to the outside. When we confess our sins, we should begin with the confession of our sinful heart attitudes. When we seek to change our direction of life, we should begin with a change in the motivations and priorities of our hearts. When we seek to change in our daily conduct and communication, we should begin with a change in the thoughts and meditations of our hearts. Yea, we must be renewed in the spirit of our minds through meditation upon the Lord our God in praise, prayer, and a conscious acknowledgement of His presence and through meditation upon the precepts, principles, and promises of His Holy Word.

96. We must not think highly of ourselves.

Romans 12:3 – *"For I say, through the grace given unto me, to every man that is among you, **not to think of himself more highly than he ought to think**; but to think soberly, according as God hath dealt to every man the measure of faith."*

223

The Lord our God requires of us that we deny any spirit of pride and self-exaltation, and that we walk before Him in a spirit of humility and lowliness of mind. In Philippians 2:3 the command is given, *"Let nothing be done through strife or vainglory; but in lowliness of mind let each esteem other better than themselves."* Also in Micah 6:8 the counsel is given, *"He hath shewed thee, O man, what is good; and what doth the LORD require of thee, but to do justly, and to love mercy, and to walk humbly with thy God?"*

Even so, from Proverbs 6:16-17 we learn that the Lord our God hates a proud look and spirit, and that such is an abomination in His sight. Yea, Proverbs 16:5 gives warning, *"Every one that is proud in heart is an abomination to the LORD: though hand join in hand, he shall not be unpunished."* Both James 4:6 & 1 Peter 5:5 declare that the Lord our God resists the proud. Psalm 12:3 warns, *"The LORD shall cut off all flattering lips, and the tongue that speaketh proud things."* Psalm 18:27 adds, *"For thou wilt save the afflicted people; but wilt bring down high looks."* Yea, the opening portion of Proverbs 15:25 declares, *"The LORD will destroy the house of the proud."* Concerning the day of judgment, Isaiah 2:11-12 proclaims, *"The lofty looks of man shall be humbled, and the haughtiness of men shall be bowed down, and the LORD alone shall be exalted in that day. For the day of the LORD of hosts shall be upon every one that is proud and lofty, and upon every one that is lifted up; and he shall be brought low."*

Concerning our daily walk upon this earth, Deuteronomy 8:14 reveals that a heart which is lifted up with pride will forget the Lord. Yea, Psalm 10:4 reveals that a spirit of pride will turn our hearts away from the Lord our God, saying, *"The wicked, through the pride of his countenance, will not seek after God: God is not in all his thoughts."* The opening half of Proverbs 13:10 indicates that a spirit of pride will bring contention into our relationships with others, saying, *"Only by pride cometh contention."* Again the opening half of Proverbs 28:25 states, *"He that is of a proud heart stirreth up strife."* Galatians 6:3 states, *"For if a man think himself to be something, when he is nothing, he deceiveth himself."* Proverbs 26:12 declares, *"Seest thou a man wise in his own conceit? There is more hope of a fool than of him."* Proverbs 11:2 reveals, *"When*

pride cometh, then cometh shame: but with the lowly is wisdom."
Finally, Proverbs 16:18 warns, "*Pride goeth before destruction, and an haughty spirit before a fall.*"

In so many areas we must take heed and beware of a proud spirit. We must take heed and beware of pride concerning our wealth and possessions. In 1 Timothy 6:17 the instruction is given, "*Charge them that are rich in this world, that they be not high-minded, nor trust in uncertain riches, but in the living God, who giveth us richly all things to enjoy.*" Also in Deuteronomy 8:11-18 the warning was given, "*Beware that thou forget not the LORD thy God, in not keeping his commandments, and his judgments, and his statutes, which I command thee this day: lest when thou hast eaten and art full, and hast built goodly houses, and dwelt therein; and when thy herds and thy flocks multiply, and thy silver and thy gold is multiplied, and all that thou hast is multiplied; then thine heart be lifted up, and thou forget the LORD thy God, which brought thee forth out of the land of Egypt, from the house of bondage; who led thee through that great and terrible wilderness, wherein were fiery serpents, and scorpions, and drought, where there was no water; who brought thee forth water out of the rock of flint; who fed thee in the wilderness with manna, which thy fathers knew not, that he might humble thee, and that he might prove thee, to do thee good at thy latter end; and thou say in thine heart, My power and the might of mine hand hath gotten me this wealth. But thou shalt remember the LORD thy God: for it is he that giveth thee power to get wealth, that he may establish his covenant which he sware unto thy fathers, as it is this day.*"

We must take heed and beware of pride concerning our abilities and advantages in life. In 1 Corinthians 4:7 the challenge is given, "*For who maketh thee to differ from another? And what hast thou that thou didst not receive? Now if thou didst receive it, why doest thou glory, as if thou hadst not received it?*" We must take heed and beware of pride concerning our position and advancements in life. In Psalm 75:5-7 the warning is given, "*Lift not up your horn on high: speak not with a stiff neck. For promotion cometh neither from the east, nor from the west, nor from the south. But God is the judge: he putteth down one, and setteth up another.*" We must take heed and beware of pride concerning our eternal salvation. In

1 Corinthians 1:26-31 the truth is revealed, *"For ye see your calling, brethren, how that not many wise men after the flesh, not many mighty, not many noble, are called: but God hath chosen the foolish things of the world to confound the wise; and God hath chosen the weak things of the world to confound the things which are mighty; and base things of the world, and things which are despised, hath God chosen, yea, and things which are not, to bring to nought things that are: that no flesh should glory in his presence. But of him are ye in Christ Jesus, who of God is made unto us wisdom, and righteousness, and sanctification, and redemption: that, according as it is written, He that glorieth, let him glory in the Lord."* We must take heed and beware of pride concerning our spiritual growth and maturity. In 1 Corinthians 10:12 the warning is given, *"Wherefore let him that thinketh he standeth take heed lest he fall."* Finally, we must take heed and beware of pride concerning our religious accomplishments. In 2 Corinthians 10:12 the counsel is given, *"For we dare not make ourselves of the number, or compare ourselves with some that commend themselves: but they measuring themselves by themselves, and comparing themselves among themselves, are not wise."*

97. We must be both dependent and diligent in fulfilling the ministry responsibility unto which the Lord our God has called us, doing all for the glory of the Lord our God.

Romans 12:3-8 – *"For I say, through the grace given unto me, to every man that is among you, not to think of himself more highly than he ought to think; **but to think soberly, according as God hath dealt to every man the measure of faith**. For as we have many members in one body, and all members have not the same office: so we, being many, are one body in Christ, and every one members one of another. Having then gifts differing according to the grace that is given to us, whether prophecy, let us prophesy according to the proportion of faith; or ministry, let us wait on our ministering: or he that teacheth, on teaching; or he that exhorteth, on exhortation: he that giveth, let him do it with simplicity; he that ruleth, with diligence; he that sheweth mercy, with cheerfulness."*

226

1 Timothy 4:14 – "***Neglect not the gift that is in thee***, *which was given thee by prophecy, with the laying on of the hands of the presbytery.*"

2 Timothy 1:6 – "***Wherefore I put thee in remembrance that thou stir up the gift of God***, *which is in thee by the putting on of my hands.*"

1 Peter 4:10-11 – "***As every man hath received the gift, even so minister the same one to another, as good stewards of the manifold grace of God***. *If any man speak, let him speak as the oracles of God; if any man minister, let him do it as of the ability which God giveth: that God in all things may be glorified through Jesus Christ, to whom be praise and dominion for ever and ever. Amen.*"

In Romans 12:3 we find two contrasting commands, the first instructing us how we are not to think of ourselves and the second instructing us how we are to think concerning ourselves. In the first place, every one of us is instructed not to think highly of ourselves. As such, we would expect that the contrasting command would then instruct us to think lowly of ourselves. However, the actual instruction of this passage is a little different than we would expect. It is that we are to think soberly concerning ourselves.

Yet what does it mean for us to think soberly concerning ourselves? Basically sober thinking means thinking appropriately and seriously concerning ourselves with a Biblical balance. Yet such appropriate and serious thinking requires some form of context. Even so, in the flow of thought of this passage, Romans 12:4-5 reveals that context, saying, "*For as we have many members in one body, and all members have not the same office: so we, being many, are one body in Christ, and every one members one of another.*" Thus the context for the instruction in verse three specifically concerns our ministry responsibility toward one another as fellow believers in the body of Christ. So then, from the full truth of this passage, we find four elements that are necessary for true, Biblical balance in our thinking concerning ourselves in relation to our ministry responsibility toward one another.

First, we must maintain a surrendered mindset. With regard to our ministry responsibility in the body of Christ, we must each recognize that we ourselves do not choose our place of responsibility. Indeed, we must recognize that the Lord our God is the One who calls us unto that place of ministry responsibility which He chooses for us. With the closing line of Romans 12:3, we find the phrase, "*According as God hath dealt to every man* the measure of faith;" and with the opening line of Romans 12:6, we find the phrase, "*Having then gifts differing according to the grace that is given* to us." Furthermore, with the opening line of 1 Peter 4:10, we find the phrase, "*As every man hath received* the gift." Finally, 1 Corinthians 12:18 declares, "*But now hath God set the members* every one of them in the body, *as it hath pleased him.*" Therefore, we ourselves must not be high-minded in this matter. We must not think that we know better than the Lord our God Himself concerning the ministry responsibility that we should be given. We must not think that we deserve some "higher" place of ministry responsibility than that unto which He has called us. Rather, we must surrender ourselves unto the will and calling of the Lord our God in our lives, no matter what it may be and no matter how "high" or "low" we may perceive it to be. We must think soberly; we must maintain a surrendered mindset.

Second, we must maintain a dependent mindset. With regard to our ministry responsibility in the body of Christ, we must each recognize that we cannot fulfill our responsibility aright in and of ourselves, but that we can only do so in and by the grace of the Lord our God. Again with the closing line of Romans 12:3, we find the phrase, "*According as **God hath dealt** to every man the measure of faith;*" and again with the opening line of Romans 12:6, we find the phrase, "*Having then gifts differing **according to the grace** that is given to us.*" Furthermore, with the closing line of 1 Peter 4:10, we find the phrase, "*As good stewards of **the manifold grace of God.***" Finally, 2 Corinthians 3:5 declares, "*Not that we are sufficient of ourselves to think any thing as of ourselves; but our sufficiency is of God.*" "*And,*" 2 Corinthians 9:8 adds, "*God is able to make all grace abound toward you; that ye, always having all sufficiency in all things, may abound to every good work.*" Therefore, we ourselves must not be high-minded in this matter. We must not think that we are self-sufficient. We must not be self-confident. We must not lean

228

upon our own understanding. We must not trust in our strength. Rather, we must be wholly dependent upon our Lord's direction and strength for our sufficiency. Our mindset must always be governed by the truth that without abiding in Christ we can do nothing, but that through abiding in Christ we can do all things specifically because then He will strengthen us out of His almighty strength. (See John 15:5 & Philippians 4:13) We must think soberly; we must maintain a dependent mindset.

In addition, with regard to our ministry responsibility in the body of Christ, we must each recognize that we ourselves need the ministry of our fellow believers for the sake of our own spiritual growth and for the fulfillment of our own ministry responsibility. In Romans 12:5 the truth is revealed, "*So we, being many, are one body in Christ, and every one members one of another.*" Therefore, we must not be high-minded in this matter. We must not think that our own place of ministry responsibility is somehow more important than another's place of ministry responsibility. We must not think that we have no need for another's efforts of ministry in our own lives. We must not think that we are somehow above them and their efforts of ministry. Rather, we must recognize that we are all members one of another, and that we all are to minister in unity one with another and one toward another, not for self-advancement and self-glory, but all for the glory of Christ's name and the advancement of Christ's work. Even so, the closing portion of 1 Peter 4:11 states, "*That God in all things may be glorified through Jesus Christ, to whom be praise and dominion for ever and ever. Amen.*" We must think soberly; we must maintain a dependent mindset.

Third, we must maintain a diligent mindset. With regard to our ministry responsibility in the body of Christ, we must each be seriously committed and diligent to fulfill that ministry responsibility aright. Indeed, we must each recognize that although our ministry responsibility will be different than that of others, we each have been given some ministry responsibility in the work of the Lord. Again with the closing line of Romans 12:3, we find the phrase, "*According as God hath dealt **to every man the measure of faith**.*" Furthermore, 1 Corinthians 12:11 declares, "*But all these worketh that one and the selfsame Spirit, **dividing to every man** severally as* *he will."* In addition, we must each recognize that our ministry responsibility is God's own will for our lives. Therefore, we must be diligent to fulfill that responsibility. In Romans 12:6-8 the instruction is given, *"Having then gifts differing according to the grace that is given to us, whether prophecy, let us prophesy according to the proportion of faith; or ministry, let us wait on our ministering: or he that teacheth, on teaching; or he that exhorteth, on exhortation: he that giveth, let him do it with simplicity; he that ruleth, with diligence; he that sheweth mercy, with cheerfulness."* With the opening line of 1 Timothy 4:14, the instruction was given, *"Neglect not the gift that is in thee;"* and in the opening portion of 2 Timothy 1:6, the encouragement was given, *"Wherefore I put thee in remembrance that thou stir up the gift of God."* Finally, in 1 Peter 4:11 the instruction is given, *"If any man speak, let him speak as the oracles of God; if any man minister, let him do it as of the ability which God giveth: that God in all things may be glorified through Jesus Christ, to whom be praise and dominion for ever and ever. Amen."* Whatever our God-given ministry responsibility might be, we must be diligent to do it. We must not neglect it. Rather, we must stir it up to use it diligently for our Lord's glory. We must think soberly; we must maintain a diligent mindset.

Finally, we must maintain a ministering mindset. With regard to our ministry responsibility in the body of Christ, we must each recognize that we are not to seek for the exaltation of self, but are to seek for edification of others. Again we consider the instruction of Romans 12:6-8, *"Having then gifts differing according to the grace that is given to us, whether prophecy, let us prophesy according to the proportion of faith; or ministry, let us wait on our ministering: or he that teacheth, on teaching; or he that exhorteth, on exhortation: he that giveth, let him do it with simplicity; he that ruleth, with diligence; he that sheweth mercy, with cheerfulness."* The one who is called unto the ministry responsibility of prophesying is to concentrate, not on self-exaltation, but on actually proclaiming the truth of God's Word for the edification of others. The one who is called unto the ministry responsibility of ministering is to concentrate, not on self-exaltation, but on actually ministering unto the growth of others. The one who is called unto the ministry responsibility of teaching is to concentrate, not on self-exaltation, but on actually teaching the doctrine of God's Word for the learning of others. The one who is called unto the ministry responsibility of exhorting is to concentrate, not on self-exaltation, but on exhorting others to walk aright with the Lord. The one who is called unto the ministry responsibility of giving is to concentrate, not on self-exaltation, but on giving with the single motivation of love in order to meet the needs of others. The one who is called unto the ministry responsibility of ruling is to concentrate, not on self-exaltation, but on ruling with a zealous motivation to advance the Lord's work in the lives of others. The one who is called unto the ministry responsibility of mercy-showing is to concentrate, not on self-exaltation, but on showing mercy with a cheerful motivation to help others. We must think soberly; we must maintain a ministering mindset.

98. We must "abhor that which is evil" and "cleave to that which is good."

Romans 12:9 – "*Let love be without dissimulation.* ***Abhor that which is evil; cleave to that which is good.***"

1 Peter 3:11 – "***Let him eschew*** [hate and avoid] ***evil, and do good;*** *let him seek peace, and ensue it.*"

All that is contrary to our Lord's will is evil; all that is according to our Lord's will is good. Thus, on the one hand, we are to abhor, to utterly hate and avoid, all that is contrary to our Lord's will. Thus, on the other hand, we are to cleave unto, to fervently and faithfully cling to and follow after, all that is according to our Lord's will. Furthermore, all that is of our selfish, sinful flesh is evil; for in our flesh there dwells no good thing. (See Romans 7:18) On the other hand, all that is of the Holy Spirit is good. Thus we are to abhor, to utterly hate and avoid, all that is of our selfish, sinful flesh. Thus also we are to cleave unto, to fervently and faithfully cling to and follow after, all that is of the Holy Spirit. All of the desires of the flesh must be utterly hated. All of the directions of the Spirit must be fervently and faithfully loved, clung to, followed after, and obeyed. In this light we find that this principle applies, not only

231

unto external words, activities, and behavior, but also unto internal thoughts, attitudes, and desires. We must utterly hate even the sinful, selfish, fleshly thoughts, attitudes, and desires of our own hearts. We must fervently and faithfully follow after the loving, righteous, holy thoughts, attitudes, and desires of the indwelling Holy Spirit.

99. We must have kind affection for our fellow brothers and sisters in Christ.

Romans 12:10 – "***Be kindly affectioned one to another with brotherly love****; in honour preferring one another.*"

Herein the context is brotherly love. It is the family love of God's own spiritual family. It is the love of fellow brothers and sisters in Christ for one another. Even so, in this context of family love, we are instructed to "*be kindly affectioned one to another.*" Now, the word "affection" here means "fond or tender feeling; warm liking." As such, our Lord desires for us to develop and maintain a tender heart, a fond feeling, and a warm interest toward our fellow brothers and sisters in Christ. Thus it is not acceptable for us to say – "I love such-and-such brother or sister in Christ; I just do not like him or her." Certainly we may not "like" some of the actions that a fellow believer might do, some of the things that a fellow believer might say, or some of the attitudes that a fellow believer might have. In fact, if these actions, words, and attitudes are contrary to God's Word of truth, then true, godly love will not "like" them or rejoice in them. (See 1 Corinthians 13:6) Yet since the individual himself or herself is a fellow brother or sister in Christ, we are required to develop an attitude of affection toward him or her as an individual.

100. We must prefer others in honor.

Romans 12:10 – *"Be kindly affectioned one to another with brotherly love; **in honour preferring one another**."*

Now, there are two aspects unto this instruction. In the first place, when honor is being given, we are to prefer that another receive that honor rather than ourselves. We are to prefer that others be recognized, complimented, praised, and rewarded before ourselves. In the second place, we are to prefer to give honor unto others rather than to receive honor from others. We are to be quick to give out compliments and praise unto others and slow to seek after such compliments and praise from others. We are to prefer to give out recognition and rewards unto others rather than to receive such recognition and rewards from others.

101. We must not be slothful in our responsibilities, but fervent, ever motivated by service to our Lord.

Romans 12:11 – *"**Not slothful in business; fervent in spirit; serving the Lord**."*

All three of these instructions are to be taken together. The first two present a contrast to one another. The first instruction presents how we are not to behave, and the second presents how we are to behave. The third instruction then presents the foundational motivation for that behavior. Now, there are three elements of this three-fold instruction that must be considered for understanding.

First, we must understand that all three instructions deal with the matter of our "business." In our time we tend to narrow our view of the word "business" as that in which we are involved for financial benefit. Often we use it in the context of "one's work, occupation, or profession." Or, we use it in the context of "the buying and selling of goods and services." Or, we use it in the context of "a commercial or industrial establishment, a store, factory, etc." Indeed, all of these are to be included in the definition of the word. However, there is another aspect for the definition of the word "business" that is less often recognized. The word "business" may refer to a "rightful responsibility" in any given area of our lives. Indeed, such is the intent of the word in the context of Romans 12:11. This verse is dealing with how we handle our God-given responsibilities in life.

What responsibilities might these be? If a man is a husband, then he has God-given responsibilities as a husband toward his wife. If a woman is a wife, then she has God-given responsibilities as a wife toward her husband. If a man is a father, then he has God-given responsibilities as a father toward his children. If a woman is a mother, then she has God-given responsibilities as a mother toward her children. The children also have God-given responsibilities in the home toward their parents. As citizens of our country, we have God-given responsibilities toward our country. As employers and employees, we have God-given responsibilities on the job. As the children of God, we have God-given responsibilities to meditate in God's Word every day, to rejoice in the Lord always, to give thanks for all things, to pray without ceasing, to walk humbly before our Lord, to love Him with all our hearts, and to obey His commandments faithfully. As the ambassadors for Christ, we have God-given responsibilities to be the salt of the earth, to be the light of the world, and to be witnesses of the gospel of Jesus Christ. As members of God the Father's family and of God the Son's body, the church, we have God-given responsibilities to love one another and to edify one another in love. Oh yes, we have many God-given responsibilities in our lives, in the church, in our private walk, in our homes, on the job, in public, etc. Such is the subject matter about which Romans 12:11 gives instruction.

Second, we must understand that we are to pursue the fulfillment of our "business," of our rightful, God-given responsibilities, with the right spirit. We are not to have a slothful spirit (a lazy spirit) in this matter. Rather, we are to have a fervent spirit in this matter. We should seek to fulfill our God-given responsibilities in every area of our lives with all of our hearts and with all of our might. Even so, the opening portion of Ecclesiastes 9:10 declares, "*Whatsoever thy hand findeth to do, do it with thy might.*" Yea, whatever our Lord has put into our hand to do, we should do it with all of our might.

Even so also, the warning is given in Proverbs 10:26, "*As vinegar to the teeth, and as smoke to the eyes, so is the sluggard* [the slothful, lazy individual] *to them that send him.*" Yea, when we are slothful in our God-given responsibilities, we become a provoking aggravation unto our Lord who called us and sent us. Yet the promise is given in Proverbs 22:29, "*Seest thou a man diligent in his business* [in his responsibilities]? *He shall stand before kings; he shall not stand before mean men.*" Yea, when we are fervently diligent to fulfill our God-given responsibilities, we shall stand rewarded before the King of kings and Lord of lords, our Lord Jesus Christ, at His judgment seat.

Third, we must understand that we are to be motivated in fulfilling our "business," in fulfilling our rightful, God-given responsibilities, as service unto our Lord. It is all to be viewed as service unto Him who died for us and thereby saved us eternally from our sins. Husbands, you are not simply to be good husbands toward our wives, but to serve the Lord our God and Savior as godly husbands toward our wives. Wives, you are not simply to be good wives toward your husbands, but to serve the Lord our God and Savior as godly wives toward your husbands. Parents, you are not simply to be good parents toward our children, but to serve the Lord our God and Savior as godly parents toward your children. Children, you are not simply to be good children toward your parents, but to serve the Lord your God and Savior as godly children toward your parents. Brethren, we are not simply to be good citizens of our country, but to serve the Lord our God and Savior as godly citizens of our country. Brethren, we are not simply to be good employers or employees on the job, but to serve the Lord our God and Savior as godly employers or employees on the job. Brethren, we are not simply to be good ministers in the ministry of the church, but to serve the Lord our God and Savior as godly ministers in the ministry of the church. Whatever we do, we are to do all to the glory of the Lord our God and Savior. (See 1 Corinthians 10:31) Yea, whatever we do, we are to do it heartily (fervently), not as men pleasers, "*but as the servants of Christ, doing the will of God from the heart.*" (See Ephesians 6:6-7 & Colossians 3:23). Also we must do nothing in service to sin, to our sinful flesh, to selfish lust and pleasure, and to the world; for such is in direct opposition to serving the Lord.

102. We must ever rejoice in our hope as believers.

Romans 12:12 – "***Rejoicing in hope***; *patient in tribulation; continuing instant in prayer.*"

Yet what is this hope in which we believers are to continue rejoicing? In Scripture the word "hope" means more than "wishful dreaming." In Scripture the word "hope" carries the meaning of "a promised certainty." What then is this hope of the believer, this promised certainty, in which we believers are ever to be rejoicing? What is the nature of this hope?

In the first place, 1 Peter 1:3-4 gives answer, saying, "Blessed be the God and Father of our Lord Jesus Christ, which according to his abundant mercy hath begotten us again unto a lively [that is – living] *hope by the resurrection of Jesus Christ from the dead, to an inheritance incorruptible, and undefiled, and that fadeth not away, reserved in heaven for you.*" Our hope as believers, yea *our living hope*, is an inheritance from God our heavenly Father unto us His dear children that He has reserved in heaven for us. It is an incorruptible inheritance, one that cannot decay in substance. It is an undefiled inheritance, one that is not and cannot be defiled by sin. It is an unfading inheritance, one that cannot fade over time in beauty or glory.

In the second place, Titus 2:13-14 gives answer, saying, "*Looking for that blessed hope, and the glorious appearing of the great God and our Savior Jesus Christ; who gave himself for us, that he might redeem us from all iniquity, and purify unto himself a peculiar people, zealous of good works.*" Our hope as believers, yea *our blessed hope*, is the glorious appearing of God the Son, our Lord and Savior Jesus Christ at His second coming. Even so, 1 John 3:1-3 brings these two aspects of our hope together, saying, "*Behold, what manner of love the Father hath bestowed upon us, that we should be called the sons of God: therefore the world knoweth us not, because it knew him not. Beloved, now are we the sons of God, and it doth not yet appear what we shall be: but we know that, when he shall appear, we shall be like him; for we shall see him as he is. And every man that hath this hope in him purifieth himself, even as he is pure.*"

Even so, Titus 3:7 declares, *"That being justified by his grace, we should be made heirs according to the hope of eternal life."* This is our hope as believers – the hope of eternal life. Yes, from the moment of our faith in Christ for salvation from sin, we possess eternal life and are made the dear children of God the Father. Yet in this life we only experience these things in a foretaste. We do not yet experience our eternal life in all of its fullness. It does not yet appear what we shall be in all fullness as the dear children of God the Father. Thus the closing portion of Romans 8:23 states, *"Even we ourselves groan within ourselves, waiting for the adoption, to wit, the redemption of our body."* That complete and perfect fullness of eternal life as God's dear children is our hope as believers. It is our incorruptible, undefiled, unfading inheritance that we shall receive in all of its fullness at the appearing of our Lord and Savior Jesus Christ. At that day we shall be made perfectly holy and righteous in body, soul, and spirit, even as our Lord Jesus Christ is perfectly holy and righteous. At that day we shall be like Him in perfect righteousness and holiness, *"for we shall see him as he is."* At that day the glory of God shall be fully manifested in us. This is our hope as believers – ever to be with our Lord and ever to be without sin; and in this hope we are ever to be rejoicing.

Furthermore, this hope is absolutely certain because of its source and foundation. Who then is the Source of our hope as believers? Again 1 Peter 1:3 gives answer, *"Blessed be the God and Father of our Lord Jesus Christ, which according to his abundant mercy hath begotten us again unto a lively hope by the resurrection of Jesus Christ from the dead."* God the Father is the Source of our hope. He Himself has begotten us as His own dear children unto the hope of our inheritance from Him. Indeed, this He did according to His own abundant mercy. In addition, 1 Peter 1:5 states concerning us, *"Who are kept by the power of God through faith unto salvation ready to be revealed in the last time."* Yea, by the almighty power of God the Father, we are kept unto that day of Christ's appearing, unto that moment wherein the glory of God will be fully revealed in us. Finally, Titus 1:2 proclaims, *"In hope of eternal life, which God, that cannot lie, promised before the world began."* The Source of our hope is God our heavenly Father Himself – through His abundant mercy, His almighty power, and His absolute promise.

What then is the Foundation of our hope as believers? Or better – Who then is the foundation of our hope as believers? 1 Timothy 1:1 gives answer, saying, *"Paul, an apostle of Jesus Christ by the commandment of God our Saviour, and Lord Jesus Christ, which is our hope."* Yet again 1 Peter 1:3 declares, *"Blessed by the God and Father of our Lord Jesus Christ, which according to his abundant mercy hath begotten us again unto a lively hope by the resurrection of Jesus Christ from the dead."* Thus our hope is founded upon our Lord's death for us and upon His resurrection from the dead. In addition, Colossians 1:26-27 reveals, *"Even the mystery which hath been hid from ages and from generations, but now is made manifest to his saints: to whom God would make known what is the riches of the glory of this mystery among the Gentiles; which is Christ in you, the hope of glory."* Thus our hope is founded upon our Lord's indwelling presence through His indwelling Holy Spirit. Finally, speaking of our Lord's appearing at His second coming, 1 John 3:1 states, *"And every man that hath this hope in him purifieth himself, even as he is pure."* Thus our hope is founded upon our Lord's coming to receive us unto Himself. Oh, how sure is our God the Father as the Source of our hope and God the Son as the foundation of our hope! Let us then ever rejoice in our hope.

103. We must patiently and joyfully remain faithful in the will and work of God through the tribulations of this life.

Romans 12:12 – *"Rejoicing in hope;* **patient in tribulation***; continuing instant in prayer."*

Hebrews 12:1 – *"Wherefore seeing we also are compassed about with so great a cloud of witnesses, let us lay aside every weight, and the sin which doth so easily beset us,* **and let us run with patience the race that is set before us.***"*

James. 1:2-4 – *"**My brethren, count it all joy when ye fall into divers temptations***; knowing this, that the trying of your faith worketh patience."*

James 5:10-11 – "***Take, my brethren, the prophets, who have spoken in the name of the Lord, for an example of suffering affliction, and of patience.*** *Behold, we count them happy which endure. Ye have heard of the patience of Job, and have seen the end of the Lord; that the Lord is very pitiful, and of tender mercy.*"

This life is a life that is full of trouble and tribulation. In Job 14:1 the man of God Job declared, "*Man that is born of a woman is of few days, and full of trouble.*" Certainly the Lord our God did not originally create this universe to be full of such trouble. Rather, He Himself characterized His completed creation as "very good." Yet from the moment that Adam sinned against God, the human race and the created universe were plunged under the curse of trouble, tribulation, decay, and death. As long as we remain in this life, we will suffer under this curse of trouble and tribulation. It may come in various forms, such as circumstantial trouble, health trouble, relational trouble, financial trouble, emotional trouble, spiritual trouble, or persecution trouble; but it will come. Even so, in Romans 12:12 we are instructed to be patient, to endure patiently, to remain patiently faithful in the midst of these tribulations and troubles. Also in James 1:2-4 we are instructed to "*count it all joy,*" to be joyfully faithful in the midst of these tribulations and troubles.

Yet how can we maintain such a patient endurance of faithfulness and joyfulness as the tribulations and troubles of this life rise up high and crash down heavy against us? First, we must recognize the good purpose of the Lord our God in such tribulations. In Romans 8:28 the assurance is given, "*And we know that all things* [yes, all things – including the tribulations and troubles of this life] *work together for good to them that love God, to them who are the called according to His purpose.*" So then, what is the good purpose of the Lord our God in our tribulations? Romans 5:3-4 gives answer, saying, "*And not only so, but we glory in tribulations also, knowing that tribulation worketh patience; and patience, experience; and experience, hope.*" Again James 1:2-4 gives answer, saying, "*My brethren, count it all joy when ye fall into divers temptations; knowing this, that the trying of your faith worketh patience. But let patience have her perfect work, that ye may be perfect and entire, wanting* [lacking] *nothing.*"

Faith in the Lord our God is absolutely necessary for our Christian lives. Even so, the opening line of Hebrews 11:6 proclaims, *"But without faith it is impossible to please him."* Certainly we must set our faith in the Lord Jesus Christ as Savior for the gift of eternal salvation and eternal life. Yet this is not to be the end of our faith, but the beginning. We also must set our faith in the Lord our God for each step of our daily Christian walk. However, our faith is often small. Our faith is often weak. Our faith is often faltering. Thus the Lord our God graciously performs His work of trying and purifying our faith. This He does through the tribulations and troubles of life.

Even so, 1 Peter 1:6-7 states, *"Wherein ye greatly rejoice, though now for a season, if need be, ye are in heaviness through manifold temptations: that the trial of your faith, being much more precious than of gold that perisheth, though it be tried with fire, might be found unto praise and honour and glory at the appearing of Jesus Christ."* Just as gold is tried and purified through fire, even so our faith is tried and purified through tribulations and troubles. In addition, just as when gold is tried and purified through fire, it becomes more valuable, even so when our faith is tried and purified through tribulations and troubles, it is found unto greater *"praise and honour and glory at the appearing of Jesus Christ."* Furthermore, this trying and purifying of our faith will develop in us a greater level of spiritual endurance (patience); and as we grow in spiritual endurance, so also we grow in spiritual maturity. This is our Lord God's good purpose in the tribulations and troubles of this life. *"Tribulation worketh patience* [spiritual endurance]*; and patience, experience* [spiritual maturity]*."* *"The trying of your faith* [through tribulations and troubles] *worketh patience* [spiritual endurance]*;"* and when we allow patience to have her perfect work and good purpose in us, we shall be *"perfect and entire* [spiritually mature]*, wanting* [lacking] *nothing."*

Second, we must look unto our Lord Jesus Christ as our perfect example of and as our empowering strength for patient endurance in tribulation. In Hebrews 12:1-3 we are instructed, *"Wherefore seeing we also are compassed about with so great a cloud of witnesses, let us lay aside every weight, and the sin which doth so easily beset us, and let us run with patience the race that is set before us,*

240

looking unto Jesus *the author and finisher of our faith; who for the joy that was set before him endured the cross, despising the shame, and is set down at the right hand of the throne of God.* **For consider him** *that endured such contradiction of sinners against himself,* **lest ye be wearied and faint in your minds**." Again in Colossians 1:10-11 the prayer is lifted up, "*That ye might walk worthy of the Lord unto all pleasing, being fruitful in every good work, and increasing in the knowledge of God;* **strengthened with all might, according to his glorious power, unto all patience and longsuffering with joyfulness**."

Third, we must meditate in the truth and teaching of God's Holy Word. In Romans 15:4 the truth is revealed, "*For whatsoever things were written aforetime were written for our learning,* **that we through patience and comfort of the scriptures might have hope**."

Fourth, we must set our trust in the tender mercies of the Lord our God. In James 5:10-11 we are encouraged, "*Take, my brethren, the prophets, who have spoken in the name of the Lord, for an example of suffering affliction, and of patience. Behold, we count them happy which endure. Ye have heard of the patience of Job,* **and have seen the end of the Lord; that the Lord is very pitiful, and of tender mercy**."

Fifth, we must remember the hope and the reward that is set before us at the appearing of our Lord Jesus Christ in His second coming. In Hebrews 10:35-37 the message is given, "*Cast not away therefore your confidence,* **which hath great recompence of reward**. *For ye have need of patience, that, after ye have done the will of God,* **ye might receive the promise**. *For yet a little while, and he that shall come will come, and will not tarry*." Again in Romans 8:14-18 the truth is revealed, "*For as many as are led by the Spirit of God, they are the children of God. For ye have not received the spirit of bondage again to fear; but ye have received the Spirit of adoption, whereby we cry, Abba, Father. The Spirit itself beareth witness with our spirit, that we are the children of God:* **and if children, then heirs; heirs of God, and joint-heirs with Christ; if so be that we suffer with him, that we may be also glorified together**. *For I reckon that the sufferings of this present time are not to be compared with*

241

the glory which shall be revealed in us." Yet again in James 1:12 the promise is given, "**Blessed is the man that endureth temptation: for when he is tried, he shall receive the crown of life,** *which the Lord hath promised to them that love him.*"

Indeed, for each one of us, the Lord our God has set the course of His will before us. Along that course every responsibility of our fellowship with Him and of our service for Him is encompassed. Yet that course is not a quick sprint. Rather, that course is a marathon run throughout the daily details of our entire lives upon this earth. Furthermore, that course passes through the manifold trials and tribulations of this life. Therefore, as we run the course that the Lord our God has set before us, we must do so with a patient and joyful endurance to finish our course without becoming weary in well doing. Yea, we must so run the course that the Lord our God has set before us in order that we might receive the reward. We must so run in order that at the end of our lives, we might join with the apostle Paul from 2 Timothy 4:7-8 in saying, "*I have fought a good fight, I have finished my course, I have kept the faith: henceforth there is laid up for me a crown of righteousness, which the Lord, the righteous judge, shall give me at that day: and not to me only, but unto all them also that love his appearing.*"

104. We must be "given to hospitality."

Romans 12:13 – "*Distributing to the necessity of saints;* **given to hospitality.**"

Hebrews 13:2 – "**Be not forgetful to entertain strangers**: *for thereby some have entertained angels unawares.*"

1 Peter 4:9 – "**Use hospitality one to another without grudging.**"

The idea of being "given to" such hospitality carries the picture of "pursuing after" it. We are to give ourselves, to give forth our energy and our efforts, in the pursuit of hospitality. Furthermore, the word "hospitality" refers to a spirit and manner of friendliness, kindness, and generosity toward guests, visitors, and strangers. Thus we are to give forth our energy and our efforts to pursue a manner of friendliness, kindness, and generosity toward guests, visitors, and strangers. We are not to be so inward focused that we have no time or consideration for these guests, visitors, and strangers. Rather, we are ever to be focused outwardly in kindness toward them. We are not to require them to come unto us in friendliness and kindness. Rather, we are to pursue after them in friendliness and kindness. Indeed, we are ungrudgingly to demonstrate kindness and helpfulness toward those around us, even if we do not know them personally.

105. We must maintain a unity of care and compassion for one another as fellow believers.

Romans 12:15 – "***Rejoice with them that do rejoice, and weep with them that weep.***"

1 Peter 3:8 – "***Finally, be ye all of one mind, having compassion one of another, love as brethren, be pitiful, be courteous.***"

As believers we are fellow members in the body of Christ. Even so, 1 Corinthians 12:12-13 declares, "*For as the body* [that is – the physical body] *is one, and hath many members, and all the members of that one body, being many, are one body: so also is Christ. For by one Spirit are we all baptized into one body, whether we be Jews or Gentiles, whether we be bond or free; and have been all made to drink into one Spirit.*" Yea, it is God our heavenly Father Himself who has placed each one of us into this church body according to His own perfect wisdom and good will. Even so, 1 Corinthians 12:18 declares, "*But now hath God set the members every one of them in the body, as it hath pleased him.*" In addition, it is God our heavenly Father Himself who knits each individual member of this church body with each other member. Even so, 1 Corinthians 12:24 declares, "*For our comely parts have no need, but God hath tempered the body together, having given more abundant honour to that part which lacked.*"

So then, what is our Lord God's purpose for placing us and knitting us into this church body? 1 Corinthians 12:25-26 gives answer, saying, *"That there should be no schism in the body; but that the members should have the same care one for another. And whether one member suffer, all the members suffer with it; or one member be honoured, all the members rejoice with it."* We are not truly functioning as a church body in accord with our Lord's purpose until our hearts are so knit together with one another that when one member suffers hurt, we all weep with him or her, or when one member is honored, we all rejoice with him or her. This is our Lord's desire for us – that there should be no division in this church body, but that we all should maintain a unity of care and compassion for one another. This is our Lord's command to us – that we should *"rejoice with them that do rejoice, and weep with them that weep."* Even so, we are instructed in 1 Peter 3:8, *"Finally, be ye all of one mind, having compassion one of another, love as brethren, be pitiful, be courteous."*

106. **We must maintain a Spirit-filled unity of mindset and love for, toward, and with one another as fellow believers in accord with the will of our Lord Jesus Christ.**

Romans 12:16 – *"**Be of the same mind one toward another.** Mind not high things, but condescend to men of low estate. Be not wise in your own conceits."*

1 Corinthians 1:10 – *"**Now I beseech you, brethren, by the name of our Lord Jesus Christ, that ye all speak the same thing, and that there be no divisions among you; but that ye be perfectly joined together in the same mind and in the same judgment.**"*

2 Corinthians 13:11 – *"Finally, brethren, farewell. Be perfect, be of good comfort, **be of one mind**, live in peace; and the God of love and peace shall be with you."*

Ephesians 4:3 – *"**Endeavouring to keep the unity of the Spirit in the bond of peace.**"*

Philippians 2:1-2 – "*If there be therefore any consolation in Christ, if any comfort of love, if any fellowship of the Spirit, if any bowels and mercies, **fulfil ye my joy, that ye be likeminded, having the same love, being of one accord, of one mind.***"

Philippians 3:15-16 – "*Let us therefore, as many as be perfect, be thus minded: and if in any thing ye be otherwise minded, God shall reveal even this unto you. **Nevertheless, whereto we have already attained, let us walk by the same rule, let us mind the same thing.***"

In the opening portion of Romans 12:16 we are instructed, "*Be of the same mind one toward another.*" Yet this can never occur if our minds are each set upon self and the things of self. If the mindset of one individual is set upon himself, and if the mindset of another is set upon himself, then they each possess a different mindset. In fact, such a selfish mindset will only result in strifes and divisions among a body of believers. Even so, in 1 Corinthians 1:10 the instruction and warning is given, "*Now I beseech you, brethren, by the name of our Lord Jesus Christ, that ye all speak the same thing, and that there be no divisions among you; but that ye be perfectly joined together in the same mind and in the same judgment.*"

Yet the only way that an entire body of believers can have one mindset is if they all are conformed and governed by one standard mindset. Whose mindset then should be that standard, governing mindset for all of us? In the apostle's prayer of Romans 15:5 for the believers at Rome, we find the answer – "*Now the God of patience and consolation grant you to be likeminded one toward another according to Christ Jesus.*" The will of our Lord Jesus Christ is to be the standard mindset unto which we all are to submit ourselves, by which we all are to be governed, and through which we all may have unity with one another.

Furthermore, it is the excellency of the knowledge (or, fellowship) of Christ Jesus our Lord that is to be the central objective of our unified mindset. In Philippians 3:15-16 the instruction is given, "*Let us therefore, as many as be perfect, be thus minded: and if in any thing ye be otherwise minded, God shall reveal even this unto you. Nevertheless, whereto we have already attained, let us walk by the* same rule, let us mind the same thing." Yet what is that "same rule" by which we all are to walk, and what is that same mindset by which we all are to be thus minded? In Philippians 3:7-14 the apostle has already revealed the answer, saying, "*But what things were gain to me, those I counted loss for Christ. Yea doubtless, and I count all things but loss for the excellency of the knowledge of Christ Jesus my Lord: for whom I have suffered the loss of all things, and do count them but dung, that I may win Christ, and be found in him, not having mine own righteousness, which is of the law, but that which is through the faith of Christ, the righteousness which is of God by faith: that I may know him, and the power of his resurrection, and the fellowship of his sufferings, being made conformable unto his death; if by any means I might attain unto the resurrection of the dead. Not as though I had already attained, either were already perfect: but I follow after, if that I may apprehend that for which also I am apprehended of Christ Jesus. Brethren, I count not myself to have apprehended: but this one thing I do, forgetting those things which are behind, and reaching forth unto those things which are before, I press toward the mark for the prize of the high calling of God in Christ Jesus.*"

Why then does our Lord desire such a unified mindset among us? In the first place, we are to have a unified mindset in order that we might be knit together in our worship of God our heavenly Father. Romans 15:5-6 declares, "*Now the God of patience and consolation grant you to be likeminded one toward another according to Christ Jesus: that ye may with one mind and one mouth glorify God, even the Father of our Lord Jesus Christ.*"

In the second place, we are to have a unified mindset in order that we might advance the gospel of Christ before a spiritually lost world. In John 17:20-23 our Lord Jesus Christ prayed to the Father, saying, "*Neither pray I for these* [the apostles] *alone, but for them also which shall believe on me through their word; that they all may be one; as thou, Father, art in me, and I in thee, that they also may be one in us: that the world may believe that thou hast sent me. And the glory which thou gavest me I have given them; that they may be one, even as we are one: I in them, and thou in me, that they may be made perfect in one; and that the world may know that thou hast sent me, and hast loved them, as thou hast loved me."* Also in Philippians 1:27 the apostle Paul encouraged the believers at Philippi, saying, *"Only let your conversation be as it becometh the gospel of Christ: that whether I come and see you, or else be absent, I may hear of your affairs, that ye stand fast in one spirit, with one mind striving together for the faith of the gospel."*

In the third place, we are to have a unified mindset in order that we might spiritually edify (build up) one another as fellow believers. Ephesians 4:15-16 declares, *"But speaking the truth in love, may grow up into him in all things, which is the head, even Christ: from whom the whole body fitly joined together and compacted by that which every joint supplieth, according to the effectual working in the measure of every part, maketh increase of the body unto the edifying of itself in love."*

In the fourth place, we are to have a unified mindset in order that we might bring joy unto the heart of our Lord and His appointed leaders. In Philippians 2:1-2 the apostle Paul charged the believers at Philippi, saying, *"If there be therefore any consolation in Christ, if any comfort of love, if any fellowship of the Spirit, if any bowels and mercies, fulfil ye my joy, that ye be likeminded, having the same love, being of one accord, of one mind."*

However, we must understand that such unity of mindset for, toward, and with one another in accord with the standard of our Lord's will is not produced through our own determination and ability. Certainly, Ephesians 4:3 indicates that we are to be *"endeavouring to keep the unity of the Spirit in the bond of peace."* Yet that "endeavoring" cannot be in our own strength. Rather, it must be through the power of the Holy Spirit. In Ephesians 4:3 we learn that this unity is *"the unity of the Spirit."* It is not a natural unity that is manufactured by the will of man. Rather, it is a spiritual unity that is produced through us and among us by the power of the Holy Spirit. Thus we understand that it will only be produced through us and among us as we each walk in the Spirit moment by moment. Furthermore, we must understand that such a unity will only be maintained "in the bond of peace." It requires that we maintain a Spirit-filled attitude of peaceableness toward one another.

Indeed, in Philippians 2:2 we are instructed to "*be likeminded,*" to have "*the same love,*" to be "*of one accord,*" and to be "*of one mind.*" Again in Philippians 1:27 we are instructed to stand fast "*in one spirit*" and to strive together for the faith of the gospel "*with one mind.*" Yet again in Philippians 3:16 we are instructed to "*walk by the same rule*" and to "*mind the same thing.*" Finally, in Philippians 4:2 the apostle gave instruction unto two women at the church of Philippi who were in division against each other, saying, "*I beseech Euodias, and beseech Syntyche, that they be of the same mind in the Lord.*" Clearly, our Lord desires that we should abide in loving, Spirit-filled unity with one another.

107. We must not set our focus upon high honors among men, but must willingly abide with the lowly.

Romans 12:16 – "*Be of the same mind one toward another.* ***Mind not high things, but condescend to men of low estate.*** *Be not wise in your own conceits.*"

The word "mind" in this verse refers to our mind set, to the set and focus of our thinking and purpose for life. Thus we are not to set our thinking and focus upon "high things." Furthermore, the "high things" of this verse do not refer unto the "high things" of God. Certainly according Colossians 3:1-2 we are to seek after and to set our focus and affections upon things above. Certainly according to Philippians 3:14 we are to "*press toward the mark for the prize of the high calling of God in Christ Jesus.*" Rather, the "high things" of this verse refer unto the "high things" of this world, that is – to the high honors of this world. The "high things" of this verse refer to the praises of men, or to prestige among men, or to power over men, or to positions of advancement in this world, or to acquisition of more possessions than others, etc. Thus we are commanded by the Lord our God in this passage not to set our thinking and focus upon the high honors of this world.

On the other hand, we are to "*condescend to men of low estate.*" This does not mean that we are to be condescending in our attitude

248

against the lowly. Rather, it means that we ourselves are to descend voluntarily unto the level of the lowly and to abide willingly with the lowly in their lowly position. We are commanded by the Lord our God to abide willingly in the lowly place and to abide in unity with others in the lowly place. Our mindset should never be to disregard or even mistreat the humble and lowly in order that we might advance ourselves unto a higher position. Rather, our mindset should be to honor and fellowship with the humble and lowly while walking in humility ourselves.

108. We must not think highly of, or trust in our own wisdom.

Romans 12:16 – *"Be of the same mind one toward another. Mind not high things, but condescend to men of low estate. **Be not wise in your own conceits**."*

In the closing portion of Romans 12:16 the instruction is given, *"Be not wise in your own conceits."* In like manner, we are instructed in Proverbs 3:5-7, *"Trust in the LORD with all thine heart; and lean not unto thine own understanding. In all thy ways acknowledge him, and he shall direct thy paths. Be not wise in thine own eyes: fear the LORD, and depart from evil."* We must not lean upon our own understanding, but must trust in the direction of the Lord our God. We must not think highly of our own wisdom, but must walk in the fear of the Lord our God. Even so, Proverbs 28:26 gives the warning, *"He that trusteth in his own heart is a fool: but whoso walketh wisely* [that is – not after the wisdom of his own heart, but after the wisdom of God's Word], *he shall be delivered."* Again Proverbs 26:12 gives the warning, *"Seest thou a man wise in his own conceit? There is more hope of a fool than of him."* Yet again Isaiah 5:21 gives the warning, *"Woe unto them that are wise in their own eyes, and prudent in their own sight!"* The fiery judgment of the Lord our God will be poured out upon all such individuals.

109. We must purposefully pursue and perform that which is good, right, true, and honest in the sight of all men.

Romans 12:17 – "*Recompense to no man evil for evil.* **Provide things honest in the sight of all men.**"

Galatians 6:10 – "**As we have therefore opportunity, let us do good unto all men, especially unto them who are of the household of faith.**"

1 Thessalonians 5:15 – "*See that none render evil for evil unto any man;* **but ever follow that which is good, both among yourselves, and to all men.**"

Titus 3:1 – "*Put them in mind to be subject to principalities and powers, to obey magistrates,* **to be ready to every good work.**"

Titus 3:8 – "*This is a faithful saying, and these things I will that thou affirm constantly,* **that they which have believed in God might be careful to maintain good works.** *These things are good and profitable unto men.*"

Titus 3:14 – "**And let ours also learn to maintain good works for necessary uses,** *that they be not unfruitful.*"

1 Peter 2:11-12 – "*Dearly beloved, I beseech you as strangers and pilgrims, abstain from fleshly lusts, which war against the soul;* **having your conversation honest among the Gentiles**: *that, whereas they speak against you as evildoers, they may by your good works, which they shall behold, glorify God in the day of visitation.*"

1 Peter 2:17 – "**Honour all men.** *Love the brotherhood. Fear God. Honour the king.*"

1 Peter 3:11 – "*Let him eschew evil,* **and do good**; *let him seek peace, and ensue it.*"

In all that we do we must pursue and perform that which is good, right, true, and honest, not only in our dealings with the Lord our God, but also in all of our dealings with all men. We must "*provide things honest in the sight of all men.*" We must "ever follow that which is good," must "*be ready to every good work,*" must "*do good unto all men,*" especially unto those who are our fellow believers. Indeed, we must "learn to maintain good works for necessary uses," in order that we not be spiritually unfruitful. On the other hand, there must be no hypocrisies, no deceptions, no dishonesty, no cheating, no unkindness, no harshness, no mistreatment, no selfishness in our dealings with others. This we must do for the testimony and glory of our Lord's name.

Specifically as we interact with the lost world around us, we must maintain a godly testimony by interacting toward every single individual with honesty, integrity, morality, honor, and godliness, not with dishonesty, hypocrisy, immorality, dishonor, and selfishness. We must especially maintain such a godly testimony as we engage with individuals who are hostile toward the Lord, toward His Word, toward His way of righteousness, and toward us as His servants. Indeed, it is specifically through such a godly testimony of our right and good dealings with them that lost souls, including even some who speak with hostility and hatred against us, might be influenced to repent of their sins and to receive the Lord as Savior.

110. We must submit ourselves unto our government authority.

Romans 13:1-5 – "*Let every soul be subject unto the higher powers. For there is no power but of God: the powers that be are ordained of God. Whosoever therefore resisteth the power, resisteth the ordinance of God: and they that resist shall receive to themselves damnation. For rulers are not a terror to good works, but to the evil. Wilt thou then not be afraid of the power? Do that which is good, and thou shalt have praise of the same: for he is the minister of God to thee for good. But if thou do that which is evil, be afraid; for he beareth not the sword in vain: for he is the minister of God, a revenger to execute wrath upon him that doeth evil. Wherefore ye must needs be subject, not only for wrath, but also for conscience sake.*"

Titus 3:1 – *"**Put them in mind to be subject to principalities and powers, to obey magistrates**, to be ready to every good work."*

1 Peter 2:13-17 – *"**Submit yourselves to every ordinance of man for the Lord's sake**: whether it be to the king, as supreme; or unto governors, as unto them that are sent by him for the punishment of evildoers, and for the praise of them that do well. **For so is the will of God**, that with well doing ye may put to silence the ignorance of foolish men: as free, and not using your liberty for a cloke of maliciousness, but as the servants of God. Honour all men. Love the brotherhood. Fear God. **Honour the king**."*

In the opening portion of Romans 13:1, the instruction is given, *"Let every soul be subject unto the higher powers."* Again in the opening portion of 1 Peter 2:13, the instruction is given, *"Submit yourselves to every ordinance of man for the Lord's sake."* Indeed, 1 Peter 2:13-14 proceeds to apply this instruction unto the officials at every level of government. Then throughout Romans 13:1-5 we encounter a two-fold reason for this instruction.

In the first place, we are to submit ourselves unto our government authority because the Lord our God Himself has ordained *the power* of government. Romans 13:1-2 reveals the truth, *"Let every soul be subject unto the higher powers. For there is no power but of God: the powers that be are ordained of God. Whosoever therefore resisteth the power, resisteth the ordinance of God: and they that resist shall receive to themselves damnation."* Every government official of every people, tribe, or nation within this world is in office by the governing hand of the Lord of lords and King of kings. *"He removeth kings, and setteth up kings."* (See Daniel 2:21) He removes government officials, and sets up government officials. He is the most high God. He *"ruleth in the kingdom of men, and giveth it to whomsoever he will."* (See Daniel 4:32) Thus when we resist the government that the Lord our God has personally and purposefully placed over us, we resist the very ordaining will of the Lord our God Himself. Even so, when we resist the government that the Lord our God has placed over us, we bring our Lord's judgment upon us.

In the second place, we are to submit ourselves unto our government authority because the Lord our God Himself has ordained *the principle* of government. In Romans 13:3-4 we read, "*For rulers are not a terror to good works, but to the evil. Wilt thou then not be afraid of the power? Do that which good, and thou shalt have praise of the same: for he is the minister of God to thee for good. But if thou do that which is evil, be afraid; for he beareth not the sword in vain: for he is the minister of God, a revenger to execute wrath upon him that doeth evil.*" The foundational reason and principle for which the Lord our God ordained human government is to execute punishment upon those who do evil within a society, and thereby to protect those who do good. Thus when we proceed to break the laws of the land, we should be afraid of government authority and of its punishing sword. Government authority has been established by the Lord our God as a ministry of the Lord our God, yea as "*a revenger to execute wrath upon him the doeth evil.*"

So then, for the sake of our peace in the land (because government authority is divinely ordained to punish wrong doing) and for the sake of our walk with the Lord (because He Himself has divinely ordained the government authority over us), we must submit ourselves unto our government authority. Even so, Romans 13:5 declares, "*Wherefore ye must needs be subject, not only for wrath* [our peace in the land]*, but also for conscience sake* [our walk with the Lord]."

Yet there are some times when disobedience unto the laws of the land are appropriate and necessary before God. Such times occur when the government authority commands us to do something that the Lord our God through His Word specifically forbids, or when the government authority forbids us to do something that the Lord our God through His Word specifically commands. In the opening portion of 1 Peter 2:13, we are instructed to submit ourselves unto governmental authority "*for the Lord's sake.*" On the one hand, this means that we are to submit ourselves unto governmental authority out of a good testimony for our Lord. On the other hand, this means that we are not to submit ourselves when we are instructed directly to disobey the Lord; for such disobedience would certainly not be "for our Lord's sake." At such times the principle that the apostle

Peter and the other apostles followed in Acts 5:29 must apply – *"We ought to obey God rather than men."* However, this principle only applies at those times when a law of the land contradicts a specific command of God's Holy Word. It does not apply when we ourselves simply think that the law is unreasonable or overly invasive of our personal freedoms.

Yet what if we might claim that as believers we are the children of God and the citizens of heaven and should not then have to obey earthly authorities? In answer to this wrong and ungodly attitude, 1 Peter 2:16 indicates that we are not to use our spiritual freedom *"as a cloak of maliciousness"* against earthly authorities or against people around us. In addition, 1 Peter 2:16 reminds us that our spiritual freedom does not grant us the authority to do our own will because we are still *"the servants of God."* So then, what is the will of God in this matter? 1 Peter 2:15 gives answer, *"For so is the will of God, that with well doing ye may put to silence the ignorance of foolish men."* Indeed, the testimony of our Lord's name is bound up with our submission unto government authority.

---

111. We must render unto our government authority what is due unto them in tribute, custom, respect, and honor.

Romans 13:6-7 – *"For for this cause pay ye tribute also: for they are God's ministers, attending continually upon this very thing. **Render therefore to all their dues: tribute to whom tribute is due; custom to whom custom; fear to whom fear; honour to whom honour.**"*

We are required by the Lord our God to pay our taxes faithfully and to demonstrate respect toward our government officials. This does not mean that we must agree with every decision that they make. It also does not mean that we should bow down in worship of any government official; for such worship is not the rightful due of any man, but only of God. Yet it does mean that we must ever maintain a respectful and honoring attitude toward our government officials, and it does mean that we must ever give unto them the customary respects and honors that are due them by their position.

112. We must cast off all the works of our sinful flesh.

Romans 13:11-13 – *"And that, knowing the time, that now it is high time to awake out of sleep* [that is – to be awake out of our spiritual lethargy and to walk in the zeal of revived Christian living]*: for now is our salvation nearer than when we believed* [not the possession of our salvation, which we have at the very moment of our faith in Christ for salvation, but the full experience of our salvation in eternal glory]. *The night is far spent* [the time of this present evil age], *the day is at hand* [the day of our Lord's return]*: **let us therefore cast off the works of darkness**, and let us put on the armour of light. Let us walk honestly, as in the day; **not in rioting and drunkenness, not in chambering and wantonness, not in strife and envying**."*

Ephesians 4:22 – *"**That ye put off concerning the former conversation the old man, which is corrupt according to the deceitful lusts**."*

Ephesians 4:25 – *"**Wherefore putting away lying**, speak every man truth with his neighbour: for we are members one of another."*

Ephesians 4:31 – *"**Let all bitterness, and wrath, and anger, and clamour, and evil speaking, be put away from you, with all malice**."*

Ephesians 5:3-4 – *"**But fornication, and all uncleanness, or covetousness, let it not be once named among you, as becometh saints; neither filthiness, nor foolish talking, nor jesting**, which are not convenient: but rather giving of thanks."*

Colossians 3:5-10 – *"**Mortify therefore your members which are upon the earth; fornication, uncleanness, inordinate affection, evil concupiscence, and covetousness, which is idolatry**: for which things' sake the wrath of God cometh on the children of disobedience: in the which ye also walked some time, when ye lived in them. **But now ye also put off all these; anger, wrath, malice, blasphemy, filthy communication out of your mouth. Lie not one to another**, seeing that ye have put off the old man with his deeds; and have put on the new man, which is renewed in knowledge after the image of him that created him."*

Titus 2:11-12 – "*For the grace of God that bringeth salvation hath appeared to all men, **teaching us that, denying ungodliness and worldly lusts**, we should live soberly, righteously, and godly, in this present world.*"

Hebrews 12:1 – "*Wherefore seeing we also are compassed about with so great a cloud of witnesses, **let us lay aside every weight, and the sin which doth so easily beset us**, and let us run with patience the race that is set before us.*"

Hebrews 12:15-16 – "***Looking diligently lest any man fail of the grace of God; lest any root of bitterness springing up trouble you**, and thereby many be defiled; **lest there be any fornicator, or profane person**, as Esau, who for one morsel of meat sold his birthright.*"

James 1:21 – "***Wherefore lay apart all filthiness and superfluity of naughtiness**, and receive with meekness the engrafted word, which is able to save your souls.*"

1 Peter 2:1 – "***Wherefore laying aside all malice, and all guile, and hypocrisies, and envies, and all evil speakings.***"

1 Peter 2:11 – "*Dearly beloved, I beseech you as strangers and pilgrims, **abstain from fleshly lusts, which war against the soul**.*"

In Romans 13:12 we believers are instructed to "*cast off the works of darkness.*" These works of darkness are the works of sinfulness. They are the works that spring forth out of our sinful flesh. These works of darkness, these sinful, fleshly works in whatever form, must be put off from our lives and cast away. So then, what are these works of our sinful flesh that we are to cast off?

Romans 13:13 reveals the answer, saying, "*Let us walk honestly, as in the day; not in rioting and drunkenness, not in chambering and wantonness* [lustfulness], *not in strife and envying.*" Again Galatians 5:19-21 reveals the answer, saying, "*Now the works of the flesh are manifest, which are these; Adultery, fornication, uncleanness, lasciviousness* [lustfulness], *idolatry, witchcraft, hatred, variance* [contentiousness], *emulations* [jealousy], *wrath, strife, seditions* [divisiveness], *heresies, envyings, murders, drunkenness, revellings, and such like: of the which I tell you before, as I have also told you in time past, that they which do such things shall not inherit the kingdom of God.*" In addition, the opening line of Ephesians 4:25 gives the instruction, "*Wherefore putting away lying;*" and Ephesians 4:31 adds, "*Let all bitterness, and wrath, and anger, and clamour* [speaking complaint against others], *and evil speaking* [speaking harshness against others], *be put away from you, with all malice.*" Again Ephesians 5:3-4 gives the instruction, "*But fornication, and all uncleanness, or covetousness, let it not be once named among you, as becometh saints; neither filthiness* [shameful behavior], *nor foolish talking, nor jesting* [biting or vulgar humor], *which are not convenient: but rather giving of thanks.*"

Yet again Colossians 3:5 gives the instruction, "*Mortify therefore your members which are upon the earth; fornication, uncleanness, inordinate affection* [unrestrained passion], *evil concupiscence* [evil lusts], *and covetousness, which is idolatry;*" and Colossians 3:8-9 adds, "*But now ye also put off all these; anger, wrath, malice, blasphemy, filthy communication out of your mouth. Lie not one to another, seeing that ye have put off the old man with his deeds.*" Yet again Hebrews 12:15-16 gives the instruction and warning, "*Looking diligently lest any man fail of the grace of God; lest any root of bitterness springing up trouble you, and thereby many be defiled; lest there be any fornicator, or profane* [worldly minded] *person, as Esau, who for one morsel of meat sold his birthright.*" Finally, 1 Peter 2:1 gives the instruction, "*Wherefore laying aside all malice, and all guile, and hypocrisies, and envies, and all evil speakings.*"

As the children of God, we are no longer to walk in the old, sinful ways of our old, sinful flesh. According to Ephesians 4:22 these ways are corrupt ways, corrupted by the deceitful lusts of our selfish, sinful flesh. Such behavior brings down the wrath of God upon the children of darkness, and such behavior is not appropriate for the children of God. Our Lord Jesus Christ died to save us from these old, corrupt ways. Before our salvation we were the children of darkness; now we are the children of light. (See Ephesians 5:8) Thus we are to walk as the children of light, not like the children of darkness.

Our old, sinful spirit has been put off from us. It has been spiritually crucified with Christ. (See Romans 6:6) We are no longer to walk in the old, corrupt, sinful deeds of that old man. A new spirit, which is created after God's image *"in righteousness and true holiness,"* has been put within us. (See Ephesians 4:24) We have been raised up spiritually to walk in newness of spiritual life. (See Romans 6:4) Now, through faith in our Lord for our daily walk, we are to put off the old, corrupt ways of our sinful flesh from our daily character and conduct. We are no longer to live in these old, corrupt ways of selfish, sinful lusts.

Even so, in Hebrews 12:1 we are instructed to lay aside (to cast off) two categories of spiritual hindrance in our lives. First, we are to lay aside any weight of this world that might slow down and hinder our growth forward in our fellowship with the Lord and in our service for the Lord. Such weights of this world may not be inherently sinful in themselves, but they serve as a spiritual hindrance to us. Anything of this world that hinders our spiritual growth should be cast aside from our lives. Second, we are lay aside whatever sin that so easily besets us, to which we find ourselves so easily yielding in temptation. Such besetting sins must be specifically, fervently, and daily targeted in our spiritual warfare against sin and our sinful flesh. Indeed, as we daily deny ourselves in order to serve our Lord, we must specifically, fervently, and daily deny the desires of our sinful flesh concerning these besetting sins, whatever they may be for each one of us.

Therefore, in the opening portion of James 1:21, we are instructed, *"Wherefore lay apart all filthiness and superfluity of naughtiness."* Indeed, we must put apart from ourselves, through confessing and forsaking, any spiritual filthiness that is in our character. In addition, we must put apart from ourselves, through confessing and forsaking, any spiritual naughtiness that is in our conduct through the overflowing of the spiritual filthiness in our character. Yea, all of the characteristics of our sinful flesh must be cut off and cast away through broken-hearted confession and whole-hearted forsaking. In fact, according to the flow of thought in James 1:21 and 1 Peter 2:1-2, this is a necessary part of preparing and motivating our hearts to receive the truth of God's Word. On the other hand, when our hearts are filled with the lusts and corruptions of our sinful flesh, our hearts will be dull toward the truth of God's Holy Word. Also according to 1 Peter 2:11 the selfish lusts of our selfish flesh engage in a war against the spiritual character of our souls. Therefore, if we intend to maintain and grow in godliness, holiness, and righteousness of character, then we must deny and abstain from the selfish lusts that rise up within our hearts from our own sinful flesh.

113. We must put on the spiritual armor of righteousness.

Romans 13:12 – "*The night is far spent, the day is at hand: let us therefore cast off the works of darkness, **and let us put on the armour of light**.*"

Ephesians 4:24 – "***And that ye put on the new man, which after God is created in righteousness and true holiness***.*"

Ephesians 6:11 – "***Put on the whole armour of God***, *that ye may be able to stand against the wiles of the devil.*"

Ephesians 6:13-17 – "***Wherefore take unto you the whole armour of God***, *that ye may be able to withstand in the evil day, and having done all, to stand.* **Stand therefore, having your loins girt about with truth, and having on the breastplate of righteousness; and your feet shod with the preparation of the gospel of peace; above all, taking the shield of faith**, *wherewith ye shall be able to quench all the fiery darts of the wicked.* **And take the helmet of salvation, and the sword of the Spirit, which is the word of God**.*"

1 Thessalonians 5:7-8 – "*For they that sleep sleep in the night; and they that be drunken are drunken in the night. But let us, who are of the day, be sober, **putting on the breastplate of faith and love; and for an helmet, the hope of salvation**.*"

In Ephesians 4:24 we are instructed to put off the old, corrupt ways of our sinful flesh, and in their place to put on the new, righteous ways of the Lord our God. In Christ Jesus our Lord and Savior, we are made new spiritual creatures; and now we possess within us the very nature of our Lord God's own righteousness and true holiness. Thus we are instructed to put on that new man, that new nature, in our daily walk. No longer are we to walk in the ways of the old man. Henceforth we are to walk in the ways of the new man, and it is all determined by the spirit of our minds. If we hold onto the old mind-set of the flesh, then we walk in the old, corrupt ways of the old man. Yet if we give up the old mind-set of the flesh and take up the new mind-set of the Spirit instead, then we walk in the new, righteous ways of the new man.

Even so, in Romans 13:12 we are instructed to "put on the armour of light." This armor of light is the spiritual means by which we may stand victorious over our sinful flesh and our adversary the devil. It is the spiritual armor that we receive from the Lord our God Himself, and it is mighty through God to give us the spiritual victory. Thus in 2 Corinthians 10:3-5 we are given the assurance, *"For though we walk in the flesh* [in physical bodies]*, we do not war after the flesh: (for the weapons of our warfare are not carnal* [not of the flesh]*, but mighty through God to the pulling down of* [spiritual] *strong holds;) casting down imaginations, and every high thing that exalteth itself against the knowledge of God, and bringing into captivity every thought to the obedience of Christ."* So then, what is this spiritual armor of light (of righteousness) that we have received from God and that is mighty through God?

The answer is revealed in Ephesians 6:13-17 and 1 Thessalonians 5:7-8. In Romans 13:12 a reference is made simply to "the armour;" whereas in Ephesians 6:11 & 13 a reference is made to "the whole armour." As such, the focus of Romans 13:12 is upon the single piece of armor that a Roman soldier would wear upon his body – his breastplate armor. However, the focus of Ephesians 6:13-17 is upon the entire outfit that a Roman soldier would wear, including his belt, breastplate, shoes, helmet, shield, and sword. Even so, Ephesians 6:14-17 provides a descriptive list of these six pieces of our spiritual armor and instructs us to put on this whole armor of God.

In the first place, we are to have *"our loins girt about with* [the belt] *of truth."* This is the foundational element of our spiritual armor.

Yet what is this spiritual belt of truth, and what does it mean to have our loins girt about with it? First, this spiritual belt of truth is our Lord Jesus Christ. In John 14:6 our Lord declared, "*I am the way, the truth, and the life.*" Also Ephesians 4:21 states, "*If so be ye have heard him, and have been taught by him, as the truth is in Jesus.*" Second, this spiritual belt of truth is God's Holy Word. In John 17:17 our Lord Jesus Christ prayed unto the Father concerning His disciples, saying, "*Sanctify them through thy truth: thy word is truth.*" Also in Psalm 119:151 the psalmist declared, "*Thou art near, O LORD; and all thy commandments are truth.*" Third, this spiritual belt is the indwelling Holy Spirit. In 1 John 5:6 God's Word declares, "*This is he that came by water and blood, even Jesus Christ; not by water only, but by water and blood. And it is the Spirit that beareth witness, because the Spirit is truth.*" Also in 1 John 2:27 God's Word declares, "*But the anointing which ye have received of him abideth in you* [that is – the indwelling Holy Spirit]*, and ye need not that any man teach you: but as the same anointing teacheth you of all things, and is truth, and is no lie, and even as it hath taught you, ye shall abide in him.*" So then, to have our loins girt about with this spiritual belt of truth means to have our heart rooted in fellowship with our Lord Jesus Christ, in obedience to God's Holy Word, and in submission to the indwelling Holy Spirit.

In the second place, we are to have on "*the breastplate of righteousness.*" This piece of our spiritual armor is directly connected to the spiritual belt of truth. As we have seen, Romans 13:12 speaks of this breastplate armor, saying, "*The night is far spent, the day is at hand: let us therefore cast off the works of darkness, and let us put on the armour of light.*" Then the opening portion of Romans 13:14 reveals a definition for this spiritual "armour of light" when it gives the instruction, "*But put ye on the Lord Jesus Christ.*" Furthermore, the opening portion of 1 Thessalonians 5:8 speaks of this breastplate, saying, "*But let us, who are of the day, be sober, putting on the breastplate of faith and love.*" Now, this breastplate of righteousness exists because of the eternal righteousness that we have in Christ Jesus our Savior. Even so, Romans 3:21-22 declares, "*But now the righteousness of God without the law is manifested, being witnessed by the law and the prophets; even the righteousness of God which is by faith of Jesus Christ unto all and upon all them that believe:*

for there is no difference." Again 2 Corinthians 5:21 proclaims, "*For he* [God the Father] *hath made him* [God the Son] *to be sin for us, who knew no sin; that we might be made the righteousness of God in him.*" Yet this breastplate of righteousness, of faith in and love for our Lord, must be put on in our daily Christian walk through three interrelated responsibilities. First, we must put on our Lord Jesus Christ through daily abiding and trusting in Him. (See Romans 13:14; 1 Thessalonians 5:8) Second, we must walk in Biblical love for our Lord through faithful obedience to Him. (See 1 Thessalonians 5:8). Third, we must cast off and reject the lusts and works of our sinful flesh. (See Romans 13:12-14) Even so, this breastplate of righteousness, of faith in and love for our Lord, is given to us for the protection of our hearts. As we maintain our trust in the Lord with full assurance and our love for the Lord through faithful obedience, our hearts shall be protected from spiritual corruption.

In the third place, we are to have our "*feet shod with the preparation of the gospel of peace.*" This piece of our spiritual armor reveals the foundation upon which we stand and the truth for which we stand. As believers, our faith in "the gospel of peace," the gospel of Jesus Christ our Lord and Savior, is our only foundation for the assurance of eternal life with God in heaven and for the experience of godly living in our daily walk. Therefore, we must ever prepare ourselves to stand on that ground against the devil's attacks. Yet there is more. The gospel of peace, the gospel of Jesus Christ our Lord and Savior, is not only the truth for our foundation, but is also the truth for our proclamation. Even so, Romans 10:8-15 proclaims, "*But what saith it? The word is nigh thee, even in thy mouth, and in thy heart: that is, the word of faith, which we preach; that if thou shalt confess with thy mouth the Lord Jesus, and shalt believe in thine heart that God hath raised him from the dead, thou shalt be saved. For with the heart man believeth unto righteousness; and with the mouth confession is made unto salvation. For the Scripture saith, Whosoever believeth on him shall not be ashamed. For there is no difference between the Jew and the Greek: for the same Lord over all is rich unto all that call upon him. For whosoever shall call upon the name of the Lord shall be saved. How then shall they call on him in whom they have not believed? And how shall they believe in him of whom they have not heard? And how shall they* hear without a preacher? And how shall they preach, except they be sent? As it is written, How beautiful are the feet of them that preach the gospel of peace, and bring glad tidings of good things!"* Indeed, our feet must be prepared every day to go and preach the gospel unto this spiritually lost world.

In the fourth place, we are to take up *"the shield of faith, whereby* [we] *shall be able to quench all the fiery darts of the wicked."* This piece of our spiritual armor represents our daily heart-trust in our Lord's almighty strength, everlasting mercy, all-sufficient grace, tender love, and unfailing faithfulness toward us who are His own dear children. Even so, Proverbs 30:5 gives the promise, *"Every word of God is pure: he is a shield unto them that put their trust in him."* He alone is our hope and shield for this life. We must set all of our faith, trust, dependence, and hope in Him for every step of our daily Christian walk. Then we shall find that this shield of faith in our Lord is an absolutely perfect protection. When we have taken up this shield of heart-trust in our Lord, *all* the fiery darts of our wicked adversary the devil will be quenched. Without this shield of faith we will be pierced through and burned deeply. Yet behind this shield of heart-trust in our Lord, we will not even be pricked by a single dart or singed by a single flame. Yea, in Psalm 28:7 David gave the testimony, *"The LORD is my strength and my shield; my heart trusted in him, and I am helped: therefore my heart greatly rejoiceth; and with my song will I praise him."* Again in Psalm 33:20-22 the psalmist declared, *"Our soul waiteth for the LORD: he is our help and our shield. For our heart shall rejoice in him, because we have trusted in his holy name. Let thy mercy, O LORD, be upon us, according as we hope in thee."* Yet again in Psalm 84:11-12 the psalmist proclaimed, *"For the LORD God is a sun and shield: the LORD will give grace and glory: no good thing will he withhold from them that walk uprightly. O LORD of hosts, blessed is the man that trusteth in thee."*

In the fifth place, we are to *"take the helmet of salvation."* This piece of our armor represents our assurance of eternal life with God in heaven. Even so, 1 Thessalonians 5:8-10 gives the instruction and the promise, *"But let us, who are of the day, be sober, putting on the breastplate of faith and love; and for an helmet, the hope of salvation.*

For God hath not appointed us to wrath, but to obtain salvation by our Lord Jesus Christ, who died for us, that, whether we wake or sleep, we should live together with him." Herein this helmet of salvation is described as the helmet of "the hope of salvation." In addition, this hope of salvation is further defined as that future time when we who are saved through faith in Christ shall "live together with him." This hope, this certain assurance, flows out of the context of 1 Thessalonians 4:13-18 and is founded upon the promise of the rapture that is given therein. Thus we read, *"But I would not have you to be ignorant, brethren, concerning them which are asleep, that ye sorrow not, even as others which have no hope. For if we believe that Jesus died and rose again, even so them also which sleep in Jesus will God bring with him. For this we say unto you by the word of the Lord, that we which are alive and remain unto the coming of the Lord shall not prevent* [precede] *them which are asleep. For the Lord himself shall descend from heaven with a shout, with the voice of the archangel, and with the trump of God: and the dead in Christ shall rise first: then we which are alive and remain shall be caught up together with them in the clouds, to meet the Lord in the air: and so shall we ever be with the Lord. Wherefore comfort one another with these words."*

In like manner, our Lord Jesus Christ proclaimed in John 6:39-40, *"And this is the Father's will which hath sent me, that of all which he hath given me I should lose nothing, but should raise it up again at the last day. And this is the will of him that sent me, that every one which seeth the Son, and believeth on him, may have everlasting life: and I will raise him up at the last day."* Again in John 14:1-3 our Lord Jesus Christ gave the assurance, *"Let not your heart be troubled: ye believe in God, believe also in me. In my Father's house are many mansions: if it were not so, I would have told you. I go to prepare a place for you. And if I go and prepare a place for you, I will come again, and receive you unto myself; that where I am, there ye may be also."* Yet again in 1 John 3:1-2 the assurance is given, *"Behold, what manner of love the Father hath bestowed upon us, that we should be called the sons of God: therefore the world knoweth us not, because it knew him not. Beloved, now are we the sons of God, and it doth not yet appear what we shall be: but we know that, when he shall appear, we shall be like him; for we shall see him as he is.*" Every day of our Christian walk upon this earth, we must take up the helmet of the hope of our eternal salvation, the hope that we shall ever live with our Lord in glory. Even so, this helmet of the hope of our salvation is given to us for the protection of our minds. As we maintain our hope in our Lord's Second Coming, our minds shall be protected from the discouragements of this life.

In the sixth place, we are to take up *"the sword of the Spirit, which is the word of God."* Among the pieces of our spiritual armor, this is the one and only piece of attack. All of the other pieces are for our defense from the wiles, attacks, and fiery darts of our wicked adversary, the devil. However, this sword of the Spirit is our weapon of attack against our wicked adversary, the devil; and this sword of the Spirit is the Word of God. Now, this is not a reference unto the truth of God's Word is some general sense. Rather, this is a reference unto pointed thrusts of specific truths from God's Holy Word. Just as our Lord Jesus Christ quoted specifically applicable truths out of God's Holy Word in His defense against the devil's temptation (see Matthew 4:1-11; Luke 4:1-13), even so we also must resist the devil's wiles and drive back the devil's temptations with specific truths from God's Holy Word. The specific truths of God's Holy Word are a sharp, two-edged sword against our adversary the devil. Even so, when we employ these specific truths, this sharp, two-edged sword, under the filling influence of God the Holy Spirit, our adversary the devil will be pierced deeply and will flee from us. Yet this requires that we learn the specific truths of God's Word, that we meditate upon the specific truths of God's Word through each day, and that we govern our thoughts by the specific truths of God's Word.

114. We must walk honestly (honorably) before our Lord and toward others, having a good conscience before God and having a good conversation (behavior) before others.

Romans 13:13 – *"**Let us walk honestly, as in the day**; not in rioting and drunkenness, not in chambering and wantonness, not in strife and envying."*

1 Peter 3:16-17 – "***Having a good conscience****; that, whereas they speak evil of you, as of evildoers, they may be ashamed that falsely accuse your good conversation in Christ. For it is better, if the will of God be so, that ye suffer for well doing, than for evil doing.*"

The English word "honestly" finds its roots in the word "honorably." In this passage we are commanded to "*walk honestly, as in the day.*" This means that in our daily lives we are to walk in a manner that is honorable before the Lord our God and that is honorable toward those around us. We are to live and walk every day in a manner that is upright, just, fair, unselfish, sincere, decent, pure, and honorable. We are to live and walk every day in a manner that is honest rather than deceitful or hypocritical. We are to live and walk every day in a manner that is upright rather than worldly and unruly (as revealed in the truth that we are not to walk "in rioting and drunkenness"). We are to live and walk every day in a manner that is pure rather than corrupt and immoral (as revealed in the truth that we are not to walk "in chambering and wantonness"). We are to live and walk every day in a manner that is peaceable rather than selfish and contentious (as revealed in the truth that we are not to walk "in strife and envying"). Every day we are to cast off the works of our sinful flesh and to put on the armor of our Lord's righteousness in order that we might walk throughout each day in a manner that is honorable before our Lord and toward others.

115. We must not make any provision for the flesh to fulfill its sinful lusts.

Romans 13:14 – "*But put ye on the Lord Jesus Christ, **and make not provision for the flesh, to fulfil the lusts thereof.***"

We are not simply to cast off the sinful works of darkness through repentance and confession after we commit them. We must also learn to cast off the sinful works of darkness through righteousness and uprightness before we commit them. Too often we foolishly or purposefully make provision to fulfill the sinful lusts of our flesh. We do so foolishly when we are not vigilant to establish and follow spiritual boundaries in our lives that may guard our hearts and lives from those sinful lusts. We do so purposefully when meditate upon the pleasures of a particular sin until we plan ahead, provide the tools, and prepare the way to fulfill the sinful lusts of our flesh. Thereby we fail to purposefully put on our Lord Jesus Christ and to starve out our sinful flesh. Rather, we allowed our sinful flesh to be provisioned. Even so, the more that we provision our sinful flesh, the stronger it will grow in our daily living. Now, so much of this begins with the thoughts of our hearts. Thus in Proverbs 4:23 we are instructed, *"Keep thy heart with all diligence; for out of it are the issues of life."* Furthermore, in 2 Corinthians 10:5 we learn that we must be *"casting down imaginations, and every high thing that exalteth itself against the knowledge* [fellowship] *of God, and bringing into captivity **every thought** to the obedience of Christ."*

116. We must not be judgmental toward others over questionable matters.

Romans 14:1-4 – *"Him that is weak in the faith receive ye, but not to doubtful disputations. For one believeth that he may eat all things: another, who is weak, eateth herbs. **Let not him that eateth despise him that eateth not; and let not him which eateth not judge him that eateth: for God hath received him.** Who art thou that judgest another man's servant? To his own master he standeth or falleth. Yea, he shall be holden up: for God is able to make him stand."*

In various areas of our lives, matters of question arise concerning a good and right standard of behavior. At the time in which the apostle Paul wrote this passage to the believers at Rome, some were disputing over whether a believer could or could not eat meat or whether a believer should or should not become a strict vegetarian. Concerning such a matter, God the Holy Spirit inspired the apostle to instruct these believers that they should not be judgmental of one another over such a thing. The one who believed that eating meat was acceptable was not to despise the one who believed that he must be a vegetarian, and the one who believed that he must be a vegetarian was not to judge the one who believed that eating meat was acceptable.

In like manner, we have matters of question in our time. In the matter of recreation, some question whether reading secular fiction or watching any television is or is not acceptable. In the matter of sports, some question whether boxing, hockey, or football is or is not acceptable because of their violent nature. In the matter of game playing, some question whether it is or is not acceptable for a believer to play pool or to play card games. In the matter of attire, some question whether it is or is not acceptable for women to "do their hair" or to have pierced ears. In the matter of holidays, some question whether it is or is not acceptable to celebrate Christmas or to go "trick-or-treating" on Halloween. And the questions continue. To all such "doubtful disputations" the instruction of God's Word is that we not be judgmental against one another. It is not our place to judge one another as brothers and sisters in Christ. Rather, it is our Lord's place to judge His own. Thus Romans 14:10-12 declares, *"But why dost thou judge thy brother? Or why dost thou set at nought thy brother? For we shall all stand before the judgment seat of Christ. For it is written, As I live, saith the Lord, every knee shall bow to me, and every tongue shall confess to God. So then every one of us shall give account of himself to God."*

117. We must each have full faith before the Lord concerning a questionable matter.

Romans 14:5-9 – *"One man esteemeth one day above another: another esteemeth every day alike. **Let every man be fully persuaded in his own mind.** He that regardeth the day, regardeth it unto the Lord; and he that regardeth not the day, to the Lord he doth not regard it. He that eateth, eateth to the Lord, for he giveth God thanks; and he that eateth not, to the Lord he eateth not, and giveth God thanks. For none of us liveth to himself, and no man dieth to himself. For whether we live, we live unto the Lord; and whether* *we die, we die unto the Lord: whether we live therefore, or die, we are the Lord's. For to this end Christ both died, and rose, and revived, that he might be Lord both of the dead and living."*

Romans 14:22-23 – "**Hast thou faith? Have it to thyself before God**. *Happy is he that condemneth not himself in that thing which he alloweth. And he that doubteth is damned if he eat, because he eateth not of faith: for whatsoever is not of faith is sin."*

If there is any doubt in your own heart and mind concerning a questionable matter, then that particular matter is forbidden to you. You yourself must not participate therein. If you have any doubt, then you would have to participate without faith before the Lord; and "whatsoever is not of faith is sin." By participating you would bring down our Lord's chastening hand against yourself.

118. We must never cause "a stumblingblock or an occasion to fall" for a fellow believer by participating in a questionable matter.

Romans 14:13-21 – *"Let us not therefore judge one another any more: **but judge this rather, that no man put a stumblingblock or an occasion to fall in his brother's way**. I know, and am persuaded by the Lord Jesus, that there is nothing unclean of itself: but to him that esteemeth any thing to be unclean, to him it is unclean. But if thy brother be grieved with thy meat, now walkest thou not charitably. **Destroy not him with thy meat, for whom Christ died. Let not then your good be evil spoken of**: for the kingdom of God is not meat and drink; but righteousness, and peace, and joy in the Holy Ghost. For he that in these things serveth Christ is acceptable to God, and approved of men. **Let us therefore follow after the things which make for peace, and things wherewith one may edify another**. **For meat destroy not the work of God**. All things indeed are pure; but it is evil for that man who eateth with offence. **It is good neither to eat flesh, nor to drink wine, nor any thing whereby thy brother stumbleth, or is offended, or is made weak**."*

Romans 15:1 – "***We then that are strong ought to bear the infirmities of the weak, and not to please ourselves.***"

1 Corinthians 8:4-13 – "*As concerning therefore the eating of those things that are offered in sacrifice unto idols, we know that an idol is nothing in the world, and that there is none other God but one. For though there be that are called gods, whether in heaven or in earth, (as there be gods many, and lords many,) but to us there is but one God, the Father, of whom are all things, and we in him; and one Lord Jesus Christ, by whom are all things, and we by him. Howbeit there is not in every man that knowledge: for some with conscience of the idol unto this hour eat it as a thing offered unto an idol; and their conscience being weak is defiled. But meat commendeth us not to God: for neither, if we eat, are we the better; neither, if we eat not, are we the worse. **But take heed lest by any means this liberty of yours become a stumblingblock to them that are weak.** For if any man see thee which hast knowledge sit at meat in the idol's temple, shall not the conscience of him which is weak be emboldened to eat those things which are offered to idols; and through thy knowledge shall the weak brother perish, for whom Christ died? But when ye sin so against the brethren, and wound their weak conscience, ye sin against Christ. Wherefore, if meat make my brother to offend, I will eat no flesh while the world standeth, lest I make my brother to offend.*"

The spiritual progress of our fellow brothers and sisters in Christ must always be more important to us than our personal enjoyment of some questionable matter. This is the primary principle that should govern our behavior in such things – We must never cause a spiritual stumblingblock or an occasion to fall for a fellow believer by our behavior. Such would destroy that fellow believer's walk with God. Such would destroy the work of God in that fellow believer's life. Such would be evil in the sight of the Lord our God. It is far better to give up our enjoyment completely than to destroy a fellow believer spiritually. Thus Romans 15:1 gives the instruction, "*We then that are strong ought to bear the infirmities of the weak, and not to please ourselves.*"

119. We must ever pursue the spiritual edification of our fellow believers.

Romans 14:19 – "***Let us therefore follow after*** *the things which make for peace, and **things wherewith one may edify another**.*"

Romans 15:1-3 – "***We then that are strong ought to bear the infirmities of the weak, and not to please ourselves. Let every one of us please his neighbour for his good to edification.*** *For even Christ pleased not himself; but, as it is written, The reproaches of them that reproached thee fell on me.*"

1 Corinthians 10:23-24 – "*All things are lawful for me, but all things are not expedient: all things are lawful for me, but all things edify not.* ***Let no man seek his own, but every man another's wealth***.*"

Our Lord and Savior Jesus Christ is our example. He sacrificed His own pleasure for our salvation, and now we are to walk in His steps. We are to sacrifice our own pleasure for the spiritual edification of our fellow believers.

120. We must receive one another as fellow believers with an attitude of godly love and unity.

Romans 15:7 – "***Wherefore receive ye one another***, *as Christ also received us to the glory of God.*"

Romans 16:1-2 – "*I commend unto you Phebe our sister, which is a servant of the church which is at Cenchrea:* ***that ye receive her in the Lord, as becometh saints, and that ye assist her in whatsoever business she hath need of you***: *for she hath been a succourer of many, and of myself also.*"

Romans 16:16 – "***Salute one another with an holy kiss***. *The churches of Christ salute you.*"

2 Corinthians 13:12-13 – "***Greet one another with an holy kiss.*** *All the saints salute you.*"

Philippians 4:21 – "***Salute every saint in Christ Jesus.*** *The brethren which are with me greet you.*"

Colossians 4:15 – "***Salute the brethren which are in Laodicea, and Nymphas, and the church which is in his house.***"

1 Thessalonians 5:26 – "***Greet all the brethren with an holy kiss.***"

2 Timothy 4:19 – "***Salute Prisca and Aquila, and the household of Onesiphorus.***"

Titus 3:15 – "*All that are with me salute thee.* ***Greet them that love us in the faith.*** *Grace be with you all. Amen.*"

Hebrews 13:24 – "***Salute all them that have the rule over you, and all the saints.*** *They of Italy salute you.*"

1 Peter 5:14 – "***Greet ye one another with a kiss of charity.*** *Peace be with you all that are in Christ Jesus. Amen.*"

3 John 1:5-8 – "*Beloved, thou doest faithfully whatsoever thou doest to the brethren, and to strangers; which have borne witness of thy charity before the church: whom if thou bring forward on their journey after a godly sort, thou shalt do well: because that for his name's sake they went forth, taking nothing of the Gentiles.* ***We therefore ought to receive such, that we might be fellowhelpers to the truth.***"

3 John 1:14 – "*But I trust I shall shortly see thee, and we shall speak face to face. Peace be to thee. Our friends salute thee.* ***Greet the friends by name.***"

We are to receive one another as fellow believers in Christ and as fellow servants of Christ. Indeed, we are to do so with an attitude of spiritual, godly, holy like-mindedness through Christ and for Christ. We are not to avoid one another, but to receive one another with kindness and love. We are not to reject one another, but to rejoice in one another's ministry for our Lord. We are not to strive with one another, but to assist one another in serving the Lord.

~~~~~~~

121. We must fervently and faithfully pray for those who minister in the work of the Lord.

Romans 15:30-32 – "*Now I beseech you, brethren, for the Lord Jesus Christ's sake, and for the love of the Spirit, **that ye strive together with me in your prayers to God for me**; that I may be delivered from them that do not believe in Judaea; and that my service which I have for Jerusalem may be accepted of the saints; that I may come unto you with joy by the will of God, and may with you be refreshed.*"

Ephesians 6:18-20 – "***Praying always with all prayer and supplication in the Spirit, and watching thereunto with all perseverance and supplication for all saints; and for me**, that utterance may be given unto me, that I may open my mouth boldly, to make known the mystery of the gospel, for which I am an ambassador in bonds: that therein I may speak boldly, as I ought to speak.*"

Colossians 4:3-4 – "***Withal praying also for us**, that God would open unto us a door of utterance, to speak the mystery of Christ, for which I am also in bonds: that I may make it manifest, as I ought to speak.*"

1 Thessalonians 5:25 – "***Brethren, pray for us.***"

2 Thessalonians 3:1-2 – "***Finally, brethren, pray for us**, that the word of the Lord may have free course, and be glorified, even as it is with you: and that we may be delivered from unreasonable and wicked men: for all men have not faith.*"

Hebrews 13:18-19 – "***Pray for us**: for we trust we have a good conscience, in all things willing to live honestly. But I beseech you the rather to do this, that I may be restored to you the sooner.*"

The central reason for our fervent and faithful prayers on the behalf of those who minister in the work of the Lord is for our Lord Jesus Christ's sake, that His name and His truth and His kingdom may be advanced. Thus we are to pray for the success of their ministry for the Lord, that is – that they may be delivered from those who would resist their ministry, that they would make progress in the efforts of their ministry, and that they might be refreshed in the fellowship of the ministry. In addition, we are to pray for them that they may have spiritual boldness in proclaiming the truth of God's Word. In the third place, we are to pray for them that they might have an open door of utterance in proclaiming the truth of God's Word. Finally, we are to pray for them that the Word of God might have free course and be glorified through their ministry.

122. We must mark and avoid those who "cause divisions and offenses" that are contrary to the truth of God's Word.

Romans 16:17-18 – "***Now I beseech you, brethren, mark them which cause divisions and offences contrary to the doctrine which ye have learned; and avoid them.*** *For they that are such serve not our Lord Jesus Christ, but their own belly; and by good words and fair speeches deceive the hearts of the simple.*"

1 Timothy 6:3-5 – "*If any man teach otherwise, and consent not to wholesome words, even the words of our Lord Jesus Christ, and to the doctrine which is according to godliness; he is proud, knowing nothing, but doting about questions and strifes of words, whereof cometh envy, strife, railings, evil surmisings, perverse disputings of men of corrupt minds, and destitute of the truth, supposing that gain is godliness:* ***from such withdraw thyself.***"

2 Timothy 3:1-9 – "*This know also, that in the last days perilous times shall come. For men shall be lovers of their own selves, covetous, boasters, proud, blasphemers, disobedient to parents, unthankful, unholy, without natural affection, trucebreakers, false accusers, incontinent, fierce, despisers of those that are good, traitors, heady, highminded, lovers of pleasures more than lovers of God; having a*

*form of godliness, but denying the power thereof: **from such turn away**. For of this sort are they which creep into houses, and lead captive silly women laden with sins, led away with divers lusts, ever learning, and never able to come to the knowledge of the truth. Now as Jannes and Jambres withstood Moses, so do these also resist the truth: men of corrupt minds, reprobate concerning the faith. But they shall proceed no further: for their folly shall be manifest unto all men, as theirs also was."*

2 Timothy 4:14-15 – *"Alexander the coppersmith did me much evil: the Lord reward him according to his works: **of whom be thou ware also**; for he hath greatly withstood our words."*

Titus 3:10-11 – *"**A man that is an heretick after the first and second admonition reject**; knowing that he that is such is subverted, and sinneth, being condemned of himself."*

2 John 1:7-11 – *"For many deceivers are entered into the world, who confess not that Jesus Christ is come in the flesh. This is a deceiver and an antichrist. **Look to yourselves, that we lose not those things which we have wrought, but that we receive a full reward**. Whosoever transgresseth, and abideth not in the doctrine of Christ, hath not God. He that abideth in the doctrine of Christ, he hath both the Father and the Son. **If there come any unto you, and bring not this doctrine, receive him not into your house, neither bid him God speed**: for he that biddeth him God speed is partaker of his evil deeds."*

We must ever be alert, on our guard, and careful concerning such false teachers in the world. They will not come in open contradiction, but will come in deception. They will come with "good words and fair speeches," and through such "good words and fair speeches" they will "deceive the hearts of the simple," that is – those who are not spiritually mature and deeply grounded in the truth. Yea, in Matthew 7:15 our Lord Jesus Christ commanded us to beware of such false teachers, who will come *"in sheep's clothing"* with the outward appearance of good, but who will inwardly be *"ravening wolves."*

2 Corinthians 11:13-15 also warns us concerning the deception of such false teachers, saying, *"For such are false apostles, deceitful*

workers, transforming themselves into the apostles of Christ. And no marvel; for Satan himself is transformed into an angel of light. Therefore it is no great thing if his ministers also be transformed as the ministers of righteousness; whose end shall be according to their works." They will appear as the ministers of righteousness, but they will actually be the ministers of the devil. They will seek to beguile and deceive with enticing words. (See Colossians 2:4) They will speak with the name of Christ, but will not speak to serve Christ. They will speak with Biblical quotes, but will speak contrary to the wholesome truth of Christ in order to lead many away from Christ. They will speak with Biblical terminology, but will speak contrary to the pure doctrine of godliness in order to lead many away from godly living. They will seek privately to *"bring in damnable heresies,"* even denying the Lord Himself and causing the way of truth to be spoken against. (See 2 Peter 2:1-2)

Thus we are not simply commanded to beware of such individuals, but also to withdraw ourselves from them and to avoid them. Indeed, 1 Timothy 6:3-5 describes such false teachers as proud individuals, being *"of corrupt minds"* and being *"destitute of the truth."* They will dote *"about questions and strifes of words"* out of which will come forth *"envy, strife, railings, evil surmisings,* [and] *perverse disputings,"* all to turn people aside from our Lord Jesus Christ and from the doctrine which leads to genuine godly living. Yea, such false teachers and deceivers will not be rare in these perilous times. Rather, they shall abound more and more and grow worse and worse. Even so, God's Word proclaims in 2 Timothy 3:13, *"But evil men and seducers shall wax worse and worse, deceiving and being deceived."*

We must beware of them. We must be on our guard against them. We must be alert to their deceptions. We must take notice of them and mark them as false teachers. We must withdraw ourselves and turn aside from them. We must avoid them and stay away from them. Yes, according to Titus 3:10-11 we must admonish them. Yet if they will not be corrected, we must reject them from our fellowship. Indeed, according to 2 John 1:7-11 we must not even receive such individuals into our houses, nor to bid them to have a good day. Indeed, according to Galatians 1:8-9 we must view them as accursed of God.

123. **We must not glory in ourselves, but must glory alone in the Lord Jesus Christ our Savior.**

1 Corinthians 1:17-31 – *"So that ye come behind in no gift; waiting for the coming of our Lord Jesus Christ: who shall also confirm you unto the end, that ye may be blameless in the day of our Lord Jesus Christ. God is faithful, by whom ye were called unto the fellowship of his Son Jesus Christ our Lord.* **Now I beseech you, brethren, by the name of our Lord Jesus Christ, that ye all speak the same thing, and that there be no divisions among you; but that ye be perfectly joined together in the same mind and in the same judgment.** *For it hath been declared unto me of you, my brethren, by them which are of the house of Chloe, that there are contentions among you. Now this I say, that every one of you saith, I am of Paul; and I of Apollos; and I of Cephas; and I of Christ. Is Christ divided? Was Paul crucified for you? Or were ye baptized in the name of Paul? I thank God that I baptized none of you, but Crispus and Gaius; lest any should say that I had baptized in mine own name. And I baptized also the household of Stephanas: besides, I know not whether I baptized any other. For Christ sent me not to baptize, but to preach the gospel: not with wisdom of words, lest the cross of Christ should be made of none effect. For the preaching of the cross is to them that perish foolishness; but unto us which are saved it is the power of God. For it is written, I will destroy the wisdom of the wise, and will bring to nothing the understanding of the prudent. Where is the wise? Where is the scribe? Where is the disputer of this world? Hath not God made foolish the wisdom of this world? For after that in the wisdom of God the world by wisdom knew not God, it pleased God by the foolishness of preaching to save them that believe. For the Jews require a sign, and the Greeks seek after wisdom: but we preach Christ crucified, unto the Jews a stumblingblock, and unto the Greeks foolishness; but unto them which are called, both Jews and Greeks, Christ the power of God, and the wisdom of God. Because the foolishness of God is wiser than men; and the weakness of God is stronger than men. For ye see your calling, brethren, how that not many wise men after the flesh, not many mighty, not many noble, are called: but God hath chosen the foolish things of the world to confound the wise; and God hath chosen the weak things of the world to*

confound the things which are mighty; and base things of the world, and things which are despised, hath God chosen, yea, and things which are not, to bring to nought things that are: that no flesh should glory in his presence. But of him are ye in Christ Jesus, who of God is made unto us wisdom, and righteousness, and sanctification, and redemption: **that, according as it is written, He that glorieth, let him glory in the Lord.**"

2 Corinthians 10:17-18 – "**But he that glorieth, let him glory in the Lord.** *For not he that commendeth himself is approved, but whom the Lord commendeth.*"

There is no part of our salvation from sin in which we can take glory unto ourselves. In God's way of salvation, all of the glory is due unto Him. In His grace and love by His almighty power, He saves us from our sin and unrighteousness. We contribute nothing to the work of our salvation. Our salvation is not even in the smallest degree out of our own wisdom, or out of our own power, or out of our own nobility. Thus no single one of us has any legitimate right to glory in ourselves. All of the glory for our salvation belongs unto the Lord our God and Savior. Even so, in Galatians 6:14 the apostle Paul exclaimed, "*But God forbid that I should glory, save in the cross of our Lord Jesus Christ, by whom the world is crucified unto me, and I unto the world.*" In addition, all of the glory for our spiritual ministry belongs unto the Lord. We do not accomplish His work out of ourselves. Rather, He accomplishes His work through us; for without Him we can do nothing. (See John 15:4-5) So then, "*he that glorieth, let him glory in the Lord.*" Indeed, it is not the one who "commendeth himself" that is approved before the Lord, but it is the one "whom the Lord commendeth" that is approved.

124. We must take heed how we build upon the foundation of our salvation in Christ.

1 Corinthians 3:5-15 – "*Who then is Paul, and who is Apollos, but ministers by whom ye believed, even as the Lord gave to every man? I have planted, Apollos watered; but God gave the increase. So*

*then neither is he that planteth any thing, neither he that watereth; but God that giveth the increase. Now he that planteth and he that watereth are one: and every man shall receive his own reward according to his own labour. For we are labourers together with God: ye are God's husbandry, ye are God's building. According to the grace of God which is given unto me, as a wise masterbuilder, I have laid the foundation, and another buildeth thereon. **But let every man take heed how he buildeth thereupon.** For other foundation can no man lay than that is laid, which is Jesus Christ. Now if any man build upon this foundation gold, silver, precious stones, wood, hay, stubble; every man's work shall be made manifest: for the day shall declare it, because it shall be revealed by fire; and the fire shall try every man's work of what sort it is. If any man's work abide which he hath built thereupon, he shall receive a reward. If any man's work shall be burned, he shall suffer loss: but he himself shall be saved; yet so as by fire."*

There is coming a time in which we all as believers shall stand before the Judgment Seat of Christ and shall give account of ourselves before Him. On that day of judgment, our work for the Lord in this life shall be tried by the fire of our Lord to determine what sort of work it was – whether it was spiritually valuable work (that is – "gold, silver, precious stone" work) or whether it was spiritually worthless work (that is – "wood, hay, stubble" work). Now, if our work in this life is spiritually valuable work ("gold, silver, precious stone" work), it shall abide through the trying of our Lord's fire; and we shall receive a reward at our Lord's hand. On the other hand, if our work in this life is spiritually worthless work ("wood, hay, stubble" work), it shall be burned up by the trying of our Lord's fire; and we shall suffer loss, not the loss of our eternal salvation, but the loss of eternal reward at our Lord's hand. Thus we who are saved must take heed how we live our daily Christian lives and how we work in the service of our Lord. We shall be required to give account. Our Lord will judge our work for Him. Receiving reward from Him or suffering loss before Him is at stake.

125. We must become foolish in the wisdom of this world that we may grow in the wisdom of God.

1 Corinthians 3:18-20 – *"Let no man deceive himself. If any man among you seemeth to be wise in this world, let him become a fool, that he may be wise. For the wisdom of this world is foolishness with God. For it is written, He taketh the wise in their own craftiness. And again, The Lord knoweth the thoughts of the wise, that they are vain."*

The wisdom of this world is contrary to the Lord our God and to the wisdom of God. In the sight of the Lord our God, the wisdom of this world is foolishness and emptiness. Yea, in the sight of the Lord our God, the very thoughts of those who are wise in the wisdom of this world are vain (empty-headed) thoughts. Therefore, we must make a choice – Will we be wise in the wisdom of this world and be foolish in the sight of God, or will we be wise in the wisdom of God and be foolish in the sight of this world? If we choose to be wise in the wisdom of this world, we will become self-deceived. We will think ourselves to be wise, when we will actually be foolish and empty-headed. However, if we choose to be wise in the wisdom of God, then we must cast aside the wisdom of this world and must become fools in the wisdom of this world. Yea, we must empty ourselves of this world's wisdom in order that the Lord our God may fill us with His true wisdom. Only then will we become wise in the wisdom of God. Only then will we grow in the wisdom of God. Thus our Lord instructs us to stop deceiving ourselves into thinking that we are wise because we are full of this world's wisdom. Rather, He instructs us to become fools in this world's wisdom in order that we may become wise in His wisdom.

126. We must not glory in the human leadership that the Lord our God has placed over us, but must view them simply as the servants of Christ and the stewards of God's Word.

1 Corinthians 3:21 - 4:6 – *"Therefore let no man glory in men. For all things are yours; whether Paul, or Apollos, or Cephas, or*

the world, or life, or death, or things present, or things to come; all are yours; and ye are Christ's; and Christ is God's. **Let a man so account of us, as of the ministers of Christ, and stewards of the mysteries of God.** *Moreover it is required in stewards, that a man be found faithful. But with me it is a very small thing that I should be judged of you, or of man's judgment: yea, I judge not mine own self. For I know nothing by myself; yet am I not hereby justified: but he that judgeth me is the Lord.* **Therefore judge nothing before the time, until the Lord come**, *who both will bring to light the hidden things of darkness, and will make manifest the counsels of the hearts: and then shall every man have praise of God. And these things, brethren, I have in a figure transferred to myself and to Apollos for your sakes;* **that ye might learn in us not to think of men above that which is written, that no one of you be puffed up for one against another**."

The believers at Corinth were comparing the qualities of various God-given, human leaders. Then they were glorying in those human leaders and becoming puffed up with pride that they had chosen to follow the one whom they deemed as the "best" among those leaders. Yet God's Word indicates that we are never to glory in our God-given, human leadership, no matter how good or gifted they may appear in our opinion. Rather, we are ever to glory in the Lord our God Himself. Furthermore, we are to view the human leadership that He places over us simply as His ministers, that is – as His servants, and as the stewards of His truth. It is not about them, but about Him. It is not about them, but about the truth of His Holy Word. Even so, in servants and stewards the one primary characteristic is faithfulness unto one's Lord and Master. Thus it is not about how much more "gifted" one human leader is above another, but about how faithful each human leader is to our Lord's calling in his life. Finally, the full depths of judgment concerning any man's faithfulness includes more than his outward behavior. It also includes "the hidden things of darkness" and "the counsels of the heart." Even so, the only One who is able to judge such matters is our Lord Himself. Thus we need to learn in our time, even as the believers at Corinth needed to learn in their time, *"not to think of men above that which is written* [in God's Word], *that no one of* [us] *be puffed up for one* [leader] *against another."*

127. We must be followers of our God-given leadership and of other faithful believers as they follow after our Lord Jesus Christ.

1 Corinthians 4:14-17 – *"I write not these things to shame you, but as my beloved sons I warn you. For though ye have ten thousand instructors in Christ, yet have ye not many fathers: for in Christ Jesus I have begotten you through the gospel.* **Wherefore I beseech you, be ye followers of me.** *For this cause have I sent unto you Timotheus, who is my beloved son, and faithful in the Lord, who shall bring you into remembrance of my ways which be in Christ, as I teach every where in every church."*

1 Corinthians 11:1 – *"**Be ye followers of me, even as I also am of Christ.**"*

Philippians 3:17-19 – *"**Brethren, be followers together of me, and mark them which walk so as ye have us for an ensample.** (For many walk, of whom I have told you often, and now tell you even weeping, that they are the enemies of the cross of Christ: whose end is destruction, whose God is their belly, and whose glory is in their shame, who mind earthly things.)"*

Philippians 4:9 – *"**Those things, which ye have both learned, and received, and heard, and seen in me, do**: and the God of peace shall be with you."*

Hebrews 13:7 – *"**Remember them which have the rule over you, who have spoken unto you the word of God: whose faith follow, considering the end of their conversation.**"*

The Lord our God places His leadership in our lives with the intent that we should follow them. Their responsibility is to be faithful servants for Him, faithfully following after Him. Our responsibility is to follow after them as they follow after Christ. For this very reason the apostle Paul had sent Timothy unto the believers at Corinth to remind them of his ways which were in Christ, which he taught in every church. Even so, Hebrews 13:7 instructs us to remember and follow after the godly teaching and godly example of the godly leadership that God has placed over us. In like manner, Philippians 3:17 instructs us to take note of those around us who are setting an example of godliness, an example of a faithful walk with the Lord, after the Lord, and for the Lord. In addition, our Lord desires that we should be followers of them, even as they also are followers of our Lord Jesus Christ. We are to search for such godly examples, to consider carefully such godly examples, to learn from such godly examples, and to follow after such godly examples.

On the other hand, the apostle Paul added the contrasting warning of Philippians 3:18-19, saying, "*For many walk, of whom I have told you often, and now tell you even weeping, that they are the enemies of the cross of Christ: whose end is destruction, whose God is their belly, and whose glory is in their shame, who mind earthly things.*" There are many around us, even within the church ministry, who are not walking in the right way. There are many around us, even within the church ministry, who are not walking as an example of godliness. There are many around us, even within the church ministry, who have the affection of their minds set upon earthly things. There are many around us, even within the church ministry, who glory in the shameful pleasures of sin. There are many around us, even within the church ministry, whose true god is their own selfish desires. The end of their path is spiritual destruction. Although they may be the children of God through faith in Christ for salvation, they are walking as the enemies of the cross of Christ in their daily behavior. They are not walking in godliness, but in worldliness. They are not the example that we are to follow.

128. We must put away from among us and not keep company with fellow believers who are living a lifestyle of immorality.

1 Corinthians 5:1-13 – "*It is reported commonly that there is fornication among you, and such fornication as is not so much as named among the Gentiles, that one should have his father's wife. And ye are puffed up, and have not rather mourned, that he that hath done this deed might be taken away from among you. For I*

verily, as absent in body, but present in spirit, have judged already, as though I were present, concerning him that hath so done this deed, in the name of our Lord Jesus Christ, when ye are gathered together, and my spirit, with the power of our Lord Jesus Christ, to deliver such an one unto Satan for the destruction of the flesh, that the spirit may be saved in the day of the Lord Jesus. Your glorying is not good. Know ye not that a little leaven leaveneth the whole lump? **Purge out therefore the old leaven, that ye may be a new lump, as ye are unleavened.** *For even Christ our passover is sacrificed for us:* **therefore let us keep the feast, not with old leaven, neither with the leaven of malice and wickedness; but with the unleavened bread of sincerity and truth.** *I wrote unto you in an epistle not to company with fornicators: yet not altogether with the fornicators of this world, or with the covetous, or extortioners, or with idolaters; for then must ye needs go out of the world.* **But now I have written unto you not to keep company, if any man that is called a brother be a fornicator, or covetous, or an idolater, or a railer, or a drunkard, or an extortioner; with such an one no not to eat.** *For what have I to do to judge them also that are without? Do not ye judge them that are within? But them that are without God judgeth.* **Therefore put away from among yourselves that wicked person.**"

Herein a case of immorality is revealed in the church at Corinth. A fellow believer in that church at that time was committing fornication. In addition, the believers at Corinth, rather than mourning with spiritual grief over the matter, were puffed up with pride over the matter. Thus the apostle Paul rebuked them in verse 6 for their sinful pride and spiritual ignorance, saying, *"Your glorying is not good. Know ye not that a little leaven* [a little corruption of sin] *leaveneth the whole lump* [will spread the corruption of sin among the whole church]." Furthermore, in verses 3-5 the apostle pronounced his own judgment of the case according to the leading of the Holy Spirit in the name of the Lord Jesus Christ *"to deliver such an one unto Satan for the destruction of the flesh, that the spirit may be saved in the day of the Lord Jesus."* Finally, in verses 7-13 the apostle instructed them on what to do concerning such a case of immorality among the believers of the church.

In the first place, he declared in verse 7, "*Purge out therefore the old leaven, that ye may be a new lump, as ye are unleavened.*" We must judge the sinful corruption of such immorality within the church by putting away from among us those believers who would commit such things. Even so, in verses 12-13 God's Word proclaims, "*For what have I to do to judge them also that are without? Do not ye judge them that are within? But them that are without God judgeth. Therefore put away from among yourselves that wicked person.*" It is our responsibility before God to judge those within the church who commit such immorality. We must put them out of the church fellowship, and then the Lord our God will judge those who are without the church fellowship.

In the second place, the apostle declared in verse 11, "*But now I have written unto you not to keep company, if any man that is called a brother be a fornicator, or covetous, or an idolater, or a railer, or a drunkard, or an extortioner; with such an one no not to eat.*" We must not only put away from the church fellowship those believers who live in such immorality. We must also keep no company with them, that is – with any believers who are living as "a fornicator, or covetous, or an idolater, or a railer [a slanderer, or verbally abusive person], or a drunkard, or an extortioner [robber, or swindler]." In fact, it appears from this passage that we are to be even more strict in not keeping company with believers who are involved in such immoral behavior, than even with unbelievers who are involved in such behavior.

129. We must flee the sin of fornication.

1 Corinthians 6:12-20 – "*All things are lawful unto me, but all things are not expedient: all things are lawful for me, but I will not be brought under the power of any. Meats for the belly, and the belly for meats: but God shall destroy both it and them. Now the body is not for fornication, but for the Lord; and the Lord for the body. And God hath both raised up the Lord, and will also raise up us by his own power. Know ye not that your bodies are the members of*

Christ? Shall I then take the members of Christ, and make them the members of an harlot? God forbid. What? Know ye not that he which is joined to an harlot is one body? For two, saith he, shall be one flesh. But he that is joined unto the Lord is one spirit. **Flee fornication.** *Every sin that a man doeth is without the body; but he that committeth fornication sinneth against his own body. What? Know ye not that your body is the temple of the Holy Ghost which is in you, which ye have of God, and ye are not your own? For ye are bought with a price:* **therefore glorify God in your body, and in your spirit, which are God's.***"*

1 Corinthians 10:8 – "***Neither let us commit fornication***, *as some of them committed, and fell in one day three and twenty thousand.*"

1 Thessalonians 4:3 – "***For this is the will of God, even your sanctification, that ye should abstain from fornication.***"

Herein we learn that our bodies were not made for fornication, but for service unto our Lord. In the second place, we learn that if we are in Christ through faith, then our bodies are the members of Christ. In the third place, we learn that the sin of fornication is a sin against our own bodies. In the fourth place, we learn that if we are children of God through faith in Christ, then our bodies are each the temple of God the Holy Spirit who dwells in us. Finally, we learn that through salvation our bodies are not our own possession, but are the possession of God our heavenly Father who bought us with the price of His beloved Son's precious blood. Thus we are not to involve our bodies in the sin of fornication. Yea, we must flee any involvement in fornication whatsoever. To involve our bodies in fornication is not to serve the Lord with our bodies. To involve our bodies in fornication is to defile a member of Christ. To involve our bodies in fornication is to defile the body that God has given to us in stewardship. To involve our bodies in fornication is to defile the temple of God the Holy Spirit. To involve our bodies in fornication is to defile the possession of God. To involve our bodies in fornication is to dishonor the precious blood of Christ by which we were bought. We must flee fornication with all of the spiritual energy that is within us. This is the will of the Lord our God for us, that we keep our bodies sanctified unto Him.

130. We must glorify God in our bodies and in our spirits because they are God's.

1 Corinthians 6:20 – "*For ye are bought with a price: **therefore glorify God in your body, and in your spirit, which are God's**.*"

1 Corinthians 10:31 – "***Whether therefore ye eat, or drink, or whatsoever ye do, do all to the glory of God.***"

God the Father has purchased us as the temple of His Holy Spirit through the shed blood and sacrificial death of His beloved Son. We are not our own. We are God's own. Therefore, we must live as God's own. We must live for Him. We must live to glorify Him. In all things – in all of our thoughts, in all of our desires, in all of attitudes, in all of our decisions, in all of our words, in all of our behavior, in whatsoever we do, we must live for His glory.

131. Married couples must regularly render unto one another the due benevolence of sexual relations.

1 Corinthians 7:1-5 – "*Now concerning the things whereof ye wrote unto me: It is good for a man not to touch a woman. Nevertheless, to avoid fornication, **let every man have his own wife, and let every woman have her own husband. Let the husband render unto the wife due benevolence: and likewise also the wife unto the husband**. The wife hath not power of her own body, but the husband: and likewise also the husband hath not power of his own body, but the wife. **Defraud ye not one the other, except it be with consent for a time, that ye may give yourselves to fasting and prayer; and come together again, that Satan tempt you not for your incontinency**.*"

Having warned against the sin of fornication in 1 Corinthians 6:13-19, and having instructed God's people in 1 Corinthians 6:20 to glorify God in both body and spirit, the apostle Paul then gave instruction unto married couples in 1 Corinthians 7:1-5. Within this context the word "touch" in verse 1 refers unto the physical relationship between a man and a woman. Even so, the Lord our God has established a very specific boundary for that physical relationship. In Hebrews 13:4 God's Holy Word proclaims, *"Marriage is honourable in all, and the bed undefiled: but whoremongers and adulterers God will judge."* The marriage relationship is God's boundary for the physical, sexual relationship between a man and a woman. Anything outside of that boundary is sin and will most certainly bring the judgment of the Lord our God.

On the other hand, God's Word declares that the physical, sexual relationship between a married couple, between a husband and his wife, is not only undefiled in the sight of our Lord, but is actually worthy of honor in the sight of our Lord. In fact, speaking concerning the physical relationship between a husband and wife, 1 Corinthians 7:2 directly commands a husband to have [to physically possess] his own wife and directly commands a wife to have [to physically possess] her own husband. Yet again in 1 Corinthians 7:3 God's Holy Word commands a husband to render unto his wife the due benevolence of this physical, sexual relationship and commands a wife to render unto her husband the due benevolence of this physical, sexual relationship.

Herein also we take note that God's Word speaks of this physical relationship as a "due benevolence." From our Lord's perspective, this physical relationship between a husband and wife is a matter of both responsibility and lovingkindness toward one another. Thus in 1 Corinthians 7:5 God's Word specifically prohibits a husband and wife from defrauding [cheating] one another out of this physical, sexual relationship. In fact, the only Biblically acceptable reason for a husband and wife not to engage in regular physical relations is if they both consent for a specified period of time to refrain, specifically in order that they might give themselves unto prayer and fasting. Furthermore, God's Holy Word instructs that as soon as that previously established period of time is ended, the husband and wife are immediately to come together again in their physical, sexual relationship with one another. This is the command of God's HOLY Word. As such, to do otherwise is to commit sin against the Lord our God. (Indeed, God's people are to be sexually pure; but they are not to be sexually prudish.)

132. Divorced individuals must remain unmarried or be reconciled to their original spouse.

1 Corinthians 7:10-11 – "*And unto the married I command, yet not I, but the Lord, Let not the wife depart from her husband: but and if she depart,* **let her remain unmarried, or be reconciled to her husband**: *and let not the husband put away his wife.*"

God's Holy Word is very specific in this matter of divorce and remarriage. Only two options are granted – to remain unmarried or to be reconciled unto the original marriage. Any other option is contrary to God's Holy Word. Any other option is to commit sin against the Lord our God.

133. A believer who is married to an unbeliever must not pursue after a divorce, but must not fight against a divorce if the unbeliever desires it.

1 Corinthians 7:12-16 – "*But to the rest speak I, not the Lord: If any brother hath a wife that believeth not, and she be pleased to dwell with him,* **let him not put her away**. *And the woman which hath an husband that believeth not, and if he be pleased to dwell with her,* **let her not leave him**. *For the unbelieving husband is sanctified by the wife, and the unbelieving wife is sanctified by the husband: else were your children unclean; but now are they holy.* **But if the unbelieving depart, let him depart**. *A brother or a sister is not under bondage in such cases: but God hath called us to peace. For what knowest thou, O wife, whether thou shalt save thy husband? or how knowest thou, O man, whether thou shalt save thy wife?*"

In a situation wherein one spouse received the Lord as Savior and the other did not the question would arise – Should the believing spouse separate from the unbelieving spouse in order not to be unequally yoked together with an unbeliever? The answer of God's Holy Word is – No, the believing spouse should remain married to the unbelieving spouse; for through the believers presence in the marriage and family our Lord might have a greater means to work upon the heart of the unbelieving spouse and upon the hearts of the children. Yet what if the unbelieving spouse does not want to remain married to the believing spouse and chooses to pursue after a divorce? The answer of God's Holy Word is that the believing spouse should let the unbelieving spouse depart, and is that the believing spouse "is not under bondage" in the sight of the Lord in such a case. Yea, God's Holy Word declares that in such a case the Lord our God has called us to peace, and not to conflict. Thus in such a case the Lord our God will not hold the believing spouse accountable for the sin of a divorce.

134. We must materially take care of those who minister God's Word unto us.

1 Corinthians 9:3-14 – "*Mine answer to them that do examine me is this, Have we not power to eat and to drink? Have we not power to lead about a sister, a wife, as well as other apostles, and as the brethren of the Lord, and Cephas? Or I only and Barnabas, have not we power to forbear working? Who goeth a warfare any time at his own charges? Who planteth a vineyard, and eateth not of the fruit thereof? Or who feedeth a flock, and eateth not of the milk of the flock? Say I these things as a man? Or saith not the law the same also? For it is written in the law of Moses, Thou shalt not muzzle the mouth of the ox that treadeth out the corn. Doth God take care for oxen? Or saith he it altogether for our sakes? For our sakes, no doubt, this is written: that he that ploweth should plow in hope; and that he that thresheth in hope should be partaker of his hope. If we have sown unto you spiritual things, is it a great thing if we shall reap your carnal things? If others be partakers of this power over you, are not we rather? Nevertheless we have not used this power; but suffer all things, lest we should hinder the gospel of Christ. Do ye not know that they which minister about holy things live of the things of the temple? And they which wait at the altar are partakers with the altar? Even so hath the Lord ordained that they which preach the gospel should live of the gospel.*"

Galatians 6:6 – "***Let him that is taught in the word communicate*** [materially] ***unto him that teacheth in all good things***."

1 Timothy 5:17-18 – "***Let the elders*** [the pastoral leadership] ***that rule well be counted worthy of double honour, especially they who labour in the word and doctrine***. *For the scripture saith, Thou shalt not muzzle the ox that treadeth out the corn. And, The labourer is worthy of his reward*."

In Galatians 6:6 the word "communicate" is used with regard to the giving and receiving of material support, even as it is used in Philippians 4:15. There the apostle Paul stated unto the believers at Philippi, "*Now ye Philippians know also, that in the beginning of the gospel, when I departed from Macedonia, no church communicated with me as concerning giving and receiving, but ye only*." This then is the principle and precept of the Lord our God – that those who faithfully minister God's Word unto us should be materially supported by us. Indeed, those who are taught in the Word of God are to communicate material support unto those who have taught them. Truly, "the labourer is worthy of his reward." Even so, those who labor in Word and doctrine are certainly worthy of a material reward from our hand. They minister unto us spiritually; therefore, we should minister unto them materially.

135. We must pursue the Christian life with spiritual discipline, keeping the desires of our body under subjection to our Lord's cause.

1 Corinthians 9:24-27 – "*Know ye not that they which run in a race run all, but one receiveth the prize? **So run, that ye may obtain**. And every man that striveth for the mastery is temperate* [disciplined] *in all things. Now they do it to obtain a corruptible crown; but we an incorruptible. I therefore so run, not as uncertainly; so fight I, not as one that beateth the air: but I keep under my body, and bring it into subjection: lest that by any means, when I have preached to others, I myself should be a castaway*."

Each one of us as believers has the course of the Christian life set before us. In addition, each one of us is called by our Lord to run that course with faithfulness, ever pressing *"toward the mark for the prize of the high calling of God in Christ Jesus."* (See Philippians 3:14) Yet we will not run with such faithfulness if we do not run with spiritual discipline. In the sports world, runners who strive for victory must be temperate (self-disciplined) in all things, and they do this in order to win a corruptible reward. Even more so, in our spiritual lives we who strive for spiritual victory must also be temperate (spiritually disciplined) in all things, in order that we might win an incorruptible reward from the hand of our Lord. We must deny ourselves and keep under (beat down) the desires of our flesh. We must bring our flesh into subjection unto the will, and purpose, and cause of our Lord Jesus Christ. On the other hand, if we are not so spiritually disciplined, we may spiritually minister unto others now; but we shall ourselves become spiritual castaways before the Lord. We shall not be cast away from our eternal salvation, but shall be cast away from spiritual usefulness in our daily lives.

136. We must not lust after evil (selfish) things.

1 Corinthians 10:6 – *"Now these things were our examples, **to the intent we should not lust after evil things, as they also lusted.**"*

In 1 Corinthians 10:1-5 the apostle Paul presented a reminder of God's dealings with His people Israel during the time of the Old Testament. There we read, *"Moreover, brethren, I would not that ye should be ignorant, how that all our fathers were under the cloud, and all passed through the sea; and were all baptized unto Moses in the cloud and in the sea; and did all eat the same spiritual meat; and did all drink the same spiritual drink: for they drank of that spiritual Rock that followed them: and that Rock was Christ. But with many of them God was not well pleased: for they were overthrown in the wilderness."* Then in verses 6-11 the apostle revealed that these things are an example unto us for our learning, and he applied them to our present lives through a series of warnings.

292

The first of these warnings is found in the closing portion of verse 6 – "*To the intent that we should not lust after evil things, as they also lusted.*" Now, the occasion when the children of Israel went to lusting is found in Numbers 11. Even so, in Numbers 11:4-6 we read, "*And the mixt multitude that was among them fell a lusting: and the children of Israel also wept again, and said, Who shall give us flesh to eat? We remember the fish, which we did eat in Egypt freely; the cucumbers, and the melons, and the leeks, and the onions, and the garlick: but now our soul is dried away: there is nothing at all, beside this manna, before our eyes.*" Herein we find that the children of Israel complained because they desired more variety in their diet. The Lord had provided them manna from heaven every week-day morning except the Sabbath Day. Yet they were not satisfied with the Lord's provision. They "fell a lusting" after the provisions of Egypt – the fish, and the cucumbers, and the melons, and the leeks, and the onions, and the garlic.

Then in 1 Corinthians 10:6 God's Word warns us not to lust after evil things as the children of Israel lusted. Are such types of food evil things? No, these things are not evil in themselves. Ye they were not the provision of the Lord for the children of Israel at that time. Even so, to set the desires of our hearts upon those things that the Lord our God has not provided for us is to lust after evil things, not because all such things are evil in themselves, but because the selfish desire to have what our Lord has not provided is evil. As our Lord Jesus Christ instructed in Matthew 6:33, our responsibility is to seek first "the kingdom of God and his righteousness," and then to trust our Lord to provide the things that are truly best for us. We must set the desires of our hearts upon the things of the Lord, not upon the things of this world. On the other hand, if we set the desires of our hearts upon the things of this world instead of upon our Lord, then these things are indeed evil things unto us.

137. We must flee the sin of idolatry.

1 Corinthians 10:7 – "***Neither be ye idolaters***, *as were some of them; as it is written, The people sat down to eat and drink, and rose up to play.*"

1 Corinthians 10:14 – "***Wherefore, my dearly beloved, flee from idolatry.***"

1 John 5:21 – "***Little children, keep yourselves from idols***. *Amen.*"

The warning of 1 Corinthians 10:7 refers to the occasion at Mount Sinai when Aaron formed the golden calf for the children of Israel to worship. Thereby the children of Israel sinned a great sin against the Lord their God, and thereby the wrath of God was kindled against them. Even so, we must take heed unto the instructions of 1 Corinthians 10:14 and 1 John 5:21 – not only to keep ourselves from all forms of idolatry, but actually to *flee* from idolatry.

138. We must not tempt (provoke) our Lord Jesus Christ by questioning His presence, His purpose, His power, or His promise.

1 Corinthians 10:9 – "***Neither let us tempt Christ***, *as some of them also tempted, and were destroyed of serpents.*"

The occasion of this warning is recorded in Numbers 21:4-9 where we read, "*And they journeyed from mount Hor by the way of the Red sea, to compass the land of Edom: and the soul of the people was much discouraged because of the way. And the people spake against God, and against Moses, Wherefore have ye brought us up out of Egypt to die in the wilderness? For there is no bread, neither is there any water; and our soul loatheth this light bread. And the LORD sent fiery serpents among the people, and they bit the people; and much people of Israel died. Therefore the people came to Moses, and said, We have sinned, for we have spoken against the LORD, and against thee; pray unto the LORD, that he take away the serpents from us. And Moses prayed for the people. And the* LORD *said unto Moses, Make thee a fiery serpent, and set it upon a pole: and it shall come to pass, that every one that is bitten, when he looketh upon it, shall live. And Moses made a serpent of brass, and put it upon a pole, and it came to pass, that if a serpent had bitten any man, when he beheld the serpent of brass, he lived.*"

Speaking about this same occasion, Psalm 78:18-19 states, "*And they tempted God in their heart by asking meat for their lust. Yea, they spake against God; they said, Can God furnish a table in the wilderness?*" Even so, Psalm 78:56-57 declares, "*Yet they tempted and provoked the most high God, and kept not his testimonies: but turned back, and dealt unfaithfully like their fathers: they were turned aside like a deceitful bow.*" On a number of occasions God's Word reveals that the children of Israel tempted (provoked) the Lord. Even so, on each occasion they presented some complaint and challenge against the Lord by questioning Him. They questioned His presence among them, or His purpose in guiding them, or His power to take care of them, or His promises being faithfully fulfilled for them. Thus we are warned not to tempt (not to challenge and provoke) our Lord by questioning Him.

139. We must not murmur or complain about anything.

1 Corinthians 10:10 – "***Neither murmur ye***, *as some of them also murmured, and were destroyed of the destroyer.*"

Philippians 2:14-16 – "***Do all things without murmurings and disputings***: *that ye may be blameless and harmless, the sons of God, without rebuke, in the midst of a crooked and perverse nation, among whom ye shine as lights in the world; holding forth the word of life; that I may rejoice in the day of Christ, that I have not run in vain, neither laboured in vain.*"

On various occasions the children of Israel engaged in murmuring and complaining about one matter or another, and in every case it displeased and angered the Lord. Even so, the Lord our God instructs us to "do all things without murmurings and disputings." No matter what we might face in this life, we must proceed without murmuring and complaining. All things must be done without it. Nothing is allowed for it. On the other hand, when we have a complaining spirit about us, we are not "blameless and harmless" as the children of God, without rebuke, in the midst of this sinful world. When we have a complaining spirit about us, we are not shining forth as spiritual lights in this spiritually dark world. Rather, when we have a complaining spirit about us, we are worthy of blame and rebuke by this world; and we are causing harm to the light of the gospel in this world.

140. We must not think highly of our spiritual condition lest we fall through the sin of pride.

1 Corinthians 10:12 – "***Wherefore let him that thinketh he standeth take heed lest he fall.***"

There is never a time that we should become high-minded about our spiritual progress, our spiritual stability, and/or our spiritual accomplishments in life. The moment that we do become high-minded about these things, spiritual failure will strike; and we will fall spiritually through the sin of pride. In fact, the very moment that we think highly of our spiritual progress, stability, and/or accomplishments, we have already failed and fallen spiritually in the sin of pride. So then, let us take heed lest we fall!

141. We must limit our personal rights and liberties by the conscience of the lost around us that we might not offend them spiritually and thus hinder them from coming unto salvation.

1 Corinthians 10:25-33 – "*Whatsoever is sold in the shambles, that eat, **asking no question for conscience sake**: for the earth is the*

*Lord's, and the fulness thereof. If any of them that believe not bid you to a feast, and ye be disposed to go; whatsoever is set before you, eat, **asking no question for conscience sake**. But if any man say unto you, This is offered in sacrifice unto idols, **eat not for his sake that shewed it, and for conscience sake**: for the earth is the Lord's, and the fulness thereof: **Conscience, I say, not thine own, but of the other**: for why is my liberty judged of another man's conscience? For if I by grace be a partaker, why am I evil spoken of for that for which I give thanks? Whether therefore ye eat, or drink, or whatsoever ye do, do all to the glory of God. **Give none offence, neither to the Jews, nor to the Gentiles, nor to the church of God**: even as I please all men in all things, not seeking mine own profit, but the profit of many, that they may be saved.*"

There are many areas in which we may have liberty before the Lord our God. Yet at times the conscience of the lost around us judges that God's people ought not to be involved in such activities. When this occurs, we should give up our personal "liberties" and should not involve ourselves in those activities. This we should do, not because the judgment of their conscience against the activity makes it sinful in itself, but because our involvement in that activity will offend their conscience and hinder them from coming unto Christ for salvation. In such cases we must not seek our own personal profit and pleasure at the expense of lost souls. Rather, we must seek the spiritual profit of the lost by removing from our lives any hindrance unto their salvation. Indeed, the souls of the lost must be far more important unto us than our personal rights and liberties.

142. A woman who ministers in the public services of the church must do so in a manner that honors the headship of her husband.

1 Corinthians 11:3-10 – "*But I would have you know, that the head of every man is Christ; and the head of the woman is the man; and the head of Christ is God. Every man praying or prophesying, having his head covered, dishonoureth his head. But every woman that*

prayeth or prophesieth with her head uncovered dishonoureth her head: for that is even all one as if she were shaven. For if the woman be not covered, let her also be shorn: but if it be a shame for a woman to be shorn or shaven, let her be covered. For a man indeed ought not to cover his head, forasmuch as he is the image and glory of God: but the woman is the glory of the man. For the man is not of the woman; but the woman of the man. Neither was the man created for the woman; but the woman for the man. **For this cause ought the woman to have power on her head because of the angels.**"

At times much contention has arisen among God's people over this matter of head coverings on women. Yet it is not the purpose of this book to consider all of the details in these contentions. Rather, it is the purpose of this book to consider the foundational principle of the passage – that a woman who ministers (prays or prophecies) in the public ministry of the church must do so in a manner that honors the headship of her husband. This is the underlying issue concerning head coverings. The head of the wife is her husband (see verse 3), and the glory of the husband is his wife (see verse 7). Therefore, a wife who ministers in the public services of the church ought not to have her head uncovered because that would dishonor her husband (see verse 5). Rather, the wife ought to have her head covered as a symbol of her submission unto her husband's authority (see verse 10). Yes, the underlying issue of the passage is whether a wife will be in honor or dishonor to her husband's headship as she ministers in the public services of the church. Even so, the Lord our God desires that she always minister in a manner that will honor her husband's headship.

143. We must be motivated by charity (godly love in behavior toward others) in all of our ministry efforts.

1 Corinthians 14:1 – "***Follow after charity***, *and desire spiritual gifts, but rather that ye may prophesy.*"

1 Corinthians 16:14 – "***Let all your things be done with charity.***"

In 1 Corinthians 12:27-31 the apostle Paul spoke concerning various gifts of ministry within the church, saying, "*Now ye are the body of Christ, and members in particular. And God hath set some in the church, first apostles, secondarily prophets, thirdly teachers, after that miracles, then gifts of healings, helps, governments, diversities of tongues. Are all apostles? Are all prophets? Are all teachers? Are all workers of miracles? Have all the gifts of healing? Do all speak with tongues? Do all interpret? But covet earnestly the best gifts: and yet shew I unto you a more excellent way.*" So then, what is this "more excellent way" than all of these ministry gifts? 1 Corinthians 13:1-3 presents the answer, saying, "*Though I speak with the tongues of men and of angels, and have not charity, I am become as sounding brass, or a tinkling cymbal. And though I have the gift of prophecy, and understand all mysteries, and all knowledge; and though I have all faith, so that I could remove mountains, and have not charity, I am nothing. And though I bestow all my goods to feed the poor, and though I give my body to be burned, and have not charity, it profiteth me nothing.*"

No matter how great may be our gifts of ministry, our efforts of ministry are nothing and profit nothing if they are not motivated by Biblical charity (by godly, Spirit-filled love in our attitudes and behavior toward others). Even so, 1 Corinthians 13:4-7 reveals the true character of Biblical charity, saying, "*Charity suffereth long, and is kind; charity envieth not; charity vaunteth not itself, is not puffed up, doth not behave itself unseemly, seeketh not her own, is not easily provoked, thinketh no evil; rejoiceth not in iniquity, but rejoiceth in the truth; beareth all things, believeth all things, hopeth all things, endureth all things.*" This must be the character of our motivation in all of our ministry efforts, or else our ministry efforts will be of no spiritual profit. Thus 1 Corinthians 14:1 gives the instruction that in all of our ministry efforts, we must "*follow after charity,*" that is – in all we must be motivated by charity. Indeed, according to 1 Corinthians 16:14, not only in our ministry efforts, but in everything that we do, all must "*be done with charity.*"

144. We must use our gifts of ministry for the purpose of edification.

1 Corinthians 12:31 – "***But covet earnestly the best gifts***: *and yet shew I unto you a more excellent way.*"

1 Corinthians 14:1-5 – "*Follow after charity,* **and desire spiritual gifts, but rather that ye may prophesy.** *For he that speaketh in an unknown tongue speaketh not unto men, but unto God: for no man understandeth him; howbeit in the spirit he speaketh mysteries. But he that prophesieth speaketh unto men to edification, and exhortation, and comfort. He that speaketh in an unknown tongue edifieth himself; but he that prophesieth edifieth the church. I would that ye all spake with tongues, but rather that ye prophesied: for greater is he that prophesieth than he that speaketh with tongues, except he interpret, that the church may receive edifying.*"

1 Corinthians 14:12 – "*Even so ye, forasmuch as ye are zealous of spiritual gifts,* **seek that ye may excel to the edifying of the church.**"

1 Corinthians 14:26 – "*How is it then, brethren? When ye come together, every one of you hath a psalm, hath a doctrine, hath a tongue, hath a revelation, hath an interpretation.* **Let all things be done unto edifying.**"

1 Corinthians 12:31 instructs us to "*covet earnestly the best gifts.*" Yet what are these "best gifts" that we are to covet so earnestly? According to 1 Corinthians 14:1-5 they are the gifts of ministry whereby "the church may receive edifying." We are to speak and minister in the church for the "edification, and exhortation, and comfort" of others (see verse 3). Indeed, in our ministry efforts we are to do all unto the edifying of others; and we are to seek that we may excel in our ministries "to the edifying of the church." So then, if it does not edify others, it does not have a place in the ministry of the church. Every use of our ministry gifts within the church, whether we sing, or teach, or preach, or testify, or exhort, or interpret, etc., must be for the purpose of edifying others, that is – for the purpose of building up others spiritually.

145. We must do all things "decently and in order" in the ministry of the church.

1 Corinthians 14:40 – "***Let all things be done decently and in order.***"

In 1 Corinthians 14:26-35 the apostle Paul delivered a series of rules and regulations for the services of the church at Corinth, saying, "*How is it then, brethren? When ye come together, every one of you hath a psalm, hath a doctrine, hath a tongue, hath a revelation, hath an interpretation. Let all things be done unto edifying. If any man speak in an unknown tongue, let it be by two, or at the most by three, and that by course; and let one interpret. But if there be no interpreter, let him keep silence in the church; and let him speak to himself, and to God. Let the prophets speak two or three, and let the other judge. If any thing be revealed to another that sitteth by, let the first hold his peace. For ye may all prophesy one by one, that all may learn, and all may be comforted. And the spirits of the prophets are subject to the prophets. For God is not the author of confusion, but of peace, as in all churches of the saints. Let your women keep silence in the churches: for it is not permitted unto them to speak; but they are commanded to be under obedience, as also saith the law. And if they will learn any thing, let them ask their husbands at home: for it is a shame for women to speak in the church.*" Then in verse 40 he provided the conclusion that all things should "*be done decently and in order.*" The Lord our God is not the Author of confusion. Rather, He is the Author of peace and order. Therefore, the services of the church must represent Him and honor Him. Indeed, every part of them must be done "decently and in order."

146. We must awaken out of our spiritual lethargy unto a committed pursuit of righteousness.

1 Corinthians 15:34 – "***Awake to righteousness, and sin not***; *for some have not the knowledge of God: I speak this to your shame.*"

Far too often in our daily Christian walk, we become weary in well doing and spiritually lethargic, lazy, and lax in our pursuit after righteousness. In truth, at such times we have allowed the deceitful voice of our sinful flesh to turn the focus of our hearts away from abiding in our Lord, to dull our ears against the guidance of the Holy Spirit, and to woo our lives into a state of spiritual sleepiness. At such times we stop running the race that our Lord has set before us in His will. (See Hebrews 12:1) At such times we stop pressing *"toward the mark for the prize of the high calling of God in Christ Jesus."* (See Philippians 3:14) At such times we stop presenting ourselves as a living sacrifice to live wholly unto our Lord. (See Romans 12:1) At such times we stop pursuing first and foremost after the kingdom of God and His righteousness. (See Matthew 5:33) At such times we stop abounding always in the work of the Lord. (See 1 Corinthians 15:58) At such times we stop bringing forth much fruit unto the glory of our heavenly Father. (See John 15:8)

Why is this so? It is so because at such times we have turned away from our first love of abiding in fellowship with our Lord. (See Revelation 2:4) This is to our shame. So then, what are we to do at such times? We are to awaken out of this spiritual sleepiness. We are to remember the path of righteousness from which have fallen. We are to repent of the sin of our spiritual lethargy. We are to return again unto a committed pursuit of righteousness and a committed resistance of our sinful flesh. We are to "awake to righteousness, and sin not."

147. We must be "stedfast, unmoveable, always abounding in the work of the Lord."

1 Corinthians 15:58 – *"Therefore, my beloved brethren, be ye stedfast, unmoveable, always abounding in the work of the Lord, forasmuch as ye know that your labour is not in vain in the Lord."*

1 Corinthians 16:13 – *"Watch ye, stand fast in the faith, quit you like men, be strong."*

2 Timothy 4:5 – "***But watch thou in all things, endure afflictions,*** *do the work of an evangelist, make full proof of thy ministry.*"

Hebrews 6:10-12 – "*For God is not unrighteous to forget your work and labour of love, which ye have shewed toward his name, in that ye have ministered to the saints, and do minister.* ***And we desire that every one of you do shew the same diligence to the full assurance of hope unto the end: that ye be not slothful****, but followers of them who through faith and patience inherit the promises.*"

Revelation 2:24-25 – "*But unto you I say, and unto the rest in Thyatira, as many as have not this doctrine, and which have not known the depths of Satan, as they speak; I will put upon you none other burden.* ***But that which ye have already hold fast till I come.***"

Revelation 3:11 – "*Behold, I come quickly:* ***hold that fast which thou hast****, that no man take thy crown.*"

The cares of this life and the pleasures of this world are ever at work to entangle us and to turn us aside from a steadfast pursuit after righteousness. Furthermore, our adversary the devil and the desires of our flesh are ever at work to move us away from the narrow path of righteousness. Yet our Lord commands us to be steadfast in righteousness and to be unmoved from righteousness. Indeed, He commands us to be always abounding in His work of righteousness. There is never a moment that we are to turn aside from it, and there is never a moment that we are to slow down at it. We are to be *always* involved in our Lord's work, and we are to be *abundantly* involved in our Lord's work. "Always abounding."

Even so, our Lord commands us ever to be alert and watching against those things that might turn us away from such an abounding work in righteousness. He commands us to stand fast in the faith, being wholly committed unto Him. He commands us to be spiritually courageous, finding all of our strength in Him. He commands us not to be slothful in His work of righteousness, but to be diligent "through faith and patience." Yea, He commands us always to be diligent, steadfast, and abounding in the work and labor of His righteousness, having "full assurance of hope unto the end."

Yet what is our "full assurance of hope"? It is that our diligent, steadfast, and abounding work and labor of righteousness "is not in vain in the Lord." Indeed, our labor in our Lord's righteousness will be for His glory and will be for our good. No matter how things may appear to us, we may ever be assured that our labor in our Lord's righteousness is right in our Lord's sight and shall be rewarded by our Lord's hand. He will not be unrighteous to forget our work and labor of love for the sake of His name. Rather, in His righteousness He will remember and will reward our work and labor of love for Him. This is our motivation to remain alertly steadfast. This is our motivation to be courageously unmoved. This is our motivation to be always abounding. This is our motivation to be patiently diligent.

148. We must give materially unto the work of the Lord "upon the first day of the week" according as God has prospered us.

1 Corinthians 16:1-2 – *"Now concerning the collection for the saints, as I have given order to the churches of Galatia, even so do ye.* **Upon the first day of the week let every one of you lay by him in store, as God hath prospered him,** *that there be no gatherings when I come."*

Two great principles of truth are presented herein concerning our responsibility to give materially unto our Lord's work. First, we are to give "upon the first day of the week." Second, we are to give "as God hath prospered [us]." As we assemble ourselves together on the first day of the week, we need to be prepared to give materially unto the work of the Lord. In addition, the manner by which we determine the material amount to give should be in accord with how much the Lord our God has prospered us throughout the previous week. Let us here take note and clearly understand that all of our material prosperity is indeed from the hand of our Lord. He is the One who has prospered us; and in gratitude and honor unto Him, we should be abundantly and cheerfully willing to give back unto His work. Furthermore, we should give according to a percentage of how much He has prospered us in the previous week. This means that the more He has prospered us, the more we should give. Now, the basic percentage of giving that we find throughout God's Holy Word is the tithe (or, tenth) of our increase. So then, at the end of every week we should consider how much our Lord has prospered us; and on the first day of the week, we should give a tithe and offering of that increase unto Him and His work.

149. We must not despise faithful ministers of the Lord, but must conduct them forth in peace.

1 Corinthians 16:10-11 – *"Now if Timotheus come, **see that he may be with you without fear**: for he worketh the work of the Lord, as I also do. **Let no man therefore despise him: but conduct him forth in peace,** that he may come unto me: for I look for him with the brethren."*

As we continue in the ministry of our Lord, at various times other faithful ministers of the Lord shall pass through our community and our company. The man of God Timothy was just such a faithful minister of the Lord who was to pass through the company of the believers at Corinth. How then are we to behave toward these faithful ministers of our Lord? 1 Corinthians 16:11 reveals that we are not in any way to hinder them, to cause them fear, to despise them, or to make things difficult for them. Even so, our Lord gave the warning in Luke 10:16 concerning His faithful ministers, saying, *"He that heareth you heareth me; and he that despiseth you despiseth me; and he that despiseth me despiseth him that sent me."* To despise one of our Lord's faithful ministers is to despise both our Lord Jesus Christ and God our heavenly Father.

Rather, we are to conduct forth such faithful ministers of our Lord in peace, helping them along their way. We are to follow the godly example of Gaius, whom the apostle John commended in 3 John 1:5-8, saying, *"Beloved, thou doest faithfully whatsoever thou doest to the brethren, and to strangers; which have borne witness of thy charity before the church: whom if thou bring forward on their journey after a godly sort, thou shalt do well: because that for his name's sake they went forth, taking nothing of the Gentiles. We therefore ought to receive such, that we might be fellowhelpers to the truth.*" We are to behave with all charity toward these faithful ministers of the Lord, giving of ourselves to them as much as we are able and helping them forward on their journey after "a godly sort." Yea, we are to minister unto them and help them forward in a manner that is worthy of the Lord our God, because it is for His name's sake that they have gone forth in ministry. Thereby we ourselves become fellow-helpers unto our Lord's truth.

On the other hand, we must not follow the evil way of Diotrephes, whom the apostle John condemned in 3 John 1:9-11, saying, "*I wrote unto the church: but Diotrephes, who loveth to have the preeminence among them, receiveth us not. Wherefore, if I come, I will remember his deeds which he doeth, prating against us with malicious words: and not content therewith, neither doth he himself receive the brethren, and forbiddeth them that would, and casteth them out of the church. Beloved, follow not that which is evil, but that which is good. He that doeth good is of God: but he that doeth evil hath not seen God.*"

150. We must submit ourselves to those who are faithful ministers in the work of the Lord.

1 Corinthians 16:15-16 – "*I beseech you, brethren, (ye know the house of Stephanas, that it is the firstfruits of Achaia, and that they have addicted themselves to the ministry of the saints,)* **that ye submit yourselves unto such, and to every one that helpeth with us, and laboureth.**"

Hebrews 13:17 – "**Obey them that have the rule over you, and submit yourselves**: *for they watch for your souls, as they that must give account, that they may do it with joy, and not with grief: for that is unprofitable for you.*"

We often find this word "submission" to be a difficult word to accept in our lives. Yet in various areas of our lives our Lord has divinely established roles of leadership and roles of submission. This is true in the home, in national government, and also in church ministry. Indeed, concerning church ministry our Lord instructs us to submit ourselves unto those whom He has placed over us in church leadership and unto those who addict themselves unto the ministry of the saints and the work of our Lord. This submission is the will of our Lord; and this submission is pleasing in His sight. Therefore, God's Holy Word beseeches us that we might submit ourselves unto such individuals – that we might obey them that have this God-established rule over us in the ministry of the Lord, and submit ourselves unto their godly leadership. Furthermore, this submission is important because these individuals have the God-given responsibility to watch and care for our souls, that is – for our spiritual growth. Indeed, they have a continuing responsibility to give account unto the Lord concerning our spiritual progress. Even so, we should obey them and submit ourselves unto their leadership in order that they may give account "with joy, and not with grief;" for if they must give account concerning us "with grief," it will be unprofitable for us before the Lord our God.

151. We must highly commend and honor those who are faithful ministers of the Lord.

1 Corinthians 16:17-18 – *"I am glad of the coming of Stephanas and Fortunatus and Achaicus: for that which was lacking on your part they have supplied. For they have refreshed my spirit and yours:* ***therefore acknowledge*** *[commend]* ***ye them that are such****."*

Philippians 2:25-30 – *"Yet I supposed it necessary to send to you Epaphroditus, my brother, and companion in labour, and fellow-soldier, but your messenger, and he that ministered to my wants. For he longed after you all, and was full of heaviness, because that ye had heard that he had been sick. For indeed he was sick nigh unto death: but God had mercy on him; and not on him only, but* on me also, lest I should have sorrow upon sorrow. I sent him therefore the more carefully, that, when ye see him again, ye may rejoice, and that I may be the less sorrowful. **Receive him therefore in the Lord with all gladness; and hold such in reputation** [honor]: because for the work of Christ he was nigh unto death, not regarding his life, to supply your lack of service toward me."

1 Thessalonians 5:12-13 – "**And we beseech you, brethren, to know them which labour among you, and are over you in the Lord, and admonish you; and to esteem them very highly in love for their work's sake.** And be at peace among yourselves."

Hebrews 13:24 – "**Salute all them that have the rule over you, and all the saints.** They of Italy salute you."

Our Lord expects us to love, esteem, honor, and commend those who are faithful ministers in the work of our Lord.

152. We must consider those who do not love our Lord Jesus Christ to be accursed.

1 Corinthians 16:22 – "**If any man love not the Lord Jesus Christ, let him be Anathema Maranatha.**"

If any individual rejects the Lord Jesus Christ, opposes the Lord Jesus Christ, and has no interest or affection for the Lord Jesus Christ as God the Son who died for him, then that individual has no part in the Lord Jesus Christ as Savior. Such an individual most certainly is anathema (accursed) in the sight of the Lord our God. Even so, such an individual should also be considered anathema (accursed) in our sight. Even so also, such an individual should be considered unacceptable to our spiritual fellowship and should have no place in our spiritual fellowship.

153. We must forgive repentant believers, comforting them and confirming our love toward them.

2 Corinthians 2:6-11 – "*Sufficient to such a man is this punishment, which was inflicted of many.* **So that contrariwise ye ought rather to forgive him, and comfort him**, *lest perhaps such a one should be swallowed up with overmuch sorrow.* **Wherefore I beseech you that ye would confirm your love toward him**. *For to this end also did I write, that I might know the proof of you, whether ye be obedient in all things. To whom ye forgive any thing, I forgive also: for if I forgave any thing, to whom I forgave it, for your sakes forgave I it in the person of Christ; lest Satan should get an advantage of us: for we are not ignorant of his devices.*"

This passage speaks of a believer who had entered into a lifestyle of sin and had been disciplined from the church fellowship. Yet this particular believer had come unto repentance of that sinful lifestyle. Thus the apostle Paul declared in verse 6, "*Sufficient to such a man is this punishment, which was inflicted of many.*" The discipline was sufficient to bring this believer unto repentance. How then were the believers at Corinth to treat this repentant believer? The answer is given in verses 7-8, "*So that contrariwise ye ought rather to forgive him, and comfort him, lest perhaps such a one should be swallowed up with overmuch sorrow. Wherefore I beseech you that ye would confirm your love toward him.*" As a church body they had disciplined him from the church fellowship. Now as a church body they were to forgive him and to restore him unto the church fellowship. Now that he had repented of his sinful ways, they were to comfort him in the grace of God and to confirm their own love toward him. Even so, when a fellow brother or sister in Christ repents of some sinful way of backsliding or immorality, we also are to forgive that one, to comfort that one in God's grace, and to confirm our love toward that one. When such an individual comes unto repentance, we are to grant them restoration. Indeed, we are to do so "*lest perhaps such a one should be swallowed up with overmuch sorrow*" (see verse 7); and we are to do so "*lest Satan should get an advantage of us: for we are not ignorant of his devices*" (see verse 9).

154. We must not be joined in fellowship and communion with unbelievers.

2 Corinthians 6:14-18 – "***Be ye not unequally yoked together with unbelievers****: for what fellowship hath righteousness with unrighteousness? And what communion hath light with darkness? And what concord hath Christ with Belial? Or what part hath he that believeth with an infidel? And what agreement hath the temple of God with idols? For ye are the temple of the living God; as God hath said, I will dwell in them, and walk in them; and I will be their God, and they shall be my people. **Wherefore come out from among them, and be ye separate**, saith the Lord, and touch not the unclean thing; and I will receive you, and will be a Father unto you, and ye shall be my sons and daughters, saith the Lord Almighty.*"

Just as light and darkness cannot mix in fellowship and communion, just as righteousness and unrighteousness cannot mix in fellowship and communion, just as Christ and Satan cannot mix in fellowship and communion, even so we believers are not to be in a place of fellowship and communion with unbelievers. We are to "come out from among them," even as Israel was required to come out from among the Egyptians. We are to be separate from them in anything that requires intimacy of fellowship and spirituality of communion. Now, this does not mean that we are to behave in an unfriendly manner toward the lost around us. Nor does this mean that we are to separate ourselves from all contact and acquaintance with the lost around us. In fact, in 1 Corinthians 5:9-10 God's own Word indicates otherwise, saying, "*I wrote unto you in an epistle not to company with fornicators: yet not altogether with the fornicators of this world, or with the covetous, or extortioners, or with idolaters; for then must ye needs go out of the world.*" Yet it does mean that we must not be yoked together with the lost around us in such matters as business ownership, marriage, or ministry.

155. We must have no part whatsoever with spiritually unclean things.

2 Corinthians 6:17-18 – *"Wherefore come out from among them, and be ye separate, saith the Lord, **and touch not the unclean thing**; and I will receive you, and will be a Father unto you, and ye shall be my sons and daughters, saith the Lord Almighty."*

Ephesians 5:11-12 – *"**And have no fellowship with the unfruitful works of darkness**, but rather reprove them. For it is a shame even to speak of those things which are done of them in secret."*

2 Timothy 2:19 – *"Nevertheless the foundation of God standeth sure, having this seal, The Lord knoweth them that are his. And, **Let every one that nameth the name of Christ depart from iniquity**."*

2 Timothy 2:21-22 – *"If a man therefore purge himself from these, he shall be a vessel unto honour, sanctified, and meet for the master's use, and prepared unto every good work. **Flee also youthful lusts**: but follow righteousness, faith, charity, peace, with them that call on the Lord out of a pure heart."*

Jude 1:23 – *"And others save with fear, pulling them out of the fire; **hating even the garment spotted by the flesh**."*

We are to have **no** fellowship, **no** part, **no** contact with the spiritually unclean, spiritually unfruitful, spiritually unrighteous works and ways of sinful darkness. We are to reject such works and ways. We are to avoid such works and ways. We are to flee such works and ways. We are to be completely separate from such works and ways. As such, we are not to be conformed unto the sinful ways of this world. Indeed, we are not to partake with sinners in their sin, nor to have any fellowship with the works of sin themselves.

156. We must cleanse ourselves through repentance from all spiritual filthiness in our actions and attitudes.

2 Corinthians 7:1 – "*Having therefore these promises, dearly beloved, let us cleanse ourselves from all filthiness of the flesh and spirit, perfecting holiness in the fear of God.*"

James 4:8-9 – "***Draw nigh to God****, and he will draw nigh to you. **Cleanse your hands, ye sinners; and purify your hearts, ye double minded. Be afflicted, and mourn, and weep: let your laughter be turned to mourning, and your joy to heaviness***."

Wherever we may find the filthiness of sin in the activities of our flesh or in the attitudes of our spirit, we must humbly repent with a broken heart before the Lord our God over our sin. We must be afflicted in heart over our sin. We must have a spirit of mourning and weeping over our sin. Our carnal happiness and joy in our sin must be exchanged for a spiritual mourning and grief over our sin. Indeed, this is the true character of Biblical repentance for the believer; and such broken-hearted repentance is the first step whereby a sinning believer may draw nigh unto the Lord for restoration of fellowship. Without broken-hearted repentance over sin, such a believer cannot enter into a walk of spiritual fellowship with the Lord. Then we can be assured that the Lord our God Himself will cleanse us of all unrighteousness and will make us spiritually as white as snow. Indeed, the promise is given in 1 John 1:9, "*If we confess our sins, he is faithful and just to forgive us our sins, and to cleanse us from all unrighteousness.*"

157. We must be perfect by surrendering unto our Lord's perfecting work within us.

2 Corinthians 13:11 – "*Finally, brethren, farewell. **Be perfect**, be of good comfort, be of one mind, live in peace; and the God of love and peace shall be with you.*"

The opening instruction of 2 Corinthians 13:11 is just this – *"Be perfect."* Yet how is it possible for us sinners to "be perfect"? The answer is found in Hebrews 13:20-21 – *"Now the God of peace, that brought again from the dead our Lord Jesus, that great shepherd of the sheep, through the blood of the everlasting covenant, make you perfect in every good work to do his will, working in you that which is wellpleasing in his sight, through Jesus Christ; to whom be glory for ever and ever. Amen."* Again the answer is found in 1 Peter 5:10 – *"But the God of all grace, who hath called us unto his eternal glory by Christ Jesus, after that ye have suffered a while, make you perfect, stablish, strengthen, settle you."* We are able to "be perfect" as the Lord our God, the God of all grace and peace, performs His perfecting work within us and as we surrender ourselves unto that perfecting work.

158. We must be of good comfort by receiving our Lord's gift of comfort for us.

2 Corinthians 13:11 – *"Finally, brethren, farewell. Be perfect, **be of good comfort**, be of one mind, live in peace; and the God of love and peace shall be with you."*

The second instruction in 2 Corinthians 13:11 is just this – *"Be of good comfort."* Yet in this world of trouble how is it possible for us to "be of good comfort"? The answer is found in 2 Corinthians 1:3-5 – *"Blessed be God, even the Father of our Lord Jesus Christ, the Father of mercies, and the God of all comfort; who comforteth us in all our tribulation, that we may be able to comfort them which are in any trouble, by the comfort wherewith we ourselves are comforted of God. For as the sufferings of Christ abound in us, so our consolation also aboundeth by Christ."* We are able to "be of good comfort" as the Lord our God, the God of all comfort and mercy, grants His gift of comfort unto us and as we receive that gift of comfort through faith.

159. We must consider those who preach any "gospel" other than the Biblical gospel to be accursed.

Galatians 1:8-9 – *"But though we, or an angel from heaven, preach any other gospel unto you than that which we have preached unto you, **let him be accursed**. As we said before, so say I now again, If any man preach any other gospel unto you than that ye have received, **let him be accursed**."*

In Galatians 1:6-7 the apostle Paul expressed his surprise at the believers of Galatia, saying, *"I marvel that ye are so soon removed from him that called you into the grace of Christ unto another gospel: which is not another; but there be some that trouble you, and would pervert the gospel of Christ."* Apparently there were some false teachers who had entered into the churches of Galatia, preaching and teaching another "gospel" than that which they had received by the Word of the Lord through His chosen apostle. Yet the apostle made clear that this "other gospel" was no true gospel at all. There is only one true gospel of salvation through faith in the Lord Jesus Christ alone. Furthermore, the apostle indicated that these individuals were perverting the true gospel of Christ and were thereby troubling the believers of Galatia with their false teaching.

Thus, under the inspiration of God the Holy Spirit, the apostle Paul gave instruction in Galatians 1:8, *"But though we, or an angel from heaven, preach any other gospel unto you than that which we have preached unto you, let him be accursed."* Then just to make the point abundantly clear, the apostle repeated the instruction under the inspiration of God the Holy Spirit in verse 9 – *"As we said before, so say I now again, If any man preach any other gospel unto you than that we have received, let him be accursed."* Such a teacher or preacher of a false gospel is not of God. Rather, such a teacher or preacher is under the curse of the Lord our God. Furthermore, such a teacher or preacher of a false gospel is to be viewed as accursed in our sight, such that we will have no fellowship with him or her and will allow him or her to have no part in fellowship with us.

Yet what is the true gospel of Jesus Christ? It is that our Lord Jesus Christ, God the Son Himself in human flesh, *"died for our sins according to the scriptures; and that he was buried, and that he rose again the third day according to the scriptures."* (See 1 Corinthians 15:3-4) Furthermore, it is that we are saved by God's grace through our faith in Christ alone, not of our own self-goodness or of our own good works. (See Ephesians 2:8-9) Any other "gospel" is not the true, Biblical gospel. Any such false "gospels" are to be rejected, and any who preach and teach such false "gospels" are to viewed as accursed of God. In fact, the apostle revealed in Galatians 5:10 that such false preachers and teachers shall indeed suffer under the judgment of God, saying, *"I have confidence in you through the Lord, that ye will be none otherwise minded: but he that troubleth you shall bear his judgment, whosoever he be."* In addition, in Galatians 5:12 the apostle indicated, under the inspiration of God the Holy Spirit, his own desire that such false preachers and teachers would be cut off by the judgment of God, saying, *"I would they were even cut off which trouble you."*

160. We must stand fast in the spiritual liberty of salvation through faith in Christ alone, and not be entangled with the spiritual bondage of justification through the works of the Law.

Galatians 5:1-6 – *"**Stand fast therefore in the liberty wherewith Christ hath made us free, and be not entangled again with the yoke of bondage**. Behold, I Paul say unto you, that if ye be circumcised, Christ shall profit you nothing. For I testify again to every man that is circumcised, that he is a debtor to do the whole law. Christ is become of no effect unto you, whosoever of you are justified by the law; ye are fallen from grace. For we through the Spirit wait for the hope of righteousness by faith. For in Jesus Christ neither circumcision availeth any thing, nor uncircumcision; but faith which worketh by love."*

315

Galatians 5:1 instructs us to *"stand fast therefore in the liberty wherewith Christ hath made us free, and be not entangled again with the yoke of bondage."* Yet what is this liberty wherewith Christ hath made us free and wherein we are to stand fast? In addition, what is this yoke of bondage wherewith we might be entangled? To what do these two things refer? The further revelation of verses 2-6 reveals the answer. Therein we learn that the yoke of bondage centers around justification by the works of the Law. Even so, if an individual seeks this path of justification before God, he has the responsibility to keep the whole Law perfectly. To him the work of Christ is of no profit, and he has no part in God's saving grace. On the other hand, we learn that the matter of liberty centers around justification through faith in Christ. Even so, if an individual seeks this path of justification before God, he has an assured part in the hope of righteousness through the Holy Spirit by faith in Christ. Therefore, we must stand fast in the Biblical doctrine of salvation through faith in Christ alone and not by the works of the Law at all. Yea, let us never, ever waver from this Biblical doctrine of salvation or turn aside from it.

This is the true gospel according to God's Word of truth. Romans 3:19-28 – *"Now we know that what things soever the law saith, it saith to them who are under the law: that every mouth may be stopped, and all the world may become guilty before God. Therefore by the deeds of the law there shall no flesh be justified in his sight: for by the law is the knowledge of sin. But now the righteousness of God without the law is manifested, being witnessed by the law and the prophets; even the righteousness of God which is by faith of Jesus Christ unto all and upon all them that believe: for there is no difference: for all have sinned, and come short of the glory of God; being justified freely by his grace through the redemption that is in Christ Jesus: whom God hath set forth to be a propitiation through faith in his blood, to declare his righteousness for the remission of sins that are past, through the forbearance of God; to declare, I say, at this time his righteousness: that he might be just, and the justifier of him which believeth in Jesus. Where is boasting then? It is excluded. By what law? Of works? Nay: but by the law of faith. Therefore we conclude that a man is justified by faith without the deeds of the law."*

Romans 4:4-5 – "*Now to him that worketh is the reward not reckoned of grace, but of debt. But to him that worketh not, but believeth on him that justifieth the ungodly, his faith is counted for righteousness.*" Romans 11:5-6 – "*Even so then at this present time also there is a remnant according to the election of grace. And if by grace, then is it no more of works: otherwise grace is no more grace. But if it be of works, then is it no more grace: otherwise work is no more work.*" Galatians 2:16 – "*Knowing that a man is not justified by the works of the law, but by the faith of Jesus Christ, even we have believed in Jesus Christ, that we might be justified by the faith of Christ, and not by the works of the law: for by the works of the law shall no flesh be justified.*" Ephesians 2:4-9 – "*But God, who is rich in mercy, for his great love wherewith he loved us, even when we were dead in sins, hath quickened us together with Christ, (by grace ye are saved;) and hath raised us up together, and made us sit together in heavenly places in Christ Jesus: that in the ages to come he might shew the exceeding riches of his grace in his kindness toward us through Christ Jesus. For by grace are ye saved through faith; and that not of yourselves: it is the gift of God: not of works, lest any man should boast.*" Titus 3:4-7 – "*But after that the kindness and love of God our Saviour toward man appeared, not by works of righteousness which we have done, but according to his mercy he saved us, by the washing of regeneration, and renewing of the Holy Ghost; which he shed on us abundantly through Jesus Christ our Saviour; that being justified by his grace, we should be made heirs according to the hope of eternal life.*"

161. We must not use our spiritual liberty for an occasion to the flesh.

Galatians 5:13 – "*For, brethren, ye have been called unto liberty; **only use not liberty for an occasion to the flesh**, but by love serve one another.*"

Yes, as those who are justified by God's grace through faith in Christ alone, we are set at spiritual liberty from the obligation, curse, and condemnation of the Law. The obligation of the Law is that we must obey every command of God perfectly in order to be justified. Yet we all have sinned and have become guilty before God of transgression against the Law of God. Even so, as sinners against the Law, we are all under the curse and condemnation of the Law. *"For it is written, Cursed is every one that continueth not in all things which are written in the book of the law to do them."* (See Galatians 3:10) However, by God's grace through faith in Christ as our eternal Savior, we are redeemed from our sins and from the curse and condemnation of the Law against our sinfulness. Even so, being spiritually redeemed, we are set at spiritual liberty from the obligation of the Law to be perfectly obedient in order to be justified in God's sight.

Yet this spiritual liberty by God's grace is not intended to grant us the license to live and act according to our selfish, sinful flesh. God forbid! We must not use this spiritual liberty that we have by God's grace in Christ our Savior for an occasion to the flesh. Yet many do turn this grace of God into a license for sinful flesh. (See Jude 1:4) Indeed, many turn this grace of God into a license to involve themselves in the works of the flesh, which are revealed in Galatians 5:19-21 – *"Now the works of the flesh are manifest, which are these; Adultery, fornication, uncleanness, lasciviousness, idolatry, witchcraft, hatred, variance, emulations, wrath, strife, seditions, heresies, envyings, murders, drunkenness, revellings, and such like: of the which I tell you before, as I have also told you in time past, that they which do such things shall not inherit the kingdom of God."* Therein, while they claim spiritual liberty, they become *"the servants of corruption."* (See 1 Peter 2:19) These things ought not so to be, and they will not be if we refuse to use our spiritual liberty for an occasion to serve our selfish, sinful flesh.

162. We must serve one another by love.

Galatians 5:13-14 – *"For, brethren, ye have been called unto liberty; only use not liberty for an occasion to the flesh, **but by love serve***

318

one another. For all the law is fulfilled in one word, even in this; Thou shalt love thy neighbour as thyself."

This is to be one of the governing principles of our new life in Christ. We now possess spiritual liberty in Christ. Yet we are not to use that spiritual liberty in order to serve our flesh in sin. Rather, we are now to use the spiritual liberty of our new life in Christ in order to serve others in love. Indeed, this is the true fulfillment of the Law, even as Galatians 5:14 declares, *"For all the Law is fulfilled in one word, even in this; Thou shalt love thy neighbor as thyself."* We are no longer to serve the flesh and to serve sin in selfishness. Now we are to serve the Lord and to serve others in love. This is the new standard for our lives in the newness of life that we have in Christ.

163. We must take heed that we "be not consumed one of another" through backbiting and harshness.

Galatians 5:15 – *"But if ye bite and devour one another, **take heed that ye be not consumed one of another**."*

If we choose not to use our spiritual liberty in Christ in order to serve our Lord and others in love, if we choose rather to use our spiritual liberty for an occasion to our selfish, sinful flesh, then in our selfish ways we will backbite, strive, and tear down one another. Furthermore, when we so behave according to our selfish, sinful flesh, we will consume one another spiritually, rather than build one another up spiritually. Yea, we ourselves, as fellow brothers and sisters in Christ, will become the very means of one another's spiritual destruction. Such behavior will destroy our family unity, our Christian fellowship, and our church ministry. Certainly this ought not so to be. Certainly this is not what God our heavenly Father intends. Thus He commands us to take heed, to beware, to be on our guard against the desires of our own sinful flesh, that we not engage in such selfish, sinful behavior. Yes, we must ever take heed and beware that we might not backbite and behave harshly against one another.

319

164. We must walk after the Holy Spirit in order not to fulfill the desires of our flesh, but in order to walk in the wisdom of our Lord.

Galatians 5:16-25 – *"This I say then, **Walk in the Spirit, and ye shall not fulfil the lust of the flesh**. For the flesh lusteth against the Spirit, and the Spirit against the flesh: and these are contrary the one to the other: so that ye cannot do the things that ye would. But if ye be led of the Spirit, ye are not under the law. Now the works of the flesh are manifest, which are these; Adultery, fornication, uncleanness, lasciviousness, idolatry, witchcraft, hatred, variance, emulations, wrath, strife, seditions, heresies, envyings, murders, drunkenness, revellings, and such like: of the which I tell you before, as I have also told you in time past, that they which do such things shall not inherit the kingdom of God. But the fruit of the Spirit is love, joy, peace, longsuffering, gentleness, goodness, faith, meekness, temperance: against such there is no law. And they that are Christ's have crucified the flesh with the affections and lusts. **If we live in the Spirit, let us also walk in the Spirit**."*

Ephesians 5:18 – *"And be not drunk with wine, wherein is excess; **but be filled with the Spirit**."*

As we have seen, we are not to give any occasion unto the sinfulness of our selfish flesh, not to follow after the selfish, sinful desires of our flesh, not to be backbiting and harsh toward others in the selfishness of our flesh. Rather, we are to serve the Lord our God and others around us by love. Yet how shall we find the spiritual power to resist the natural selfishness and sinfulness of our flesh and to actually serve our Lord and others by love? The answer is found in Galatians 5:16 where the instruction and promise is given, *"This I say then, Walk in the Spirit, and ye shall not fulfil the lust of the flesh."*

Certainly every true believer experiences the spiritual battle between the indwelling Holy Spirit and the indwelling sinful flesh. Thus Galatians 5:17 reports, *"For the flesh lusteth against the Spirit, and the Spirit against the flesh: and these are contrary the one to the other: so that ye cannot do the things that ye would."* Yet the power of God the Holy Spirit is infinitely greater than the power of our sinful flesh. Therefore, when we surrender ourselves to walk in the Spirit, that is – to walk moment by moment after the direction of the Holy Spirit, then we shall be filled with the Holy Spirit's power to overcome the affections and lusts (desires) of our sinful flesh. Even so, Galatians 5:24 declares, "*And they that are Christ's have crucified the flesh with the affections and lusts.*" Even so also, Galatians 5:16 gives the promise, "*This I say then, Walk in the Spirit, and ye shall not fulfil the lust of the flesh.*" Thus in the power of the Holy Spirit we are indeed able to deny the natural selfishness of the sinful flesh in our daily living. Furthermore, when we surrender ourselves to walk after the Holy Spirit's direction and to depend upon His power, then we shall also bring forth the fruit of the Spirit as it is described in Galatians 5:22-23. Thus in the power of the Holy Spirit we are indeed able to be servant-minded through godly love in our daily living. Finally, as we surrender ourselves under the holy influence of the Holy Spirit, we shall grow abundantly in godliness. Indeed, then we shall glean the wisdom of God's Word, understand the will of our Lord, and be empowered to follow in the way of His will.

165. We must not be "desirous of vain glory," and thereby "provoking one another" and "envying one another."

Galatians 5:26 – "*Let us not be desirous of vain glory, provoking one another, envying one another.*"

So then, what is this "vain glory" that we are not to be desiring? In this context the word "vain" refers to that which is empty and worthless in the estimation of the Lord our God. Often it may have the appearance of substance and value in the sight of man, yet it lacks the reality of substance and value in the sight of God. So then, what kind of glory appears to have substance and value in the sight of man, while lacking the reality of substance and value in the sight of God? The answer is just this – glory for self among mankind. In the sight and estimation of the Lord our God, when we desire and seek after glory for ourselves among men, it is spiritually vain (yea, spiritually empty and worthless). In fact, such glory is the very opposite of that glory which the Lord our God approves and values. In Galatians 6:14 the Word of God reveals the type of glory that the Lord our God approves and values when the apostle Paul gave declaration under the inspiration of God the Holy Spirit, saying, *"But God forbid that I should glory, save in the cross of our Lord Jesus Christ, by whom the world is crucified unto me, and I unto the world."*

The Lord our God does not at all approve or value the glory that we receive unto ourselves among men. Such glory is vain, that is – spiritually empty and worthless, in His sight. Rather, the Lord our God approves and values the glory of His Son, our Lord Jesus Christ, and the glory of the cross of our Lord Jesus Christ. Thus our Lord instructs us not even to desire such "vain glory." Furthermore, our Lord warns us that such "vain glory" will only involve us in the practice of "provoking one another" and "envying one another." When we desire such "vain glory" for ourselves, then we will envy all others who acquire that glory over us and will seek to undercut (provoke) all others in order that we might rise in glory over them. This is the way of our selfish, sinful flesh. This is not the way of the indwelling Holy Spirit. This is the way of sinful selfishness, not the way of godly love. Thus the Lord our God instructs us not to desire any form of "vain glory" and thereby to avoid the selfish and sinful ways of provoking and envying one another.

166. We who walk in the Spirit must restore in the spirit of meekness a fellow believer who is overtaken by sin.

Galatians 6:1 – *"Brethren, if a man be overtaken in a fault, **ye which are spiritual, restore such an one in the spirit of meekness**; considering thyself, lest thou also be tempted."*

When we are aware of a fellow brother or sister in Christ who has been overtaken by and has fallen to a sinful fault, we should not rejoice in their spiritual downfall, but should seek after their spiritual restoration. We should not abuse them while they are fallen into sin, but should help them to walk again in the Spirit. Certainly, this process of restoration may require reproof and rebuke in accord with the truth of God's Holy Word in order that the overtaken one may see the sinfulness of his or her sin and be convicted thereby. Yet the purpose must always be the loving desire for the other's spiritual restoration. Thus it is necessary that our involvement in such cases always be while walking in the Spirit and with a spirit of meekness. God's Word clearly declares, "*Ye which are spiritual restore such an one in the spirit of meekness.*" We are not to involve ourselves in such cases when we ourselves are in the flesh; for in the flesh we will only destroy, and not restore. Furthermore, we are not to involve ourselves in such cases with a spirit of pride or superiority; for again in the pride of our flesh we will only destroy, and not restore. Yea, in the pride of our sinful flesh we ourselves will also be tempted and overtaken by sin.

167. We must lovingly bear one another's burdens.

Galatians 6:2 – "*Bear ye one another's burdens, and so fulfil the law of Christ.*"

Now, "the law of Christ" is His command that we are to love one another, even as our Lord and Savior Jesus Christ has loved us. Thus in bearing one another's burdens, we demonstrate godly love toward one another and obey our Lord's command. So then, what does it mean to bear one another's burdens? It means that when a fellow believer is weighed down under the burdens of this life in whatever sort it may be, we are to come along side and to help him or her as much as we able in bearing that burden.

323

168. We must prove our own work before the Lord in bearing our own responsibilities from the Lord.

Galatians 6:3-5 – *"For if a man think himself to be something, when he is nothing, he deceiveth himself.* ***But let every man prove his own work****, and then shall he have rejoicing in himself alone, and not in another. For every man shall bear his own burden."*

In these verses we find a contrast between an individual who thinks himself to be something, when he is nothing, and thereby deceives himself, and an individual who actually fulfills his own work of responsibility and thereby finds rejoicing in himself alone before the Lord. In the first case the individual compares himself to others and glories in himself over others. In the second case the individual just performs his God-given responsibility and finds joy in the pleasure of the Lord. Now, according to the instruction of our Lord, we are to follow in the way of the second individual. We are not to think ourselves to be something. We are just to bear the weight of our responsibility. We are not to glory in ourselves over others. We are just to seek the joy of pleasing our Lord. We are not to seek the joy of comparing ourselves unto others and finding ourselves to be something more than others. Rather, we are to seek the joy of simply being a good and faithful servant of our Lord.

169. We must not be deceived into thinking that we can get away with sowing unto our sinful flesh.

Galatians 6:7-8 – *"****Be not deceived****; God is not mocked: for whatsoever a man soweth, that shall he also reap. For he that soweth to his flesh shall of the flesh reap corruption; but he that soweth to the Spirit shall of the Spirit reap life everlasting."*

Here we find the instruction that we are not to be deceived. Yet about what are we not to be so deceived? We are not to be deceived into thinking that the Lord our God, the righteous Judge of all the earth, can be mocked as we sin and get away with it. No, the Lord our God is not mocked; for no one can sin and just get away with it.

Whatever an individual sows spiritually, that shall he or she also reap spiritually. No one can sin without consequences. If an individual sows to the sinfulness of his or her sinful flesh, then that individual shall reap the corruption of that sinfulness. This is a certain principle of God's government over this world.

Indeed, this principle rings throughout God's Holy Word. We hear it in Proverbs 1:24-32 as the personified wisdom of God cries forth her judgment, saying, "*Because I have called, and ye refused; I have stretched out my hand, and no man regarded; but ye have set at nought all my counsel, and would none of my reproof: I also will laugh at your calamity; I will mock when your fear cometh; when your fear cometh as desolation, and your destruction cometh as a whirlwind; when distress and anguish cometh upon you. Then shall they call upon me, but I will not answer; they shall seek me early, but they shall not find me: for that they hated knowledge, and did not choose the fear of the LORD: they would none of my counsel: they despised all my reproof. Therefore shall they eat of the fruit of their own way, and be filled with their own devices. For the turning away of the simple shall slay them, and the prosperity of fools shall destroy them.*"

Again we hear it in Proverbs 6:12-15 – "*A naughty person, a wicked man, walketh with a froward mouth. He winketh with his eyes, he speaketh with his feet, he teacheth with his fingers; frowardness is in his heart, he deviseth mischief continually; he soweth discord. Therefore shall his calamity come suddenly; suddenly shall he be broken without remedy.*" Yet again we hear it in the opening half of Proverbs 14:14 – "*The backslider in heart shall be filled with his own ways.*" And yet again we hear it in the opening half of Proverbs 22:8 – "*He that soweth iniquity shall reap vanity.*"

We hear it in Jeremiah 2:19 – "*Thine own wickedness shall correct thee, and thy backslidings shall reprove thee: know therefore and see that it is an evil thing and bitter, that thou hast forsaken the LORD thy God, and that my fear is not in thee, saith the Lord GOD of hosts.*" Again we hear it in the opening portion of Hosea 8:7 – "*For they have sown the wind, and they shall reap the whirlwind.*" Yet again we hear it in the opening portion of Hosea 10:13 – "*Ye have plowed wickedness, ye have reaped iniquity.*" And yet again we hear it in the first half of Romans 8:13 – "*For if ye live after the flesh, ye shall die.*" Finally, we hear it in James 1:14-15 – "*But every man is tempted, when he is drawn away of his own lust, and enticed. Then when lust hath conceived, it bringeth forth sin: and sin, when it is finished, bringeth forth death.*" Truly our sin will find us out.

⌒〰〰⌒

170. We must not be weary in well doing because in due season we will reap reward.

Galatians 6:8-9 – "*For he that soweth to his flesh shall of the flesh reap corruption; but he that soweth to the Spirit shall of the Spirit reap life everlasting. And let us not be weary in well doing: for in due season we shall reap, if we faint not.*"

2 Thessalonians 3:13 – "*But ye, brethren, be not weary in well doing.*"

Hebrews 12:12-13 – "*Wherefore lift up the hands which hang down, and the feeble knees; and make straight paths for your feet, lest that which is lame be turned out of the way; but let it rather be healed.*"

This also is a certain principle of God's government over this world. Yea, this principle of promise is just as certain as the previous principle of warning in Galatians 6:7-8. If an individual sows unto the things of God the Holy Spirit, then that individual will reap the blessing and reward of God. Now, this blessing and reward does not come immediately. Rather, it comes "in due season." Thus we are instructed not to become weary in well doing as that blessing and reward may appear to tarry long. Our labor in well doing "*is not in vain in the Lord.*" (See 1 Corinthians 15:58) In fact, our Lord has promised a "*great recompence of reward.*" (See Hebrews 10:35) Indeed, although our outward man may perish under the afflictions of this life, yet as we sow to the Spirit, our inward man will be renewed from day to day. (See 2 Corinthians 4:16) Even so, the promise is given in Romans 8:13, "*For if ye live after the flesh, ye* shall die: but if ye through the Spirit do mortify the deeds of the body,* *ye shall live* [that is – ye shall experience abundant spiritual life]." Furthermore, as we remain faithful under the afflictions of this life, it shall work for us "*a far more exceeding and eternal weight of glory.*" (See 2 Corinthians 4:17)

On the other hand, if we have already become weary in well doing, if we have already become faint in our minds, if we have already become discouraged in our hearts, if we have already become depressed in our Christian walk so that our hands "hang down" and our knees are "feeble," then we must beware lest we completely turn aside and depart from the way of our Lord's fellowship and righteousness. Rather, we must confess the unrighteousness of our discouragement and depression, and must refocus our pursuit upon the straight path of righteousness, and must find spiritual healing and encouragement from the Lord our God.

171. We must remember our lost spiritual condition before we were saved, and the way by which we were saved from that lost condition.

Ephesians 2:11-13 – "*Wherefore remember, that ye being in time past Gentiles in the flesh, who are called Uncircumcision by that which is called the Circumcision in the flesh made by hands; that at that time ye were without Christ, being aliens from the commonwealth of Israel, and strangers from the covenants of promise, having no hope, and without God in the world: but now in Christ Jesus ye who sometimes were far off are made nigh by the blood of Christ.*"

We are to remember that in our lost condition we were "without Christ," that is – having been without eternal salvation through Christ Jesus our Lord and Savior. We are to remember that at that time we were "aliens from the commonwealth of Israel," that is – having had no part among the people of God. We are to remember that at that time we were "strangers from the covenants of promise," that is – having had no claim on the blessed promises of God. We are to remember that at that time we had "no hope," that is – having had no spiritual hope for the life to come. We are to remember that at that time we were "without God in the world," that is – having had no possibility of any fellowship with God or any approval from God in this life. We are to remember that at that time we were spiritually lost in our sin and had no possible way to save ourselves from that lost spiritual condition.

Yet we are also to remember that a way of salvation was provided unto us in Christ Jesus. We are to remember that in Christ Jesus our Lord and Savior, through faith in Him, we who were spiritually afar from God the Father were made spiritually nigh unto God the Father. We are to remember that in Christ we who were the spiritual enemies of God were reconciled unto God and adopted into God's family as His own dear children. We are to remember that in Christ we now have eternal peace with God. Indeed, we are to remember that God the Son, our Lord and Savior Jesus Christ, provided this way of eternal salvation unto us by His own shed blood and sacrificial death on the cross. "Wherefore remember;" and never forget!

***

172. We must walk worthy of our eternal calling into the family and fellowship of God.

Ephesians 4:1 – *"I therefore, the prisoner of the Lord, **beseech you that ye walk worthy of the vocation wherewith ye are called**."*

Ephesians 4:17-21 – *"This I say therefore, and testify in the Lord, **that ye henceforth walk not as other Gentiles walk**, in the vanity of their mind, having the understanding darkened, being alienated from the life of God through the ignorance that is in them, because of the blindness of their heart: who being past feeling have given themselves over unto lasciviousness, to work all uncleanness with greediness. But ye have not so learned Christ; if so be that ye have heard him, and have been taught by him, as the truth is in Jesus."*

Ephesians 5:8 – *"For ye were sometimes darkness, but now are ye light in the Lord: **walk as children of light**."*

In Ephesians 4:1 we are beseeched with great emotional intensity to "walk worthy of the vocation [the calling] wherewith [we] are called." What then is this vocation (this calling) wherewith we have been called by the Lord our God? The answer is revealed in Ephesians 2:19-22 – "*Now therefore ye are no more strangers and foreigners, but fellowcitizens with the saints, and of the household of God; and are built upon the foundation of the apostles and prophets, Jesus Christ himself being the chief corner stone; in whom all the building fitly framed together groweth unto an holy temple in the Lord: in whom ye also are builded together for an habitation of God through the Spirit.*" Through salvation in Christ Jesus our Lord and Savior we are now "fellowcitizens with the saints, and of the household of God." We are now a part of God's own people and children in God's own family. Furthermore, we are now "an holy temple in the Lord," "an habitation of God through the Spirit." We are now able to experience the closest of communion and fellowship with God the Father in God the Son, the Lord Jesus Christ, through God the Holy Spirit who indwells us. Yes, at the moment of eternal salvation through faith in Christ, we were eternally called into the family and fellowship of God.

Now then, each moment of our daily walk in this life, we are to walk worthy of that calling. We are no longer to walk in the sinful, selfish ways of this spiritually dark world. Even so, Ephesians 4:17-21 instructs us not to walk henceforth "*as other Gentiles walk.*" We are no longer to walk in the selfish vanity of our mind. We are no longer to walk without spiritual understanding. We are no longer to walk in sinfulness, working "all uncleanness with greediness [selfishness]." We are no longer to walk as the children of spiritual darkness. Through faith in Christ we have been saved and called out of the old walk of sinfulness. Now we have been called to walk in newness of spiritual life. Now we have been called as the children of God and the children of light. We are no longer the children of spiritual darkness, and we are no longer to walk as the children of spiritual darkness. We are now the children of God, and we are to walk as the children of God. We are now the children of light, and we are to walk as the children of light. We are to walk worthy of our eternal calling into the family and fellowship of God our heavenly Father.

329

173. We must walk "with all lowliness and meekness."

Ephesians 4:1-2 – "*I therefore, the prisoner of the Lord, **beseech you that ye walk** worthy of the vocation wherewith ye are called, **with all lowliness and meekness**, with longsuffering, forbearing one another in love.*"

Colossians 3:12 – "***Put on therefore**, as the elect of God, holy and beloved, bowels of mercies, kindness, **humbleness of mind, meekness**, longsuffering.*"

1 Timothy 6:11 – "*But thou, O man of God, flee these things; **and follow after** righteousness, godliness, faith, love, patience, **meekness**.*"

1 Peter 5:5 – "*Likewise, ye younger, submit yourselves unto the elder. Yea, all of you be subject one to another, **and be clothed with humility**: for God resisteth the proud, and giveth grace to the humble.*"

The Lord our God would have us ever to maintain an attitude and spirit of Biblical humility in our daily walk. In Matthew 11:29 our Lord Jesus Christ revealed that this was His own attitude and spirit as He walked upon the earth. Therein He declared, "*Take my yoke upon you, and learn of me; for I am meek and lowly of heart: and ye shall find rest unto your souls.*" Thus we are called to learn of Him and walk in His steps, to be meek and lowly of heart like Him. Each day we are to put on humbleness of mind and meekness of spirit. Each day we are to be clothed with Biblical humility and meekness. Indeed, we are to follow and pursue after humbleness of mind and meekness of spirit throughout each day.

174. We must walk "with longsuffering, forbearing one another in love."

Ephesians 4:1-2 – "*I therefore, the prisoner of the Lord, **beseech you that ye walk** worthy of the vocation wherewith ye are called, with all lowliness and meekness, **with longsuffering, forbearing one another in love**.*"

Colossians 3:12-13 – "***Put on therefore***, *as the elect of God, holy and beloved, bowels of mercies, kindness, humbleness of mind, meekness,* ***longsuffering; forbearing one another***, *and forgiving one another, if any man have a quarrel against any: even as Christ forgave you, so also do ye.*"

1 Thessalonians 5:14 – "*Now we exhort you, brethren, warn them that are unruly, comfort the feebleminded, support the weak,* ***be patient toward all men***."

The Lord our God would have us ever to maintain an attitude and spirit of Biblical longsuffering in our dealings with one another. Certainly in this life people shall do us wrong and shall mistreat us at times. Such may come from our friends or from our enemies, from our family or from our neighbors, from fellow believers or from lost sinners. Yet in every case and toward every individual, we are called unto a spirit of longsuffering and an attitude of forbearance. In any quarrel we are to maintain an attitude of godly forbearance; and toward every individual we are to maintain a spirit of patient longsuffering. We are not to be quick unto anger, but to be long in patience. We are not to be quick to strike back, but to be long in bearing up under the suffering.

175. We must be renewed in the spirit of our mind.

Ephesians 4:23 – "***And be renewed in the spirit of your mind***."

As believers we need the spirit of our minds changed and made new. We need a new mental spirit. We need the old mind-set of the flesh to be taken away and the new mind-set of the Spirit to take its place. We need to give up the old mind-set of the flesh and to take hold of the new mind-set of the Spirit. We need no longer to enjoy the pleasures of sin, but to rejoice in the fellowship of our Lord. We need no longer to corrupt our hearts with sinful lusts, but to cleanse our hearts in Christ's blood through broken confession. We need no longer to seek after our own will, but to submit ourselves unto our Lord's will. We need no longer to hold a stubborn spirit against our Lord, but to hold a surrendered spirit before our Lord. We need no longer to walk in disobedience and rebellion, but to walk in obedience and humility. We need no longer to walk in the unrighteousness of our selfish flesh, but to walk in the righteousness of our Lord's ways. Then through this renewed spirit of mind, we shall be spiritually transformed unto the holy image of our Lord Jesus Christ. Even so, the opening portion of Romans 12:2 declares, *"And be not conformed to this world: but be ye transformed by the renewing of your mind."*

Yet how shall we be renewed in the spirit of our minds? In the first place, we must allow the Word of Christ to abide in our hearts and minds richly in all wisdom. In the opening half of John 15:7 our Lord Jesus Christ said, *"If ye abide in me, and my words abide in you."* In the opening portion of Colossians 3:16 the instruction is given, *"Let the Word of Christ dwell in you richly in all wisdom."* In Hebrews 4:12 the truth is revealed, *"For the word of God is quick, and powerful, and sharper than any twoedged sword, piercing even to the dividing asunder of soul and spirit, and of the joints and marrow, and is a discerner of the thoughts and intents of the heart."* In Psalm 19:7 the further truth is revealed, *"The law of the LORD is perfect, converting the soul* [renewing the heart and mind]*: that testimony of the LORD is sure, making wise the simple."* Only as we receive the truth and wisdom of God's Holy Word into our hearts to do its work of correction and instruction will we be renewed in the spirit of our minds.

In the second place, we must walk after the spiritual guidance of the indwelling Holy Spirit. In Romans 8:4-6 the truth is revealed, *"That the righteousness of the law might be fulfilled in us, who walk not after the flesh, but after the Spirit. For they that are after the flesh do mind the things of the flesh; but they that are after the Spirit the things of the Spirit. For to be carnally* [fleshly] *minded is death; but to be spiritually minded is life and peace."* In Galatians 5:16 the instruction is given, *"This I say then, Walk in the Spirit, and ye shall not fulfil the lust of the flesh."* In 2 Corinthians 3:18 the truth is revealed, *"But we all, with open face beholding as in a glass the glory of the Lord, are changed into the same image from glory to glory, even as by the Spirit of the Lord."* Only as we yield ourselves unto the holy influence and guidance of the Holy Spirit for our daily living will we be renewed in the spirit of our minds.

In the third and final place, we must bring into captivity every thought unto the obedience of Christ. In 2 Corinthians 10:5 the instruction is given, *"Casting down imaginations, and every high thing that exalteth itself against the knowledge of God, and bringing into captivity every thought to the obedience of Christ."* Many of the thoughts and imaginations of our hearts and minds are at war with the knowledge of God. They are contrary to and exalt themselves against the knowledge of God. Thus God's Holy Word instructs us to cast down such thoughts and imaginations. Every time that our thoughts and imaginations rise up against the knowledge of God we must forcefully cast them down. Furthermore, we must purposefully bring into captivity every thought of our hearts and minds unto the obedience of Christ. Yes, every thought of our minds must be made to conform unto the will of the Lord our God. In addition, every thought of our minds that will not conform unto the will of our Lord must be cast down. Only then will we be renewed in the spirit of our minds.

176. We must put away all falsehood and "speak every man truth with his neighbor."

Ephesians 4:25 – *"**Wherefore putting away lying, speak every man truth with his neighbour**: for we are members one of another."*

Colossians 3:9 – *"**Lie not one to another**, seeing that ye have put off the old man with his deeds."*

In Proverbs 6:16-19 God's Holy Word lists seven things that are a hateful abomination in our Lord's sight. The second of these is *"a lying tongue."* In fact, the matter of speaking falsehood is mentioned twice on this list; for the list not only includes *"a lying tongue"* as second on the list, but also includes *"a false witness that speaketh lies"* as sixth on the list. In addition, Proverbs 12:22 proclaims,

"*Lying lips are abomination to the* LORD: *but they that deal truly are his delight.*" Yea, one of the reasons that the Lord our God will refuse to hear the cry of His people's prayer and will refuse to help His people in their time of need is because of the sin of lying and deception. In Isaiah 59:1-4 our Lord delivers His warning unto His people, saying, "*Behold, the* LORD'S *hand is not shortened, that it cannot save; neither his ear heavy, that it cannot hear: but your iniquities have separated between you and your God, and your sins have hid his face from you, that he will not hear.* [What sins, and what iniquities?] *For your hands are defiled with blood, and your fingers with iniquity; your lips have spoken lies, your tongue hath muttered perverseness. None calleth for justice, nor any pleadeth for truth: they trust in vanity, and speak lies; they conceive mischief, and bring forth iniquity.*" According to our Lord Jesus Christ from John 8:44, the devil is the father of all lies. Every lie finds its source in him. Thus we who are God's children are commanded to put away lying, and rather to "*speak every man truth with his neighbor.*" Through faith in our Lord Jesus Christ for eternal salvation, we have been delivered from the spiritual darkness and deeds of our sinful flesh. Let us then put away all lying. We are now the children of spiritual light. So then, let every one of us on every occasion speak the truth with everyone around us.

177. We must be angry at unrighteousness, in a God-honoring manner, not in a self-serving manner.

Ephesians 4:26 – "***Be ye angry, and sin not****: let not the sun go down upon your wrath.*"

Indeed, there is a righteous and godly anger at all unrighteousness; for all unrighteousness stands against the Lord our God. In fact, throughout God's Word we observe the Lord our God Himself displaying this righteous anger quite regularly, even in a fiery and fierce manner. Yet there is also an unrighteous anger; for James 1:20 provides the warning, "*For the wrath of man worketh not the righteousness of God.*" Even so, through this verse we can understand the difference between these two forms of anger. Unrighteous anger is rooted in the selfishness of our flesh. Unrighteous anger is not concerned with the righteousness of God. Unrighteous anger does not produce the righteousness of God. Unrighteous anger does not honor the righteousness of God. On the other hand, righteous anger centers itself on the righteousness of God, pursues after the righteousness of God, and seeks to exalt the righteousness of God. Yet even in righteous anger against unrighteousness there is a great temptation to turn in our attitude and actions away from that which honors God unto that which serves ourselves. Thus the command is given with the warning, "Be ye anger, and sin not."

178. We must not allow any anger to germinate through even one day into the sin of bitterness.

Ephesians 4:26-27 – "*Be ye angry, and sin not: **let not the sun go down upon your wrath: neither give place to the devil**.*"

Hebrews 12:15 – "***Looking diligently lest any man fail of the grace of God; lest any root of bitterness springing up trouble you, and thereby many be defiled***."

The sin of bitterness is a serious matter in our lives. It will trouble our spiritual walk with the Lord our God. It will grant our adversary the devil a place in our lives to devour us spiritually. It will defile our relationships with so many of those around us, destroying our ability to be used of our Lord in ministering aright to their lives. Thus God's Holy Word instructs us to be ever "looking diligently" in this matter. We must be always on our guard, always watching to prevent any root of bitterness at all, including even the smallest of this bitterness root, from springing up in our hearts. So then, what is the seed of bitterness? It is fleshly anger. How long does it take for this seed of anger to germinate into a root bitterness? God's Holy Word warns us not even to allow an attitude of anger to pass from one day into the next. "*Let not the sun go down upon your wrath.*" In a case wherein our anger is selfish, fleshly anger, we must repent quickly. In a case wherein our anger is righteous indignation against that which is contrary unto our Lord and His righteousness, and wherein we have the authority and ability to act against it, we must act for the honor of our Lord and according to the direction of the Holy Spirit. Finally, in a case wherein our anger is righteous indignation against that which is contrary unto our Lord and His righteousness, but we have no authority or ability to act against it, we must trust our Lord to act as He will in His righteous anger and vengeance. Yet in all we must not allow an attitude of anger to linger beyond the immediate day.

179. We must not steal, but must work with our hands "the thing which is good" in order that we might give to the needs of others.

Ephesians 4:28 – "*Let him that stole steal no more: but rather let him labour, working with his hands the thing which is good, that he may have to give to him that needeth.*"

The Lord our God has given commandment – "*Thou shalt not steal.*" The Lord our God is against any form of stealing. In addition, if we have engaged in any form of stealing, then He commands us to stop! "*Let him that stole steal no more.*" Yet our Lord does not simply command us to stop the practice of stealing, but He also commands us to replace that practice with another. He instructs us to stop stealing with our hands and rather to start working with our hands. In addition, He instructs us to stop taking the goods of others away from them through stealing, and rather to start giving our own hard earned goods unto others in need. We must replace stealing and taking for self with working and giving unto others. This our Lord instructs because He desires not simply that we should stop a bad habit, but also that we should learn a new desire. Yea, He desires that we should leave behind the selfish desire to take away from others and should learn the loving desire to give unto others.

180. We must not speak with corrupt communication, but only with "that which is good to the use of edifying."

Ephesians 4:29-30 – "***Let no corrupt communication proceed out of your mouth, but that which is good to the use of edifying, that it may minister grace unto the hearers. And grieve not the holy Spirit of God***, *whereby ye are sealed unto the day of redemption.*"

Colossians 4:6 – "***Let your speech be alway with grace, seasoned with salt***, *that ye may know how ye ought to answer every man.*"

In Ephesians 4:29 the word "corrupt" simply refers to that which is not of good use, to that which is worthless, offensive, or harmful. It is anything which is the opposite of "*that which is good to the use of edifying, that it may minister grace* [God's grace] *to the hearers.*" Certainly corrupt communication includes taking the name of the Lord in vain, speaking reproachfully against the Lord, and speaking with vulgar and obscene language. Yet it includes more than this. It also includes lofty words that are proud, arrogant, and self-exalting. It includes grievous words that are harsh, hurtful and stir up anger. It includes contentious words that produce strife and discord. It includes froward and perverse words that are selfish, willful, stubborn, and contrary to the truth and righteousness of God. It includes piercing words that are harsh, biting, malicious, and violent. It includes foolish words that are to no profit, but only for the sake of attention. It includes jesting words that are cutting, discouraging, and dishonoring. Even so, such corrupt communication is never to proceed out of our mouths. Yea, in Ephesians 4:30 we are warned to avoid all such corrupt communication in order not to grieve the indwelling Holy Spirit of God.

Rather, we are ever to speak with good communication. So then, how is good communication to be defined? It is defined as that which is unto "the use of edifying, that it may minister grace to the hearers." It is that which is useful for building up others spiritually. It is that which draws others closer to the Lord and that which ministers the Lord's grace unto others.

Certainly good communication includes exalting the name of our Lord, praising the works of our Lord, and honoring the truth of our Lord. Thus the man of God David expressed his commitment in Psalm 34:1-2, saying, "*I will bless the LORD at all times: his praise shall continually be in my mouth. My soul shall make her boast in the LORD: the humble shall hear thereof, and be glad;*" and again in Psalm 145:5, "*I will speak of the glorious honour of thy majesty, and of thy wondrous works.*" Thus also the psalmist Ethan expressed his commitment in Psalm 89:1, saying, "*I will sing of the mercies of the LORD for ever: with my mouth will I make known thy faithfulness to all generations.*" Again the commitment is expressed in Psalm 71:15-16, "*My mouth shall shew forth thy righteousness and thy salvation all the day; for I know not the numbers thereof. I will go in the strength of the Lord GOD: I will make mention of thy righteousness, even of thine only.*" Yet again the psalmist expressed his commitment in Psalm 119:172, saying, "*My tongue shall speak of thy word: for all thy commandments are righteousness.*"

Good communication also includes gracious words that are motivated by a loving, gracious spirit and that minister grace unto the other's spirit. Even so, Colossians 4:6 gives the instruction, "*Let your speech be alway with grace, seasoned with salt, that ye may know how ye ought to answer every man.*" Such is the character of the wise man's words, even as the opening half of Ecclesiastes 10:12 reveals, "*The words of a wise man's mouth are gracious.*" Our speech must be always filled with the grace of God in order that it might minister God's grace unto the hearers. Indeed, our speech must ever be helpful and gracious. Even when we must deliver rebuke, reproof, and correction, although our speech may be hard, it must not be harsh. Even then our speech must be filled with God's grace. Our speech must be "seasoned with salt." Its character must not be corrupting or damaging, but must be purifying and preserving. This all is necessary in order that we might relate aright both unto our fellow believers and unto the lost world. Concerning our fellow believers, our speech must be always with God's grace for the sake of ministry and edification. Concerning the lost world, our speech must be always with God's grace for the sake of testimony and witness.

Good communication includes pleasant words that are rooted in purity and that encourage the other's spirit. Even so, Proverbs 15:26 declares, *"The thoughts of the wicked are an abomination to the LORD: but the words of the pure are pleasant words;"* and Proverbs 16:24 adds, *"Pleasant words are as an honeycomb, sweet to the soul, and health to the bones."* Good communication includes soft, gentle words that turn away anger and promote peace. Even so, Proverbs 15:1 declares, *"A soft answer turneth away wrath: but grievous words stir up anger."* Good communication includes sweet words that enhance and encourage learning. Even so, Proverbs 16:21 declares, *"The wise in heart shall be called prudent: and the sweetness of the lips increaseth learning."* Good communication includes wholesome words that comfort and encourage. Even so, Proverbs 12:25 declares, *"Heaviness in the heart of man maketh it stoop: but a good word maketh it glad;"* and the opening half of Proverbs 15:4 adds, *"A wholesome tongue is a tree of life."* Good communication includes wise words that counsel and guide in accord with God's truth and wisdom. Even so, the opening half of Proverbs 10:13 declares, *"In the lips of him that hath understanding wisdom is found;"* and the opening half of verse 31 adds, *"The mouth of the just bringeth forth wisdom."* Good communication includes truthful words. Even so, the opening half of Proverbs 12:17 declares, *"He that speaketh truth sheweth forth righteousness;"* and verse 22 adds, *"Lying lips are abomination to the LORD: but they that deal truly are his delight."* Finally, good communication includes hearty counsel and loving correction. Even so, Proverbs 27:9 declares, *"Ointment and perfume rejoice the heart: so doth the sweetness of a man's friend by hearty counsel."* Furthermore, Proverbs 27:5 states, *"Open rebuke is better than secret love;"* and the opening half of verse 6 adds, *"Faithful are the wounds of a friend."*

181. We must be kind to one another.

Ephesians 4:32 – *"**And be ye kind one to another**, tenderhearted, forgiving one another, even as God for Christ's sake hath forgiven you."*

Colossians 3:12 – "***Put on therefore****, as the elect of God, holy and beloved, bowels of mercies, **kindness**, humbleness of mind, meekness, longsuffering.*"

In Ephesians 4:32 a three-fold instruction is given, and the first of these is that we must be "*kind one to another.*" This means that we must ever be inclined to do others good and not evil. We are to be alert to take every opportunity for doing others good. We are to be courteous, friendly, generous, gentle, gracious, sympathetic, etc. toward one another. Yea, as the children of God we are to put on this spirit of kindness so that is characterizes every moment of our behavior. In fact, this is one of the key ingredients of godly love toward others; for the opening line of 1 Corinthians 13:4 teaches us that "*charity suffereth long, and is kind.*" Indeed, we are even to demonstrate this spirit of kindness toward those who are ungrateful and unkind; for we are to be followers of God our heavenly Father, who according to the closing line of Luke 6:35 is "*kind unto the unthankful and to the evil.*"

182. We must be tenderhearted toward one another.

Ephesians 4:32 – "***And be ye*** *kind one to another, **tenderhearted**, forgiving one another, even as God for Christ's sake hath forgiven you.*"

Now, it is not just that we are to maintain kind action toward one another, but also that we are to maintain a tenderhearted attitude toward one another. We are ever to be well intentioned toward one another. We are ever to be sweet spirited toward one another. We are ever to be graciously motivated toward one another. On the other hand, we are never to harden our hearts against one another. We are never to be resentful against one another. We are never to be bitter against one another.

183. We must be followers (or, imitators) of the Lord our God.

Ephesians 5:1 – "***Be ye therefore followers of God, as dear children.***"

Through faith in our Lord Jesus Christ as personal Savior, we have been spiritually born again into God's family as His dear children. Thus we are now to behave like our heavenly Father. We are to follow after His direction and His example. We are to imitate His righteousness. We are to be holy as our heavenly Father is holy. (See 1 Peter 1:15-16) We are to be perfect as our heavenly Father is perfect. (See Matthew 5:48) We are to be merciful as our heavenly Father is merciful. (See Luke 6:35-36) We are to be forgiving as our heavenly Father is forgiving. (See Ephesians 4:32). We are to be loving as our heavenly Father is loving. (See 1 John 4:7-11) We are to walk in the light as our heavenly Father walks in the light. (See 1 John 1:7) We are now the children of God and of light; therefore, we are to walk after God as children of light. Even so, Ephesians 5:8 declares, *"For ye were sometimes darkness, but now are ye light in the Lord: walk as children of light."*

184. We must reprove the works of darkness through our walk in light.

Ephesians 5:11-13 – *"And have no fellowship with the unfruitful works of darkness, **but rather reprove them**. For it is a shame even to speak of those things which are done of them in secret. But all things that are reproved are made manifest by the light: for whatsoever doth make manifest is light."*

Our very walk in light and righteousness reproves the sinful works of darkness and unrighteousness. This passage is not instructing us to go about verbally reproving all of the sinful works of this world (especially not if we ourselves are partakers in them). Rather, this passage is instructing us ever to live and behave is such a righteous manner that our very character and conduct shines the light of reproof upon the works of darkness.

185. We must walk carefully in wisdom and thereby redeem the time from this evil world.

Ephesians 5:15-16 – *"See then that ye walk circumspectly, not as fools, but as wise, redeeming the time, because the days are evil."*

Colossians 4:5 – *"Walk in wisdom toward them that are without, redeeming the time."*

The word "circumspectly" means "to act with careful exactness, to be careful to consider all related circumstance before acting, deciding, etc." In addition, Ephesians 5:15 reveals that such a circumspect walk is the way of the wise, not the way of fools. Even so, a wise man carefully considers a matter before he makes any decisions; whereas a foolish man makes decisions hastily without careful consideration. Now, the Lord our God has called us to walk as wise individuals, not as fools. Thus we must walk in every step of life with careful consideration of every matter and every decision. We must not just "go with the flow" or just "follow the crowd." We must not just do whatever seems good at the moment. We must not make hasty decisions. We must carefully consider every matter according to the standard of our Lord God's Word and will.

Thereby we shall redeem our time out of the evil of this world, rather than waste our time on the evil of this world. Furthermore, thereby we shall maintain a godly testimony before the lost of this world, rather than dishonor the name of Christ before the lost of this world. The continual direction of this world is not toward godliness, but away from godliness. Thus if we just "go with the flow," and "follow the trends," and accept the world's influence, we ourselves will move away from godliness, destroy our testimony as the light of this world, and waste the time of our Christian lives upon worldliness. On the other hand, if we walk carefully in Biblical wisdom every day, then we will move toward godliness, shine brightly as the light of this world, and invest the time of our Christian lives in eternity.

186. We must understand the will of our Lord in order to walk in wisdom.

Ephesians 5:17 – "***Wherefore be ye not unwise, but understanding what the will of the Lord is.***"

Herein we find a direct contrast between being spiritually unwise and understanding the will of the Lord. Thus we may conclude that understanding the will of the Lord and being spiritually wise are equivalent to one another. In fact, God's Word indicates this very truth in Psalm 111:10, saying, "*The fear of the LORD is the beginning of wisdom: a good understanding have all they that do his commandments: his praise endureth for ever.*" Indeed, from Psalm 111:10 we also learn how we might come to understand the will of our Lord – through obedience to the commandments of his Word. The Word of God is our spiritual wisdom for this life. Full assurance of faith in its truth and teachings and full commitment of obedience to its commands and counsels, precepts and principles, statutes and standards is the wise way. Doubting and disobedience is the way of foolishness. Therefore, if we would walk carefully in spiritual wisdom for every step of our lives, we must walk obediently in faith for every step.

187. We must not be drunk with alcohol.

Ephesians 5:18 – "***And be not drunk with wine***, *wherein is excess; but be filled with the Spirit.*"

In Ephesians 5:17 we were instructed not to be unwise and walk in spiritual foolishness, but to understand and obey our Lord's will and walk in spiritual wisdom. Now in the opening portion of Ephesians 5:18 we are instructed not to be "drunk with wine." So then, what is the connection between this instruction and the need to walk in spiritual wisdom? Proverbs 20:1 reveals the answer, saying, "*Wine is a mocker, strong drink is raging: and whosoever is deceived thereby is not wise.*" In like manner, Proverbs 23:19-21 gives the warning, "*Hear thou, my son, and be wise, and guide thine heart in the way.*

Be not among winebibbers; among riotous eaters of flesh: for the drunkard and the glutton shall come to poverty: and drowsiness shall clothe a man with rags." Then to this Proverbs 23:29-35 add, "*Who hath woe? Who hath sorrow? Who hath contentions? Who hath babbling? Who hath wounds without cause? Who hath redness of eyes? They that tarry long at the wine; they that go to seek mixed wine. Look not thou upon the wine when it is red, when it giveth his colour in the cup, when it moveth itself aright. At the last it biteth like a serpent, and stingeth like an adder. Thine eyes shall behold strange women, and thine heart shall utter perverse things. Yea, thou shalt be as he that lieth down in the midst of the sea, or as he that lieth upon the top of a mast. They have stricken me, shalt thou say, and I was not sick; they have beaten me, and I felt it not: when shall I awake? I will seek it yet again.*" Even so, Isaiah 5:11-12 proclaims, "*Woe unto them that rise up early in the morning, that they may follow strong drink; that continue until night, till wine inflame them! And the harp, and the viol, the tabret, and pipe, and wine, are in their feasts: but they regard not the work of the LORD, neither consider the operation of his hands.*" Alcohol will turn us away from the will and ways of the Lord our God; thus alcohol will move us down the path of foolishness and ungodliness. Alcohol will only cause an excess of ungodliness; thus we must never be "under the influence."

188. We must sing in joyful praise unto the Lord our God, both with one another publicly and from our hearts privately.

Ephesians 5:19 – "***Speaking to yourselves in psalms and hymns and spiritual songs, singing and making melody in your heart to the Lord.***"

Colossians 3:16 – "*Let the word of Christ dwell in you richly in all wisdom; teaching and admonishing one another in psalms and hymns and spiritual songs, **singing with grace in your hearts to the Lord**.*"

We are to be a people who sing forth the praises of the Lord our God. Even so, Psalm 9:11 gives the instruction, "*Sing praises to the LORD, which dwelleth in Zion: declare among the people his doings;*" and

Psalm 30:4 adds, "*Sing unto the LORD, O ye saints of his, and give thanks at the remembrance of his holiness.*" Again Psalm 33:1-5 gives the instruction, "*Rejoice in the LORD, O ye righteous: for praise is comely for the upright. Praise the LORD with harp: sing unto him with the psaltery and an instrument of ten strings. Sing unto him a new song; play skilfully with a loud noise. For the word of the LORD is right; and all his works are done in truth. He loveth righteousness and judgment: the earth is full of the goodness of the LORD.*" Yet again Psalm 47:6-7 gives the instruction, "*Sing praises to God, sing praises: sing praises unto our King, sing praises. For God is the King of all the earth: sing ye praises with understanding;*" and Psalm 68:3-4 adds, "*But let the righteous be glad; let them rejoice before God: yea, let them exceedingly rejoice. Sing unto God, sing praises to his name: extol him that rideth upon the heavens by his name JAH, and rejoice before Him.*"

And yet again Psalm 95:1-3 gives the instruction, "*O come, let us sing unto the LORD: let us make a joyful noise to the rock of our salvation. Let us come before his presence with thanksgiving, and make a joyful noise unto him with psalms. For the LORD is a great God, and a great King above all gods;*" and Psalm 105:1-3 adds, "*O give thanks unto the LORD; call upon his name: make known his deeds among the people. Sing unto him, sing psalms unto him: talk ye of all his wondrous works. Glory ye in his holy name: let the heart of them rejoice that seek the LORD.*" Finally, Psalm 135:1-3 gives the instruction, "*Praise ye the LORD. Praise ye the name of the LORD; praise him, O ye servants of the LORD. Ye that stand in the house of the LORD, in the courts of the house of our God, Praise the LORD; for the LORD is good: sing praises unto his name; for it is pleasant;*" and Psalm 149:1-5 adds, "*Praise ye the LORD. Sing unto the LORD a new song, and his praise in the congregation of saints. Let Israel rejoice in him that made him: let the children of Zion be joyful in their King. Let them praise his name in the dance: let them sing praises unto him with the timbrel and harp. For the LORD taketh pleasure in his people: he will beautify the meek with salvation. Let the saints be joyful in glory: let them sing aloud upon their beds.*"

Yea, according to Ephesians 5:19 & Colossians 3:16 we are to sing forth such praises in two specific realms. First, we are to sing forth the praises of our Lord in the congregation of the saints to and with one another. Second, we are to sing forth the praises of our Lord privately in our own hearts unto the Lord. In addition, we are to sing forth such praises for two specific reasons. First, we are to sing forth the praises of our Lord in honor of His name. Second, we are to sing forth the praises of our Lord in order to teach and admonish one another.

189. We must give thanks always in and for all things unto God our heavenly Father in the name of our Lord Jesus Christ.

Ephesians 5:20 – "***Giving thanks always for all things unto God and the Father in the name of our Lord Jesus Christ.***"

Philippians 4:6 – "*Be careful for nothing; but in every thing by prayer and supplication **with thanksgiving** let your requests be made known unto God.*"

Colossians 3:17 – "*And whatsoever ye do in word or deed, do all in the name of the Lord Jesus, **giving thanks to God and the Father by him.***"

Colossians 4:2 – "*Continue in prayer, and watch in the same **with thanksgiving.***"

1 Thessalonians 5:18 – "***In every thing give thanks: for this is the will of God in Christ Jesus concerning you.***"

Hebrews 13:15 – "***By him*** [by our Lord Jesus Christ] ***therefore let us offer the sacrifice of praise to God continually, that is, the fruit of our lips giving thanks to his name.***"

We are to be a thankful people, "*giving thanks always for all things unto God.*" In fact, it is with the word of thanksgiving that we are to replace foolish talking and unprofitable jesting; for in Ephesians

5:4 the instruction is given, *"Neither filthiness, nor foolish talking, nor jesting, which are not convenient: but rather giving of thanks."* Even so, Psalm 92:1-2 declares, *"It is a good thing to give thanks unto the LORD, and to sing praises unto thy name, O most High: to shew forth thy lovingkindness in the morning, and thy faithfulness every night;"* and Psalm 97:11-12 adds, *"Light is sown for the righteous, and gladness for the upright in heart. Rejoice in the LORD, ye righteous; and give thanks at the remembrance of his holiness."* Yea, in Psalm 100:4-5 the instruction is given, *"Enter into his gates with thanksgiving, and into his courts with praise: be thankful unto him, and bless his name. For the LORD is good; his mercy is everlasting; and his truth endureth to all generations;"* and Psalm 107:1-2 adds, *"O give thanks unto the LORD, for he is good: for his mercy endureth for ever. Let the redeemed of the LORD say so, whom he hath redeemed from the hand of the enemy."* Indeed, according to Philippians 4:6 and Colossians 4:2 our prayer lives are also to be thanksgiving lives. In everything we are to continue in prayer, making request unto the Lord our God for help in time of need. Yet as we continue in prayer and supplication, we are also to continue therein with thanksgiving, expressing gratitude unto the Lord our God for the help that He grants us. We are to be continually praying with continual thanksgiving.

190. We must submit ourselves "one to another in the fear of God" and in godly humility.

Ephesians 5:21 – *"**Submitting yourselves one to another in the fear of God**."*

1 Peter 5:5 – *"Likewise, ye younger, submit yourselves unto the elder. **Yea, all of you be subject one to another, and be clothed with humility**: for God resisteth the proud, and giveth grace to the humble."*

The Lord our God Himself calls us to submit ourselves to one another. We are not to strive against one another in order to get our own way or to get honor unto ourselves. Rather, we are to submit ourselves unto one another in order to give honor unto others and to give up our own way for their sake. Yea, we are to be motivated unto such a walk of humble submission by the fear of the Lord our God. Out of reverence for His Person and honor to His authority we must submit ourselves unto one another. Even so, if we do not submit ourselves one to another, then it is foremost a disrespect, not of them, but of Him.

---

191. The wife must submit herself under her husband's headship in everything as unto the Lord with a meek and quiet spirit of reverence toward her husband.

Ephesians 5:22-24 – "***Wives, submit yourselves unto your own husbands, as unto the Lord.*** *For the husband is the head of the wife, even as Christ is the head of the church: and he is the saviour of the body. Therefore as the church is subject unto Christ,* **so let the wives be to their own husbands in every thing.**"

Ephesians 5:33 – "*Nevertheless let every one of you in particular so love his wife even as himself;* **and the wife see that she reverence her husband.**"

Colossians 3:18 – "***Wives, submit yourselves unto your own husbands, as it is fit in the Lord.***"

Titus 2:5 – "*To be discreet, chaste, keepers at home, good,* **obedient to their own husbands**, *that the word of God be not blasphemed.*"

1 Peter 3:1-4 – "***Likewise, ye wives, be in subjection to your own husbands;*** *that, if any obey not the word, they also may without the word be won by the conversation of the wives; while they behold your chaste conversation coupled with fear. Whose adorning let it not be that outward adorning of plaiting the hair, and of wearing of gold, or of putting on of apparel;* **but let it be the hidden man of the heart, in that which is not corruptible, even the ornament of a meek and quiet spirit, which is in the sight of God of great price.**"

From these five New Testament passages we learn a number of truths concerning this matter. In the first place, we learn that the wife is to submit herself unto her own husband because the Lord our God has set him in the role of headship and leadership within the marriage and home relationship.

In the second place, we learn that the wife is to submit herself unto her own husband willingly. In both Ephesians 5:22 and Colossians 3:18 the instruction is given to each wife herself to submit herself unto her own husband. This is not to be a submission that is forced upon her by her husband, but a submission that she willingly offers unto her husband. She herself is willingly to arrange herself in both her attitude and her actions under her husband's headship and leadership authority.

In the third place, we learn that the wife is to submit herself unto her own husband "in every thing." (See Ephesians 5:24) Now, certainly if the husband requires his wife to do something that is directly contrary to a specific command of God's Holy Word, then the wife should follow the principle of Acts 5:17 – "*We ought to obey God rather than men.*" Yet even in such a case the wife should apply this principle with "a meek and quiet spirit." (See 1 Peter 3:4) In addition, the wife should never use this principle selfishly as a weapon against her husband to get her own way in a matter. Nor should she ever apply this principle to matters of her own formulation that are not specifically presented in God's Word. Such cases are to be subject only unto the direct declaration of God's Word, and not unto her own interpretations of right and wrong. Rather, in everything else except a case in which something is directly contrary to God's Word, the wife is to submit herself completely unto her own husband. Indeed, such submission "in every thing" not only includes submission to her husband's stated decisions, but also to her husband's unstated desires and direction.

In the fourth place, we learn that the wife is to submit herself unto her own husband "as unto the Lord." (See Ephesians 5:22) Just as the wife would give respect and submission unto the Lord Himself, even so she should give such respect and submission unto her husband. Yet a wife might defend an unsubmissive spirit with the claim that her husband is not actually worthy of such a high level of respect and submission. However, the instruction of God's Holy Word does not give any such exception to the rule. The wife is to grant this respect and submission unto her husband, not because he himself is so worthy, but because the Lord Jesus Christ, who indeed is abundantly worthy, requires it.

In the fifth place, we learn that the wife is to submit herself unto her own husband with reverence. (See Ephesians 5:33) Her submission is not simply to be demonstrated in acts of obedience, but also in an attitude of reverence. What then does it mean for the wife to reverence her husband? It means that she is to maintain a spirit and attitude of respect, esteem, and honor toward him. She is to hold him in an exalted place within her heart and to treat him with honor through her behavior. She is not to be critical of him, but to lift him up with honor. She is to adore him as her husband, to be attentive unto his thoughts and desires, and to be supportive of him and his pursuits. She is to be ever concerned to please him and to be ever cautious not to offend him. Although the wife will certainly be aware of her husband's weaknesses and unworthiness, yet in her submission unto him she is to maintain a spirit of reverence toward him "as unto the Lord."

In the sixth place, we learn that the wife is to submit herself unto her own husband because it is proper and pleasing in the sight of the Lord. (See Colossians 3:18) The Lord our God Himself established the institution of marriage, and He Himself set the husband in the role of headship and leadership within the marriage. Thus it is proper and pleasing in our Lord's sight when the wife submits herself unto the leadership of her husband, for in doing so she also submits herself unto the will of our Lord. If the wife desires, not only to have a proper marriage relationship with her husband, but also to have a proper Christian walk before her Lord, then she must submit herself unto her own husband. Such may not be proper and pleasing in the sight of this world, but it most certainly is proper and pleasing in the sight of our Lord.

In the seventh place, we learn that the wife is to submit herself unto her own husband because it is the divinely established means by which she may influence her husband toward the things of God. (See 1 Peter 3:1-2) Often we believe that the way to influence others is by leading them and instructing them. Yet in the case of the wife's spiritual influence upon her husband, the Lord our God declares that her way of influence is by submitting herself unto her husband's headship and leadership. In fact, in 1 Peter 3:1 this is presented as the means of the wife's influence upon her husband specifically when he is in direct disobedience to the Word of God, including even the gospel message. "Without the word" (that is – without words of instruction, correction, rebuke, or nagging) she is to win the heart of her husband unto obedience toward the Lord through her faithful, submissive, pure, respectful behavior. This is her divinely established means of spiritual influence upon him.

In the eighth place, we learn that the wife is to submit herself unto her own husband with "a meek and quiet spirit." (See 1 Peter 3:3-4) This is an ornament of true, incorruptible beauty. This is the adorning of "the hidden man of the heart." Indeed, this ornament, this adorning of the heart, has the highest value set upon it; for the Lord our God Himself considers this ornament of a meek and quiet spirit to be "of great price." Oh, how great, how glorious, how beautiful, how worthwhile is this ornament that the Lord our God Himself would value it as "of great price!" Yet what is a meek and quiet spirit? First, it is not simply an external show, but a true attitude of heart. Second, it is an attitude of heart that governs the external behavior of the life. Third, it is an attitude of meekness – not of selfish manipulation or abrasive demeanor, but of humble selflessness and patient gentleness. Fourth, it is an attitude of quietness – not self-assertive or contentious, but peaceable and harmonious. It is the spirit of one who is not pushing to get her own way, but who is ever giving up her own way for the sake of peace. It is the spirit of one who is not pushing herself forward to take the lead, but who is yielding herself unto the lead of her husband.

In the ninth and final place, we learn that the wife is to submit herself unto her own husband in order that the Word of God might not be blasphemed by the world. (See Titus 2:5) The people of this lost world are ever watching the behavior of those who claim to be God's own people. They are watching our behavior in public, on the job, in our recreation, in our family relationships, and in our marriage relationships. With regard to our marriage relationships, they are ever watching how those who claim to be men of God relate to their wives and how those who claim to be women of God relate to their husbands. Thus when the wife who claims to be a woman of God does not relate to her husband in the Biblical manner, it creates an occasion for the truth of God's Word as a whole to be slandered, disrespected, and rejected by this lost world. On the other hand, when the wife who claims to be a woman of God does relate to her husband in the Biblical manner, it creates an occasion for the truth of God's Word as a whole to be exalted, honored, and received by this lost world.

192. The husband must love his wife as Christ loved the church, giving up of himself to nourish her, cherish her, dwell at harmony with her, and give honor unto her.

Ephesians 5:25-33 – "***Husbands, love your wives, even as Christ also loved the church, and gave himself for it****; that he might sanctify and cleanse it with the washing of water by the word, that he might present it to himself a glorious church, not having spot, or wrinkle, or any such thing; but that it should be holy and without blemish. **So ought men to love their wives as their own bodies***. He that loveth his wife loveth himself. For no man ever yet hated his own flesh; but nourisheth and cherisheth it, even as the Lord the church: for we are members of his body, of his flesh, and of his bones. For this cause shall a man leave his father and mother, and shall be joined unto his wife, and they two shall be one flesh. This is a great mystery: but I speak concerning Christ and the church. **Nevertheless let every one of you in particular so love his wife even as himself***; and the wife see that she reverence her husband.*"

Colossians 3:19 – "***Husbands, love your wives, and be not bitter against them***."

1 Peter 3:7 – "***Likewise, ye husbands, dwell with them according to knowledge, giving honour unto the wife****, as unto the weaker*

vessel, and as being heirs together of the grace of life; that your prayers be not hindered."

From these three New Testament passages we learn a number of truths concerning this matter. In the first place, we learn that the husband is to love his wife unto the same extent as our Lord Jesus Christ loved the church. So then, to what extent did our Lord Jesus Christ love the church? He completely gave up His life for it. In like manner, the Lord our God commands the husband to give up his own life completely for his wife. Yet this is not simply a matter of the husband's dying physically for his wife, or even of being willing to do so. Rather, this is a matter of the husband's daily giving up of himself in humility in order to serve his wife. Concerning the matter of true, godly love Galatians 5:13 declares, *"For, brethren, ye have been called unto liberty; only use not liberty for an occasion to the flesh, but by love serve one another."*

So then, for the husband to walk in true, godly love toward his wife he must give up the ways of the flesh (the ways of selfishness and self-serving) and must give himself in service to his wife. Every day and every moment he is to give up his time, his energy, his interests, his rights, etc. in service to his wife. He is to humble himself and take upon himself the form of a servant in his relationship toward his wife. Furthermore, lest the husband might claim that he cannot take upon himself the form of a servant in his relationship toward his wife because he is divinely called as her head, let him remember that our Lord Jesus Christ humbled Himself and took upon Himself the form of a servant although He Himself is God the Son, the second Person of the eternal Godhead. So then, just as our Lord Jesus Christ loved the church and gave Himself for it, even so the husband is to love his wife and to give himself for her.

In the second place, we learn that the husband is to love his wife by nourishing her as Christ nourishes the church. (See Ephesians 5:28-29) Since his wife is one with him in the one-flesh relationship of the marriage, the husband should nourish her as his very own flesh, even as our Lord nourishes His own body, the church. Indeed, this should be an on-going, daily matter. Throughout every day of their marriage relationship, a husband should seek to be nourishing his wife. Yet what does it mean for a husband to nourish his wife? The word "nourish" here has reference unto cultivation. Thus the husband is to cultivate his wife's growth in maturity just as an individual might cultivate a beautiful flower. He is to plant her in the best of soil, that is – in a relationship with a truly Spirit-filled husband.

Indeed, the "soil" in which a wife is planted is the husband himself. Her father has given her away into his hand. God her heavenly Father has joined her in a one-flesh relationship with him. She is now bone of his bone and flesh of his flesh. She is now a part of him. She is now his helpmeet. He is the "soil" in which she has now been planted; and for that "soil" to be the most nourishing to her growth, he must be a truly Spirit-filled husband. Yea, as the "soil" for his wife he must bring forth the spiritual fruit of love, joy, peace, longsuffering, gentleness, goodness, faith, meekness, and temperance that she might be nourished thereby. (See Galatians 5:22-23) Furthermore, the husband is to provide his wife with every other necessary ingredient for growth. In every way possible he is to cultivate his wife so that she might blossom into the most beautiful wife, mother, and woman of God possible. Even so, when a man's wife does not blossom into such beauty of godliness and maturity, it is often the fault of his own failure in nourishing her.

In the third place, we learn that the husband is to love his wife by cherishing her as Christ cherishes the church. (See Ephesians 5:28-29) Again since his wife is one with him in the one-flesh relationship of the marriage, the husband should cherish her as his very own flesh, even as our Lord cherishes His own body, the church. Indeed, this also should be an on-going, daily matter. Throughout every day of their marriage relationship a husband should seek to be cherishing his wife. Yet what does it mean for a husband to cherish his wife? The only other New Testament passage in which we find this word "cherish" might help us come to an understanding of the matter. Thus in 1 Thessalonians 2:7-8 we read, *"But we were gentle among you, even as a nurse cherisheth her children: so being affectionately desirous of you, we were willing to have imparted unto you, not the gospel of God only, but also our own souls, because ye were dear unto us."*

Now, the Greek word that is translated "cherish" literally means "to keep warm." It was often used of the manner in which a mother might care for her newborn child, holding that child close in order to keep that child warm. Thus she held her child close to her heart, cherishing him. Even so, the apostle Paul employed this picture to illustrate his own relationship with the believers at Thessalonica; and in relation to this illustration, he presented four phrases of explanation. First, the apostle indicated that he had been gentle among the believers at Thessalonica. Second, he indicated that he had been affectionately desirous of them. Third, he indicated that he had imparted his own soul unto them. Finally, he indicated that they were dear unto him. In like manner, the husband is to cherish his wife by being gentle toward her, by being affectionately desirous of his wife, by being willing and well pleased to impart his own soul unto his wife, and by holding his wife dear unto his heart.

In the fourth place, we learn that the husband is to love his wife by dwelling at harmony with her. The opening line of 1 Peter 3:7 gives the instruction, *"Likewise, ye husbands, dwell with them according to knowledge."* The word "dwell" here means "to live in a home with another." When used in a context where the emphasis is less upon the location and more upon the relationship, the word conveys the idea of living at home with another. In our present day we might think of this as living at harmony with another. Thus the husband is to live at harmony with his wife. He is to develop and maintain a unity of friendship and fellowship with her.

So then, upon what ground will the husband be able to develop and maintain this harmony, this unity of friendship and fellowship, with his wife? The prepositional phrase "according to knowledge" reveals the answer. The husband must come to know his own wife. He must put forth the effort and energy to know his own wife as an individual – to know her individual personality, her individual joys and burdens, her individual likes and dislikes, her individual delights and annoyances, her individual pleasures and pains, her individual strengths and weaknesses, her individual hopes and fears. In addition, the husband must come to know how his own wife thinks and feels differently from himself. Certainly this will require that he lovingly, attentively, and faithfully communicate with

355

his wife, and especially that he carefully and considerately listen to his wife. Then as the husband comes to know these things, he must dwell in harmony with her in accord with that knowledge. When he comes to know that something bothers his wife, he should put forth every Biblically acceptable effort to avoid that thing. When he comes to know that something pleases his wife, he should put forth every Biblically acceptable effort to pursue that thing. The husband must be considerate of his wife, considering her individual desires and needs and acting accordingly.

In the fifth place, we learn that the husband is to love his wife by giving honor unto her. In 1 Peter 3:7 the instruction continues, *"Likewise, ye husbands, dwell with them according to knowledge, giving honour unto the wife."* Not only is the husband to give affection unto his wife, but also he is to give honor unto her. In addition, this honor is not simply to be granted unto her upon a rare occasion or an assigned holiday. Rather, this honor is to be poured out daily unto her in specific, tangible ways. Each day throughout every step of the day the husband is to prize his wife as a precious treasure. Furthermore, this honor is not to be granted in a grudging manner. Rather, this honor is to be poured out from the fullness of the husband's heart in attitude, word, and action.

Thus the husband is not to take his wife and her efforts for granted, nor is he to treat her as an unimportant inferior or as a worthless possession. Rather, as Romans 12:10 teaches, in honor he is to prefer her above himself. Furthermore, the husband is not to tear down or tear into his wife verbally. Rather, he is to bless her and praise her for the fruit of her hands and the faithfulness of her work. Finally, the husband is not to mistreat, misuse, marginalize, manipulate, malign, mock, menace, or manhandle his wife. Rather, he is to behave toward his wife in such a manner as to magnify her and to minister unto her. In all, the husband should express and demonstrate respect and appreciation for his wife's thoughts, feelings, opinions, suggestions, time, efforts, labor, and submission.

In the sixth and final place, we learn that the husband is to love his wife in order that his prayers be not hindered. (See 1 Peter 3:7) When a husband either neglects or refuses to love his wife aright, his prayer life will become ineffective and unavailing. The Lord our God Himself will neglect and refuse to hear that husband's prayers. According to 1 Corinthians 11:4, the head of the wife is the husband; and the Head of the husband is the Lord. Thus when the husband does not treat his wife aright, his Head and Lord will hold that husband accountable and will reject his prayers.

193. Children must ever maintain a spirit of honor toward their father and mother, obeying their parents while they abide under their parents' authority.

Ephesians 6:1-3 – "*Children, obey your parents in the Lord: for this is right.* **Honour thy father and mother**; *(which is the first commandment with promise;) that it may be well with thee, and thou mayest live long on the earth.*"

Colossians 3:20 – "*Children, obey your parents in all things: for this is well pleasing unto the Lord.*"

In the first place, we learn that children are to obey the authority of their parents in all things while they are yet under their parent's authority. "This is right" before the Lord, and "this is well pleasing unto the Lord." Certainly, if a parent requires a child to do something that is directly contrary unto a specific command of God's Holy Word, then the child should follow the principle of Acts 5:17 – "*We ought to obey God rather than men.*" Yet even in such a case, that child should apply this principle with a spirit of honor toward the parent's position of authority. In addition, that child should never use this principle selfishly as a weapon against his or her parent to get his or her own way in a matter. Nor should that child ever apply this principle unto matters of his or her own formulation that are not specifically presented in God's Word. Such cases are to be subject only to the direct declaration of God's Word, and not to his or her own interpretations of right and wrong. Rather, in all things except a case in which something is directly contrary unto God's Word, a child is to obey completely the authority of his or her parent. Furthermore, unto those children who refuse to obey the authority of their parents the warning of God's judgment is graphically delivered in Proverbs 30:17 – "*The eye that mocketh at his father, and despiseth to obey his mother, the ravens of the valley shall pick it out, and the young eagles shall eat it.*"

In the second place, we learn that children are to maintain a spirit of honor toward their parents at all times. Yea, this is the fifth of the Ten Commandments that the Lord our God delivered to Israel in Exodus 20 – "*Honour thy father and thy mother: that thy days may be long upon the land which the* LORD *thy God giveth thee.*" Both in the past time of the Old Testament and in the present time of the New Testament, the Lord our God has promised His blessing upon those children who will maintain a spirit of honor toward their parents. Yet this honor is not just an outward behavior of obedience, for the Lord our God looks upon the heart. Thus this honor must be a sincere attitude of respect and love in the heart, out of which a behavior of faithful obedience will flow forth. Yea, this honor must especially govern the manner in which a child speaks toward and about his or her parents. In Leviticus 20:9 the warning was given to the children of Israel, "*For every one that curseth* [or, speaks disrespectfully against] *his father or his mother shall be surely put to death: he hath cursed* [or, spoken disrespectfully against] *his father or his mother; his blood shall be upon him.*" Again in Proverbs 20:20 the warning of God's wisdom is given to all of us, "*Whoso curseth* [or, speaks disrespectfully against] *his father or his mother, his lamp shall be put out in obscure darkness.*"

In the third place, we learn that children are to honor and not to forsake the good instruction of their parents even after they reach adulthood. Unto a young adult son, the wisdom of God's Word declares in Proverbs 1:8-9, "*My son, hear the instruction of thy father, and forsake not the law of thy mother: for they shall be an ornament of grace unto thy head, and chains about thy neck.*" Again in Proverbs 6:20-23 the wisdom of God's Word declares, "*My son, keep thy father's commandment, and forsake not the law of thy mother: bind them continually upon thine heart, and tie them about thy neck. When thou goest, it shall lead thee; when thou sleepest, it shall keep thee; and when thou awakest, it shall talk with thee. For the commandment is a lamp; and the law is light; and reproofs of instruction are the way of life."* Yet again in Proverbs 23:22 the wisdom of God's Word declares, *"Hearken unto thy father that begat thee, and despise not thy mother when she is old."*

In the fourth place, we learn that children are to maintain a spirit of honor toward their parents throughout all of their lifetime. In the closing half of Proverbs 23:22, the wisdom of God's Word declares, *"And despise not thy mother when she is old."* Even so, our Lord Jesus Christ rebuked the adult Pharisees in Mark 9:7-13, saying, *"Full well ye reject the commandment of God, that ye may keep your own tradition. For Moses said, Honour thy father and thy mother; and, Whoso curseth father or mother, let him die the death: but ye say, If a man shall say to his father or mother, It is Corban, that is to say, a gift, by whatsoever thou mightest be profited by me; he shall be free. And ye suffer him no more to do ought for his father or his mother; making the word of God of none effect through your tradition, which ye have delivered: and many such like things do ye."* Thus our Lord Jesus Christ indicated that God's command to honor thy father and mother continues even throughout the child's adult years, and He rebuked the Pharisees for creating a false, manmade "loophole" against such honor.

194. Fathers must not provoke their children to wrath, lest they be discouraged, but must "bring them up in the nurture and admonition of the Lord."

Ephesians 6:4 – *"And, ye fathers, provoke not your children to wrath: but bring them up in the nurture and admonition of the Lord."*

Colossians 3:21 – *"Fathers, provoke not your children to anger, lest they be discouraged."*

In the first place, we learn that the father is primarily responsible for the spiritual upbringing of his children. In Ephesians 5:22-24 instruction was given to the wives concerning their responsibility toward their own husbands, and in turn in Ephesians 5:25-33 instruction was given to the husbands concerning their responsibility toward their own wives. Then in Ephesians 6:1-3 instruction was given to the children concerning their responsibility toward their parents, and in turn in verse 4 we would expect an instruction to the parents concerning their responsibility toward their children. Yet verse 4 does not begin with the words, "And, ye parents." Rather, it begins with the words, "And, ye fathers." This focus reveals that the Lord our God holds the father primarily responsible for the spiritual upbringing of his children. Certainly, mothers have a responsibility in this matter; for the children are required to obey and honor the mother's authority as well as the father's authority. Yet the mother's primary responsibility is to be a helper who is meet for her husband in helping him to fulfill his God-given responsibility to bring up their children "in the nurture and admonition of the Lord." The responsibility for the upbringing of the children is his; the responsibility to help him is hers.

In the second place, we learn that the father is not to provoke his children unto anger and thus also unto discouragement. Yet how might a father so provoke and discourage his children? From Proverbs 15:1 we learn that he might do so through grievous words; for there we read, "*A soft answer turneth away wrath: but grievous words stir up anger.*" Thus fathers must refrain from all that the Word of God would define as being grievous words; for these will provoke and discourage the children. Again from the opening portion of Proverbs 28:25 we learn that he might do so through a proud attitude; for there we read, "*He that is of a proud heart stirreth up strife*." Thus fathers must refrain from all that the Word of God would define as being of a proud attitude; for such an attitude will provoke and discourage the children. Yet again from Proverbs 15:18 we learn that he might do so through an angry attitude; for there we read, "*A wrathful man stirreth up strife: but he that is slow to anger appeaseth strife.*" Thus fathers must refrain from all that the Word of God would define as fleshly anger; for such an attitude will provoke and discourage the children. And yet again from Proverbs 30:33 we learn that he might do so through unnecessary aggravation; for there we read, "*Surely the churning of milk bringeth forth butter, and the wringing of the nose bringeth forth blood: so the forcing of wrath bringeth forth strife.*" Thus fathers must refrain from aggravating our children unnecessarily; for such aggravation will provoke and discourage the children. Finally, from the opening portion of Proverbs 16:28 we learn that he might do so through ungodly behavior; for there we read, "*A froward man soweth strife.*" Thus fathers must refrain from any walk in ungodliness; for such ungodliness will provoke and discourage the children.

On the other hand and in the third place, we learn that the father must bring up his children "in the nurture and admonition of the Lord." This requires that the father himself walk in love for and service to the Lord his God; for Deuteronomy 6:4-5 declares, "*Hear, O Israel: The LORD our God is one LORD: and thou shalt love the LORD thy God with all thine heart, and with all thy soul, and with all thy might.*" This also requires that the father himself root the truth of God's Word in his own heart; for Deuteronomy 6:6 adds, "*And these words, which I command thee this day, shall be in thine heart.*" Then this requires that the father diligently teach the truth of God's Word unto his children; for Deuteronomy 6:7 continues, "*And thou shalt teach them diligently unto thy children, and shalt talk of them when thou sittest in thine house, and when thou walkest by the way, and when thou liest down, and when thou risest up.*" Yet again this requires that the father hold forth the truth of God's Word as the governing principle for the entire household; for Deuteronomy 6:8-9 declares, "*And thou shalt bind them for a sign upon thine hand, and they shall be as frontlets between thine eyes. And thou shalt write them upon the posts of thy house, and on thy gates.*" Finally, this requires that the father faithfully discipline his children for any disobedience against the precepts and principles of God's Word; for Proverbs 3:12 declares, "*For whom the LORD loveth he correcteth; even as a father the son in whom he delighteth;*" and Proverbs 13:24 adds, "*He that spareth his rod hateth his son: but he that loveth him chasteneth him betimes.*" Yea, Proverbs 19:18 declares, "*Chasten thy son while there is hope, and let not thy soul spare for his crying;*" and Proverbs 23:13-14 adds, "*Withhold not correction from the child: for if thou beatest him with the rod, he shall not die. Thou shalt beat him with the rod, and shalt deliver his soul from hell.*"

195. **Servants (or, employees) must be obedient and submissive to their masters (or, employers) in all things as unto the Lord with honor and respect, not argumentatively or grudgingly, but pleasantly and heartily, not with eye service, but with commitment of heart, not embezzling, but with faithful responsibility.**

Ephesians 6:5-8 – "*Servants, be obedient to them that are your masters according to the flesh, with fear and trembling, in singleness of your heart, as unto Christ; not with eyeservice, as menpleasers; but as the servants of Christ, doing the will of God from the heart; with good will doing service, as to the Lord, and not to men*: knowing that whatsoever good thing any man doeth, the same shall he receive of the Lord, whether he be bond or free."

Colossians 3:22-25 – "*Servants, obey in all things your masters according to the flesh; not with eyeservice, as menpleasers; but in singleness of heart, fearing God: and whatsoever ye do, do it heartily, as to the Lord, and not unto men*; knowing that of the Lord ye shall receive the reward of the inheritance: for ye serve the Lord Christ. But he that doeth wrong shall receive for the wrong which he hath done: and there is no respect of persons."

1 Timothy 6:1-2 – "*Let as many servants as are under the yoke count their own masters worthy of all honour, that the name of God and his doctrine be not blasphemed. And they that have believing masters, let them not despise them, because they are brethren; but rather do them service, because they are faithful and beloved, partakers of the benefit*. These things teach and exhort."

Titus 2:9-10 – "*Exhort servants to be obedient unto their own masters, and to please them well in all things; not answering again; not purloining, but shewing all good fidelity*; that they may adorn the doctrine of God our Saviour in all things."

1 Peter 2:18 – "*Servants, be subject to your masters with all fear; not only to the good and gentle, but also to the froward.*"

From these five New Testament passages we learn a nine truths concerning this matter. In the first place, we learn that employees are to be obedient and submissive unto their employers because it is the will of God. Ephesians 6:5-6 declares, "*Servants, be obedient to them that are your masters according to the flesh, with fear and trembling, in singleness of your heart, as unto Christ; not with eyeservice, as menpleasers; but as the servants of Christ, **doing the will of God from the heart**.*" Colossians 3:22 adds, "*Servants, obey in all things your masters according to the flesh; not with eyeservice, as menpleasers; but in singleness of heart, **fearing God**.*"

In the second place, we learn that employees are to be obedient and submissive unto their employers "in all things." (See Colossians 3:22) Certainly, if the employer requires the employee to do something that is directly contrary to a specific command of God's Holy Word, then the employee should follow the principle of Acts 5:17 – "*We ought to obey God rather than men.*" Yet even in this case the employee should apply this principle while demonstrating "all honour" unto the employer. (See 1 Timothy 6:1) In addition, the employee should never use this principle selfishly as a weapon against the employer to get his or her own way in a matter. Nor should the employee ever apply this principle unto matters of his or her own formulation that are not specifically presented in God's Word. Such cases are to be subject only unto the direct declaration of God's Word, and not unto the employee's own interpretations of right and wrong. Rather, in everything else except a case in which something is directly contrary to God's Word, the employee is to be obedient and submissive unto the authority of the employer, even if the requirement is distasteful, or "unfair," or contrary to one's job-description.

In the third place, we learn that employees are to be obedient and submissive unto their employers "as to the Lord." Three times in the three verses of Ephesians 6:5-7 this truth is emphasized – "*Servants, be obedient to them that are your masters according to the flesh, with fear and trembling, in singleness of your heart, **as unto Christ**; not with eyeservice, as menpleasers; **but as the servants of Christ**, doing the will of God from the heart; with good will doing service, **as to the Lord**, and not to men.*" Again in Colossians

3:22-23 this truth is given – *"Servants, obey in all things your masters according to the flesh; not with eyeservice, as menpleasers; but in singleness of heart, fearing God: and whatsoever ye do, do it heartily, **as to the Lord**, and not unto men."* Just as the employee would give obedience, submission, commitment, good-will, hearty labor, honor, and respect unto the Lord, even so he or she should give such unto his or her employer. Yea, the employee is ever to work as if the Lord Himself was his or her employer. Thus the employee is ever to work with the attitude and quality of which the Lord Himself is worthy. We are the servants of Christ; and on the job we are to work, not simply as the employees of some human employer or company, but as the servants of our Lord Jesus Christ Himself.

In the fourth place, we learn that employees are to be obedient and submissive unto their employers with honor and respect. Ephesians 6:5-8 declares, *"Servants, be obedient to them that are your masters according to the flesh, **with fear and trembling** [with all due respect], in singleness of your heart, as unto Christ."* 1 Timothy 6:1 adds, *"Let as many servants as are under the yoke **count their own masters worthy of all honour**, that the name of God and His doctrine be not blasphemed."* Finally, 1 Peter 2:18 proclaims, *"Servants, be subject to your masters **with all fear** [with all respect]; not only to the good and gentle, but also to the froward."* Yes, this honor and respect is to be given, not only unto those employers who "earn" it through their good and gentle character, but also unto those employers who are of an unrighteous and mean-spirited character.

In the fifth place, we learn that employees are to be obedient and submissive unto their employers, not argumentatively or grudgingly, but pleasantly and heartily. Ephesians 6:5-7 declares, *"Servants, be obedient to them that are your masters according to the flesh, with fear and trembling, in singleness of your heart, as unto Christ; not with eyeservice, as menpleasers; but as the servants of Christ, doing the will of God from the heart; **with good will doing service**, as to the Lord, and not to men."* Colossians 3:22-23 adds, *"Servants, obey in all things your masters according to the flesh; not with eyeservice, as menpleasers; but in singleness of heart, fearing God: and whatsoever ye do, **do it heartily**, as to the Lord, and not unto* men." Finally, Titus 2:9-10 proclaims, "*Exhort servants to be obedient unto their own masters, **and to please them well in all things; not answering again*** [that is – not being argumentative in word or grudging in attitude]."

In the sixth place, we learn that employees are to be obedient and submissive unto their employers, not with eyeservice (working aright only when the boss is watching), but with commitment of heart (at all times). Ephesians 6:5-6 declares, "*Servants, be obedient to them that are your masters according to the flesh, with fear and trembling, **in singleness of your heart*** [with commitment of heart], *as unto Christ; **not with eyeservice, as menpleasers***; *but as the servants of Christ, doing the will of God from the heart.*" Colossians 3:22-23 adds, "*Servants, obey in all things your masters according to the flesh; **not with eyeservice, as menpleasers; but in singleness of heart*** [with commitment of heart], *fearing God: and whatsoever ye do, do it heartily, as to the Lord, and not unto men.*"

In the seventh place, we learn that employees are to be obedient and submissive unto their employers, not embezzling materials or time, but with faithful responsibility. Titus 2:9-10 declares, "*Exhort servants to be obedient unto their own masters, and to please them well in all things; not answering again; **not purloining*** [not embezzling or stealing], ***but shewing all good fidelity*** [demonstrating all faithfulness in responsibility]; *that they may adorn the doctrine of God our Saviour in all things.*"

In the eight place, we learn that employees are to be obedient and submissive unto their employers as those who shall be rewarded or disciplined by the Lord. Ephesians 6:5-8 declares, "*Servants, be obedient to them that are your masters according to the flesh, with fear and trembling, in singleness of your heart, as unto Christ; not with eyeservice, as menpleasers; but as the servants of Christ, doing the will of God from the heart; with good will doing service, as to the Lord, and not to men: **knowing that whatsoever good thing any man doeth, the same shall he receive of the Lord**, whether he be bond or free.*" Colossians 3:22-25 adds, "*Servants, obey in all things your masters according to the flesh; not with eyeservice, as menpleasers; but in singleness of heart, fearing God: and whatsoever* *ye do, do it heartily, as to the Lord, and not unto men;* **knowing that of the Lord ye shall receive the reward of the inheritance: for ye serve the Lord Christ. But he that doeth wrong shall receive for the wrong which he hath done: and there is no respect of persons.**" Brethren, it matters not if things are always just and fair on the job. Our Lord is watching, and He has promised to reward us for our faithfulness as employees. On the other hand, it matters not if we are "getting away" with a wrong attitude, or a wasting of time, or some other wrong behavior on the job. Our Lord is watching, and He will indeed discipline us for our unfaithfulness as employees.

In the ninth and final place, we learn that employees are to be obedient and submissive unto their employers in order that our Lord God's name and doctrine might not be blasphemed by the world, but might be adorned before the world. 1 Timothy 6:1 declares, "*Let as many servants as are under the yoke count their own masters worthy of all honour,* **that the name of God and His doctrine be not blasphemed.**" Titus 2:9-10 adds, "*Exhort servants to be obedient unto their own masters, and to please them well in all things; not answering again; not purloining, but shewing all good fidelity;* **that they may adorn the doctrine of God our Saviour in all things.**" The people of this lost world are ever watching the behavior of those who claim to be God's own people. Yes, on the job they are ever watching how those who claim to be men and women of God work as employees. Thus when an employee who claims to be one of God's own is unfaithful on the job, it creates an occasion for the name of God and the truth of God to be slandered, disrespected, and rejected by this lost world. On the other hand, when an employee who claims to be one of God's own is faithful on the job, it creates an occasion for the name of God and the truth of God to be adorned, honored, and received by this lost world.

196. Masters (or, employers) must treat their servants (or, employees) with good will in submission to the Lord their Master, not being quick tempered or mean spirited, but being just and fair.

Ephesians 6:9 – "***And, ye masters, do the same things unto them, forbearing threatening***: *knowing that your Master also is in heaven; neither is there respect of persons with him."*

Colossians 4:1 – "***Masters, give unto your servants that which is just and equal***; *knowing that ye also have a Master in heaven."*

In the first place, we learn that employers are to maintain an attitude of good will toward their employees. The instruction of Ephesians 6:9 begins, "*And, ye masters, do the same things unto them* [that is – unto the servants]." This indicates that there was something which the servants had previously been instructed to do in verses 5-8 that the masters are also to do. What might that be? Were the masters to be obedient unto the servants as the servants had been instructed to be obedient unto the masters? No, for the servants are in the role of submission and the masters are in the role of leadership. Were the masters to focus upon "doing the will of God from the heart" as the servants had been instructed to do? Yes, for as believers the masters also are the servants of Christ. Were the masters to maintain "good will" in their treatment of the servants as the servants were instructed to do in their submission toward the masters? Yes, for as believers masters are to remember that they also have a Master, the Lord Himself in heaven. Thus our Lord and Master in heaven requires that believing employers should maintain an attitude of good will and a spirit of pleasantness toward their employees.

In the second place, we learn that employers are to refrain from a quick-tempered or mean-spirited attitude toward their employees. In Ephesians 6:9 the instruction continues, "*And, ye masters, do the same things unto them, forbearing threatening."* An angry, threatening manner is not to be the means by which an employer attempts to motivate employees. Even when an employee makes a mistake, or does something annoying, or fails in a matter, the employer must maintain a spirit of godly forbearance toward that employee.

In the third place, we learn that employers are to give unto their employees what is just and fair. The opening portion of Colossians 4:1 declares, *"Masters, give unto your servants that which is just and equal."* First, this means that employers are not to treat their employees with unnecessary harshness. Second, this means that employers are not to place unreasonable expectations or unreasonable responsibilities upon their employees. Third, this means that employers are to reward and promote those employees who are worthy of reward and promotion. Fourth, this means that employers are to discipline, and even remove, those employees who are worthy of discipline or removal (not simply for the sake of the business, but even more out of fairness to the other hard-working employees). Fifth, this means that employers are not to favor some employees over others out of "respect of persons." Yea, in the closing portion of Ephesians 6:9 this truth is specifically revealed through a reference to the example of our Lord in heaven. There we read, *"And, ye masters, do the same things unto them, forbearing threatening: knowing that your Master also is in heaven; neither is there respect of persons with him."*

Sixth, this means that employers are to pay their employees in a faithful and timely manner. In Deuteronomy 24:14-15 the instruction was given, *"Thou shalt not oppress an hired servant that is poor and needy, whether he be of thy brethren, or of thy strangers that are in thy land within thy gates: at his day thou shalt give him his hire, neither shall the sun go down upon it; for he is poor, and setteth his heart upon it: lest he cry against thee unto the LORD, and it be sin unto thee."* Again in James 5:1-4 the rebuke is given, *"Go to now, ye rich men, weep and howl for your miseries that shall come upon you. Your riches are corrupted, and your garments are motheaten. Your gold and silver is cankered; and the rust of them shall be a witness against you, and shall eat your flesh as it were fire. Ye have heaped treasure together for the last days. Behold, the hire of the labourers who have reaped down your fields, which is of you kept back by fraud, crieth: and the cries of them which have reaped are entered into the ears of the Lord of sabaoth."*

In the fourth and final place, we learn that employers are to remember that they must give account unto their Lord and Master in heaven.

In Ephesians 6:9 the reminder is given, "*And, ye masters, do the same things unto them, forbearing threatening: knowing that your Master also is in heaven; neither is there respect of persons with him.*" Again in Colossians 4:1 it is given, "*Masters, give unto your servants that which is just and equal; knowing that ye also have a Master in heaven.*"

197. We must be "strong in the Lord, and in the power of His might."

Ephesians 6:10 – "*Finally, my brethren, be strong in the Lord, and in the power of his might.*"

2 Timothy 2:1 – "*Thou therefore, my son, be strong in the grace that is in Christ Jesus.*"

In the first place, we must humbly recognize our own inability. Ephesians 6:10 indicates that we are to "*be strong in the Lord, and in the power of His might.*" The focus here is upon our Lord and upon His strength. There is no mention whatsoever of our strength or our ability. In fact, our own strength and ability is completely ignored and excluded. This is because our own spiritual strength, understanding, and ability is nothing. Even so, our Lord Jesus Christ proclaimed in the closing portion of John 15:5, "*For without me ye can do nothing.*" It is all about our Lord's strength, and not at all about our own; for our own spiritual ability is nothing. Thus we are instructed in Proverbs 3:5, "*Trust in the LORD with all thine heart; and lean not unto thine own understanding.*" In like manner, the apostle Paul gave testimony in 2 Corinthians 12:7-10, "*And lest I should be exalted above measure through the abundance of the revelations, there was given to me a thorn in the flesh, the messenger of Satan to buffet me, lest I should be exalted above measure* [that is – in order to teach him humility]. *For this thing I besought the Lord thrice, that it might depart from me. And he said unto me, my grace is sufficient for thee: for my strength is made perfect in weakness. Most gladly therefore will I rather glory in my infirmities, that the power of Christ may rest upon me. Therefore I take pleasure*

369

in infirmities, in reproaches, in necessities, in persecutions, in distresses for Christ's sake: for when I am weak, then am I strong." Our Lord's strength is made perfect in our hearts and lives when we recognize our own weakness, when we stop attempting to proceed in our ability, but start relying upon our Lord's strength.

In the second place, we must humbly trust in our Lord God's grace. Ephesians 6:10 indicates that we are to *"be strong in the Lord."* Also 2 Timothy 2:1 indicates that we are to *"be strong in the grace that is in Christ Jesus."* Even so, in the opening portion of 2 Corinthians 12:9 the Lord gave answer to the apostle Paul's prayer concerning the thorn in his flesh, saying, *"My grace is sufficient for thee: for my strength is made perfect in weakness."* We can do nothing to earn the outpouring of God's enabling and empowering grace upon us. It is all out of His grace. It is none out of our merit. He must graciously give in the abundance of His mercy and love, and we must humbly receive with full assurance of faith. It is only unto the humble that our Lord will grant the outpouring of abundant grace to enable, and empower, and help in time of need. In James 4:6 the truth is revealed, *"But he giveth more grace* [that is – all-sufficient grace and over abundant grace]. *Wherefore he saith, God resisteth the proud, but giveth grace to the humble."* Furthermore, it is unto those who humbly trust in Him that our Lord will grant His enabling and empowering grace. In Proverbs 3:5-6 the instruction is given, *"Trust in the LORD with all thine heart; and lean not unto thine own understanding. In all thy ways acknowledge him, and he shall direct* [yea, even enable and empower] *thy paths."*

In the third place, we must humbly depend upon God's Holy Spirit. Ephesians 6:10 indicates that we are to *"be strong in the Lord, and in the power of his might."* Now, the indwelling Holy Spirit that the Lord our God has given to each of us believers is the Spirit of power. He, the third Person of the eternal Godhead, is the One who will guide our paths in the truth and will empower our steps in the way of truth. Even so, in Acts 1:8, in His last words before He ascended into heaven, our Lord Jesus Christ declared, *"And ye shall receive power, after that the Holy Ghost is come upon you: and ye shall be witnesses unto me both in Jerusalem, and in all Judaea, and in Samaria, and unto the uttermost parts of the earth."*

In like manner, in Ephesians 3:14-16 the apostle Paul prayed under the inspiration of the Holy Spirit for the believers at Ephesus, saying, *"For this cause I bow my knees unto the Father of our Lord Jesus Christ, of whom the whole family in heaven and earth is named, that he would grant you, according to the riches of his glory, to be strengthened with might by his Spirit in the inner man."* We are spiritually enabled and empowered through our humble faith (trust, dependence) in God's all-sufficient grace by God's indwelling Holy Spirit. This is the reason that we are instructed in the closing half of Ephesians 5:18, *"But be filled with the Spirit;"* and again in Galatians 5:16, *"This I say then, Walk in the Spirit, and ye shall not fulfil the lust of the flesh."* To "be strong in the Lord, and in the power of his might" we must walk in and after the guidance of the Holy Spirit. We must yield ourselves unto His guidance and depend upon His empowerment.

In the fourth and final place, we must confidently follow after all God's will. Ephesians 6:10 indicates that we are to *"be strong in the Lord, and in the power of his might."* How powerful is our Lord's might? It is all-mighty power and strength. Thus our Lord declared unto the apostle Paul in 2 Corinthians 12:9, *"My grace is sufficient* [yea, is all-sufficient] *for thee."* Indeed, this is the grace and the power with which our Lord will enable and empower us. What spiritual confidence we may have in this! Humbling ourselves in our own weakness, trusting in our Lord's all-sufficient grace, and depending upon the spiritual enablement of the indwelling Holy Spirit, we should join in the confidence of the apostle Paul from Philippians 4:13, *"I can do all things through Christ which strengtheneth me."* Yea, we must hear and receive the encouraging words of our Lord as He delivered them unto Joshua in Joshua 1:9, saying, *"Have not I commanded thee? Be strong and of a good courage; be not afraid, neither be thou dismayed: for the LORD thy God is with thee withersoever thou goest."* Again we must hear and receive the encouraging words from the Lord our God in Isaiah 41:10, *"Fear thou not; for I am with thee: be not dismayed; for I am thy God: I will strengthen thee; yea, I will help thee; yea, I will uphold thee with the right hand of my righteousness."*

198. We must be persevering in prayer for our fellow believers.

Ephesians 6:18 – *"Praying always with all prayer and supplication in the Spirit,* **and watching thereunto** [unto prayer and supplication] **with all perseverance and supplication for all saints.***"

Even so, we may find great instruction through the example of the apostle Paul in this matter. In Ephesians 1:15-19 he gave report, *"Wherefore I also, after I heard of your faith in the Lord Jesus, and love unto all the saints, cease not to give thanks for you, making mention of you in my prayers; that the God of our Lord Jesus Christ, the Father of glory, may give unto you the spirit of wisdom and revelation in the knowledge of him: the eyes of your under-standing being enlightened; that ye may know what is the hope of his calling, and what the riches of the glory of his inheritance in the saints, and what is the exceeding greatness of his power to us-ward who believe, according to the working of his mighty power."*

In Ephesians 3:14-19 he gave report, *"For this cause I bow my knees unto the Father of our Lord Jesus Christ, of whom the whole family in heaven and earth is named, that he would grant you, according to the riches of his glory, to be strengthened with might by his Spirit in the inner man; that Christ may dwell in your hearts by faith; that ye, being rooted and grounded in love, may be able to comprehend with all saints what is the breadth, and length, and depth, and height; and to know the love of Christ, which passeth knowledge, that ye might be filled with all the fulness of God."*

In Philippians 1:9-11 he gave report, *"And this I pray, that your love may abound yet more and more in knowledge and in all judgment; that ye may approve things that are excellent; that ye may be sincere and without offence till the day of Christ; being filled with the fruits of righteousness, which are by Jesus Christ, unto the glory and praise of God."*

In Colossians 1:9-11 he gave report, *"For this cause we also, since the day we heard it, do not cease to pray for you, and to desire that ye might be filled with the knowledge of his will in all wisdom and spiritual understanding; that ye might walk worthy of the Lord unto all pleasing, being fruitful in every good work, and increasing in the knowledge of God; strengthened with all might, according to his glorious power, unto all patience and longsuffering with joyfulness.*"

In 1 Thessalonians 3:9-13 he gave report, "*For what thanks can we render to God again for you, for all the joy wherewith we joy for your sakes before our God; night and day praying exceedingly that we might see your face, and might perfect that which is lacking in your faith? Now God himself and our Father, and our Lord Jesus Christ, direct our way unto you. And the Lord make you to increase and abound in love one toward another, and toward all men, even as we do toward you: to the end he may stablish your hearts unblameable in holiness before God, even our Father, at the coming of our Lord Jesus Christ with all his saints.*"

In 2 Thessalonians 1:11-12 he gave report, "*Wherefore also we pray always for you, that our God would count you worthy of this calling, and fulfil all the good pleasure of his goodness, and the work of faith with power: that the name of our Lord Jesus Christ may be glorified in you, and ye in him, according to the grace of our God and the Lord Jesus Christ.*"

In 2 Timothy 1:3-4 he gave report, "*I thank God, whom I serve from my forefathers with pure conscience, that without ceasing I have remembrance of thee in my prayers night and day; greatly desiring to see thee, being mindful of thy tears, that I may be filled with joy.*"

Finally, in Philemon 1:4-6 he gave report, "*I thank my God, making mention of thee always in my prayers, hearing of thy love and faith, which thou hast toward the Lord Jesus, and toward all saints; that the communication of thy faith may become effectual by the acknowledging of every good thing which is in you in Christ Jesus.*"

199. We must have our love toward one another to abound yet more and more in Spirit-filled discernment.

Philippians 1:9 – "*And this I pray, that your love may abound yet more and more in knowledge and in all judgment.*"

1 Thessalonians 3:12 – "*And the Lord make you to increase and abound in love one toward another, and toward all men, even as we do toward you.*"

1 Thessalonians 4:9-10 – "*But as touching brotherly love ye need not that I write unto you: for ye yourselves are taught of God to love one another. And indeed ye do it toward all the brethren which are in all Macedonia: but we beseech you, brethren, that ye increase more and more.*"

We know that the Lord our God has commanded us to love one another even as He has loved us. We know that the fullness of our Lord's perfect love toward us is the God-given standard for our love toward one another. Yet none of us have yet attained unto the fullness of this perfect love toward one another. Every one of us yet falls short of this standard of love. Therefore, we all must pursue the objective that our love toward one another might increase and abound yet more and more until we attain unto the standard of the fullness of our Lord's perfect love toward us. Our present level of love toward one another is not sufficient. Our love toward one another as fellow believers must increase. Our love toward one another as fellow believers must abound. Our love toward one another as fellow believers must grow yet more and more.

Yet this must not simply be an increase and abundance of emotional love toward one another. Rather, this must be an increase and abundance of spiritual love toward one another. This increase and abundance of love must be governed by the godly wisdom and discernment of the Holy Spirit's guidance through the truth of God's Word. This increase and abundance of our love toward one another must be continually motivated unto godliness both in our own lives and in the lives of our fellow believers all for the glory of God. Just as our Lord's perfect love toward us is always governed

374

by the principles of godliness and never contradicts those principles, even so our growing love toward one another must be always governed by those principles of godliness and must never contradict them.

~~~

200. We must approve with full conviction of heart and with full commitment of life those things that are spiritually excellent.

Philippians 1:10 – "*That ye may approve things that are excellent; that ye may be sincere and without offence till the day of Christ.*"

1 Thessalonians 5:21 – "*Prove all things; hold fast that which is good.*"

Now, approving things that are excellent is a two-step process. First, to approve things that are excellent, we must prove (test) all things in order to discern if they are actually excellent or not. Not all things are actually good and excellent. Not even all things that appear on the surface to be good and excellent are actually good and excellent for us spiritually. Therefore, we must "prove all things." We must test all things according to the standard of spiritual excellence. What then is this standard of spiritual excellence? Ephesians 5:10 reveals the answer when it says, "*Proving what is acceptable unto the Lord.*" The closing portion of Romans 12:2 also reveals the answer when it says, "*That ye prove what is that good, and acceptable, and perfect, will of God.*" The standard of spiritual excellence is that which is acceptable in our Lord's sight. The standard of spiritual excellence is that which is the will of the Lord our God for our lives. His will alone is good, and acceptable, and perfect. His will alone is spiritually excellent for us. Therefore, we must first prove all things to discern if it is acceptable in our Lord's sight and if it is the will of our Lord for our lives.

Then, second, to approve things that are excellent, we must hold fast unto those things that are found actually to be spiritually good and excellent for us. If it is acceptable in our Lord's sight, then it must be acceptable in our sight. If it is the will of the Lord our God for us, then it must be that to which we hold fast. Yea, then we must hold fast to it with all the conviction of our hearts and must pursue after it with all the commitment of our lives.

201. We must walk in Spirit-filled sincerity (as opposed to flesh-filled hypocrisy), being filled with the fruits of righteousness.

Philippians 1:10-11 – *"That ye may approve things that are excellent; that ye may be sincere and without offence till the day of Christ; being filled with the fruits of righteousness, which are by Jesus Christ, unto the glory and praise of God."*

In this context the phrase "sincere and without offense" refers to that which is genuine and real, honest and pure. It refers to that which is without the hidden offenses of hypocrisy and deception. The Lord our God would have us to walk each day in sincere godliness. He does not want us to walk in a hypocritical show of godliness that denies the Spirit-filled power thereof. In fact, such a walk of hypocrisy is a great offense in His sight. Indeed, He is greatly offended when we appear to honor Him with our external show of behavior while our heart within is actually far from Him. Rather, our Lord desires that we should walk, not in the self-righteous hypocrisy of our sinful flesh, but in the true godliness of the Holy Spirit's direction.

He desires that we should be truly filled from the depths of our heart with the fruits of righteousness, that is – with the righteous fruit of the Spirit, with love, joy, peace, longsuffering, gentleness, goodness, faith, meekness. (See Galatians 5:22-23) He desires that we should continually abide in Christ through the filling of the Holy Spirit, for this is the only way in which we might be filled with the fruits of righteousness and might walk with sincere godliness. Even so, in John 15:4-5 our Lord Jesus Christ declared, *"Abide in me, and I in you. As the branch cannot bear fruit of itself, except it abide in the vine; no more can ye, except ye abide in me. I am the vine, ye are the branches: he that abideth in me, and I in him, the same bringeth forth much fruit: for without me ye can do nothing.*" Yes, the fruits of righteousness are only by Jesus Christ in our lives, and we shall be filled with them only as we abide in Him. Then our daily living shall be "unto the glory and praise of God."

202. We must conduct ourselves in a manner that is worthy of and adorning to the gospel of our Lord and Savior Jesus Christ.

Philippians 1:27 – "***Only let your conversation be as it becometh the gospel of Christ****: that whether I come and see you, or else be absent, I may hear of your affairs, that ye stand fast in one spirit, with one mind striving together for the faith of the gospel.*"

Through faith we have received the gospel of Christ's death for our sin and of Christ's resurrection for our justification. Now as the eternally redeemed and eternally saved children of God, we are called to conduct ourselves in a manner that is worthy of that saving gospel. Furthermore, as the children of God we are also called to be witnesses of our Savior Jesus Christ and of His glorious gospel unto the lost world around us. Therefore, we are called to conduct ourselves in a manner that adorns the gospel of Christ and attracts the lost world to receive it. Certainly, it is possible for us as the people of God to conduct ourselves in such a manner that we turn the lost away from the gospel. It is possible for us to conduct ourselves in such a manner that we cause the gospel of Christ to be discredited, dishonored, disregarded, and despised among them. On the other hand, it is possible for us as the people of God to conduct ourselves in such a manner that we attract the lost toward the gospel. It is possible for us to conduct ourselves in such a manner that we cause the gospel of Christ to be approved, esteemed, exalted, and accepted among them.

So then, what is involved in the manner of conduct that is worthy of and adorning to the gospel of Christ?

First, in order to conduct ourselves in a manner that is worthy of and adorning to the gospel, we must maintain holiness in character. In 1 Peter 3:15 God's Word declares, *"But sanctify the Lord God in your hearts: and be ready always to give an answer to every man that asketh you a reason of the hope that is in you with meekness and fear."* To "sanctify the Lord God in our hearts" is to present ourselves as "a living sacrifice, holy, acceptable unto God." (See Romans 12:1) Even so, such holiness in character will draw the lost to ask of us the reason of the hope that is in us, which reason is the glorious gospel of Christ.

Second, in order to conduct ourselves in a manner that is worthy of and adorning to the gospel, we must maintain goodness in behavior. In Matthew 5:14-16 our Lord Jesus Christ declared, *"Ye are the light of the world. A city that is set on an hill cannot be hid. Neither do men light a candle, and put it under a bushel, but on a candlestick; and it giveth light unto all that are in the house. Let your light so shine before men, that they may see your good works, and glorify your Father which is in heaven."* Again in 1 Peter 2:11-12 God's Word declares, *"Dearly beloved, I beseech you as strangers and pilgrims, abstain from fleshly lusts, which war against the soul; having your conversation honest among the Gentiles: that, whereas they speak against you as evildoers, they may by your good works, which they shall behold, glorify God in the day of visitation."* Both of these passages give instruction concerning our behavior before the lost world, and in both of these passages the appropriate behavior is defined as "good works." Even so, we are informed in both of these passages that our goodness in behavior will motivate the lost to glorify God our heavenly Father.

Third, in order to conduct ourselves in a manner that is worthy of and adorning to the gospel, we must maintain unity through love. In Philippians 1:27 God's Word declares, *"Only let your conversation be as it becometh the gospel of Christ: that whether I come and see you, or else be absent, I may hear of your affairs, that ye stand fast in one spirit, with one mind striving together for the faith of the gospel."* Even so, in John 17:20-21 our Lord Jesus Christ lifted up His prayer, saying, *"Neither pray I for these alone, but for them also which shall believe on me through their word; that they all may be one; as thou, Father, art in me, and I in thee, that they also may be one in us: that the world may believe that thou hast sent me.*" Godly unity among us as believers will move the lost to believe on Jesus Christ as God's way of salvation. What then is the foundational means for such godly unity among us? In Philippians 2:2 God's Word declares, "*Fulfil ye my joy, that ye be likeminded, having the same love, being of one accord, of one mind.*" The foundational means for godly unity among us is godly love toward one another. Thus in John 13:34-35 our Lord Jesus Christ declared, "*A new commandment I give unto you, That ye love one another; as I have loved you, that ye also love one another. By this shall all men know that ye are my disciples, if ye have love one to another.*"

Fourth, in order to conduct ourselves in a manner that is worthy of and adorning to the gospel, we must remain steadfast against persecution. In Philippians 1:27-28 God's Word declares, "*Only let your conversation be as it becometh the gospel of Christ: that whether I come and see you, or else be absent, I may hear of your affairs, that ye stand fast in one spirit, with one mind striving together for the faith of the gospel; and in nothing terrified by your adversaries: which is to them an evident token of perdition, but to you of salvation, and that of God.*" Again in 1 Peter 3:14-15 God's Word declares, "*But and if ye suffer for righteousness' sake, happy are ye: and be not afraid of their terror, neither be troubled; but sanctify the Lord God in your hearts: and be ready always to give an answer to every man that asketh you a reason of the hope that is in you with meekness and fear.*" Our untroubled steadfastness in the things of the Lord, especially in the face of affliction and persecution, bears powerful witness to our unwavering hope through the gospel of our Lord. Even so, this demonstration of unwavering hope will stir up lost souls to seek after that same hope through faith in the gospel of Christ.

Fifth, in order to conduct ourselves in a manner that is worthy of and adorning to the gospel, we must not have a spirit of complaining. In Philippians 2:14-16 God's Word declares, "*Do all things without murmurings and disputings: that ye may be blameless and harmless, the sons of God, without rebuke, in the midst of a crooked and perverse nation, among whom ye shine as lights in the world; holding* forth the word of life; that I may rejoice in the day of Christ, that I have not run in vain, neither laboured in vain." When we have a complaining spirit about us, we are not blameless and harmless as the children of God, without rebuke, in the midst of this sinful world. When we have a complaining spirit about us, we are not shining forth as spiritual lights in this spiritually dark world. Rather, when we have a complaining spirit about us, we are worthy of blame and rebuke by this world; and we are causing harm to the light of the gospel in this world.

Finally, in order to conduct ourselves in a manner that is worthy of and adorning to the gospel, we must not set our priority on earthly things. In Philippians 3:18-19 God's Word declares, *"(For many walk, of whom I have told you often, and now tell you even weeping, that they are the enemies of the cross of Christ: whose end is destruction, whose God is their belly, and whose glory is in their shame, who mind earthly things.)"* Such a priority on earthly pursuits, earthly pleasures, and earthly possessions will cause us to be the enemies of the gospel of Christ's cross. Such a priority is certainly not worthy of the gospel and will not attract the lost unto the gospel.

203. We must stand fast in Spirit-filled unity against suffering and persecution for our Lord's sake.

Philippians 1:27-30 – *"Only let your conversation be as it becometh the gospel of Christ: that whether I come and see you, or else be absent, I may hear of your affairs,* ***that ye stand fast in one spirit****, with one mind striving together for the faith of the gospel;* ***and in nothing terrified by your adversaries*** *[your persecutors]: which is to them an evident token of perdition, but to you of salvation, and that of God. For unto you it is given in the behalf of Christ, not only to believe on him, but also to suffer for his sake; having the same conflict which ye saw in me, and now hear to be in me."*

We must stand fast together in one spirit, that is – in the unity of the Holy Spirit (as mentioned in Ephesians 4:3). We must not strike at one another, but must stand fast with one another. We must not strive against one another in self-centered pursuits, but must support one another in Spirit-filled unity. We must yield ourselves to the Holy Spirit so that He might knit our hearts together as fellow brothers and sisters in Christ. Indeed, this we must do in order that we might encourage one another and support one another in times of suffering and persecution for our Lord's sake. In times of suffering and persecution, we need to stand fast in the faith. Even so, in such times of suffering and persecution, we can help one another to stand fast if we are knit together in Spirit-filled unity.

204. We must strive together in Spirit-filled unity "for the faith of the gospel."

Philippians 1:27 – *"Only let your conversation be as it becometh the gospel of Christ: that whether I come and see you, or else be absent, I may hear of your affairs, that ye stand fast in one spirit, **with one mind striving together for the faith of the gospel**."*

One of the great reasons that we must stand fast in Spirit-filled unity is that we might strive together to proclaim the gospel of Christ unto the lost and to lead lost sinners unto faith in Christ for salvation. We must not strive against one another to get our own way. Rather, we must strive with one another to see souls saved. Far too often the people of God spend their energy striving among themselves. This ought not so to be. Rather, we must spend our energy striving in Spirit-filled unity with one another for the spread of the gospel. We must have our spirits knit together with a burden for the lost. We must pray together for souls to be saved. We must go together in witnessing for Christ. We must give together for the support of worldwide missions. We must work together to lead souls unto faith in Christ for eternal salvation. We must walk in godly love together as a testimony concerning the life-transforming power of the gospel. We must praise the Lord together for every lost soul that is saved through our ministry. "Striving together for the faith of the gospel."

205. We must do nothing "through strife or vainglory."

Philippians 2:3 – "*Let nothing be done through strife or vainglory; but in lowliness of mind let each esteem other better than themselves.*"

In this verse God's Word instructs us to maintain a Spirit-filled unity of mindset and love for, toward, and with one another as fellow believers in accord with the will of our Lord Jesus Christ. Then in verse 3-8 we are given a number of principles whereby such a Spirit-filled unity might be pursued and preserved. The first of these "principles for Spirit-filled unity" is that we must do nothing "through strife and vainglory." Now, the word "strife" refers to a spirit of contention and fighting in order to get one's own way. In addition, the word "vainglory" refers to a spirit of desire and pursuit to get glory for one's self. Even so, these two motivations must never be a part of our character or conduct. Such motivations will only destroy Spirit-filled unity, not develop it. In Galatians 5:26 the warning is given, "*Let us not be desirous of vain glory, provoking one another, envying one another.*" Furthermore, such motivations only reveal that we are walking in the carnality of our sinful flesh, rather than in the spirituality of the Holy Spirit. In 1 Corinthians 3:3 the believers at Corinth were warned, "*For ye are yet carnal: for whereas there is among you envying, and strife, and divisions, are ye not carnal, and walk as men?*" Let nothing, not a single thing in your home life, in your church ministry, or in your public behavior, be done through the fleshly motivations of strife or vainglory.

206. We must in godly humility esteem others as better than ourselves.

Philippians 2:3 – "*Let nothing be done through strife or vainglory; but in lowliness of mind let each esteem other better than themselves.*"

This is the second of "the principles for Spirit-filled unity." This is not a spirit of hypocrisy whereby we put on a show of humility and of esteeming others. Rather, this is a true, godly spirit of humility whereby we sincerely acknowledge ourselves as lower and whereby we sincerely esteem others as better. Certainly this spirit will help in the development of Spirit-filled unity among us who are God's people. With such a spirit we will not strive against others to get for self. Rather, with such a spirit we will give up of self to serve others and to submit unto others.

---

207. We must not be self-centered, but must be others centered.

Philippians 2:4 – "*Look not every man on his own things, but every man also on the things of others.*"

Our own things (that is – our own interests, our own ideas, our own preferences, our own pursuits, our own advancement, etc.) must not be the center of our focus. Certainly, it is natural for us to center our focus upon our own things; but our Lord desires that we purposefully center our focus instead upon the things of others. We must purposefully center our focus upon the benefits of others, the edification of others, the advancement of others, the preferences of others, the honor of others, the interests of others, etc. This is the way of true, godly love toward one another; for 1 Corinthians 13:5 reveals that such true, godly love "*seeketh not her own.*" Furthermore, this is the way in which our hearts will be knit together in Spirit-filled unity with one another. Finally, this is the way that we may be most effective in our ministry of edification toward one another and in our ministry of evangelism toward the lost. In 1 Corinthians 10:23-24 God's Word teaches us, saying, "*All things are lawful for me, but all things are not expedient: all things are lawful for me, but all things edify not. Let no man seek his own, but every man another's wealth.*" In addition, in verses 32-33 God's Word teaches us, saying, "*Give none offence, neither to the Jews, nor to the Gentiles, nor to the church of God: even as I please all men in all things, not seeking mine own profit, but the profit of many, that they may be saved.*"

---

208. We must have the same servant-mindedness as our Lord Jesus Christ.

Philippians 2:5-8 – "***Let this mind be in you, which was also in Christ Jesus****: who, being in the form of God, thought it not robbery to be equal with God: but made himself of no reputation, and took upon him the form of a servant, and was made in the likeness of men: and being found in fashion as a man, he humbled himself, and became obedient unto death, even the death of the cross.*"

Although our Lord Jesus Christ, as God the Son, was eternally equal with God the Father in the glory of the Godhead, He set aside that glory and took upon Himself the form of a servant. He came to this earth, being born in human flesh, not to be ministered unto, but to minister unto us. Although He is the Lord and Master of all, He came among us as a servant. Then as a servant, He gave His life a ransom for us sinners. He humbled Himself as a servant even unto the death of the cross. This was our Lord's mindset, and this is the same mindset that we are to possess – the mindset of a servant. We must possess the mindset that chooses, no matter how high we may be, to take upon ourselves the place and purpose of a servant. We must possess the mindset that seeks, not to be ministered unto, but to minister unto others. We must possess the mindset that is willing to serve even unto great sacrifice of ourselves. Furthermore, if we will abase ourselves with the Christ-like mindset of a servant, we can be assured that the Lord our God will exalt us in due time. Concerning our Lord Jesus Christ, Philippians 2:9-11 declares, "*Wherefore God also hath highly exalted him, and given him a name which is above every name: that at the name of Jesus every knee should bow, of things in heaven, and things in earth, and things under the earth; and that every tongue should confess that Jesus Christ is Lord, to the glory of God the Father.*" Even so, in Matthew 23:12 our Lord Jesus Christ gave promise to us, saying, "*And whosoever shall exalt himself shall be abased; and he that shall humble himself shall be exalted.*"

209. We must work out of our own salvation with fear and trembling by serving the Lord our God "with reverence and godly fear."

Philippians 2:12-13 – *"Wherefore, my beloved, as ye have always obeyed, not as in my presence only, but now much more in my absence,* **work out your own salvation with fear and trembling***. For it is God which worketh in you both to will and to do of his good pleasure."*

Hebrews 12:28-29 – *"Wherefore we receiving a kingdom which cannot be moved,* **let us have grace, whereby we may serve God acceptably with reverence and godly fear***: for our God is a consuming fire."*

1 Peter 1:17-19 – *"And if ye call on the Father, who without respect of persons judgeth according to every man's work,* **pass the time of your sojourning here in fear***: forasmuch as ye know that ye were not redeemed with corruptible things, as silver and gold, from your vain conversation received by tradition from your fathers; but with the precious blood of Christ, as of a lamb without blemish and without spot."*

1 Peter 2:17 – *"Honour all men. Love the brotherhood.* **Fear God***. Honour the king."*

It is important that we do not misunderstand this instruction. We are not here instructed to work *up* our own salvation, as if we could arrange our own salvation through our own mighty efforts. God's Word clearly reveals to us that as lost sinners we were spiritually *"dead in trespasses and sins"* (Ephesians 2:1), and that as such we were without any spiritual strength to save ourselves. Yea, Romans 5:6 declares, *"For when we were yet without strength, in due time Christ died for the ungodly."* Furthermore, we are not instructed in Philippians 2:12 to work *for* our own salvation, as if we could earn our own salvation through our own righteous efforts. Ephesians 2:8-9 declares, *"For by grace are ye saved through faith; and that not of yourselves: it is the gift of God: not of works, lest any man should boast."* Again Romans 4:4-5 declares, *"Now to him that worketh* is the reward not reckoned of grace, but of debt. But to him that worketh not, but believeth on him that justifieth the ungodly, his faith is counted for righteousness." Yet again Titus 3:4-7 declares, *"But after that the kindness and love of God our Saviour toward man appeared, not by works of righteousness which we have done, but according to his mercy he saved us, by the washing of regeneration, and renewing of the Holy Ghost; which he shed on us abundantly through Jesus Christ our Saviour; that being justified by his grace, we should be made heirs according to the hope of eternal life."*

So then, what does it mean to work *out* our own salvation with fear and trembling? First, we must understand that it is a matter of obedience unto the will and Word of the Lord our God. Under the inspiration of God the Holy Spirit, the apostle Paul opened the instruction of Philippians 2:12, saying, *"Wherefore, my beloved, as ye have always obeyed."*

Second, we must understand that it is a matter of working out that which the Lord our God has already worked within us at our salvation. At the moment of our faith in Christ as Savior, we received eternal redemption, eternal salvation, and eternal life. At that very moment, we were recreated as a new spiritual creation in Christ Jesus our Lord and Savior. 2 Corinthians 5:17 declares, *"Therefore if any man be in Christ, he is a new creature: old things are passed away; behold, all things are become new."* At that very moment, we were spiritually born again by the work of God the Holy Spirit; and thereby we were given newness of spiritual life within. Yea, at that very moment, we were permanently sealed and indwelt by God the Holy Spirit for our entire walk upon this earth.

We, who had been the children of darkness, the children of the devil, the children of disobedience, the children of wrath, are now the children of light, the children of God, the children of promise. At the moment of our faith in Christ as Savior, God our heavenly Father did a mighty spiritual work of salvation within us. Now He requires us to work out in our daily walk that which He has already worked in at the moment of our salvation.

We are the children of light; that is the work that the Lord our God has already worked within us. Now we are called and commanded to walk in the light as the children of light. We are the children of God by new spiritual birth; that is the work that the Lord our God has already worked within us. Now we are called and commanded to be followers of God in obedience as His dear children. We have been delivered from the power of spiritual darkness and translated into the kingdom of God's dear Son; that is the work that the Lord our God has already worked within us. Now we are called and commanded no more to yield ourselves unto the darkness of sin, but rather to yield ourselves in service unto God.

Third, we must understand that working out our own salvation is a matter of yielding ourselves daily unto the direction that the Lord our God continues to work within us. In Philippians 2:13 the truth is revealed, *"For it is God which worketh in you both to will and to do of his good pleasure."* This is not speaking of our Lord God's mighty work within us at the moment of our salvation. Rather, this is speaking of our Lord's God daily work within us through His indwelling Holy Spirit to guide and govern our desires and our doings. Through His indwelling Holy Spirit, the Lord our God works in us daily to will (to desire) and to do of His good pleasure. Our responsibility then is to yield ourselves unto that direction, and thereby to live out in our daily walk that which the Lord our God is working in us through the direction of His indwelling Holy Spirit.

Fourth, we must understand that working out our own salvation is a matter of reverence and godly fear before the lordship authority of the Lord our God. We must have a truly humble, contrite, and submissive spirit before our Lord. In Philippians 2:12 we are instructed to work out our own salvation, to walk in obedience unto our Lord's daily direction, *"with fear and trembling."* Again in Hebrews 12:28-29 we are instructed, *"Wherefore we receiving a kingdom which cannot be moved, let us have grace, whereby we may serve God acceptably with reverence and godly fear: for our God is a consuming fire."* Yet again in 2 Corinthians 7:1 we are instructed, *"Having therefore these promises, dearly beloved, let us cleanse ourselves from all filthiness of the flesh and spirit, perfecting holiness in the fear of God."*

210. We must rejoice in our Lord always.

Philippians 3:1 – *"Finally, my brethren, **rejoice in the Lord**. To write the same things to you, to me indeed is not grievous, but for you it is safe."*

Philippians 4:4 – *"**Rejoice in the Lord alway: and again I say, Rejoice**."*

1 Thessalonians 5:16 – *"**Rejoice evermore**."*

Four times in these three verses we find the command of God's Word that we are to *rejoice*. Furthermore, from two of these verses (Philippians 4:4 & 1 Thessalonians 5:17) we find that we are to rejoice *all the time* (always) *and forever more*. Finally, from two of these verses we find that we are to rejoice *in our Lord and Savior Jesus Christ*. This rejoicing always and ever more is not to be rooted in the circumstances of our lives; for our circumstances often are not those of joy and rejoicing, but of grief and sorrow. This rejoicing always and ever more is not to be rooted in the determination of our hearts, for our hearts often are not moved to joy and rejoicing in the face of many circumstances. Rather, this rejoicing always and ever more is to be rooted in our Lord and Savior; for He alone can fill us with *"joy unspeakable and full of glory."* (See 1 Peter 1:6-8) Only as we look unto Him to fill us with His own divine joy may our joy be full. (See John 15:11)

211. We must beware of those who put their confidence in the flesh.

Philippians 3:2-14 – *"**Beware of dogs, beware of evil workers, beware of the concision**. For we are the circumcision, which worship God in the spirit, and rejoice in Christ Jesus, and have no confidence in the flesh. Though I might also have confidence in the flesh. If any other man thinketh that he hath whereof he might trust in the flesh, I more: circumcised the eighth day, of the stock of Israel, of the tribe of Benjamin, an Hebrew of the Hebrews; as* *touching the law, a Pharisee; Concerning zeal, persecuting the church; touching the righteousness which is in the law, blameless. But what things were gain to me, those I counted loss for Christ. Yea doubtless, and I count all things but loss for the excellency of the knowledge of Christ Jesus my Lord: for whom I have suffered the loss of all things, and do count them but dung, that I may win Christ, and be found in him, not having mine own righteousness, which is of the law, but that which is through the faith of Christ, the righteousness which is of God by faith: that I may know him, and the power of his resurrection, and the fellowship of his sufferings, being made conformable unto his death; if by any means I might attain unto the resurrection of the dead. Not as though I had already attained, either were already perfect: but I follow after, if that I may apprehend that for which also I am apprehended of Christ Jesus. Brethren, I count not myself to have apprehended: but this one thing I do, forgetting those things which are behind, and reaching forth unto those things which are before, I press toward the mark for the prize of the high calling of God in Christ Jesus."*

These dogs of whom the apostle speaks are not the actual animal. Rather, under the inspiration of God the Holy Spirit, the apostle uses this term "dogs" to represent those evil workers whose worship was not through the filling of the Holy Spirit and whose joy was not rooted in the Lord Jesus Christ, but whose religious confidence was in their own fleshly activities and accomplishments. So many point to their own religious activities and accomplishments as the proof that they are spiritual. Yet our spirituality is not founded upon how religiously active we are or upon how much we have religiously accomplished. Rather, our spirituality is founded upon how closely and how faithfully we walk with our Lord Jesus Christ.

Therefore, the apostle Paul stated in verses 4-6, *"Though I might also have confidence in the flesh. If any other man thinketh that he hath whereof he might trust in the flesh, I more: circumcised the eighth day, of the stock of Israel, of the tribe of Benjamin, an Hebrew of the Hebrews; as touching the law, a Pharisee; concerning zeal, persecuting the church; touching the righteousness which is in the law, blameless."* Yet in verse 7 the apostle stated in contrast, *"But what things were gain to me* [that is – what things were religiously gain to him], *those I counted loss for Christ.*" True spirituality is not defined by our religious activities and accomplishments. It is defined by the excellency of the knowledge of Christ Jesus our Lord. We must count all things loss for Christ. We must suffer the loss of all things that we may win Christ and be found in Christ. We must ever seek to know Christ, "and the power of his resurrection, and fellowship of his sufferings, being made conformable unto his death." We must never imagine that we have already attained unto the heights of spirituality and perfection, but must ever "press toward the mark for the prize of the high calling of God in Christ Jesus."

212. We must help and assist fellow believers who faithfully labor in the ministry of evangelism and edification.

Philippians 4:3 – "*And I intreat thee also, true yokefellow, help those women which laboured with me in the gospel, with Clement also, and with other my fellowlabourers, whose names are in the book of life.*"

In a similar fashion, the apostle had entreated the believers at Rome in Romans 16:1-2, saying, "*I commend unto you Phebe our sister, which is a servant of the church which is at Cenchrea: that ye receive her in the Lord, as becometh saints, and that ye assist her in whatsoever business she hath need of you: for she hath been a succourer of many, and of myself also.*" Not only are we to follow after the example of those who are faithful in the work of the Lord, but we are also to help and assist them as they labor in the work of the Lord. Whatever they might need in order to continue forward in their labor for the Lord, we are to help them. Whatever business they might pursue in their labor for the Lord, we are to assist them. In so doing, we are to labor with them and to learn from them.

213. We must maintain a moderate attitude of gentleness toward and before every one.

Philippians 4:5 – "***Let your moderation be known unto all men***. *The Lord is at hand*."

Titus 3:2 – "*To speak evil of no man, to be no brawlers,* ***but gentle***, *shewing all meekness unto all men*."

The English word "moderation" means "an avoidance of extremes" or "an absence of violence, a calmness of attitude." With the first part of that definition, the word "moderation" can be applied either to our pursuits or to our attitudes; whereas the second part of that definition is specifically applied to our attitudes. When applied to our actions, moderation means that we are not extreme in or consumed by any particular pursuit of this world. However, when applied to our attitudes, moderation means that we are not extreme in or filled with an angry, violent attitude toward anyone or anything. In this context of this command, the English word "moderation" is to be applied unto our attitudes.

The Greek word that is employed here is used only five times in the New Testament Scriptures. Here it is translated with the English word "moderation." In 1 Timothy 3:3 it is translated with the English word "patient." There we read concerning the spiritual overseer of the church (the pastor) that in character he must be "*not given to wine, no striker, not greedy of filthy lucre; but* ***patient***, *not a brawler, not covetous*." Then the three other occurrences of the Greek word are translated with the English word "gentle." In Titus 3:2 we are instructed, "*To speak evil of no man, to be no brawlers, but* ***gentle***, *shewing all meekness unto all men*." In James 3:17 God's Word declares, "*But the wisdom that is from above is first pure, then peaceable,* ***gentle***, *and easy to be intreated, full of mercy and good fruits, without partiality, and without hypocrisy*." In 1 Peter 2:18 God's Word instructs, "*Servants, be subject to your masters with all fear; not only to the good and* ***gentle***, *but also to the froward*." Thus we understand that the word "moderation" in Philippians 4:5 is intended to focus our attention upon our attitudes toward others.

We are to be known as people of moderation in our attitudes. We are to be known as people who are patient, calm, and gentle in our attitudes in the face both of circumstantial difficulty and of personal dispute. We must not be quick to anger or to fight. Rather, we must be *"gentle, shewing all meekness unto all men."* Even so, our motivation for maintaining such a moderate attitude of gentleness should be the soon return of our Lord. *"Let your moderation be known unto all men. The Lord is at hand."*

214. We must set our thoughts on whatever things are true, honest, just, pure, lovely, of good report, and of true virtue and praise.

Philippians 4:8 – *"Finally, brethren, whatsoever things are true, whatsoever things are honest, whatsoever things are just, whatsoever things are pure, whatsoever things are lovely, whatsoever things are of good report; if there be any virtue, and if there be any praise, think on these things."*

What then might fit the boundaries of such a description? Upon what then should we focus the attention of our thoughts? The answer is this – Anything of the Lord our God. The person of the Lord our God, the fellowship of the Lord our God, the character of the Lord our God, the wonders of the Lord our God, the Word of the Lord our God, the will of the Lord our God, the ways of the Lord our God, etc. These are the things upon which we are to set the focus of our thoughts. These are the things that are true, and honest, and just, and pure, and lovely, and of good report. These are the things in which there is true virtue and true praise. "Think on these things."

215. As we abide and walk in our Lord, we must be rooted and built up spiritually in Him.

Colossians 2:6-7 – "*As ye have therefore received Christ Jesus the Lord, so walk ye in him: **rooted and built up in him**, and stablished in the faith, as ye have been taught, abounding therein with thanksgiving.*"

2 Peter 3:18 – "***But grow in grace, and in the knowledge of our Lord and Saviour Jesus Christ***. *To him be glory both now and for ever. Amen.*"

In like manner, Ephesians 4:15 indicates that we need to "grow up into him in all things, which is the head, even Christ." In fact, this is the very essence of true spirituality. It is not how knowledgeable we are in the things of the Lord, or how involved we are in the ministry of the Lord, or even how obedient we are to the commands of the Lord. Certainly all of these elements are a part of true spirituality. However, the very essence of true spirituality is our growth in a daily walk of abiding fellowship with our Lord. Then as we grow in that daily walk of abiding fellowship with our Lord, we will grow accordingly in our knowledge in the things of the Lord, in our involvement in the ministry of the Lord, and in our obedience to the commands of the Lord.

216. As we abide and walk in our Lord, we must be established in the faith.

Colossians 2:6-7 – "*As ye have therefore received Christ Jesus the Lord, so walk ye in him: rooted and built up in him, **and stablished in the faith**, as ye have been taught, abounding therein with thanksgiving.*"

Jude 1:20 – "***But ye, beloved, building up yourselves on your most holy faith***, *praying in the Holy Ghost.*"

The phrase "the faith" in this context refers, not specifically to our heart of faith in the Lord, but to the body of truth upon which we are to found our faith. Even so, in this context the phrase "the faith" is described by the phrase, "as ye have been taught." Yet this phrase "the faith" does not simply refer to the information of doctrinal truth, for then the passage would have stated that we need to be established in "the doctrine." Rather, this phrase "the faith" refers to the whole realm and walk of doctrinal truth and teaching, including the objective content of the truth and teaching of God's Word, our heart commitment to the truth and teaching of God's Word, and our obedient conduct in the truth and teaching of God's Word. We must "*continue in the faith grounded and settled*," and must not be "*moved away from the hope of the gospel*." (See Colossians 1:23) As we grow in a daily walk of abiding fellowship with our Lord, we must also grow in our knowledge of God's truth and teaching, in our commitment to God's truth and teaching, and in our obedience to God's truth and teaching.

217. As we abide and walk in our Lord, we must be abounding with thanksgiving.

Colossians 2:6-7 – "*As ye have therefore received Christ Jesus the Lord, so walk ye in him: rooted and built up in him, and stablished in the faith, as ye have been taught, **abounding therein with thanksgiving**.*"

As we grow in a daily walk of abiding fellowship with our Lord, we must be filled with abundant thanksgiving toward the Lord our God. Even so, Colossians 3:17 gives the instruction, "*And whatsoever ye do in word or deed, do all in the name of the Lord Jesus, giving thanks to God and the Father by him*." Again in 2 Thessalonians 5:18 the instruction is given, "*In every thing give thanks: for this is the will of God in Christ Jesus concerning you*." Yet again in Hebrews 13:15 the instruction is given, "*By him* [by our Lord Jesus Christ] *therefore let us offer the sacrifice of praise to God continually, that is, the fruit of our lips giving thanks to his name*." In a daily walk of abiding fellowship with our Lord, we must be *"giving thanks always for all things unto God and the Father in the name of our Lord Jesus Christ."* (See Ephesians 5:20)

218. We must beware lest anyone spoil us "through philosophy and vain deceit."

Colossians 2:8 – *"**Beware lest any man spoil you through philosophy and vain deceit**, after the tradition of men, after the rudiments of the world, and not after Christ."*

The word of command in this verse is the first word, the word "beware." This word "beware" means that we are to be aware, to be continually alert and on our guard against someone or something negative. So then, against what are we to beware? Against what are we to be continually alert and on our guard? We are to beware, to be continually alert and on our guard, lest anyone spoil us spiritually. Now, in this context the word "spoil" does not refer to the corruption of our character and conduct, as in the sense of spoiling a child. Rather, in this context the word "spoil" refers to the plundering of our blessings and benefits, as in the sense of the spoils belonging unto the victor. We must beware. We must be continually alert and on our guard lest anyone steal away from us the spiritual blessings and benefits that we have in Christ for our daily walk in this life.

So then, if we are to beware, to be continually alert and on our guard, what is the avenue of attack by which this spoiling might occur? The avenue of attack is "through philosophy and vain deceit." Our great, spiritual adversary the devil is ever on the attack against us who are God's dear children. Our adversary the devil desires to devour up our Christian lives so that we live a spiritually defeated and fruitless walk. He begins this process by attempting to steal away from us our spiritual blessings and benefits in Christ for our daily walk. His avenue of attack is through false teaching, that is – through the false philosophies and vain deceits of this world.

395

So then, what is the nature of these false philosophies and vain deceits, whereby we may discern them and reject them? These false philosophies and vain deceits will be "after the tradition of men, after the rudiments [after the foundational principles] of the world," but not after Christ Jesus our Lord and Savior. Such philosophies may be social, political, educational, religious, etc. Yet in one way or another, they will be man-centered and world-centered. We do not need philosophical teachings that center our attention upon our selves or upon the interests of this world. Such teaching is vain deceit. Such teaching will plunder us spiritually. Rather, we need Biblical truth that will center our attention upon our Lord and upon His will for our lives. We need to walk daily in Him. We need to be "rooted and built up in him." Therefore, we must be continually alert and on our guard against any teaching that might turn us aside from a daily walk with our Lord.

Even so, Colossians 2:9-13 provides a significant series of truths to indicate that our Lord Jesus Christ is the foundational Source for our entire Christian walk. First, verse 9 declares, *"For in him dwelleth all the fulness of the Godhead bodily."* Second, verse 10 adds, *"And ye are complete in him, which is the head of all principality and power."* Third, verse 11 reveals, *"In whom also ye are circumcised with the circumcision made without hands, in putting off the body of the sins of the flesh by the circumcision of Christ."* Fourth, verse 12 states, *"Buried with him in baptism, wherein also ye are risen with him through the faith of the operation of God, who hath raised him from the dead."* Finally, verse 13 proclaims, *"And you, being dead in your sins and the uncircumcision of your flesh, hath he* [God the Father] *quickened together with him* [with our Lord Jesus Christ]*, having forgiven you all trespasses."*

219. We must not allow anyone to judge us according to the Old Testament religious system.

Colossians 2:16-17 – **"*Let no man therefore judge you in meat, or in drink, or in respect of an holyday, or of the new moon, or of the***

sabbath days*: which are a shadow of things to come; but the body is of Christ.*"

Herein God's Word directly indicates that in this time of the New Testament, we believers are no longer responsible for the food laws, the sacrificial laws, or the Sabbath law of the Old Testament. In the context, three reasons are revealed for this truth. The first reason is that these Old Testament laws were taken away through the cross of Christ. This is revealed in Colossians 2:13-14 – "*And you, being dead in your sins and the uncircumcision of your flesh, hath he* [God the Father] *quickened together with him* [God the Son], *having forgiven you all trespasses; blotting out the handwriting of ordinances that was against us, which was contrary to us, and took it out of the way, nailing it to his cross.*" The second reason is that these Old Testament laws were simply a shadow of greater things to come. This is revealed in the opening portion of Colossians 2:17 – "*Which are a shadow of things to come.*" The third reason is that the greater things to come have now come in the body of Christ, which is the church. This is revealed in the closing portion of Colossians 2:17 – "*But the body is of Christ.*" Therefore, we are no longer responsible before the Lord our God for these Old Testament religious laws. In fact, we are directly commanded by the Lord our God not to allow anyone to judge us (that is – to lay rules and regulations upon us) in the area of these Old Testament laws.

220. We must not allow anyone to deceive us out of our spiritual reward through the false humility of man-made religious regulations.

Colossians 2:18-23 – "***Let no man beguile you of your reward in a voluntary humility and worshipping of angels****, intruding into those things which he hath not seen, vainly puffed up by his fleshly mind, and not holding the Head, from which all the body by joints and bands having nourishment ministered, and knit together, increaseth with the increase of God. Wherefore if ye be dead with Christ from the rudiments of the world, why, as though living in the world, are*

397

ye subject to ordinances, (Touch not; taste not; handle not; which all are to perish with the using;) after the commandments and doctrines of men? Which things have indeed a shew of wisdom in will worship, and humility, and neglecting of the body; not in any honour to the satisfying of the flesh."

Herein God's Word instructs us not to allow anyone to beguile us and deceive us out of our spiritual reward. The manner by which they might attempt to beguile us and deceive is in "a voluntary humility and worshipping of angels." This "voluntary humility" is defined in verses 20-22 as being, not after the Word and will of Christ, but "after the commandments and doctrines of men." In addition, verse 19 reveals that this "voluntary humility" is not motivated for the exaltation of Christ and for the spiritual edifying of church. Rather, the closing portion of verse 18 reveals that those who teach the "voluntary humility" of these man-made religious regulations are motivated by the vain pride of their fleshly mindset. Thus we are to understand that the "voluntary humility" of these man-made religious regulations is not Christ-centered, but is self-centered. Finally, verse 23 reveals that the "voluntary humility" of these man-made religious regulations do indeed have a show of spirituality, but do not actually grant victory over our sinful flesh. All that such "voluntary humility" will accomplish in our Christian lives is to deceive us out of our spiritual and eternal reward, for such "voluntary humility" will simply focus our lives upon a show of spirituality through the power of the flesh in order to impress others for selfish recognition. Such "voluntary humility" will not produce spiritual profit, but will only produce selfish pride. Let us not be deceived thereby.

221. We must be thankful toward one another.

Colossians 3:15 – *"And let the peace of God rule in your hearts, **to the which also ye are called in one body; and be ye thankful.**"*

Throughout God's Word we are often instructed to maintain a spirit of thankfulness toward the Lord our God. However, in this verse the instruction to be thankful is connected with our calling as fellow members in the body of Christ. Even so, herein we are instructed to maintain a spirit of thankfulness toward one another as fellow believers.

222. We must "let the word of Christ dwell" in us "richly in all wisdom."

Colossians 3:16 – "*Let the word of Christ dwell in you richly in all wisdom; teaching and admonishing one another in psalms and hymns and spiritual songs, singing with grace in your hearts to the Lord.*"

1 John 2:24 – "*Let that therefore abide in you, which ye have heard from the beginning. If that which ye have heard from the beginning shall remain in you, ye also shall continue in the Son, and in the Father.*"

We must receive and root the truth of God's Word in our hearts so that it might become the governing principle for all of our thoughts, emotions, motivations, decisions, communications, and conduct. First, this is a matter of daily diligence. We must study the truth of God's Word with diligence, and must search the Scriptures daily. We must come daily unto God's Word in order to learn its wisdom with diligence. Second, this is a matter of delighting desire. We must desire with all of our heart and soul to learn the truth of God's Word, and must delight ourselves greatly in the commands of God's Word. We must delight lovingly in God's Word so as to meditate therein day and night with hungry desire. Third, this is a matter of ready reception. We must receive the truth of God's Word with meekness and submission unto it as the authority of God Himself, and we must receive the truth of God's Word with all readiness of mind to be taught and transformed thereby. Fourth, this is matter of righteous renewal. We must allow the truth of God's Word to renew the spirit of our mindset in all wisdom, and we must allow the truth of God's Word to transform us after the righteous image of our Lord Jesus Christ. We must daily and diligently search God's Word with all desire to learn its truth, with all delight to meditate in its wisdom, and with all readiness to receive its instruction in order to be renewed unto a righteous character. Yea, we must let the truth and wisdom of God's Word dwell in our hearts richly to govern us in character, to guard us from sin, and to guide us in righteousness. Finally, we learn from 1 John 2:24 that if we allow God's Word to dwell in us "richly in all wisdom" as the governing principle of our hearts and lives, then we shall continue in abiding fellowship with God the Son our Savior and with God our heavenly Father.

223. We must spiritually teach and admonish one another through the ministry of singing.

Colossians 3:16 – "*Let the word of Christ dwell in you richly in all wisdom;* **teaching and admonishing one another in psalms and hymns and spiritual songs***, singing with grace in your hearts to the Lord.*"

Our ministry of singing "psalms and hymns and spiritual songs" is not just to demonstrate praise unto the Lord our God. Our ministry of singing is also to be spiritually edifying unto fellow believers. It is to be a ministry of teaching them the Word, wisdom, will, and ways of the Lord; and it is to be a ministry of admonishing them against wandering away from the Word, wisdom, will, and ways of the Lord.

224. We must give attendance unto reading God's Word in our church services.

Colossians 4:16 – "**And when this epistle is read among you, cause that it be read also in the church of the Laodiceans; and that ye likewise read the epistle from Laodicea.**"

1 Thessalonians 5:27 – "***I charge you by the Lord that this epistle be read unto all the holy brethren***."

1 Timothy 4:13 – "*Till I come,* **give attendance to reading***, to exhortation, to doctrine.*"

225. We must "abound more and more" in a walk of obedience that pleases the Lord our God.

1 Thessalonians 4:1-2 – "***Furthermore then we beseech you, brethren, and exhort you by the Lord Jesus, that as ye have received of us how ye ought to walk and to please God, so ye would abound more and more.*** *For ye know what commandments we gave you by the Lord Jesus.*"

Certainly the Lord our God would have us to walk in obedience to that which He has commanded through His Word. Certainly such a walk of obedience would be pleasing in our Lord's sight. Yet we are not simply to take momentary steps of such obedience. Rather, we are to grow in our walk of obedience throughout our Christian lives. We are to "abound more and more" in a walk of obedience, in a walk that pleases our Lord. We are never to go away backward. We are never to depart from the faith. Rather, we are ever to grow on forward. We are ever to "abound more and more."

226. We must not defraud (cheat) our fellow believers in any matter.

1 Thessalonians 4:6-8 – "***That no man go beyond and defraud his brother in any matter***: *because that the Lord is the avenger of all such, as we also have forewarned you and testified. For God hath not called us unto uncleanness, but unto holiness. He therefore that despiseth, despiseth not man, but God, who hath also given unto us his holy Spirit.*"

We must never cheat one another as brethren in Christ, whether in money, in possessions, in time, in reputation, in relationship, in responsibility, yea in any matter whatsoever. This is a serious matter. The Lord our God has declared that He will pour out His own vengeance upon all believers who so cheat their fellow believers. In addition, verse 8 gives the warning, "He therefore that despiseth, despiseth not man, but God, who hath also given unto us his holy Spirit." To despise a fellow believer by cheating him or her is, in truth, to despise the Lord our God Himself. God the Holy Spirit dwells within that fellow believer. Thus to defraud and thereby to despise him or her is to commit a direct offense against the Holy Spirit who dwells within that fellow brother or sister in Christ.

227. We must study to be quiet in doing our business and working for our own provision.

1 Thessalonians 4:11-12 – "*And that ye study to be quiet, and to do your own business, and to work with your own hands, as we commanded you;* that ye may walk honestly toward them that are without, and that ye may have lack of nothing."

2 Thessalonians 3:10-12 – "*For we hear that there are some which walk among you disorderly, working not at all, but are busybodies. Now them that are such we command and exhort by our Lord Jesus Christ, that with quietness they work, and eat their own bread.*"

We are not to be busybodies in other people's matters. Rather, we are to study (to concentrate) on staying out of other people's business, on fulfilling our own responsibilities, and on working with our own hands. Yea, we are to concentrate on working with our own hands in order that we might be honest in paying our own bills and in order that we might be diligent in providing for our own needs. It is the principle of God Himself that he who will not work should not eat. Yes, it is our Lord's responsibility to supply all of our need "according to his riches in glory by Christ Jesus." (Philippians 4:19) However, He will not do so if we are walking disorderly in not working at all, but in being busybodies in the business of others.

228. We must comfort and exhort one another through the truth of our Lord's coming for His own in the rapture.

1 Thessalonians 4:13-18 – "*But I would not have you to be ignorant, brethren, concerning them which are asleep, that ye sorrow not, even as others which have no hope. For if we believe that Jesus died and rose again, even so them also which sleep in Jesus will God bring with him. For this we say unto you by the word of the Lord, that we which are alive and remain unto the coming of the Lord shall not prevent them which are asleep. For the Lord himself shall descend from heaven with a shout, with the voice of the archangel, and with the trump of God: and the dead in Christ shall rise first: then we which are alive and remain shall be caught up together with them in the clouds, to meet the Lord in the air: and so shall we ever be with the Lord.* **Wherefore comfort one another with these words***.*"

1 Thessalonians 5:9-11 – "*For God hath not appointed us to wrath, but to obtain salvation by our Lord Jesus Christ, who died for us, that, whether we wake or sleep, we should live together with him.* **Wherefore comfort yourselves together, and edify one another***, even as also ye do.*"

Now, in these passages the word "rapture" is not used. In fact, the word "rapture" is not found anywhere throughout the King James translation. However, the truth of the rapture is revealed within this passage. The word "rapture" means "a catching up;" and verse 17 declares, "*Then we which are alive and remain shall be caught up together with them in the clouds, to meet the Lord in the air: and so shall we ever be with the Lord.*" There is a day coming in which our Lord will come again in the air in order to receive His own unto Himself. We do not know when that day is; for our Lord has not revealed the hour, the day, the time, or the season. Yet He has promised to come again for us, and His promise is certain.

At that time our Lord Jesus Christ Himself "*shall descend from heaven with a shout, with the voice of the archangel, and with the trump of God.*" At that time our Lord will bring with Him the souls of the saved who have already died; and in that moment the bodies of those who have died in Christ shall be resurrected, glorified, and joined with their souls. Immediately after the resurrection of the dead in Christ, we believers who are yet alive at that time will also be *"be caught up together with them in the clouds, to meet the Lord in the air: and so shall we ever be with the Lord."* This is the truth by which we are to comfort one another. We are to comfort one another that our Lord is coming again for us. Indeed, we are to comfort one another in our sorrow at the death of our fellow brothers and sisters in Christ, having full assurance concerning the promised hope that they shall be resurrected and that we shall meet them in the air with our Lord at the rapture.

229. We must warn our fellow believers who are "unruly."

1 Thessalonians 5:14 – *"Now we exhort you, brethren, warn them that are unruly, comfort the feebleminded, support the weak, be patient toward all men."*

Herein the word "unruly" refers to those who are unsubmissive with regard to their authorities and to those who are unfaithful with regard to their responsibilities. When our fellow believers are either unsubmissive to authority, especially to spiritual authority, or unfaithful in responsibility, especially in spiritual responsibility, we are to warn them. We are to warn them concerning God's chastening hand upon them and concerning the destructive consequences of their way.

230. We must comfort our fellow believers who are discouraged.

1 Thessalonians 5:14 – *"Now we exhort you, brethren, warn them that are unruly, comfort the feebleminded, support the weak, be patient toward all men."*

Discouragement is a weapon that our adversary the devil often uses to destroy the spiritual progress of believers' lives. Therefore, we must be alert to the discouragement through which our adversary is attacking our fellow believers; and we must be compassionate to comfort them in the Lord through the truth of His Word.

231. We must support our fellow believers who are weak.

1 Thessalonians 5:14 – *"Now we exhort you, brethren, warn them that are unruly, comfort the feebleminded, **support the weak**, be patient toward all men."*

Some of our fellow believers are weak. Some are physically weak. Some are emotionally weak. Some are spiritually weak. It is our responsibility to support them and to help them where we are able in order that they might grow out of their weakness if possible.

232. We must not quench the work of the indwelling Holy Spirit in our hearts.

1 Thessalonians 5:19 – *"**Quench not the Spirit**."*

To quench the Holy Spirit means to reject His spiritual work in our hearts and to harden our hearts against it. It means to turn our spiritual ears away from His spiritual guidance and direction. The work of the indwelling Holy Spirit is to assure us of our new birth and eternal salvation. We must not quench this work of assurance in our hearts. The work of the indwelling Holy Spirit is to guide us in and through the truth of God's Word. We must not quench this work of guidance in our hearts and lives. The work of the indwelling Holy Spirit is to direct us in the way of obedience throughout our daily walk. We must not quench this work of direction in our hearts and lives. The work of the indwelling Holy Spirit is to produce the fruit of righteousness in and through our hearts and lives. We must not quench this work of production in and through us. The work of the indwelling Holy Spirit is to convict us of any unrighteousness in our hearts and lives. We must not quench this work of conviction upon our hearts. The work of the indwelling Holy Spirit is to empower us for spiritual victory over temptation. We must not quench this work of empowerment in our hearts and lives. Finally, the work of the indwelling Holy Spirit is to enable us for faithful witness unto the lost world. We must not quench this work of enablement in our hearts and lives.

233. We must not despise the truths of God's Word, but must desire and receive the truths of God's Word wholeheartedly and submissively.

1 Thessalonians 5:20 – "***Despise not prophesyings.***"

Hebrews 13:22 – "***And I beseech you, brethren, suffer the word of exhortation****: for I have written a letter unto you in few words.*"

James 1:21 – "*Wherefore lay apart all filthiness and superfluity of naughtiness, **and receive with meekness the engrafted word**, which is able to save your souls.*"

1 Peter 2:2 – "***As newborn babes, desire the sincere milk of the word***, *that ye may grow thereby:*"

In the context of 1 Thessalonians 5:20, the word "prophesyings" refers to that truth which the Lord our God has directly sent forth unto us. This truth of the Lord our God is now contained in the completed Word of God. Therefore, we must not despise and reject any truth or teaching, counsel or command, principle or precept, standard or statute, rebuke or reproof of God's Holy Word. Rather, we must desire with whole-heartedness and receive with meekness every truth and teaching, every counsel and command, every principle and precept, every standard and statute, every rebuke and reproof of God's Holy Word. Yea, we must not despise and reject God's Word, but desire it and receive it whether it comes to us through our own Bible study, through the ministry of the church, or through the edification of a fellow believer.

234. We must abstain from every appearance by which evil may seek to enter our lives.

1 Thessalonians 5:22 – *"**Abstain from all appearance of evil.**"*

Often this phrase is employed to indicate that we must abstain from anything that others might view as evil. Indeed, it is certainly a Biblical principle that we should be concerned about our testimony of godliness before this world. Yet there are some things that others may view as evil from which we should not abstain. For example, the Pharisees viewed it as evil for our Lord Jesus Christ to eat with publicans and sinners. Yet our Lord did not abstain from this practice. This practice was not evil, but was actually right. Rather, in 1 Thessalonians 5:22 the instruction refers to every appearance by which evil may seek to enter into our hearts and lives. The prepositional phrase "of evil" is possessive in nature. It indicates that the "appearance" mentioned in the verse is that "appearance" possessed "of evil." It is "evil's appearance." Indeed, evil will take many different appearances as it seeks to overcome us. Therefore, we must be sober and vigilant to note any and all of evil's different appearances and to abstain from all of them.

235. We must not become deceived, shaken in mind, and troubled in heart that the day of Christ has already come upon us.

2 Thessalonians 2:1-3 – *"Now we beseech you, brethren, by the coming of our Lord Jesus Christ, and by our gathering together unto him, **that ye be not soon shaken in mind, or be troubled, neither by spirit, nor by word, nor by letter as from us, as that the day of Christ is at hand. Let no man deceive you by any means**: for that day shall not come, except there come a falling away first, and that man of sin be revealed, the son of perdition."*

Apparently false teachers were falsely reporting to these believers that the day of Christ was already upon them. Apparently these false teachers had even forged a letter as from the apostle himself, in order to support their false report. Yet the apostle Paul instructed these believers at Thessalonica not to be deceived by any such false report, and not to be "soon shaken in mind, or be troubled" that the day of Christ was already upon them. In fact, this instruction is similar to that which our Lord Jesus Christ delivered unto His disciples in Matthew 24:6 that they (and we) not become troubled in heart at the signs of the times. *"And ye shall hear of wars and rumours of wars: see that ye be not troubled: for all these things must come to pass, but the end is not yet."*

Now, this matter concerning the coming of the day of Christ concerns the events of the rapture and of the seven-year tribulation period. Thus the apostle stated in verse 1, *"Now we beseech you, brethren, by the coming of our Lord Jesus Christ, and by our gathering together unto him."* When the apostle Paul had been with these believers, he had previously taught them concerning these events. Even so, in verse 5 he stated, *"Remember ye not, that, when I was yet with you, I told you these things?"* In addition, the apostle had further explained concerning the event of the rapture in his first epistle (letter) to them. Thus we read in 1 Thessalonians 4:13-18, *"But I would not have you to be ignorant, brethren, concerning them which are asleep, that ye sorrow not, even as others which have no hope. For if we believe that Jesus died and rose again, even so them also which sleep in Jesus will God bring with him. For this we say unto you by the word of the Lord, that we which are alive and remain unto the coming of the Lord shall not prevent them which are asleep. For the Lord himself shall descend from heaven with a shout, with the voice of the archangel, and with the trump of God: and the dead in Christ shall rise first: then we which are alive and remain shall be caught up together with them in the clouds, to meet the Lord in the air: and so shall we ever be with the Lord. Wherefore comfort one another with these words."*

Finally, in 1 Thessalonians 2:3 the apostle Paul revealed that two events must occur before the day of Christ comes upon the earth, saying, *"Let no man deceive you by any means: for that day shall not come, except there come a falling away first, and that man of sin be revealed, the son of perdition."* So then, we also must not become deceived, shaken in mind, and troubled in heart that the day of Christ has come upon us; for these two events have not yet occurred.

236. We must stand fast upon and hold firm to the truths that we have been taught from God's Word.

2 Thessalonians 2:15 – "*Therefore, brethren, stand fast, and hold the traditions which ye have been taught, whether by word, or our epistle.*"

2 Timothy 1:13-14 – "*Hold fast the form of sound words, which thou hast heard of me, in faith and love which is in Christ Jesus. That good thing which was committed unto thee keep by the Holy Ghost which dwelleth in us.*"

2 Timothy 3:14-17 – "*But continue thou in the things which thou hast learned and hast been assured of, knowing of whom thou hast learned them; and that from a child thou hast known the holy scriptures, which are able to make thee wise unto salvation through faith which is in Christ Jesus. All scripture is given by inspiration of God, and is profitable for doctrine, for reproof, for correction, for instruction in righteousness: that the man of God may be perfect, throughly furnished unto all good works.*"

Hebrews 2:1-4 – "*Therefore we ought to give the more earnest heed to the things which we have heard, lest at any time we should let them slip. For if the word spoken by angels was stedfast, and every transgression and disobedience received a just recompence of reward; how shall we escape, if we neglect so great salvation; which at the first began to be spoken by the Lord, and was confirmed unto us by them that heard him; God also bearing them witness, both with signs and wonders, and with divers miracles, and gifts of the Holy Ghost, according to his own will?*"

Now, 2 Thessalonians 2:15 is not speaking about religious traditions that have been passed down by the creation of men. Rather, it is speaking about Biblical traditions that we have been taught through the word and writings of the New Testament Scriptures. We must hold fast unto the truth and teaching, precepts and principles, statutes and standards, commands and counsels, wisdom and warnings of God's Holy Word. We must not allow ourselves to be moved from them or to become neglectful of them. They are the sound words and wisdom of the Lord our God Himself, given by inspiration of God. They are profitable for our eternal salvation and our spiritual growth. *"Therefore we ought to give the more earnest heed to the things which we have heard, lest at any time we should let them slip."* Indeed, we must hold firmly unto the truths and teachings of God's Holy Word by the power of the indwelling Holy Spirit with the full conviction of our hearts and with the committed obedience of our lives.

<hr />

237. We must withdraw ourselves from fellow believers who walk disorderly, living a lifestyle that is not in accord with the teachings of God's Word.

2 Thessalonians 3:6 – *"Now we command you, brethren, in the name of our Lord Jesus Christ, that ye withdraw yourselves from every brother that walketh disorderly, and not after the tradition which he received of us."*

2 Thessalonians 3:14 – *"And if any man obey not our word by this epistle, note that man, and have no company with him, that he may be ashamed."*

If a fellow believer walks in a regular lifestyle of disobedience to the basic behavioral teachings of God's Word, we are to enact church discipline upon that fellow believer. Yea, we are to give notice concerning that believer publicly, and to withdraw ourselves from that believer, and to have no friendship association ("company") with that believer.

Now, the manner in which some believers were walking disorderly among the believers at Thessalonica at that time was that they were not working at all, but were being busybodies in other people's matters. Even so, in 2 Thessalonians 3:7-11 the apostle Paul gave the report, *"For yourselves know how ye ought to follow us: for we behaved not ourselves disorderly among you; neither did we eat any man's bread for nought; but wrought with labour and travail night and day, that we might not be chargeable to any of you: not because we have not power, but to make ourselves an ensample unto you to follow us. For even when we were with you, this we commanded you, that if any would not work, neither should he eat. For we hear that there are some which walk among you disorderly, working not at all, but are busybodies.*" This then provides us with a Biblical example concerning the level of disorderly, disobedient walk that is worthy of church discipline.

238. We must not view fellow believers who walk in a disorderly, disobedient lifestyle as enemies, but must admonish them as brethren in Christ.

2 Thessalonians 3:15 – "***Yet count him not as an enemy, but admonish him as a brother***."

239. Those in pastoral leadership must authoritatively forbid anyone from teaching anything contrary to the doctrine of God's Word in the ministry for which those leaders have God-given responsibility.

1 Timothy 1:3-4 – "*As I besought thee to abide still at Ephesus, when I went into Macedonia, **that thou mightest charge some that they teach no other doctrine, neither give heed to fables and endless genealogies, which minister questions, rather than godly edifying which is in faith: so do***."

2 Timothy 2:14 – "***Of these things put them in remembrance, charging them before the Lord that they strive not about words to no profit, but to the subverting of the hearers***."

2 Timothy 2:16-18 – "***But shun profane and vain babblings***: *for they will increase unto more ungodliness. And their word will eat as doth a canker: of whom is Hymenaeus and Philetus; who concerning*

411

the truth have erred, saying that the resurrection is past already; and overthrow the faith of some."

Titus 1:10-14 – *"For there are many unruly and vain talkers and deceivers, specially they of the circumcision: **whose mouths must be stopped**, who subvert whole houses, teaching things which they ought not, for filthy lucre's sake. One of themselves, even a prophet of their own, said, The Cretians are alway liars, evil beasts, slow bellies. This witness is true. **Wherefore rebuke them sharply, that they may be sound in the faith; not giving heed to Jewish fables, and commandments of men, that turn from the truth."***

In its immediate historical context, the instruction of 1 Timothy 1:3-4 was specifically for Timothy's ministry work at Ephesus. The apostle Paul had sent Timothy under apostolic authority to serve within the pastoral leadership of the church at Ephesus and to deal with false teachers that had arisen within that church ministry. Yet the principle of this instruction has a continuing application unto the present day.

The pastoral leadership that God the Holy Spirit has placed over a church ministry is responsible before the Lord for the doctrine that is taught within that ministry. As such, that God-ordained pastoral leadership is required by the Lord our God to charge any individual who might seek to teach any doctrine that is contrary unto God's Word that they are not to do so. Herein the word "charge" indicates the authority of command. Thus God-appointed pastoral leadership must authoritatively forbid individuals from teaching any doctrine that is not Biblically rooted or not Biblically edifying. If some doctrine is not according to the teaching of God's Word, the God-appointed pastoral leadership must authoritatively forbid it. In addition, if some doctrine only ministers unending questions, and does not produce spiritual edification, the God-appointed pastoral leadership must authoritatively forbid it.

Indeed, such authoritative forbidding is necessary for the spiritual protection of the Lord's church flock. According to 2 Timothy 2:14, such false teaching will bring no spiritual profit unto the hearers, but will only subvert their spiritual walk before the Lord. Furthermore, according to 2 Timothy 2:16-18 such false teaching will "increase unto more ungodliness" and will overthrow the faith of believers. Therefore, within the qualifications for a pastor that are presented in Titus 1:5-9, verse 9 concludes with the Biblical qualification that a pastor must be "*holding fast the faithful word as he hath been taught, that he may be able by sound doctrine both to exhort and to convince the gainsayers.*" The reason for this qualification is then given in Titus 1:10-11 – "*For there are many unruly and vain talkers and deceivers, specially they of the circumcision: whose mouths must be stopped, who subvert whole houses, teaching things which they ought not, for filthy lucre's sake.*" Even so, in Titus 1:13-14 the apostle Paul instructed Titus to rebuke such false teachers "*sharply, that they may be sound in the faith; not giving heed to Jewish fables, and commandments of men, that turn from the truth.*"

240. We must faithfully fight the good fight of faith, "holding faith and a good conscience," enduring hardness "as a good soldier of Jesus Christ," and not being entangled "with the affairs of this life."

1 Timothy 1:18-19 – "*This charge I commit unto thee, son Timothy, according to the prophecies which went before on thee, **that thou by them mightest war a good warfare; holding faith, and a good conscience**; which some having put away concerning faith have made shipwreck.*"

1 Timothy 6:12-16 – "***Fight the good fight of faith**, lay hold on eternal life, whereunto thou art also called, and hast professed a good profession before many witnesses. I give thee charge in the sight of God, who quickeneth all things, and before Christ Jesus, who before Pontius Pilate witnessed a good confession; **that thou keep this commandment without spot, unrebukeable, until the appearing of our Lord Jesus Christ**: which in his times he shall shew, who is the blessed and only Potentate, the King of kings, and Lord of lords; who only hath immortality, dwelling in the light which*

no man can approach unto; whom no man hath seen, nor can see: to whom be honour and power everlasting. Amen."

2 Timothy 2:3-4 – "**Thou therefore endure hardness, as a good soldier of Jesus Christ.** *No man that warreth entangleth himself with the affairs of this life; that he may please him who hath chosen him to be a soldier.*"

Within these passages the apostle Paul instructed Timothy to "fight the good fight of faith," enduring hardness "as a good soldier of Jesus Christ." Furthermore, in 2 Timothy 4:7-8 the apostle gave testimony near the end of own his life, saying, "*I have fought a good fight, I have finished my course, I have kept the faith: henceforth there is laid up for me a crown of righteousness, which the Lord, the righteous judge, shall give me at that day: and not to me only, but unto all them also that love his appearing.*" Thus we recognize that this instruction to fight the good fight of faith was not just for Timothy, but for every believer.

Yet what does it mean to fight the good fight of faith? First, it is a fight of faith, of fighting to maintain our focus on and faith in our Lord for His enabling grace regardless of our trials, tribulations, and troubles in this life. Thus in 2 Timothy 2:1 the apostle gave instruction, saying, "*Thou therefore, my son, be strong in the grace that is in Christ Jesus;*" and in verse 3 he added, "*Thou therefore endure hardness, as a good soldier of Jesus Christ.*" In addition, it is the good fight, of fighting against worldliness and temptation to sin and of fighting for submission and service to the Lord. Thus in 2 Timothy 2:4 the apostle gave instruction, saying, "*No man that warreth entangleth himself with the affairs of this life; that he may please him who hath chosen him to be a soldier.*" Even so, in the opening portion of 1 Timothy 1:19, the apostle indicated that we must fight this good fight by "*holding faith, and a good conscience.*" Indeed, we fight the good fight of faith by holding fast unto faith in our Lord and unto godliness in our character.

241. We must fervently and faithfully pray and give thanks for all of the people around us in our lives.

1 Timothy 2:1 – "*I exhort therefore, that, first of all, supplications, prayers, intercessions, and giving of thanks, be made for all men.*"

Clearly this instruction concerns the matter of our prayer lives. Specifically, we are instructed to include "all men" in our prayers. In general this would encompass every single soul on the earth. In particular this would encompass all of those around us in our lives, whatever relationship they may have toward us. For them we are to make supplication, prayers, and intercessions. For them we are to make request unto God for their benefit. For them we are to supplicate before God with fervency and faithfulness. For them we are to intercede toward God that He might be gracious unto them.

Especially, we are to intercede for them that the Lord our God and Savior might draw them unto himself for salvation. Even so, in this very context 1 Timothy 2:3-6 declares, "*For this is good and acceptable in the sight of God our Saviour; who will have all men to be saved, and to come unto the knowledge of the truth. For there is one God, and one mediator between God and men, the man Christ Jesus; who gave himself a ransom for all, to be testified in due time.*" Yea, we are to supplicate, pray, and intercede "for all men" because God the Father "will have all men to be saved" and because our Lord Jesus Christ "gave himself a ransom for all."

Furthermore, we are to give thanks on behalf of all men. Certainly, we are to give thanks for everyone who actually comes "unto the knowledge of the truth." Yet we are also to give thanks unto the Lord our God for every benefit, no matter how small, that we might receive through others around us. In addition, we are to give thanks unto the Lord on the behalf of others for every benefit that the Lord has brought into their lives.

242. We must fervently and faithfully pray and give thanks for all of our government officials.

1 Timothy 2:1-2 – "*I exhort therefore, that, first of all, supplications, prayers, intercessions, and giving of thanks, be made for all men; for kings, and for all that are in authority; that we may lead a quiet and peaceable life in all godliness and honesty.*"

Just as we are to supplicate, pray, intercede, and even give thanks for all men, even so we are to supplicate, pray, intercede, and even give thanks for all those who are in governmental authority on any level. We are to pray for their benefit. We are to supplicate with fervency and faithfulness. We are to intercede on their behalf, especially for their eternal salvation. We are even to give thanks for whatever good is brought forth by their governing activities. This all we are to do with the desire that through them the Lord our God might allow us to "*lead a quiet and peaceable life in all godliness and honesty.*"

243. Men of God must take the leadership in public prayers with holiness of character and "without wrath and doubting."

1 Timothy 2:8 – "*I will therefore that men pray every where, lifting up holy hands, without wrath and doubting.*"

In the context this is an instruction delivered specifically to men of God, with the complementary instruction to women of God being delivered in verses 9-15. Again this instruction concerns the matter of prayer. Specifically, it concerns the matter of public praying, as the phrase "every where" would indicate. Even so, this instruction indicates that men of God are to pray "every where" in the public arena. Indeed, it indicates that men of God are to step forward and to take the lead in public praying. Yet this instruction also indicates that men of God are to lead in public prayers with spiritual character. It indicates that men of God are to lead in public prayers with "holy hands," that is – with holy character of heart and with holy conduct of life. Ungodly, unspiritual men are not to take the lead in our public praying. Rather, godly, Spirit-filled men are to take the lead in our public praying. In addition, men of God are to take the lead in public prayer "without wrath and doubting." Angry, contentious men are not to take the lead in our public praying; neither are doubting, unbelieving men to take the lead in our public praying. Rather, gracious, faith-filled men are to take the lead in our public praying. So then, men let us be the men of God that we ought to be, in order that we may take the lead in public prayers as we ought also to do.

<hr/>

244. Women of God must "adorn themselves in modest apparel, with shamefacedness and sobriety."

1 Timothy 2:9 – "***In like manner also, that women adorn themselves in modest apparel, with shamefacedness and sobriety***; *not with broided hair, or gold, or pearls, or costly array.*"

1 Peter 3:3-4 – "*Whose adorning let it not be that outward adorning of plaiting the hair, and of wearing of gold, or of putting on of apparel; but let it be the hidden man of the heart, in that which is not corruptible, **even the ornament of a meek and quiet spirit**, which is in the sight of God of great price.*"

In 1 Timothy 2:9 the word "modest" means "that which is decent, without extreme and without show." To adorn oneself with modest apparel means to adorn oneself in a manner that is moderate and reserved. It means to adorn oneself in a manner that does not to get attention. Even so, women of God are not to adorn themselves in a manner that is over-expensive, getting attention through wealthy attire. Nor are women of God to adorn themselves in a manner that is over-expressive, getting attention through greatly noticeable attire. Nor are women of God to adorn themselves in a manner that is over-enhancive, getting attention through sensually attractive attire. Nor are women of God to adorn themselves in a manner that is over-exposive, getting attention through sexually revealing attire.

Rather, women of God are to adorn themselves "in modest apparel" and to conduct themselves with "a meek and quiet spirit." Indeed, the Lord our God is not only concerned about modesty in a woman's apparel and adornment, but also in her character and conduct. Thus God's Word instructs women of God to adorn themselves specifically "with shamefacedness and sobriety" and with "the ornament of a meek and quiet spirit." Indeed, it is this very spirit of meekness, quietness, shamefacedness, and sobriety that is of great value in the sight of the Lord our God. Thus a woman of God will conduct herself with the submission of meekness, not always trying to get her way. Thus a woman of God will conduct herself with the silence of quietness, not always trying to be heard. Thus a woman of God will conduct herself with the reservation of shamefacedness, not always trying to be noticed. Thus a woman of God will conduct herself with the calmness of sobriety, not always gushing with public emotion.

245. Women of God must adorn themselves with godly behavior and good works.

1 Timothy 2:9-10 – "*In like manner also, that women adorn themselves in modest apparel, with shamefacedness and sobriety; not with broided hair, or gold, or pearls, or costly array;* **but (which becometh women professing godliness) with good works**."

Titus 2:3-5 – "**The aged women likewise, that they be in behaviour as becometh holiness**, *not false accusers, not given to much wine, teachers of good things; that they may teach the young women* **to be sober, to love their husbands, to love their children, to be discreet, chaste, keepers at home, good, obedient to their own husbands**, *that the word of God be not blasphemed*."

That which should cause a woman of God to be noticed should not be her immodest apparel or her boisterous spirit, but should be her godly behavior and her good works. Indeed, a woman of God should be adorned with Spirit-filled soberness, with godly love to her husband, with godly love to her children, with Biblical discretion and purity, with diligent keeping of her home, with obedient submission to her husband, and with abundant good works in the ministry. These are the things that truly define a woman's spiritual approval in the sight of the Lord our God.

246. Women must not teach or have authority over men within the church ministry, but must learn from and submit to the male leadership of the church ministry.

1 Timothy 2:11-15 – "*Let the woman learn in silence with all subjection. But I suffer not a woman to teach, nor to usurp authority over the man, but to be in silence. For Adam was first formed, then Eve. And Adam was not deceived, but the woman being deceived was in the transgression. Notwithstanding she shall be saved in childbearing, if they continue in faith and charity and holiness with sobriety.*"

1 Corinthians 14:34-35 – "*Let your women keep silence in the churches: for it is not permitted unto them to speak; but they are commanded to be under obedience, as also saith the law. And if they will learn any thing, let them ask their husbands at home: for it is a shame for women to speak in the church.*"

In these two passages the instruction for silence specifically concerns the public teaching ministry of the church. This instruction for silence is not intended to indicate that women cannot speak within the public ministry at all; for in 1 Corinthians 11:5-10 God's Word provides regulations for a woman of God to pray or prophesy within the public ministry. As such, this grants a woman of God Biblical permission to speak for praying or for prophesying (which has now passed away). Thus the truth of 1 Timothy 2:11-15 & 1 Corinthians 14:34-35 is not that women cannot speak at all within the public church ministry. Rather, the central truth of these passages is that women are not to fulfill a teaching role or an authority role over men within the church ministry. This is made especially clear through the instruction of 1 Timothy 2:11-12. First, in verse 11 the basic instruction is given, "*Let the woman learn in silence with all subjection.*" Then in verse 12 the contextual explanation is provided, "*But I suffer not a woman to teach, nor to usurp authority over the man, but to be in silence.*" As such, women of God are not to be in positions of teaching over men, but to be in positions of learning within the church ministry. (Note: This is specifically in regard to the adult ministry of the church that includes both men and women. Women of God are to be involved in teaching other women (see Titus 2:3-5 above) and children within the ministry of the church.) In addition, women of God are not to be in positions of leadership over men, but in a position of submission within the ministry of the church.

Now, some may contend that this precept and principle concerning the woman's role within the church ministry was only cultural for the time in which the apostle Paul had originally written unto Timothy. Yet such a position is not supported by the context of 1 Timothy 2:11-15. In verses 13-14 the apostle delivered two Biblical reasons for this precept and principle concerning the woman's role within the church ministry, and both of those reasons supersede any human culture. The first reason is delivered in verse 13 and concerns the order of the original creation – "*For Adam was first formed, then Eve.*" Thus from the original creation, the Lord our God Himself determined that the man should fulfill the role of leadership and that the woman should fulfill the role of submission. The second reason is then delivered in verse 14 and concerns the reality of mankind's original fall into sin – "*And Adam was not deceived, but the woman being deceived was in the transgression.*" This truth does not in any way commend Adam's involvement in the transgression, since it indicates that he fully understood the character and consequences of his sin, and yet rebelled against God anyway. Yet concerning the God-created nature of women, this verse does indicate that women are more susceptible to be deceived by false doctrine. Thus the Lord our God has purposed that the man should fulfill the role of leadership and that the woman should fulfill the role of submission.

On the other hand, women do possess a very strong influence upon the church ministry, as they train up their children to be the next generation of the church. Even so, verse 15 states, "*Notwithstanding she shall be saved* [that is – delivered from having no leadership influence within the church ministry] *in childbearing, if they* [the children] *continue in faith and charity and holiness with sobriety."*

～⌒⌒⌒⌒～

247. We must choose for the office of the pastorate those who meet the Biblical qualifications.

1 Timothy 3:1-7 – *"This is a true saying, If a man desire the office of a bishop, he desireth a good work.* ***A bishop then must be*** *blameless, the husband of one wife, vigilant, sober, of good behaviour, given to hospitality, apt to teach; not given to wine, no striker, not greedy of filthy lucre; but patient, not a brawler, not covetous; one that ruleth well his own house, having his children in subjection with all gravity; (For if a man know not how to rule his own house, how shall he take care of the church of God?) not a novice, lest being lifted up with pride he fall into the condemnation of the devil. Moreover he must have a good report of them which are without; lest he fall into reproach and the snare of the devil."*

Titus 1:5-9 – *"For this cause left I thee in Crete, that thou shouldest set in order the things that are wanting,* ***and ordain elders in every city, as I had appointed thee: if any be*** *blameless, the husband of one wife, having faithful children not accused of riot or unruly. For a bishop must be blameless, as the steward of God; not selfwilled, not soon angry, not given to wine, no striker, not given to filthy lucre; but a lover of hospitality, a lover of good men, sober, just, holy, temperate; holding fast the faithful word as he hath been taught, that he may be able by sound doctrine both to exhort and to convince the gainsayers."*

Through these two passages of Scripture, we learn first in general that a man must be spiritually blameless in his character and conduct in order to be Biblically qualified for the pastorate. This does not mean that he must be completely perfect; but it does mean that he must be generally above reproach, "as the steward of God." Second, we learn that a man must be characterized by a number of godly characteristics in order to be Biblically qualified for the pastorate.

He must be "vigilant, sober, of good behavior," a lover of and given to hospitality, patient, "a lover of good men," just, holy, and temperate. Third, we learn that a man must not be characterized by a number of ungodly characteristics in order to be Biblically qualified for the pastorate. He must not be "given to wine, no striker," "not a brawler, not covetous," "not selfwilled, not soon angry," and not given to and greedy of "filthy lucre."

Fourth, we learn that a man must be a godly leader in his home relationships in order to be Biblically qualified for the pastorate. He must be "the husband of one wife;" he must be "one that ruleth well his own house, having his children in subjection with all gravity; (For if a man know not how to rule his own house, how shall he take care of the church of God?);" and he must have "faithful children not accused of riot or unruly." Fifth, we learn that a man must have a godly testimony with the general public in order to be Biblically qualified for the pastorate. He must "have a good report of them which are without; lest he fall into reproach and the snare of the devil." Sixth, we learn that a man must not be a new believer or spiritually immature in order to be Biblically qualified for the pastorate. He must not be "a novice, lest being lifted up with pride he fall into the condemnation of the devil." Finally, we learn that a man must be committed to and skillful in the truth of God's Word in order to be Biblically qualified for the pastorate. He must be "apt to teach;" and he must hold fast "the faithful word as he hath been taught, that he may be able by sound doctrine both to exhort and to convince the gainsayers."

248. We must choose for the office of the deaconate those who meet the Biblical qualifications.

1 Timothy 3:8-13 – "***Likewise must the deacons be*** *grave, not doubletongued, not given to much wine, not greedy of filthy lucre; holding the mystery of the faith in a pure conscience. And let these also first be proved; then let them use the office of a deacon, being found blameless. Even so must their wives be grave, not slanderers,*

sober, faithful in all things. Let the deacons be the husbands of one wife, ruling their children and their own houses well. For they that have used the office of a deacon well purchase to themselves a good degree, and great boldness in the faith which is in Christ Jesus."

First, we learn that a man must be characterized by two godly characteristics in order to be Biblically qualified for the deaconate. He must be grave (spiritually serious), and he must hold "the mystery of the faith in a pure conscience." Second, we learn that a man must not be characterized by a number of ungodly characteristics in order to be Biblically qualified for the deaconate. He must not be "doubletongued, not given to much wine," and "not greedy of filthy lucre." Third, we learn that a man must first be examined and be found faithful and above reproach in order to be Biblically qualified for the deaconate. "And let these also first be proved; then let them use the office of a deacon, being found blameless." Fourth, we learn that a man's wife must be characterized with godly character in order for him to be Biblically qualified for the deaconate. She must be grave (spiritually serious), not a slanderer, sober, and faithful in all things. Finally, we learn that a man must be a godly leader in his home relationships in order to be Biblically qualified for the deaconate. He must be "the husband of one wife," and he must rule his own children and his own house well.

249. We must refuse to involve ourselves with doctrines that are rooted in philosophical speculations, rather than in Biblical revelation.

1 Timothy 4:7 – "***But refuse profane and old wives' fables***, *and exercise thyself rather unto godliness."*

1 Timothy 6:20-21 – *"O Timothy, keep that which is committed to thy trust, **avoiding profane and vain babblings, and oppositions of science falsely so called**: which some professing have erred concerning the faith. Grace be with thee. Amen."*

2 Timothy 2:16-18 – "***But shun profane and vain babblings****: for they will increase unto more ungodliness. And their word will eat as doth a canker: of whom is Hymenaeus and Philetus; who concerning the truth have erred, saying that the resurrection is past already; and overthrow the faith of some.*"

2 Timothy 2:23 – "***But foolish and unlearned questions avoid***, *knowing that they do gender strifes.*"

Titus 3:9 – "***But avoid foolish questions, and genealogies, and contentions, and strivings about the law****; for they are unprofitable and vain.*"

Hebrews 13:9-10 – "***Be not carried about with divers and strange doctrines****. For it is a good thing that the heart be established with grace; not with meats, which have not profited them that have been occupied therein. We have an altar, whereof they have no right to eat which serve the tabernacle.*"

In the context of 1 Timothy 4:7, the instruction to "refuse profane and old wives' fables" was delivered specifically unto Timothy as a pastoral leader in the church. Even so, in verse 6 the apostle Paul exhorted him, saying, "*If thou put the brethren in remembrance of these things, thou shalt be a good minister of Jesus Christ, nourished up in the words of faith and of good doctrine, whereunto thou hast attained.*" Then he continued with the instruction of verse 7. Thus the instruction to refuse such doctrines is especially to be applied unto the lives and ministries of those in pastoral leadership.

However, the principle of this instruction certainly has an application unto all of us. Indeed, all of us as believers should "refuse profane and old wives' fables." Yet what is meant by this description? In that day, philosophers would often ridicule the philosophies of their opponents by referring unto them as "old wives' fables." Even so, the apostle Paul, under the inspiration of God the Holy Spirit, was ridiculing all philosophical speculations as "old wives' fables." Because such philosophies are rooted in human speculations, rather than in Biblical revelation, they are spiritually profane; and we should refuse to involve ourselves therein.

In 1 Timothy 1:4 such philosophical speculations are described as doctrines *"which minister questions, rather than godly edifying which is in faith."* Thus at the conclusion of this epistle, in 1 Timothy 6:20-21 the apostle Paul again instructed and warned Timothy to avoid *"profane and vain babblings, and oppositions of science falsely so called: which some professing have erred concerning the faith. Grace be with thee. Amen."* Again in 2 Timothy 2:16 the apostle instructed and warned Timothy to *"shun profane and vain babblings: for they will increase unto more ungodliness."* Yet again in 2 Timothy 2:23 the apostle instructed and warned Timothy to avoid *"foolish and unlearned questions"* because *"they do gender strifes."* Finally, in Titus 3:9 the apostle instructed and warned Titus to *"avoid foolish questions, and genealogies, and contentions, and strivings about the law; for they are unprofitable and vain."* Even so, in Hebrews 13:9 all believers are instructed and warned to *"Be not carried about with divers and strange doctrines."*

Indeed, we must refuse, shun, avoid, and be not carried about with such philosophical speculations. This we must do because such philosophical speculations only minister questions and gender strifes, but do not promote "godly edifying" through the truth of God's Word. This we must do because such philosophical speculations will cause us to "err from the faith" (that is – from the truth of God's Word), and will overthrow the faith of fellow believers whom we influence thereby. This we must do because such philosophical speculations are spiritually "unprofitable and vain," and only "increase unto more ungodliness."

250. We must exercise ourselves unto and follow after godliness and true holiness, ever remembering that this world shall be consumed with fire and that we look forward to "new heavens and a new earth," and ever seeking to be found of our Lord "in peace, without spot, and blameless."

1 Timothy 4:7-10 – *"But refuse profane and old wives' fables, **and exercise thyself rather unto godliness**. For bodily exercise profiteth*

little: but godliness is profitable unto all things, having promise of the life that now is, and of that which is to come. This is a faithful saying and worthy of all acceptation. For therefore we both labour and suffer reproach, because we trust in the living God, who is the Saviour of all men, specially of those that believe."

1 Timothy 6:11 – *"But thou, O man of God, flee these things;* **and follow after righteousness, godliness, faith, love, patience, meekness***."*

2 Timothy 2:22 – *"Flee also youthful lusts:* **but follow righteousness, faith, charity, peace, with them that call on the Lord out of a pure heart***."*

Titus 2:11-12 – *"For the grace of God that bringeth salvation hath appeared to all men, teaching us that, denying ungodliness and worldly lusts,* **we should live soberly, righteously, and godly, in this present world***."*

Hebrews 12:14 – *"**Follow peace with all men, and holiness***, without which no man shall see the Lord."*

1 Peter 1:14-16 – *"As obedient children, not fashioning yourselves according to the former lusts in your ignorance:* **but as he which hath called you is holy, so be ye holy in all manner of conversation; because it is written, Be ye holy; for I am holy***."*

2 Peter 3:11-14 – *"Seeing then that all these things* [the things of this world] *shall be dissolved,* **what manner of persons ought ye to be in all holy conversation and godliness***, looking for and hasting unto the coming of the day of God, wherein the heavens being on fire shall be dissolved, and the elements shall melt with fervent heat? Nevertheless we, according to his promise, look for new heavens and a new earth, wherein dwelleth righteousness.* **Wherefore, beloved, seeing that ye look for such things, be diligent that ye may be found of him in peace, without spot, and blameless***."*

Rather than pursue after philosophical speculations according to the wisdom of men, we must pursue after Spirit-filled godliness according to the wisdom of God's Word. Philosophical speculations

426

are spiritually "unprofitable and vain." On the other hand, Spirit-filled godliness is spiritually "profitable unto all things." Philosophical speculations do not minister "godly edifying which is in faith," but only "increase unto more ungodliness." On the other hand, Spirit-filled godliness has "promise of the life that now is, and of that which is to come." Indeed, if we "trust in the living God, who is the Saviour of all men, specially of those that believe," then we should set our trust in His promise concerning godliness, that it is truly "profitable unto all things," for both "the life that now is" and for the life "which is to come."

Yea, on the foundation of this divine promise, we should exercise ourselves unto godliness and true holiness. We should engage in daily training for godliness and true holiness. We should daily make our practice in and our pursuit after godliness and true holiness. Indeed, we must do so in accord with the principles of God's Holy Word and in dependence upon the enablement of God's Holy Spirit. As 1 Peter 1:14-16 teaches us, we are to exercise ourselves unto holiness because God our heavenly Father is holy. We are to exercise ourselves unto holiness just as God our heavenly Father is holy. We are to exercise ourselves unto holiness as the children of God our heavenly Father. We are to exercise ourselves unto holiness by being obedient unto God our heavenly Father's will. We are to exercise ourselves unto holiness by separating ourselves from the selfish lusts of our lost condition. Indeed, we are to exercise ourselves unto holiness in every aspect of our character and conduct. Furthermore, 2 Peter 3:11-13 teaches us to do so while ever remembering that the things of this world "shall be dissolved" with fire and that we believers look forward unto "new heavens and a new earth, wherein dwelleth righteousness."

251. Those who are called to pastoral ministry must preach and teach the whole counsel of God's Word, reproving, rebuking, and exhorting "with all longsuffering and doctrine."

1 Timothy 4:11 – "*These things command and teach*."

1 Timothy 4:13 – "***Till I come, give attendance to reading, to exhortation, to doctrine.***"

1 Timothy 6:2 – "*And they that have believing masters, let them not despise them, because they are brethren; but rather do them service, because they are faithful and beloved, partakers of the benefit. **These things teach and exhort.**"*

2 Timothy 4:1-4 – "*I charge thee therefore before God, and the Lord Jesus Christ, who shall judge the quick and the dead at his appearing and his kingdom; **preach the word; be instant in season, out of season; reprove, rebuke, exhort with all longsuffering and doctrine.** For the time will come when they will not endure sound doctrine; but after their own lusts shall they heap to themselves teachers, having itching ears; and they shall turn away their ears from the truth, and shall be turned unto fables.*"

Titus 2:15 – "***These things speak, and exhort, and rebuke with all authority.** Let no man despise thee.*"

Titus 3:8 – "***This is a faithful saying, and these things I will that thou affirm constantly,** that they which have believed in God might be careful to maintain good works. These things are good and profitable unto men.*"

From these passages we learn that as those who had been called unto pastoral ministry, Timothy and Titus were required authoritatively to command and preach forth the truth of God's Word unto the flock over which God the Holy Spirit had made them spiritual overseers. In addition, they were required carefully to teach and instruct the flock in the truths of God's Word. Indeed, as those who had been called by God the Holy Spirit unto pastoral ministry, this was their responsibility before God the Father and the Lord Jesus Christ. Even so, all who are called unto pastoral ministry are required by God the Father and by the Lord Jesus Christ to preach and teach the truth of God's Word with authority. They are required to preach and teach that truth both "in season," when the people are ready of mind to hear it, and "out of season," when the people are resistant of heart to hear it. Yea, they are required by their preaching and teaching of God's

Word to reprove, to rebuke, and to exhort "with all longsuffering and doctrine." Indeed, those who are called to pastoral ministry are required to preach and teach the whole counsel of God's Holy Word. Even so, in Acts 20:26-27 the apostle Paul gave testimony, saying, *"Wherefore I take you to record this day, that I am pure from the blood of all men. For I have not shunned to declare unto you all the counsel of God."*

252. Those who are called to pastoral ministry must not allow anyone in the flock to despise them as the ministers of God's Word.

1 Timothy 4:12 – *"**Let no man despise thy youth**; but be thou an example of the believers, in word, in conversation, in charity, in spirit, in faith, in purity."*

Titus 2:15 – *"These things speak, and exhort, and rebuke with all authority. **Let no man despise thee**."*

As those who are called by God the Holy Spirit are engaged in the ministry of the Word, they must not allow anyone to despise them in that Biblical ministry.

253. Those who are called to pastoral ministry must be an example of godliness unto the members of the flock.

1 Timothy 4:12 – *"Let no man despise thy youth; **but be thou an example of the believers, in word, in conversation, in charity, in spirit, in faith, in purity**."*

Titus 2:7-8 – *"**In all things shewing thyself a pattern of good works: in doctrine shewing uncorruptness, gravity, sincerity, sound speech, that cannot be condemned**; that he that is of the contrary part may be ashamed, having no evil thing to say of you."*

1 Peter 5:3 – "*Neither as being lords over God's heritage, **but being ensamples to the flock.***"

In fact, this example of godliness is the very manner through which those in pastoral leadership are to answer and silence those who despise them as ministers of God's Word. Even so, those in pastoral leadership must be an example of godliness in relation to their communication, employing sound speech that is good and gracious unto edifying. Those in pastoral leadership must be an example of godliness in relation to their daily behavior, ever walking in a holy manner. Those in pastoral leadership must be an example of godliness in relation to those around them, demonstrating sincere, godly love toward them. Those in pastoral leadership must be an example of godliness in relation to their spirit, maintaining a Spirit-filled attitude in all things. Those in pastoral leadership must be an example of godliness in relation to the Lord, ever rooting their faith in Him. Those in pastoral leadership must be an example of godliness in relation to this world, keeping themselves pure from this present evil world's corruption. Finally, those in pastoral leadership must be an example of godliness in relation to God's Word, holding to and holding forth the doctrine of God's Word with faithfulness. Yea, those in pastoral leadership must be such an example of godliness, not only that they might lead the flock aright in walking after the Lord, but also that those who are "of the contrary part" might be ashamed because they have no legitimate accusation to present.

254. Those who are called to pastoral ministry must meditate daily upon the truths of God's Word and must give themselves wholly to learn the wisdom of God's Word.

1 Timothy 4:15 – "*Meditate upon these things; give thyself wholly to them; that thy profiting may appear to all.*"

Indeed, those in pastoral leadership must meditate upon the truths of God's Word and give themselves to learn the wisdom of God's Word so much that their continuing growth in Biblical understanding and wisdom might be apparent unto all who are around them. Those in pastoral ministry must take heed to the instruction that was delivered unto Joshua in Joshua 1:8, concerning the leadership role which he had been given over God's people Israel – "*This book of the law shall not depart out of thy mouth; but thou shalt meditate therein day and night, that thou mayest observe to do according to all that is written therein: for then thou shalt make thy way prosperous, and then thou shalt have good success.*" Yea, those in pastoral ministry must love and delight in the truth and wisdom of God's Word, so as to meditate therein all throughout the day.

255. Those who are called to pastoral ministry must take heed unto themselves to continue learning, obeying, and teaching the doctrine of God's Holy Word.

1 Timothy 4:16 – "*Take heed unto thyself, and unto the doctrine; continue in them: for in doing this thou shalt both save thyself, and them that hear thee.*"

Indeed, it is through this very habit of continuing in the doctrine of God's Holy Word that a pastoral minister may spiritually deliver himself from the ungodly desires of his own selfish flesh, from the sinful corruption of this present evil world, from the deceptive wiles of our adversary the devil, and from the destructiveness of sin itself. Yea, it is also through this very habit of continuing in the doctrine of God's Holy Word that a pastoral minister may spiritually deliver those to whom he ministers from the ungodly desires of their selfish flesh, from the sinful corruption of this present evil world, from the deceptive wiles of our adversary the devil, and from the destructiveness of sin itself.

256. We must not verbally beat down one another in correction, but must lovingly entreat one another as family members.

1 Timothy 5:1-2 – "***Rebuke not an elder, but intreat him as a father; and the younger men as brethren; the elder women as mothers; the younger as sisters, with all purity.***"

Herein the prohibition against rebuking is not a contradiction with those passages that instruct us to engage in rebuking; for in this context the word rebuke refers specifically to a manner of verbally abusing another, of verbally beating and pounding down another. Rather, when we engage in spiritual correction, we are to entreat and exhort one another with godly love. We are to speak the truth of correction with love, with longsuffering, with meekness, and with gentleness. In correction we are to entreat and exhort the older men as we would a father. In correction we are to entreat and exhort the older women as we would a mother. In correction we are to entreat and exhort the younger men as we would a brother. In correction we are to entreat and exhort the younger women as we would a sister, "with all purity."

257. As a church body, we must financially support those widows who meet the Biblical qualifications.

1 Timothy 5:3-16 – "***Honour widows that are widows indeed.*** *But if any widow have children or nephews, let them learn first to shew piety at home, and to requite their parents: for that is good and acceptable before God. Now she that is a widow indeed, and desolate, trusteth in God, and continueth in supplications and prayers night and day. But she that liveth in pleasure is dead while she liveth. And these things give in charge, that they may be blameless. But if any provide not for his own, and specially for those of his own house, he hath denied the faith, and is worse than an infidel. Let not a widow be taken into the number under threescore years old, having been the wife of one man, well reported of for good works; if she have brought up children, if she have lodged strangers, if she have washed the saints' feet, if she have relieved the afflicted, if she have diligently*

followed every good work. But the younger widows refuse: for when they have begun to wax wanton against Christ, they will marry; having damnation, because they have cast off their first faith. And withal they learn to be idle, wandering about from house to house; and not only idle, but tattlers also and busybodies, speaking things which they ought not. I will therefore that the younger women marry, bear children, guide the house, give none occasion to the adversary to speak reproachfully. For some are already turned aside after Satan. If any man or woman that believeth have widows, let them relieve them, and let not the church be charged; that it may relieve them that are widows indeed."

The church body should financially support a widow if she is over sixty years old, if she does not have family to care for her, if she is financially desolate, if she walks by faith in God and not in the pleasures of this world, if she has been "the wife of one man" (not a fornicator and not divorced), and if she is "well reported of for good works" in her past home life, church ministry, and public kindness.

258. Personally, we must financially help the older members of our family who are in financial need.

1 Timothy 5:4 – *"**But if any widow have children or nephews, let them learn first to shew piety at home, and to requite their parents**: for that is good and acceptable before God."*

1 Timothy 5:7-8 – *"**And these things give in charge, that they may be blameless**. But if any provide not for his own, and specially for those of his own house, he hath denied the faith, and is worse than an infidel."*

1 Timothy 5:16 – *"**If any man or woman that believeth have widows, let them relieve them**, and let not the church be charged; that it may relieve them that are widows indeed."*

259. Younger widows and younger women should pursue marriage and home responsibilities.

1 Timothy 5:11-14 – *"But the younger widows refuse: for when they have begun to wax wanton against Christ, they will marry; having damnation, because they have cast off their first faith. And withal they learn to be idle, wandering about from house to house; and not only idle, but tattlers also and busybodies, speaking things which they ought not.* **I will therefore that the younger women marry, bear children, guide the house***, give none occasion to the adversary to speak reproachfully."*

260. We must regard pastoral leadership who are godly in leadership and faithful in ministry as being worthy of both spiritual and financial honor.

1 Timothy 5:17-18 – ***"Let the elders that rule well be counted worthy of double honour, especially they who labour in the word and doctrine.*** *For the scripture saith, Thou shalt not muzzle the ox that treadeth out the corn. And, The labourer is worthy of his reward."*

In this context the term "elders" is employed as a title for those who serve in pastoral ministry; for the term is modified first with the phrase, "that rule well," and then with the phrase, "especially that who labour in the word and doctrine." Furthermore, the phrase "double honour" refers to a two-fold manner of giving honor. So then, the instruction is that the members of the church should count (regard) as being truly worthy of a two-fold honor any pastoral leader who rules (leads) well in godliness and who labors faithfully in the ministry of God's Word and God's doctrine. Yet what is the two-fold manner of honor for which the Lord our God indicates that they are to be regarded as worthy?

First, such godly and faithful pastoral leadership is worthy of spiritual honor. Even so, 1 Thessalonians 5:12-13 gives the instruction, *"And we beseech you, brethren, to know them which labour among you, and are over you in the Lord, and admonish you; and to esteem them very highly in love for their work's sake. And be at peace among yourselves."* In like manner, Hebrews 13:7 gives the instruction, *"Remember them which have the rule over you, who have spoken unto you the word of God: whose faith follow, considering the end of their conversation."*

Second, such godly and faithful pastoral leadership is worthy of financial honor. Even so, the following context of 1 Timothy 5:18 declares, *"For the scripture saith, Thou shalt not muzzle the ox that treadeth out the corn. And, The labourer is worthy of his reward."* In like manner, in 1 Corinthians 9:7-14 the apostle Paul stated under the inspiration of God the Holy Spirit, *"Who goeth a warfare any time at his own charges? Who planteth a vineyard, and eateth not of the fruit thereof? Or who feedeth a flock, and eateth not of the milk of the flock? Say I these things as a man? Or saith not the law the same also? For it is written in the law of Moses, Thou shalt not muzzle the mouth of the ox that treadeth out the corn. Doth God take care for oxen? Or saith he it altogether for our sakes? For our sakes, no doubt, this is written: that he that ploweth should plow in hope; and that he that thresheth in hope should be partaker of his hope. If we have sown unto you spiritual things, is it a great thing if we shall reap your carnal* [financial] *things? If others be partakers of this power over you, are not we rather? Nevertheless we have not used this power; but suffer all things, lest we should hinder the gospel of Christ. Do ye not know that they which minister about holy things live of the things of the temple? And they which wait at the altar are partakers with the altar? Even so hath the Lord ordained that they which preach the gospel should live of the gospel."* Yea, in Galatians 6:6 the instruction is given, *"Let him that is taught in the word communicate unto him that teacheth in all good things."*

261. We must not receive a public or official accusation against a pastoral leader unless it is accompanied by two or three witnesses.

1 Timothy 5:19 – "***Against an elder receive not an accusation, but before two or three witnesses.***"

Such accusations should not be made without the support of witnesses, and such accusations should not be received without the presence of witnesses. Because of the spiritual honor that our Lord places upon the position of pastoral leadership, He also places a guard upon accusations being made against pastoral leaders. Yet what about when an accusation of significant (especially, disqualifying) sin is found to be accurate against a pastoral leader?

262. We must publicly rebuke pastoral leadership that is found guilty of significant (especially disqualifying) sin.

1 Timothy 5:20 – "***Them that sin rebuke before all, that others also may fear.***"

Again because of the spiritual honor that our Lord places upon the position of pastoral leadership, He also requires that a pastoral leader who dishonors this position through sinful behavior should be publicly and distinctly rebuked. Yea, such a public and distinct rebuke is necessary so that the other members of the church might be moved unto a greater fear of sin's pathway. Yea, such a public and distinct rebuke is necessary so that the other members of the church might not think that anyone is excused from our Lord's judgment against sin, no matter what their ministry role in the church.

263. We must not handle matters either of honor or of rebuke for pastoral leadership with partiality.

1 Timothy 5:21 – "***I charge thee before God, and the Lord Jesus Christ, and the elect angels, that thou observe these things without preferring one before another, doing nothing by partiality.***"

264. We must be slow and careful in ordaining men for roles of pastoral leadership.

1 Timothy 5:22 – "***Lay hands suddenly on no man, neither be partaker of other men's sins: keep thyself pure.***"

1 Timothy 5:24-25 – "*Some men's sins are open beforehand, going before to judgment; and some men they follow after. Likewise also the good works of some are manifest beforehand; and they that are otherwise cannot be hid.*"

In this context the phrase "lay hands" refers, not unto taking hold of an individual for punishment, but unto ordaining an individual for leadership. It is that about which the apostle Paul spoke in 1 Timothy 4:14 – "*Neglect not the gift that is in thee, which was given thee by prophecy, with the laying on of the hands of the presbytery.*" It is that unto which Acts 13:1-3 refers – "*Now there were in the church that was at Antioch certain prophets and teachers; as Barnabas, and Simeon that was called Niger, and Lucius of Cyrene, and Manaen, which had been brought up with Herod the tetrarch, and Saul. As they ministered to the Lord, and fasted, the Holy Ghost said, Separate me Barnabas and Saul for the work whereunto I have called them. And when they had fasted and prayed, and laid their hands on them, they sent them away.*"

The reason that we must be slow and careful in ordaining men for roles of pastoral leadership (to "lay hands suddenly on no men") is so that we might not become a responsible partaker in, but might keep ourselves pure from the sins of those who are not spiritually qualified. Even so, in verses 24-25 the counsel is given, "*Some men's sins are open beforehand, going before to judgment; and some men they follow after. Likewise also the good works of some are manifest beforehand; and they that are otherwise cannot be hid.*" If we do not quickly ordain men for pastoral leadership, but patiently wait for our Lord's guidance, both the spiritually unqualified and the spiritually qualified will be made clear.

265. We must be content with such things as we have, recognizing that we cannot take the things of this life with us into the life to come, and recognizing that our Lord Himself is all-sufficient for our lives.

1 Timothy 6:6-8 – "*But godliness with contentment is great gain. For we brought nothing into this world, and it is certain we can carry nothing out.* **And having food and raiment let us be therewith content.**"

Hebrews 13:5-6 – "*Let your conversation be without covetousness;* **and be content with such things as ye have:** *for he hath said, I will never leave thee, nor forsake thee. So that we may boldly say, The Lord is my helper, and I will not fear what man shall do unto me.*"

Through these two passages we find three great reasons why we ought to be content with such things that we have and in whatever condition we are. First, we ought to be content because when godliness of character is joined with contentment of attitude, it is a great spiritual gain to us. Second, we ought to be content because we cannot take the things of this world with us into the life to come. Third, we ought to be content because our Lord Jesus Christ will never leave us nor forsake us, but will ever be with us as our Helper in time of need. Therefore, we must learn to be content in whatever condition our Lord leads us. Even so, in Philippians 4:11-13 the apostle Paul gave testimony, saying, "*Not that I speak in respect of want: for I have learned, in whatsoever state I am, therewith to be content. I know both how to be abased, and I know how to abound: every where and in all things I am instructed both to be full and to be hungry, both to abound and to suffer need. I can do all things through Christ which strengtheneth me.*"

266. Those who are rich in the things of this world must view their riches as a gift from God to be used according to the will of God.

1 Timothy 6:17-19 – "***Charge them that are rich in this world, that they be not highminded, nor trust in uncertain riches, but in the living God***, *who giveth us richly all things to enjoy;* ***that they do good, that they be rich in good works, ready to distribute, willing to communicate***; *laying up in store for themselves a good foundation against the time to come, that they may lay hold on eternal life.*"

Those who are rich in the things of this world must not become high minded because of their riches and must not set their trust upon those riches. Rather, they are to maintain their trust in the Lord God, ever remembering that His grace is the source for those riches. Furthermore, those who are rich in the things of this world must use their riches for the purpose of good, godly works. Thus they are to be ever ready and willing to distribute those riches unto the work of the Lord and unto others who have need. By this means, they must set their focus upon laying up eternal riches in heaven, rather than upon accumulating the riches of this world.

267. We must not be ashamed "of the testimony of our Lord" or of those who are suffering for that testimony.

2 Timothy 1:7-8 – "*For God hath not given us the spirit of fear; but of power, and of love, and of a sound mind.* ***Be not thou therefore ashamed of the testimony of our Lord, nor of me his prisoner***: *but be thou partaker of the afflictions of the gospel according to the power of God.*"

There is no need that we should ever be ashamed of the gospel truth and testimony of our Lord and Savior Jesus Christ. He is God the Son, the Almighty Creator, the Anointed Savior, and the Eternal Sovereign. His gospel is the very power of Almighty God unto eternal salvation for every believer. Even so, in Romans 1:16-17 the apostle Paul gave testimony, saying, "*For I am not ashamed of*

the gospel of Christ: for it is the power of God unto salvation to
every one that believeth; to the Jew first, and also to the Greek. For
therein is the righteousness of God revealed from faith to faith: as it
is written, The just shall live by faith.*"* In like manner, 2 Timothy
1:9-10 declares concerning God the Father, "*Who hath saved us,
and called us with an holy calling, not according to our works, but
according to his own purpose and grace, which was given us in
Christ Jesus before the world began, but is now made manifest by
the appearing of our Saviour Jesus Christ, who hath abolished death,
and hath brought life and immortality to light through the gospel.*"*
The gospel of Jesus Christ is the power of God the Father unto our
eternal salvation and our holy calling through regeneration as God's
own dear children. The gospel of Jesus Christ reveals the abundant
grace of God the Father unto us wicked, ungodly, lost, guilty, helpless
sinners. The gospel of Jesus Christ is the message of Christ's death
and resurrection, whereby He "abolished death, and brought life and
immortality to light." Therefore, any spirit of shame that we might
have toward the truth and testimony of Christ is not produced by
God the Holy Spirit, but by our selfish, sinful flesh.

268. We must be willing partakers "of the afflictions of the gospel according to the power of God."

2 Timothy 1:7-8 – "*For God hath not given us the spirit of fear; but
of power, and of love, and of a sound mind. Be not thou therefore
ashamed of the testimony of our Lord, nor of me his prisoner: **but
be thou partaker of the afflictions of the gospel according to the
power of God**.*"

Certainly, being a gospel witness will stir up hatred, reproach, and
affliction from the ungodly who oppose our Lord Jesus Christ and
His glorious gospel. Yet we should not be ashamed of the gospel
because of this affliction, nor should we shy away from proclaiming
the gospel. Rather, with full assurance of faith in the saving power
of Christ's gospel, we should faithfully proclaim it with complete
willingness to partake of the afflictions of the gospel thereby. Yea,

we should be willing partakers of those afflictions "according to the power of God" in the gospel itself to save lost sinners and "according to the power of God" upon us as Spirit-filled witnesses of that gospel. Let us then join with the apostle Paul's testimony from 2 Timothy 1:12, saying, *"For the which cause I also suffer these things: nevertheless I am not ashamed: for I know whom I have believed, and am persuaded that he is able to keep that which I have committed unto him against that day."*

269. Those who are called to pastoral ministry must commit the truths of God's Word unto other faithful men, who may in turn teach others also.

2 Timothy 2:2 – *"**And the things that thou hast heard of me among many witnesses, the same commit thou to faithful men, who shall be able to teach others also**."*

Herein we find a three-fold progression for the spiritual growth of a church ministry. First, the pastoral minister himself must grow in the truths of God's Holy Word. Second, the pastoral minister must teach the truths of God's Holy Word unto faithful men. Third, the faithful men must teach the truths of God's Holy Word unto others also. Through this progression the pastoral minister will be perfecting the saints for the work of the ministry for the edifying of the church in love. (See Ephesians 4:11-16)

270. We must be diligent in studying and rightly dividing God's Word of truth.

2 Timothy 2:15 – *"**Study to shew thyself approved unto God**, a workman that needeth not to be ashamed, **rightly dividing the word of truth**."*

441

The Lord our God not only desires that we read and meditate in His Word daily. He also desires that we search and study the truth of His Word diligently. Yea, it is through such diligent study in God's Holy Word that we shall walk before our Lord as approved, rather than ashamed, workmen. On the other hand, if we do not engage in such diligent study of God's Holy Word, we shall not be approved unto our Lord, but should be ashamed before our Lord. Furthermore, our diligent study in God's Holy Word should be for the purpose that we might rightly divide and rightly understand the truths and teachings of God's Word. Even as 2 Peter 3:16 indicates, many wrest (that is – violently twist and distort) the teachings of God's Word for their own purpose and "unto their own destruction." Yet we are to study God's Word diligently in order that we might not wrongly distort the truth of God's Word unto our spiritual destruction, but might rightly divide the truth of God's Word unto our spiritual growth. The phrase "rightly dividing" refers to a precise cutting according to an established pattern. Through inspiration God the Holy Spirit has established the pattern of truth. Even so, it is our responsibility then to understand that truth according to the precise wording and context of any given statement in God's Word.

271. We must not strive with a contentious spirit about Biblical doctrine.

2 Timothy 2:24 – "***And the servant of the Lord must not strive; but be gentle unto all men, apt to teach, patient.***"

We are actually not to strive with a contentious spirit about anything. In fact, Philippians 2:3 gives the instruction, "*Let nothing be done through strife or vainglory; but in lowliness of mind let each esteem other better than themselves.*" However, the context of the instruction in 2 Timothy 2:24 seems to be focused specifically upon the matter of Biblical doctrine. Even so, in 2 Timothy 2:23 the instruction and warning is given, "*But foolish and unlearned questions avoid, knowing that they do gender strifes.*" Then in 2 Timothy 2:24-25 the instruction continues, "*And the servant of the Lord must not*

442

strive; but be gentle unto all men, apt to teach, patient, in meekness instructing those that oppose themselves; if God peradventure will give them repentance to the acknowledging of the truth." Certainly, according to Jude 1:3 we *"should earnestly contend for the faith."* Yet in so doing, we are not to strive with a contentious spirit.

272. We must teach the truths of God's Word unto others with a spirit of gentleness, patience, and meekness.

2 Timothy 2:24-26 – *"And the servant of the Lord must not strive;* **but be gentle unto all men, apt to teach, patient, in meekness instructing those that oppose themselves;** *if God peradventure will give them repentance to the acknowledging of the truth; and that they may recover themselves out of the snare of the devil, who are taken captive by him at his will."*

Indeed, we are not to strive with a contentious spirit about Biblical doctrine. Rather, we are to teach Biblical doctrine faithfully with a spirit of gentleness, patience, and meekness. In fact, this spirit of gentleness, patience, and meekness is especially necessary when we are instructing "those that oppose themselves" through sinful and rebellious behavior. According to God's Word, it is through this means that the Lord our God might grant them an opportunity for repentance unto "the acknowledging of the truth," whereby they may be delivered from "the snare of the devil."

273. We must conduct ourselves in a manner that is adorning to the sound doctrine of God's Holy Word.

Titus 2:1-6 – *"***But speak thou the things which become** [which adorn] **sound doctrine: that the aged men be** *sober, grave, temperate, sound in faith, in charity, in patience.* **The aged women likewise, that they be** *in behaviour as becometh holiness, not false accusers, not given to much wine, teachers of good things;* **that they may teach**

the young women to be *sober, to love their husbands, to love their children, to be discreet, chaste, keepers at home, good, obedient to their own husbands, that the word of God be not blasphemed.* **Young men likewise exhort to be** *sober minded."*

Herein we find four categories of believers mentioned – the older men of God, the older women of God, the younger women of God, and the younger men of God. For each of these categories, there are spiritual characteristics by which they ought to conduct themselves in order to adorn the sound doctrine of God's Holy Word.

For the older men of God, we find a list of six characteristics. First, the older men of God are to be "sober." This means that they are to have a self-disciplined, sensible, and serious balance in mind and spirit. Second, the older men of God are to be "grave." This means that they are to behave in a manner that is worthy of spiritual honor and respect. Third, the older men of God are to be "temperate." This means that they are to have a self-discipline that is rooted in spiritual discretion and in sound judgment. Fourth, the older men of God are to be "sound in faith." This means that they are to be characterized by a godly trust in the Lord our God. Fifth, the older men of God are to be "sound . . . in charity." This means that they are to be characterized by a godly love for others around them. Finally, the older men of God are to be "sound . . . in patience." This means that they are to be characterized by a godly endurance under the pressures of life.

For the older women of God, we find a list of four characteristics. First, the older women of God are to be "in behavior as becometh holiness." This means that they are to be characterized by holiness and godliness, as women who belong to the Lord their God. Second, the older women of God are to be "not false accusers." This means that they are not to engage in gossiping and speaking hurtfully against others. Third, the older women of God are to be "not given to much wine." This means that they are not to become enslaved (addicted) to alcohol. Finally, the older women of God are to be "teachers of good things." This means that they must possess a personal and practical understanding in the truth of God's Word concerning the "good things" that they are to teach. The reason that older women of God are to be such "teachers of good things" is in order that they might be able to teach the younger women of God how they should conduct themselves in a manner that is adorning to the sound doctrine of God's Holy Word. Even so, these older women of God cannot be teachers of these "good things" unto the younger women of God, if they themselves are not characterized by these good characteristics.

For the younger women of God, we find a list of eight characteristics. First, the younger women of God must learn from the older women of God "to be sober." This means that they are to have a self-disciplined, sensible, and serious balance in mind and spirit. Second, the younger women of God must learn from the older women of God "to love their husbands." This mean that they are to have a Biblical and practical affection for their own individual husbands, ever seeking to do them good and not evil all the days of their lives. Third, the younger women of God must learn from the older women of God "to love their children." This means that they are to have a Biblical and practical affection for their own respective children, ever seeking for their children to be raised up in the nurture and admonition of the Lord. Fourth, the younger women of God must learn from the older women of God "to be discreet." This means that they are to be characterized by spiritual discretion and sound judgment.

Fifth, the younger women of God must learn from the older women of God to be "chaste." This means that they are to be characterized by spiritual and relational purity. Sixth, the younger women of God must learn from the older women of God to be "keepers at home." This means that they are to be diligent in taking care and looking well unto the ways of their households. Seventh, the younger women of God must learn from the older women of God to be "good." This means that they are to be characterized by goodness and kindness toward others. Finally, the younger women of God must learn from the older women of God to be "obedient to their own husbands." This means that they are to submit themselves under the leadership of their own individual husbands with a spirit of reverence and trustworthiness. Now, as we have noted, the fact that the older women of God are to teach these "good things" unto the younger women of God indicates that the older women of God themselves must be characterized by these same characteristics. In addition, this fact implies that younger women of God must have the humility to be taught (or, educated) in these "good things" by the older women of God.

For the younger men of God, we find a list of one characteristic. Indeed, the younger men of God must be "sober minded." This means that they are to be characterized by spiritual discretion and sound judgment. Now, this one characteristic is not presented for the young men of God because they have no need of any other characteristics. Rather, this one characteristic is presented for the young men of God because it is so significant for them that they cannot learn any other characteristics apart from learning this one. Even so, above all else young men of God must learn spiritual discretion and sound judgment in order to conduct themselves in a manner that is adorning to the sound doctrine of God's Word. Yea they must learn spiritual discernment and sound judgment for their thinking, their attitudes, their motivations, their decision, their priorities, their pursuits, their communication, their relationships, and their actions.

274. We must consider and meditate upon the truth of our Lord Jesus Christ.

Hebrews 3:1 – "*Wherefore, holy brethren, partakers of the heavenly calling,* **consider the Apostle and High Priest of our profession, Christ Jesus.**"

Hebrews 12:2-3 – "**Looking unto Jesus the author and finisher of our faith***; who for the joy that was set before him endured the cross, despising the shame, and is set down at the right hand of the throne of God.* **For consider him that endured such contradiction of sinners against himself***, lest ye be wearied and faint in your minds.*"

Indeed, we are to consider and meditate upon the truth of our Lord Jesus Christ for comfort and encouragement of heart, so that we might not become wearied in well doing and faint in our minds.

Even so, the instruction in Hebrews 3:1 to consider and meditate upon the truth of our Lord Jesus Christ as "the Apostle and High Priest of our profession" follows after the encouraging truths of Hebrews 2:9-18 – "*But we see Jesus, who was made a little lower than the angels for the suffering of death, crowned with glory and honour; that he by the grace of God should taste death for every man. For it became him, for whom are all things, and by whom are all things, in bringing many sons unto glory, to make the captain of their salvation perfect through sufferings. For both he that sanctifieth and they who are sanctified are all of one: for which cause he is not ashamed to call them brethren, saying, I will declare thy name unto my brethren, in the midst of the church will I sing praise unto thee. And again, I will put my trust in him. And again, Behold I and the children which God hath given me. Forasmuch then as the children are partakers of flesh and blood, he also himself likewise took part of the same; that through death he might destroy him that had the power of death, that is, the devil; and deliver them who through fear of death were all their lifetime subject to bondage. For verily he took not on him the nature of angels; but he took on him the seed of Abraham. Wherefore in all things it behoved him to be made like unto his brethren, that he might be a merciful and faithful high priest in things pertaining to God, to make reconciliation for the sins of the people. For in that he himself hath suffered being tempted, he is able to succour them that are tempted.*"

Again in Hebrews 4:15-16 the encouraging truths concerning the Lord Jesus Christ as our great High Priest are delivered – "*Seeing then that we have a great high priest, that is passed into the heavens, Jesus the Son of God, let us hold fast our profession. For we have not an high priest which cannot be touched with the feeling of our infirmities; but was in all points tempted like as we are, yet without sin. Let us therefore come boldly unto the throne of grace, that we may obtain mercy, and find grace to help in time of need.*" Again in Hebrews 5:7-10 the encouraging truths concerning Him are delivered, "*Who in the days of his flesh, when he had offered up prayers and supplications with strong crying and tears unto him that was able to save him from death, and was heard in that he feared; though he were a Son, yet learned he obedience by the things which he suffered; and being made perfect, he became the author of eternal salvation*

447

unto all them that obey him; called of God an high priest after the order of Melchisedec."

Again in Hebrews 7:22-8:2 the encouraging truths concerning our great High Priest, the Lord Jesus Christ, are delivered – "*By so much was Jesus made a surety of a better testament. And they* [the priesthood of Aaron] *truly were many priests, because they were not suffered to continue by reason of death: but this man* [our Lord and Savior Jesus Christ], *because he continueth ever, hath an unchangeable priesthood. Wherefore he is able also to save them to the uttermost that come unto God by him, seeing he ever liveth to make intercession for them. For such an high priest became us, who is holy, harmless, undefiled, separate from sinners, and made higher than the heavens; who needeth not daily, as those high priests, to offer up sacrifice, first for his own sins, and then for the people's: for this he did once, when he offered up himself. For the law maketh men high priests which have infirmity; but the word of the oath, which was since the law, maketh the Son, who is consecrated for evermore. Now of the things which we have spoken this is the sum: We have such an high priest, who is set on the right hand of the throne of the Majesty in the heavens; a minister of the sanctuary, and of the true tabernacle, which the Lord pitched, and not man.*"

Again in Hebrews 9:11-15 the encouraging truths concerning our great High Priest, the Lord Jesus Christ, are delivered – "*But Christ being come an high priest of good things to come, by a greater and more perfect tabernacle, not made with hands, that is to say, not of this building; neither by the blood of goats and calves, but by his own blood he entered in once into the holy place, having obtained eternal redemption for us. For if the blood of bulls and of goats, and the ashes of an heifer sprinkling the unclean, sanctifieth to the purifying of the flesh: how much more shall the blood of Christ, who through the eternal Spirit offered himself without spot to God, purge your conscience from dead works to serve the living God? And for this cause he is the mediator of the new testament, that by means of death, for the redemption of the transgressions that were under the first testament, they which are called might receive the promise of eternal inheritance.*"

Finally, in Hebrews 10:19-25 the encouragement and exhortation concerning our Lord and Savior Jesus Christ as our great High Priest are delivered – "*Having therefore, brethren, boldness to enter into the holiest by the blood of Jesus, by a new and living way, which he hath consecrated for us, through the veil, that is to say, his flesh; and having an high priest over the house of God; let us draw near with a true heart in full assurance of faith, having our hearts sprinkled from an evil conscience, and our bodies washed with pure water. Let us hold fast the profession of our faith without wavering; (for he is faithful that promised;) and let us consider one another to provoke unto love and to good works: not forsaking the assembling of ourselves together, as the manner of some is; but exhorting one another: and so much the more, as ye see the day approaching.*"

275. We must take heed to our heart character and beware that our hearts not become hardened by a spirit of unbelief.

Hebrews 3:7-13 – "*Wherefore (as the Holy Ghost saith, To day if ye will hear his voice, harden not your hearts, as in the provocation, in the day of temptation in the wilderness: when your fathers tempted me, proved me, and saw my works forty years. Wherefore I was grieved with that generation, and said, They do alway err in their heart; and they have not known my ways. So I sware in my wrath, They shall not enter into my rest.)* **Take heed, brethren, lest there be in any of you an evil heart of unbelief, in departing from the living God.** *But exhort one another daily, while it is called To day; lest any of you be hardened through the deceitfulness of sin.*"

Every day that we walk in this spiritually dark world, experiencing its troubles and its temptations, we must take heed to the character of our hearts and must beware that our hearts might not become hardened against the Lord our God. Even so, in Hebrews 3:7-13 we find five elements to this warning against the spiritual hardening of our hearts.

First, as we have already mentioned, it is a spiritual hardening that is developed against the Lord our God. It is a spiritual hardening against our daily walk in fellowship with the Lord our God. In Hebrews 3:7-10 the Old Testament warning is given, *"Wherefore (as the Holy Ghost saith, To day if ye will hear his voice, harden not your hearts, as in the provocation, in the day of temptation in the wilderness: when your fathers tempted **me**, proved **me**, and saw **my** works forty years. Wherefore **I** was grieved with that generation, and said, They do alway err in their heart; and they have not known **my** ways."*

Second, it is a spiritual hardening that is caused by an evil spirit of unbelief. It is our unbelief (our lack of faith) in the Lord our God that will produce this spiritual hardening in our hearts. In the opening portion of Hebrews 3:12, the warning is given, *"Take heed, brethren, lest there be in any of you **an evil heart of unbelief**."* Herein we learn that our unbelief (our lack of faith) in the Lord our God is indeed an evil spirit of heart. Even so, Hebrews 11:6 proclaims, *"But without faith it is impossible to please him: for he that cometh to God must believe that he is, and that he is a rewarder of them that diligently seek him."*

Third, it is a spiritual hardening that is influenced "through the deceitfulness of sin." It is through the deceitful enticement of sinful temptation that our hearts are turned away from the priority of our Lord's blessed fellowship unto the pursuit of our own selfish desires. In the closing portion of Hebrews 3:13, the warning is given, *"Lest any of you be hardened **through the deceitfulness of sin**."* As the focus of our hearts is set more and more upon the desires of self, so the faith of our hearts grows more and more dulled through sin. In turn, as the faith of our hearts grows more and more dulled through sin, so the hardening of our hearts grows more and more against the Lord our God.

Fourth, it is a spiritual hardening that results in a departure from the Lord our God. Yea, it results in a heart that is characterized by unrighteousness and in a walk that is contrary to our Lord's ways. In Hebrews 3:12 the warning is given, *"Take heed, brethren, lest there be in any of you an evil heart of unbelief, **in departing from the living God**."* Even so also, in verse 10 the Old Testament declaration is given, *"Wherefore I was grieved with that generation,* *and said,* **They do alway err in their heart; and they have not known my ways***.*" As the hardening of our hearts grows more and more against the Lord our God, so the unrighteousness of our hearts and lives will grow more and more also.

Fifth and finally, it is a spiritual hardening that will provoke the wrath of the Lord our God. It will move our Lord's heart unto grief and our Lord's hand unto chastening. In Hebrews 3:7-11 the Old Testament warning is given, "*Wherefore (as the Holy Ghost saith, To day if ye will hear his voice, harden not your hearts, as in the provocation, in the day of temptation in the wilderness: when your fathers tempted me, proved me, and saw my works forty years. Wherefore I was grieved with that generation, and said, They do alway err in their heart; and they have not known my ways.* **So I sware in my wrath, They shall not enter into my rest***.)*"

276. We must exhort one another daily not to be "hardened through the deceitfulness of sin," but to cleave unto our Lord and to pursue godly love and good works.

Hebrews 3:13 – "***But exhort one another daily****, while it is called To day; lest any of you be hardened through the deceitfulness of sin.*"

Hebrews 10:24-25 – "***And let us consider one another to provoke unto love and to good works****: not forsaking the assembling of ourselves together, as the manner of some is;* **but exhorting one another***: and so much the more, as ye see the day approaching.*"

In Acts 11:22-23 the example of Barnabas is reported, "*Then tidings of these things came unto the ears of the church which was in Jerusalem: and they sent forth Barnabas, that he should go as far as Antioch. Who, when he came, and had seen the grace of God, was glad, and exhorted them all, that with purpose of heart they would cleave unto the Lord.*" Indeed, with every opportunity that the Lord our God grants unto us, we should be exhorting one another not to fall away from the Lord our God unto the ways of unrighteousness, but to walk with the Lord our God after the ways of righteousness.

277. We must take heed unto our heart that we not come short of our Lord's promised rest unto our souls due to our unbelief.

Hebrews 4:1 – "*Let us therefore fear, lest, a promise being left us of entering into his rest, any of you should seem to come short of it.*"

Hebrews 4:9-11 – "*There remaineth therefore a rest to the people of God. For he that is entered into his rest, he also hath ceased from his own works, as God did from his. Let us labour therefore to enter into that rest, lest any man fall after the same example of unbelief.*"

In Matthew 11:29 our Lord Jesus Christ gave the promise, saying, "*Take my yoke upon you, and learn of me; for I am meek and lowly in heart: and ye shall find rest unto your souls.*" It is only as we walk in fellowship with our Lord that we may experience His promised rest unto our souls, and it is only as we walk by faith in our Lord that we may walk in fellowship with Him. Therefore, we must have a holy fear against the spirit of doubt and unbelief, lest we should lose out on this rest unto our souls. Yea, we must be ever diligent to maintain the spirit of faith and trust in our Lord, lest we fall spiritually through a spirit of doubt and unbelief.

278. We must hold fast the full assurance, daily walk, and public testimony of our faith in the Lord without wavering.

Hebrews 4:14 – "*Seeing then that we have a great high priest, that is passed into the heavens, Jesus the Son of God, let us hold fast our profession.*"

Hebrews 10:23 – "*Let us hold fast the profession of our faith without wavering; (for he is faithful that promised;)*"

The profession of our faith encompasses our attitude, our walk, and our testimony. In the realm of our attitude, the profession of our faith is to be defined as a full assurance of faith in our Lord. Furthermore, in the realm of our walk, the profession of our faith is to be defined as a daily walk of fellowship with our Lord. Finally, in the realm of our testimony, our profession of faith is to be defined as a public testimony of faithfulness unto our Lord. This is the very profession of faith that we are to hold fast without wavering; and that which should motivate us to hold fast is the truth that our Lord is ever faithful to keep His promises.

279. We must come boldly unto God's throne of grace through prayer, "that we may obtain mercy, and find grace to help in time of need."

Hebrews 4:15-16 – *"For we have not an high priest which cannot be touched with the feeling of our infirmities; but was in all points tempted like as we are, yet without sin.* **Let us therefore come boldly unto the throne of grace, that we may obtain mercy, and find grace to help in time of need***."*

Through our Lord Jesus Christ as our eternal Savior and our great High Priest, we believers have access unto the very throne of God's grace through prayer. Yea, through our Lord Jesus Christ as our eternal Savior, we are made the very children of God and are able to cry unto Him as our heavenly Father. Even so, in Romans 8:10 God's Word declares, *"And if Christ be in you, the body is dead because of sin; but the Spirit is life because of righteousness."* Then in Romans 8:15-16 God's Word adds, *"For ye have not received the spirit of bondage again to fear; but ye have received the Spirit of adoption, whereby we cry, Abba, Father. The Spirit itself beareth witness with our spirit, that we are the children of God."* In addition, through our Lord Jesus Christ as our great High Priest, we have a holy boldness and a confident access unto God our heavenly Father. Even so, concerning our Lord Jesus Christ, in Ephesians 3:12 God's Word declares, *"In whom we have boldness and access with confidence by the faith of him."* Therefore, we should come boldly through our Lord Jesus Christ unto God our heavenly Father's throne of grace through prayer, in order that we may obtain mercy and find grace from our heavenly Father to help us in our times of need.

280. We must grow forward unto spiritual maturity by using God's Word to exercise our spiritual discernment.

Hebrews 5:12 - 6:2 – *"For when for the time ye ought to be teachers, ye have need that one teach you again which be the first principles of the oracles of God; and are become such as have need of milk, and not of strong meat. For every one that useth milk is unskilful in the word of righteousness: for he is a babe. But strong meat belongeth to them that are of full age, even those who by reason of use have their senses exercised to discern both good and evil.* **Therefore leaving the principles of the doctrine of Christ, let us go on unto perfection**; *not laying again the foundation of repentance from dead works, and of faith toward God, of the doctrine of baptisms, and of laying on of hands, and of resurrection of the dead, and of eternal judgment."*

This instruction indicates that we should not remain in the place of spiritual immaturity, grasping only the first principles of our salvation through faith in Christ. Rather, this instruction indicates that we should go forward "unto perfection," that is – unto spiritual maturity in our Christian walk. The means by which this growth in spiritual maturity is made possible is revealed in Hebrews 5:14. Therein those who are "of full age" (that is – of spiritual maturity) are defined as "those who by reason of use have their senses exercised to discern both good and evil." The earlier context of Hebrews 5:12-13 reveals this activity of "use" concerns the truth of God's Word, "the word of righteousness." So then, we are instructed to grow forward unto spiritual maturity; and this growth in spiritual maturity is made possible as we faithfully use the truth of God's Word to exercise our spiritual senses that we may learn to discern between what is spiritually good and what is spiritually evil.

281. We must draw near unto the Lord our God in spiritual fellowship "with a true heart in full assurance of faith."

Hebrews 10:19-22 – "*Having therefore, brethren, boldness to enter into the holiest by the blood of Jesus, by a new and living way, which he hath consecrated for us, through the veil, that is to say, his flesh; and having an high priest over the house of God;* **let us draw near with a true heart in full assurance of faith,** *having our hearts sprinkled from an evil conscience, and our bodies washed with pure water.*"

James 4:8 – "***Draw nigh to God, and he will draw nigh to you.*** *Cleanse your hands, ye sinners; and purify your hearts, ye double minded.*"

Through the shed blood, sacrificial death, bodily resurrection, glorious exaltation, and high priestly work of the Lord Jesus Christ our Savior, we have full spiritual access unto God our heavenly Father. On the ground of that Biblical truth, we should draw near unto God our heavenly Father and Jesus Christ our Lord for daily spiritual fellowship. Indeed, we should draw near for such fellowship "in full assurance of faith," believing that our heavenly Father and our Lord Jesus Christ actually desire to walk in daily fellowship with us. Yet we should also draw near for such fellowship "with a true heart," recognizing that such daily fellowship is only possible on the path of righteousness. Indeed, from James 4:8 we find the promise of God's own Word that if we will draw near unto Him, then He will certainly respond by also drawing near unto us. Oh, what a glorious and gracious promise this is! Oh, what a glorious and gracious privilege it is to walk in fellowship with the Lord our God and Savior! Oh, what a glorious and gracious Lord God is the Lord our God and Savior that He would be so ready and willing to lift us up spiritually unto the high and holy place of His spiritual fellowship!

282. We must not "forsake the assembling of ourselves together" for church services.

Hebrews 10:25 – "***Not forsaking the assembling of ourselves together***, *as the manner of some is; but exhorting one another: and so much the more, as ye see the day approaching.*"

This instruction is actually subordinate to a more primary instruction. In Hebrews 10:24 the instruction is given, "*And let us consider one another to provoke unto love and to good works.*" Then the instruction of verse 25 follows as a necessary element for obedience to the primary instruction of verse 24. In order to engage faithfully in the ministry of provoking and exhorting one another "unto love and to good works," it is necessary that we regularly meet with one another. Thus verse 25 provides the subordinate instruction that we must not "forsake the assembling of ourselves together." Yet what does it mean not to "forsake the assembling of ourselves together"? The word "forsake" indicates a purposeful decision to turn aside from something. Even so, we are never to make a purposeful decision to turn aside from the assembling of ourselves together for church services or to allow something of this world to obtain a greater priority in our lives. Rather, we are faithfully to pursue the assembling of ourselves together for church services.

283. We must not cast away our godly confidence concerning the rewards of the life to come.

Hebrews 10:32-36 – "*But call to remembrance the former days, in which, after ye were illuminated, ye endured a great fight of afflictions; partly, whilst ye were made a gazingstock both by reproaches and afflictions; and partly, whilst ye became companions of them that were so used. For ye had compassion of me in my bonds, and took joyfully the spoiling of your goods, knowing in yourselves that ye have in heaven a better and an enduring substance. **Cast not away therefore your confidence, which hath great recompence of reward.** For ye have need of patience, that, after ye have done the will of God, ye might receive the promise.*"

The Hebrew believers to which this epistle was originally written had "endured a great fight of afflictions." They had been made "a gazingstock both by reproaches and afflictions." They had joyfully suffered "the spoiling of their goods." Indeed, they had endured all of this with a joyful spirit because they had a confident knowledge that they had in heaven a far better and more enduring reward. Even so, the instruction was given that they should not cast aside their Biblical confidence concerning that heavenly reward. Yea, the exhortation was given that they should maintain a spirit of patient endurance in doing God's will, ever keeping their focus upon that promised reward. In like manner, we also must not cast aside our Biblical confidence in the heavenly reward that the Lord our God has promised unto those who serve and obey Him faithfully in this life.

284. We must not despise or faint at the chastening of our Lord in our lives.

Hebrews 12:5-6 – "*And ye have forgotten the exhortation which speaketh unto you as unto children,* **My son, despise not thou the chastening of the Lord, nor faint when thou art rebuked of him**: *for whom the Lord loveth he chasteneth, and scourgeth every son whom he receiveth.*"

Indeed, every child of God experiences the chastening hand of our heavenly Father upon them for their sinful character and conduct. The Lord our God and heavenly Father is ever faithful to chasten his own dear children. Yet we should not despise and stubbornly resist our heavenly Father's chastening hand in our lives. Rather, we should yield to it and willingly receive its corrective purpose. We should not become faint and discouraged under our heavenly Father's chastening hand. Rather, we should be brought to humble repentance and spiritual growth by it.

First, we should recognize that our heavenly Father's chastening hand reveals His fatherly love toward us as His dear children. Even so, the opening portion of Hebrews 12:6 declares, "*For whom the Lord loveth he chasteneth.*" Therefore, we should respond unto our heavenly Father's chastening hand with repentance of sin. Second, we should recognize that our heavenly Father's chastening hand serves as evidence that we truly are children in God's family. Even so, Hebrews 12:7-8 reveals the truth, saying, *"If ye endure chastening, God dealeth with you as with sons; for what son is he whom the father chasteneth not? But if ye be without chastisement, whereof all are partakers, then are ye bastards, and not sons."* Therefore, we should respond unto our heavenly Father's chastening hand with the encouragement of this assurance.

Third, we should recognize that our heavenly Father's chastening hand is for our spiritual profit, that we might grow in His holiness. Even so, Hebrews 12:9-10 states, *"Furthermore we have had fathers of our flesh which corrected us, and we gave them reverence: shall we not much rather be in subjection unto the Father of spirits, and live? For they verily for a few days chastened us after their own pleasure; but he for our profit, that we might be partakers of his holiness."* Therefore, we should respond unto our heavenly Father's chastening hand with submission to its correction. Finally, we should recognize that although our heavenly Father's chastening is grievous in the actual experience thereof, it will produce wonderful spiritual fruit in our lives if we submit ourselves unto it. Even so, Hebrews 12:11 declares, *"Now no chastening for the present seemeth to be joyous, but grievous: nevertheless afterward it yieldeth the peaceable fruit of righteousness unto them which are exercised thereby."* Therefore, we should respond to our heavenly Father's chastening hand with joy in its results.

285. We must not rebel against the authoritative Word of our Lord Jesus Christ.

Hebrews 12:25-27 – *"**See that ye refuse not him that speaketh.** For if they escaped not who refused him that spake on earth, much more shall not we escape, if we turn away from him that speaketh from heaven: whose voice then shook the earth: but now he hath promised, saying, Yet once more I shake not the earth only, but also* heaven. *And this word, Yet once more, signifieth the removing of those things that are shaken, as of things that are made, that those things which cannot be shaken may remain."*

In Hebrews 12:18-24 the foundation for this instruction is given, *"For ye are not come unto the mount that might be touched* [that is – Mount Sinai from the Old Testament], *and that burned with fire, nor unto blackness, and darkness, and tempest, and the sound of a trumpet, and the voice of words; which voice they that heard intreated that the word should not be spoken to them any more: (For they could not endure that which was commanded, and if so much as a beast touch the mountain, it shall be stoned, or thrust through with a dart: and so terrible was the sight, that Moses said, I exceedingly fear and quake:) but ye are come unto mount Sion, and unto the city of the living God, the heavenly Jerusalem, and to an innumerable company of angels, to the general assembly and church of the firstborn, which are written in heaven, and to God the Judge of all, and to the spirits of just men made perfect, and to Jesus the mediator of the new covenant, and to the blood of sprinkling, that speaketh better things than that of Abel."*

Then in the opening portion of Hebrews 12:25 the instruction is given, *"See that ye refuse not him that speaketh."* Indeed, we must not refuse, resist, reject, or rebel against the authority of our Lord Jesus Christ and His Holy Word in our daily lives. Finally, in Hebrews 12:26-27 the warning is given, *"For if they escaped not who refused him that spake on earth, much more shall not we escape, if we turn away from him that speaketh from heaven: whose voice then shook the earth: but now he hath promised, saying, Yet once more I shake not the earth only, but also heaven. And this word, Yet once more, signifieth the removing of those things that are shaken, as of things that are made, that those things which cannot be shaken may remain."*

286. We must remember with compassion fellow believers who are suffering in prison or under persecution for the cause of Christ.

Hebrews 13:3 – *"**Remember them that are in bonds, as bound with them; and them which suffer adversity, as being yourselves also in the body**."*

In fact, an illustration and commendation of this spiritual behavior has already been presented in Hebrews 10:32-34 – *"But call to remembrance the former days, in which, after ye were illuminated, ye endured a great fight of afflictions; partly, whilst ye were made a gazingstock both by reproaches and afflictions; and partly, whilst ye became companions of them that were so used. For ye had compassion of me in my bonds, and took joyfully the spoiling of your goods, knowing in yourselves that ye have in heaven a better and an enduring substance."* In like manner, the apostle Paul commended the believers at Philippi in Philippians 4:14-18 for this spiritual behavior, saying, *"Notwithstanding ye have well done, that ye did communicate with my affliction. Now ye Philippians know also, that in the beginning of the gospel, when I departed from Macedonia, no church communicated with me as concerning giving and receiving, but ye only. For even in Thessalonica ye sent once and again unto my necessity. Not because I desire a gift: but I desire fruit that may abound to your account. But I have all, and abound: I am full, having received of Epaphroditus the things which were sent from you, an odour of a sweet smell, a sacrifice acceptable, wellpleasing to God."* Furthermore, in 2 Timothy 1:16-18 the apostle Paul commended Onesiphorus for this spiritual behavior, saying, *"The Lord give mercy unto the house of Onesiphorus; for he oft refreshed me, and was not ashamed of my chain: but, when he was in Rome, he sought me out very diligently, and found me. The Lord grant unto him that he may find mercy of the Lord in that day: and in how many things he ministered unto me at Ephesus, thou knowest very well."*

Also in Hebrews 13:18-19 the Holy Spirit inspired author made request that these believer might pray for him concerning his own imprisonment – *"Pray for us: for we trust we have a good conscience, in all things willing to live honestly. But I beseech you the rather to do this, that I may be restored to you the sooner.*" In like manner, in Ephesians 6:19-20 the apostle Paul made request for prayer concerning his own imprisonment, saying, "*And for me* [that is – pray for me], *that utterance may be given unto me, that I may open my mouth boldly, to make known the mystery of the gospel, for which I am an ambassador in bonds: that therein I may speak boldly, as I ought to speak.*" Furthermore, in Colossians 4:3-4 the apostle Paul made request for prayer concerning his own imprisonment, saying, "*Withal praying also for us, that God would open unto us a door of utterance, to speak the mystery of Christ, for which I am also in bonds: that I may make it manifest, as I ought to speak.*" Finally, with his closing remarks in Colossians 4:18, the apostle Paul gave instruction unto the believers at Colossi concerning himself, saying, "*The salutation by the hand of me Paul. Remember my bonds. Grace be with you. Amen.*" Even so, through all of this we understand that to remember with compassion our fellow believers who are suffering in prison or under persecution for the cause of Christ means to help them, encourage them, minister to, and pray for them in whatever manner that we are able.

287. We must willingly and purposefully bear the reproach of Christ in being separated unto Christ and apart from the world.

Hebrews 13:12-14 – "*Wherefore Jesus also, that he might sanctify the people with his own blood, suffered without the gate.* **Let us go forth therefore unto him without the camp, bearing his reproach.** *For here have we no continuing city, but we seek one to come.*"

In fact, an illustration of this godly behavior is presented in Hebrews 11:24-26 concerning the man of God Moses – "*By faith Moses, when he was come to years, refused to be called the son of Pharaoh's daughter; choosing rather to suffer affliction with the people of God, than to enjoy the pleasures of sin for a season; esteeming the reproach of Christ greater riches than the treasures in Egypt: for*

461

he had respect unto the recompence of the reward." Indeed, we ourselves must also esteem "the reproach of Christ" as of far greater value than any of the so-called treasures of this world, in whatever form they may present themselves. Therefore, we must choose rather to live for our Lord Jesus Christ than to live for this present evil world. Yea, we must choose rather to suffer affliction for our Lord's sake than "to enjoy the pleasures of sin for a season."

288. We must purposefully allow God's work of patience to accomplish its perfecting work in our lives.

James 1:4 – "***But let patience have her perfect work,*** *that ye may be perfect and entire, wanting nothing.*"

James 5:10-11 – "***Take, my brethren, the prophets, who have spoken in the name of the Lord, for an example of suffering affliction, and of patience.*** *Behold, we count them happy which endure. Ye have heard of the patience of Job, and have seen the end of the Lord; that the Lord is very pitiful, and of tender mercy.*"

According to James 1:3 God our heavenly Father uses the trying of our faith through the tribulations of life to perform His work of developing spiritual patience in our character. "Knowing this, that the trying of your faith worketh patience." Through this process God our heavenly Father intends to perfect us so that our spiritual character is perfectly complete, lacking nothing in righteousness. Yea, through this process He intends to perfect us in spiritual maturity unto the perfectly righteous character of His Son, our Lord Jesus Christ. Ephesians 4:13 describes this as growing "*unto a perfect man, unto the measure of the stature of the fullness of Christ.*" Thus in James 1:4 we are instructed to submit willingly and purposefully unto our Lord God's perfect and perfecting work of patience-building and maturity-building in our lives. Although this work comes through the trying of our faith, we are not to despise it, resist it, or avoid it in our lives. Rather, we are to accept it, submit unto it, and grow through it.

289. We must ask humbly of God in prayer for wisdom when we recognize our lack thereof.

James 1:5 – "***If any of you lack wisdom, let him ask of God***, *that giveth to all men liberally, and upbraideth not; and it shall be given him.*"

In the application of this instruction unto our lives, we must first humble ourselves to acknowledge how greatly we lack true wisdom for daily living. Second, we must come to the conviction that the Lord our God is the only true Source for the wisdom that we need. Third, we then must humble ourselves to ask of God through prayer for the wisdom that we so greatly lack and so desperately need. Fourth, we must set our trust upon the Lord our God to provide graciously and abundantly the wisdom that we need. Even so, the opening portion of James 1:6 adds the instruction, "*But let him ask in faith, nothing wavering.*" Finally, we must engage in this request for God's gift of wisdom consistently and constantly each day. Indeed, we must especially engage in this request for God's gift of wisdom when we are experiencing the trying of our faith.

290. Believers who have learned humility through being materially poor must rejoice in the Lord's promise of exaltation for the humble.

James 1:9 – "***Let the brother of low degree rejoice in that he is exalted***."

In this context the reference unto "the brother of low degree" is not simply unto all believers who are materially poor; for the phrase does not specify those of "poor" degree. Rather, this reference is unto all believers who have learned a humble (low) spirit through being materially poor. Unto such humble believers the Lord our God gives promise in 1 Peter 5:6, "*Humble yourselves therefore under the mighty hand of God, that he may exalt you in due time.*" Even so, in that promise believers who have learned godly humility through being materially poor are to engage in great rejoicing.

291. Believers who are materially rich must rejoice when they experience circumstances that may teach them godly humility.

James 1:10-11 – "***But the rich, in that he is made low***: *because as the flower of the grass he shall pass away. For the sun is no sooner risen with a burning heat, but it withereth the grass, and the flower thereof falleth, and the grace of the fashion of it perisheth: so also shall the rich man fade away in his ways.*"

In our walk with the Lord our God, the characteristic of godly humility is far more important than the possession of material wealth. Even so, those believers who possess material wealth are not to rejoice in their condition of material wealth, but are to rejoice in anything that teaches them the characteristic of godly humility.

292. We must never indicate or imply that the Lord our God is the source for our temptation unto sin. (Also by implication, we must never accept when any other indicates or implies that the Lord our God is the Source for temptation unto sin.)

James 1:13-14 – "***Let no man say when he is tempted, I am tempted of God***: *for God cannot be tempted with evil, neither tempteth he any man: but every man is tempted, when he is drawn away of his own lust, and enticed.*"

In the opening portion of James 1:13, God's Word clearly forbids us from ever saying, whether in thinking unto ourselves or in claiming unto others, that our temptation unto sin is "of God" as its Source. Furthermore, in declaring that we must "let no man say" this, this prohibition also indicates that we must never accept the thought when anyone else claims or teaches that the Lord our God is the Source for sinful temptation. Rather, the closing portion of James 1:13 teaches that the Lord our God, in His nature of perfect holiness and perfect righteousness, cannot be tempted unto sinful unrighteousness and never tempts another unto sinful unrighteousness.

Even so, any thought, claim, or implication that the Lord our God is the Source for sinful temptation is a direct attack against the person and character of God, and thereby is blasphemy against God. On the other hand, James 1:14 teaches that all sinful temptation actually finds its Source in the sinful, selfish character of our own hearts. Thus when we are tempted unto sinful unrighteousness, and especially when we yield unto such temptation, we must never think that the Lord our God is at fault, but must ever acknowledge that the fault is our own.

293. We must not go astray into error in relation to the doctrine of God's goodness and the doctrine of sin's corruption.

James 1:16 – "*Do not err, my beloved brethren.*"

In its immediate context, this warning is placed at the very center of a doctrinal presentation concerning God's goodness and concerning sin's corruption. Thus we understand contextually that we are not to go astray into error concerning these specific doctrinal matters from James 1:13-18 – "*Let no man say when he is tempted, I am tempted of God: for God cannot be tempted with evil, neither tempteth he any man: but every man is tempted, when he is drawn away of his own lust, and enticed. Then when lust hath conceived, it bringeth forth sin: and sin, when it is finished, bringeth forth death. Do not err, my beloved brethren. Every good gift and every perfect gift is from above, and cometh down from the Father of lights, with whom is no variableness, neither shadow of turning. Of his own will begat he us with the word of truth, that we should be a kind of firstfruits of his creatures.*"

294. We must be swift to hear, slow to speak, and slow to wrath.

James 1:19-20 – "***Wherefore, my beloved brethren, let every man be swift to hear, slow to speak, slow to wrath****: for the wrath of man worketh not the righteousness of God.*"

By our naturally selfish nature, we are slow to hear, swift to speak, and swift to wrath. Indeed, by our naturally selfish nature, we are slow to hear the thoughts, opinions, feelings, and interests of others. Furthermore, by our naturally selfish nature, we are swift to express our own thoughts, opinions, feelings, and interests. Finally, by our naturally selfish nature we are swift to wrath when our own thoughts, opinions, feelings, and interests are not honored and when we do not get our own way. Thus in James 1:19-20 the Lord our God expresses His desire that we should deny our naturally selfish nature in our relations with others and do that which is more considerate of them. Yea, herein the Lord our God instructs us to deny our naturally selfish nature by being swift to hear the communications of others, by being slow to speak forth our own mind, and by being slow to be provoked unto wrath. Even more so, the Lord our God especially warns us that "the wrath of man" (that is – the wrath that is generated by our selfish nature) does not produce the righteousness of God in our character, in our conduct, or in our communication.

295. We must be doers of God's Word, and not hearers only.

James 1:22-25 – "***But be ye doers of the word, and not hearers only, deceiving your own selves****. For if any be a hearer of the word, and not a doer, he is like unto a man beholding his natural face in a glass: for he beholdeth himself, and goeth his way, and straightway forgetteth what manner of man he was. But whoso looketh into the perfect law of liberty, and continueth therein, he being not a forgetful hearer, but a doer of the work, this man shall be blessed in his deed.*"

Certainly, we must be receptive hearers of God's Word. Yet being hearers of God's Word is not enough. We must also be obedient doers of God's Word. In fact, if we are only hearers of God's Word, then we shall be spiritually self-deceived into thinking that only our hearing of the Word makes us right with God. Yet if we are also obedient doers of God's Word, then we shall be blessed of God in our daily walk with Him.

296. We must not attempt to join our walk of faith in our Lord Jesus Christ with the practice of showing partiality against others due simply to external considerations.

James 2:1 – *"My brethren, have not the faith of our Lord Jesus Christ, the Lord of glory, with respect of persons."*

A daily walk of faith in our Lord and a practice of showing "respect of persons" are not spiritually consistent and compatible with one another. Rather, these two behaviors are spiritually contrary to one another. Thus we believers, who are called by our Lord unto a daily walk of faith in and fellowship with Him, must not be characterized by a spirit of partiality. Yet how is this sinful practice of showing "respect of persons" to be defined Biblically? The phrase "respect of persons" is translated from a Greek word that combines the noun for "face" and the verb for "receiving," literally meaning "face-receiving," or "receiving the face." As such, this phrase refers to the practice of receiving or rejecting individuals on the basis of external, superficial considerations rather than upon the basis of inner, spiritual character. It is the practice of granting special favor, regard, and respect to others based solely upon such superficial, external circumstances as social status, financial wealth, physical appeal, public popularity, racial distinction, etc.

Even so, in James 2:2-4 an example of showing such "respect of persons" is given in relation to the matter of financial wealth, that is – in relation to the practice of favoring the rich over the poor simply due to their financial condition. Indeed, in these verses the hypothetical, yet realistic, illustration is given with a concluding rebuke – *"For if there come unto your assembly a man with a gold ring, in goodly apparel, and there come in also a poor man in vile* raiment; and ye have respect to him that weareth the gay clothing, and say unto him, Sit thou here in a good place; and say to the poor, Stand thou there, or sit here under my footstool: are ye not then partial in yourselves* [showing partiality even among the assembly of the church], *and are become judges of evil thoughts?"* Yes, when we engage in the ungodly practice of showing partiality against others due simply unto external considerations, we demonstrate ourselves to be judges who possess evil thinking within our hearts. Thus in James 2:1 this characteristic and practice is expressly and firmly forbidden. Indeed, this ungodly character and practice, in any of the various forms that it may take, must never be allowed a place in our hearts and lives.

297. We must be careful both to speak and to act toward others in accord with God's law of love.

James 2:9-13 – *"But if ye have respect to persons, ye commit sin, and are convinced of the law as transgressors. For whosoever shall keep the whole law, and yet offend in one point, he is guilty of all. For he that said, Do not commit adultery, said also, Do not kill. Now if thou commit no adultery, yet if thou kill, thou art become a transgressor of the law.* **So speak ye, and so do, as they that shall be judged by the law of liberty.** *For he shall have judgment without mercy, that hath shewed no mercy; and mercy rejoiceth against judgment."*

The word "so," with which the instruction of James 2:12 begins, points back to the commendation of verse 8 and the admonition of verses 9-11. Therein God's Word declares, *"If ye fulfil the royal law according to the scripture, Thou shalt love thy neighbour as thyself, ye do well: but if ye have respect to persons, ye commit sin, and are convinced of the law as transgressors. For whosoever shall keep the whole law, and yet offend in one point, he is guilty of all. For he that said, Do not commit adultery, said also, Do not kill. Now if thou commit no adultery, yet if thou kill, thou art become a transgressor of the law."* The foundational issue here is not simply negative that we should not engage in the practice of showing partiality against others. Rather, the foundational issue is positive that we should pursue demonstrating godly love toward others. Indeed, God's law of love must be the governing principle for all of our interactions with others. We are to "so speak" and to "so do" in accord with God's law of love. Indeed, we must "so speak" and "so do" in accord with God's law of love toward others because we shall one day be judged by the Lord our God according to His law of liberty in relation to how we spoke and acted toward others. Even so, James 2:13 concludes the passage with the warning, *"For he shall have judgment without mercy, that hath shewed no mercy; and mercy rejoiceth against judgment."*

298. We must not pursue greater leadership and teaching authority than the Lord our God has granted to us.

James 3:1 – *"**My brethren, be not many masters**, knowing that we shall receive the greater condemnation."*

The opening instruction of James 3:1 means that the "many" among us should not be pursuing after positions of leadership and teaching. Then the closing portion of the verse reveals the reason, "Knowing that we shall receive the greater condemnation." This reason reveals that those who do possess some level of leadership or teaching authority will face a greater level of judgment than those who do not. Indeed, the Biblical principle and warning is just this – The greater the authority, the greater the responsibility; and the greater the responsibility, the greater the accountability before the Lord. In addition, James 3:2 strengthens the force of this warning by focusing its application upon the category of our words. *"For in many things we offend all. If any man offend not in word, the same is a perfect man, and able also to bridle the whole body."* Herein the verb "offend" carries its most basic meaning – "to break a law." Indeed, in many different ways all of us commit sinful offense against the law of the Lord our God; and this is especially true in the realm of our words. Yea, only a truly perfect individual would never commit a sinful offense through his or her words. Even so, the Biblical principle stands true – The more that we talk, the more chance there is for us to commit a sin through our words. Yet by definition an individual who possesses leadership and teaching responsibility is required to speak more abundantly. Therefore, the instruction is emphasized even more – "*My brethren, be not many masters, knowing that we* [those in leadership and teaching roles] *shall receive the greater condemnation.*"

299. We must not allow our communication both to be filled with praises toward God, yet also harsh words against others.

James 3:9-10 – "*Therewith bless we God, even the Father; and therewith curse we men, which are made after the similitude of God. Out of the same mouth proceedeth blessing and cursing. My brethren, these things ought not so to be.*"

Out of the same mouth should not proceed blessing toward God and cursing toward men. Such a practice "ought not so to be." In fact, when our communication is filled with blessing and praises toward God, but cursing and harsh words against others, our harsh words against others so taint the character of our communication that the Lord our God does not accept our blessing and praises toward Him. In James 3:11-12 an illustration is given in order to reveal this point – "*Doth a fountain send forth at the same place sweet water and bitter? Can the fig tree, my brethren, bear olive berries? Either a vine, figs? So can no fountain both yield salt water and fresh.*" In the natural world, a spring fountain does not produce both sweet water and bitter water, or both fresh water and salt water. Indeed, if bitterness enters into the water of a fountain that originally produced sweet water, then all of the water in that fountain will become corrupted by that bitterness. In like manner, if harsh, bitter words against others enter into our communication, then that harshness and bitterness will corrupt the character of our communication so that even the sweetness of blessing and praising the Lord our God will be found unacceptable in His sight.

In addition, the confrontation of James 3:9-10 is given after a significant warning is provided concerning our communication in verses 3-8. *"Behold, we put bits in the horses' mouths, that they may obey us; and we turn about their whole body. Behold also the ships, which though they be so great, and are driven of fierce winds, yet are they turned about with a very small helm, whithersoever the governor listeth. Even so the tongue is a little member, and boasteth great things. Behold, how great a matter a little fire kindleth! And the tongue is a fire, a world of iniquity: so is the tongue among our members, that it defileth the whole body, and setteth on fire the course of nature; and it is set on fire of hell. For every kind of beasts, and of birds, and of serpents, and of things in the sea, is tamed, and hath been tamed of mankind: but the tongue can no man tame; it is an unruly evil, full of deadly poison."* Through this passage we are brought to understand that harsh, bitter words against others are characteristic of a tongue that is being used as an instrument of fire. Such a fiery tongue will bring spiritual defilement upon the character of the individual who employs it. Furthermore, such a fiery tongue will set on fire the course of the relationships around it and will produce great destruction thereby. Finally, such a fiery tongue is itself set on fire through the fires of hell and the influence of the devil. Indeed, such a fiery tongue is to be Biblically described as "a world of iniquity" and as "an unruly evil, full of deadly poison." Even so, such a fiery tongue reveals that the individual who employs it is not spiritually submitted to and tamed by the filling influence of God the Holy Spirit. Certainly, "these things ought not so to be" in our lives.

300. If we think ourselves to possess spiritual wisdom, then we must demonstrate it through the reality of good behavior and a meek spirit.

James 3:13 – *"Who is a wise man and endued with knowledge among you?* **Let him shew out of a good conversation his works with meekness of wisdom.***"*

First, we are confronted with the question, *"Who is a wise man and endued with knowledge among you?"* If we think that we can answer affirmatively to that question, if we think of ourselves as actually possessing spiritual wisdom and Biblical knowledge, then the instruction applies to us – *"Let him shew out of a good conversation his works with meekness of wisdom."* If we think ourselves to possess spiritual wisdom and Biblical knowledge, then we should show it – not so much through our words, but much more so through our works. Yea, then we should show the reality of our spiritual wisdom and Biblical knowledge through works that flow out of good character and conduct and that are accompanied with a spirit of meekness. In fact, the Biblical phrase "meekness of wisdom" reveals that meekness is an integral characteristic of true, spiritual wisdom. Indeed, James 3:17-18 further describes such true, spiritual wisdom, saying, *"But the wisdom that is from above is first pure, then peaceable, gentle, and easy to be intreated, full of mercy and good fruits, without partiality, and without hypocrisy. And the fruit of righteousness is sown in peace of them that make peace."* Spiritual purity, peaceableness, gentleness, selflessness, mercifulness, goodness, fairness, integrity – These are the characteristics by which true, spiritual wisdom demonstrates itself.

301. If we possess "bitter envying and strife" in the character of our hearts and lives, then we must stop glorying in our supposed wisdom, and thus lying "against the truth."

James 3:14 – *"But if ye have bitter envying and strife in your hearts, glory not, and lie not against the truth."*

Being placed in direct contrast to the principle of James 3:13, this instruction specifically concerns any claim that we might make concerning the possession of spiritual wisdom. If we think and claim that we possess spiritual wisdom, and yet we are characterized by "bitter envying and strife," then we must stop thinking and claiming such about ourselves. Indeed, when we are characterized by "bitter envying and strife," any claim to spiritual wisdom that we might make is revealed to be a lie against God's truth. In such a case, we might possess worldly, self-centered, ungodly wisdom; but we do not possess true, spiritual, godly wisdom. Indeed, James 3:15-16 further describes the type of wisdom that is characterized by "bitter envying and strife," saying, *"This wisdom descendeth not from above, but is earthly, sensual, devilish. For where envying and strife is, there is confusion and every evil work."*

302. We must humbly submit ourselves in dependence upon and obedience to the Lord our God.

James 4:6-7 – *"But he giveth more grace. Wherefore he saith, God resisteth the proud, but giveth grace unto the humble.* **Submit yourselves therefore to God***. Resist the devil, and he will flee from you."*

James 4:10 – *"****Humble yourselves in the sight of the Lord****, and he shall lift you up."*

1 Peter 5:6-7 – *"****Humble yourselves therefore under the mighty hand of God****, that he may exalt you in due time: casting all your care upon him; for he careth for you."*

Specifically because the Lord our God resists the proud, but gives grace unto the humble, we should humbly submit ourselves under His authority to obey His will. Furthermore, specifically because the Lord our God gives more and more (yea, even more abundant grace) unto the humble, we should humbly submit ourselves under His goodness to depend upon His grace.

303. Having submitted ourselves unto the Lord our God, we must faithfully resist the spiritual attacks of our adversary the devil.

James 4:7 – "*Submit yourselves therefore to God.* **Resist the devil, and he will flee from you.**"

1 Peter 5:6-9 – "*Humble yourselves therefore under the mighty hand of God, that he may exalt you in due time: casting all your care upon him; for he careth for you.* **Be sober, be vigilant;** *because your adversary the devil, as a roaring lion, walketh about, seeking whom he may devour:* **whom resist stedfast in the faith**, *knowing that the same afflictions are accomplished in your brethren that are in the world.*"

As we humbly submit ourselves unto the Lord our God in dependence upon and obedience to Him, we will be empowered by His abundant grace to resist the devil with great victory. Indeed, through the strength of our Lord God's almighty power, administered unto us through His abundant grace, we will be able to resist our adversary the devil with such great victory that he will actually flee from us. Therefore, we are commanded, not to cower and submit before our adversary the devil, and not even to turn and flee from our adversary the devil, but to stand firmly and faithfully in resistance against our adversary the devil. Yet we are only instructed to do this after first being instructed to submit ourselves unto the Lord our God, for we cannot resist the devil successfully and victoriously through our own strength. Rather, we can only resist the devil successfully and victoriously when we humbly depend upon the Lord our God so as to be strong in His power and might through His grace.

304. We must not speak evil, harsh, biting words against one another.

James 4:11 – "***Speak not evil one of another, brethren.*** *He that speaketh evil of his brother, and judgeth his brother, speaketh evil of the law, and judgeth the law: but if thou judge the law, thou art not a doer of the law, but a judge.*"

Ephesians 4:31 – "*Let all bitterness, and wrath, and anger, and clamour,* ***and evil speaking, be put away from you****, with all malice.*"

1 Peter 2:1 – "***Wherefore laying aside*** *all malice, and all guile, and hypocrisies, and envies,* ***and all evil speakings.***"

1 Peter 3:10 – "*For he that will love life, and see good days****, let him refrain his tongue from evil****, and his lips that they speak no guile.*"

305. We must not be presumptuous concerning our plans for the future, but must ever recognize the sovereignty of the Lord our God concerning the circumstances of our lives.

James 4:13-17 – "***Go to now****, ye that say, To day or to morrow we will go into such a city, and continue there a year, and buy and sell, and get gain: whereas ye know not what shall be on the morrow. For what is your life? It is even a vapour, that appeareth for a little time, and then vanisheth away.* ***For that ye ought to say, If the Lord will, we shall live, and do this, or that****. But now ye rejoice in your boastings: all such rejoicing is evil. Therefore to him that knoweth to do good, and doeth it not, to him it is sin.*"

Herein a Biblical warning is delivered to those who proceed to make plans for their future without having any consideration of God's sovereign authority in and over their lives. Indeed, God's Word firmly confronts such individuals in James 4:13, saying, "*Go to now, ye that say, To day or to morrow we will go into such a city, and continue there a year, and buy and sell, and get gain.*" Such an attitude that we can make our plans for the future without any consideration of our Lord's sovereign will and work implies that we can be the masters of our own destiny. As such, this attitude and this practice is a sin of proud presumption against our Lord God's eternal and almighty sovereignty. It is the sinful evil of arrogant boasting in the very face of the Lord our God. Even so, in James 4:16 God's Word firmly rebukes those with such an attitude and practice, saying, *"But now ye rejoice in your boastings: all such rejoicing is evil."*

Certainly, it is wise for us to make realistic plans for our future and to discipline our behavior thereby. Yet we must not be presumptuous in making such plans, acting as if we ourselves can bring our plans into fulfillment by our own abilities. In fact, no matter how well developed our plans may be, we cannot actually know what the next day or even the present day might hold for our lives. Even so, in James 4:14 God's Word declares, *"Whereas ye know not what shall be on the morrow. For what is your life? It is even a vapour, that appeareth for a little time, and then vanisheth away."* Truly, what are our lives in relation to the whole process of time and eternity? Our lives are just like a vapor of smoke that appears for a passing moment and then quickly vanishes away. How quickly can the vapor of our lives be brought to an end, and all of our plans for the future with them? How quickly can one unplanned circumstance alter the entire direction of our lives and our plans for days, weeks, months, and even years to come? Thus James 4:15 gives the instruction, *"For that ye ought to say, If the Lord will, we shall live, and do this, or that."*

Now, this instruction does grant us permission to make plans for our future that we might pursue doing this or that as our lives proceed. Yet this instruction indicates that we must govern our planning for the future by our recognition of our Lord God's sovereign will and working in and over our lives. In making our plans for the future, we must ever submit ourselves under the Biblical truths that the Lord our God is the all-sovereign God, that He can do whatever He pleases in our lives, that our plans will only be fulfilled as He permits, and that He can alter our plans however He pleases. In making our plans for the future, we must ever be humble before the sovereign authority of the Lord our God to recognize that we are not at all the masters of our own destiny, but that He is the sovereign ruler over the circumstances of our lives to govern them as He pleases.

306. The wealthy of this world that have become arrogant in their wealth and oppressive over others should take serious heed concerning their future judgment (even to take heed unto repentance).

James 5:1-6 – "***Go to now, ye rich men, weep and howl for your miseries that shall come upon you.*** *Your riches are corrupted, and your garments are motheaten. Your gold and silver is cankered; and the rust of them shall be a witness against you, and shall eat your flesh as it were fire. Ye have heaped treasure together for the last days. Behold, the hire of the labourers who have reaped down your fields, which is of you kept back by fraud, crieth: and the cries of them which have reaped are entered into the ears of the Lord of sabaoth. Ye have lived in pleasure on the earth, and been wanton; ye have nourished your hearts, as in a day of slaughter. Ye have condemned and killed the just; and he doth not resist you.*"

First, as we consider this passage, it is worthy to note that there is no specific contextual indication whether these "rich men" are or are not believers. Second, we find a two-fold condemnation against these "rich men."

In the first place, they are condemned, not because they possess the wealth of this world, but because they have centered their hearts and lives upon that wealth of this world. Even so, in James 5:5 the condemnation is delivered, "*Ye have lived in pleasure on the earth, and been wanton; ye have nourished your hearts, as in a day of slaughter.*" They were not simply enjoying the benefits of wealth in this world (which our Lord does not strictly oppose – see 1 Timothy 6:17). Rather, they had become selfishly and sinfully wanton (self-pleasing and self-indulgent, living for pleasure) through the benefits of wealth in this world. Indeed, they had given over their hearts to the pleasures of their worldly wealth, nourishing their hearts upon it, rather than upon the Lord. Thus in James 5:2-3 God's Word warns them that their worldly wealth is an empty, worthless, and even damaging substance in relation to eternity, saying, "*Your riches are corrupted, and your garments are motheaten. Your gold and silver is cankered; and the rust of them shall be a witness against you, and shall eat your flesh as it were fire.*"

In the second place, they are condemned because they had become oppressive against their laborers and against the righteous. Even so, in James 5:4 the condemnation is delivered, *"Behold, the hire of the labourers who have reaped down your fields, which is of you kept back by fraud, crieth: and the cries of them which have reaped are entered into the ears of the Lord of sabaoth."* Yet again in verse 6 the condemnation is delivered, *"Ye have condemned and killed the just; and he doth not resist you."* Thus in verse 1 these "rich men" are instructed to take serious heed even unto weeping over the misery that will come upon them at the last days when the Lord of Sabaoth (the Lord of Hosts) shall move against them in judgment. Yet since they are instructed in the present tense to weep concerning that coming judgment, this would seem to imply that they ought to take heed with weeping even unto broken-hearted repentance in order that they might flee the wrath to come.

<hr />

307. We must establish our hearts in patient endurance under the afflictions of this life with a focus upon the return of our Lord.

James 5:7-8 – *"**Be patient therefore, brethren, unto the coming of the Lord**. Behold, the husbandman waiteth for the precious fruit of the earth, and hath long patience for it, until he receive the early and latter rain. **Be ye also patient; stablish your hearts: for the coming of the Lord draweth nigh**."*

Twice in these two verses we are instructed to "be patient." Under the many afflictions of this life, we are to establish our hearts with patient endurance. Indeed, we are to establish our hearts with patient endurance unto the coming return of our Lord. Yet we are not simply to be patient unto our Lord's coming return, but also to be patient because of our Lord's coming return. Our patient endurance should be rooted in our certain hope of our Lord's coming return. We must ever remember that when our Lord returns, He shall bring reward with Him for those who have remained faithful unto His name. Therefore, with a continual focus upon our Lord's promised return, we should ever establish our hearts in patient endurance and our lives in faithful obedience, being ever motivated by the promise of reward from our Lord's own hand. Just as a farmer patiently endures unto the fruitful reward of the harvest, even so we should patiently endure unto the blessed reward of our Lord's coming return.

308. We must not hold grudges against one another.

James 5:9 – "*Grudge not one against another, brethren, lest ye be condemned*: *behold, the judge standeth before the door.*"

The coming return of our Lord not only serves as an encouragement unto faithfulness, but also as a warning against sin and unfaithfulness. When our Lord returns, He will certainly return with reward in His hand for His faithful servants. Yet just as certainly, He will also return with judgment in His hand for His unfaithful servants. Thus we are warned not to hold a grudge against another brother or sister in Christ, lest we fall under our Lord's judgment and condemnation at His return for our sinful attitude toward another believer. Now, to hold a grudge means "to store up a strong, continuing attitude of anger, bitterness, and ill-will against another over some perceived grievance (whether real or imagined)." This we must not do.

309. We must follow the example of the Biblical prophets in suffering affliction with patient endurance.

James 5:10-11 – "*Take, my brethren, the prophets, who have spoken in the name of the Lord, for an example of suffering affliction, and of patience*. *Behold, we count them happy which endure. Ye have heard of the patience of Job, and have seen the end of the Lord; that the Lord is very pitiful, and of tender mercy.*"

Indeed, through the example of these godly men, we are able to learn that the Lord our God is "very pitiful [compassionate], and of tender mercy" toward His faithfully and patiently enduring servants. Indeed, we are able to learn that in His abundant compassion and tender mercies, the Lord our God will bring the afflictions of His faithful servants to an end and will greatly bless His faithful servants at that end (which, according to the context, is primarily at the time of our Lord's coming return).

310. If we are in circumstances of affliction, we must pray unto the Lord about it.

James 5:13 – "*Is any among you afflicted? Let him pray. Is any merry? Let him sing psalms.*"

311. If we are in circumstances of happiness, we must sing psalms of praise unto our Lord.

James 5:13 – "*Is any among you afflicted? Let him pray. **Is any merry? Let him sing psalms**.*"

312. If we are in circumstances of significant illness, we must call for the leadership of the church to pray over us.

James 5:14-15 – "***Is any sick among you? Let him call for the elders of the church; and let them pray over him, anointing him with oil in the name of the Lord***: *and the prayer of faith shall save the sick, and the Lord shall raise him up; and if he have committed sins, they shall be forgiven him.*"

In this context the anointing of oil appears to be a reference unto the medicinal oils that were employed at that time. Thus it is worthy of recognition that both prayer and medicine are appropriate in such cases. However, it is also worthy of notice that it is not the medicine itself that will deliver the sick one from his or her illness; but it is the power of God through godly prayer that will ultimately deliver the sick one from his or her illness. It is also worthy of notice that the sick one may need to repent of sinfulness in order for deliverance to be provided by God.

313. We must confess unto one another the sinful faults that we have committed against them.

James 5:16 – "***Confess your faults one to another***, *and pray one for another, that ye may be healed. The effectual fervent prayer of a righteous man availeth much.*"

In relation to this context, it is especially worthy of notice that this confession one to another is necessary if we desire for our Lord to heal us from our illnesses and to deliver us from our afflictions. It is "the effectual fervent prayer of a righteous man" that avails much, and we can only be found in the class of the righteous when we are willing to confess unto one another the sinful faults that we have committed against them.

314. We must pray for the healing of our fellow brothers and sisters in Christ.

James 5:16 – "*Confess your faults one to another,* ***and pray one for another, that ye may be healed****. The effectual fervent prayer of a righteous man availeth much.*"

315. We must maintain a mindset of confident hope in our Lord's promises concerning our eternal future.

1 Peter 1:13 – "***Wherefore gird up the loins of your mind, be sober, and hope to the end for the grace that is to be brought unto you at the revelation of Jesus Christ.***"

Now, "the grace" that is to be brought forth unto us believers in the end at the revelation (the Second Coming) of our Lord and Savior Jesus Christ has been revealed already in 1 Peter 1:3-5. Therein God's Word declares, "*Blessed be the God and Father of our Lord Jesus Christ, which according to his abundant mercy hath begotten us again unto a lively hope by the resurrection of Jesus Christ from the dead, to an inheritance incorruptible, and undefiled, and that fadeth not away, reserved in heaven for you, who are kept by the power of God through faith unto salvation ready to be revealed in the last time.*" What is the living hope unto which God our heavenly Father has begotten us again by the resurrection power of our Lord and Savior Jesus Christ? It is a heavenly inheritance that is incorruptible, undefiled, and unfading. It is a heavenly inheritance that is even now reserved in heaven for us believers. It is the eternal security of our eternal salvation through faith whereby we believers are kept by the almighty power of the Lord our God Himself. It is the eternal security of our eternal salvation wherein the Lord our God Himself is keeping us until we are glorified in His sight with all heavenly glory and godliness.

Even so, we are instructed in 1 Peter 1:13 to establish the steady focus of our hearts and minds with unshakable confidence upon that living hope. This is the living hope that the Lord our God has given to us as a spiritual anchor for our souls, "both sure and steadfast." (See Hebrews 6:19) This is the living hope of our eternal salvation that the Lord our God has given to us as a spiritual helmet to guard the thinking and attitudes of our mindset. (See 1 Thessalonians 5:8) This is the living hope of our eternal salvation in our Savior Jesus Christ that when He shall appear, we shall be like Him in perfect righteousness and holiness. (See 1 John 3:2) Even so, we are to establish our mindset upon this hope, such that our confidence in it is ever steadfast and unmoveable.

482

316. We must follow our Lord Jesus Christ's example of taking it patiently when we suffer wrongfully for righteousness' sake.

1 Peter 2:19-25 – *"For this is thankworthy, if a man for conscience toward God endure grief, suffering wrongfully. For what glory is it, if, when ye be buffeted for your faults, ye shall take it patiently? But if, when ye do well, and suffer for it, ye take it patiently, this is acceptable with God. **For even hereunto were ye called: because Christ also suffered for us, leaving us an example, that ye should follow his steps**: who did no sin, neither was guile found in his mouth: who, when he was reviled, reviled not again; when he suffered, he threatened not; but committed himself to him that judgeth righteously: who his own self bare our sins in his own body on the tree, that we, being dead to sins, should live unto righteousness: by whose stripes ye were healed. For ye were as sheep going astray; but are now returned unto the Shepherd and Bishop of your souls."*

Herein we learn the truth that it is acceptable with the Lord our God and worthy of His approval when for His sake we endure wrongful (unjust) grief and suffering. Herein we learn that is it acceptable with Him and worthy of His approval when we take patiently any suffering for well doing and for righteousness' sake. Yea, herein we learn that we have been specifically called by the Lord our God unto just such a pathway of suffering for His sake and for His righteousness' sake. Indeed, herein we are specifically instructed to walk after the example of our Lord Jesus Christ in His patient suffering for our sakes, in order that He might fulfill the righteous will of God the Father in providing eternal salvation for us sinners.

So then, what is the example of our Lord Jesus Christ in this matter? First, He "did no sin, neither was guile found in his mouth." He did not use His wrongful suffering as an excuse for sinning in either His conduct or His communication; and we must follow His example. Second, "when he was reviled," He "reviled not again." When He was verbally abused for righteousness' sake, He did not respond back with verbal abuse; and we must follow His example. Third, "when he suffered, he threatened not." When He was physically abused for righteousness' sake, He did not respond back even with a threat of physical violence; and we must follow His example. Fourth, when He suffered wrongfully for righteousness' sake, He "committed himself to him that judgeth righteously." He committed Himself unto the loving care of God the Father, and He committed His case unto the perfect justice of God the Father; and we must follow His example.

So then, what motivation is given that we should actually follow our Lord's example? We should be motivated because He suffered all that He suffered for our sakes, in order to bear our sins on the cross, in order to save us through His stripes, in order to give us newness of spiritual life unto righteousness of life. Yea, He suffered all that He suffered for our sakes even though we were rebellious sinners, "as sheep going astray." Yea, He suffered all that He suffered for our sakes, in order to seek us, save us, and return us unto God and Himself. So then, if He could take it patiently when He suffered all of the wrongful suffering that He suffered for our sakes as wicked sinners, should not we then take it patiently when we suffer wrongfully for His sake as our Savior?

---

317. We must "be ready always to give an answer" concerning "the hope that is in us with meekness and fear."

1 Peter 3:15 – *"But sanctify the Lord God in your hearts:* ***and be ready always to give an answer to every man that asketh you a reason of the hope that is in you with meekness and fear.***"

Herein the specific instruction is that we "be ready always to give an answer." Yet the instruction also continues concerning the specific subject about which we might be asked, saying "to give an answer to every man that asketh you a reason of the hope that is in you." Thus the matter about which we should be expecting others to ask us and about which we should always be ready to give an answer is the matter of our hope. Yet if people are going to ask us concerning our hope, then they must first be able to observe that we actually have hope in the face of trouble and affliction. They must be able to observe that we have a spirit of happiness and joy

484

even in the face of suffering for the sake of righteousness. They must be able to observe that we do not have a spirit of trouble or fear in the face of reproach and persecution. They must be able to observe that the Lord our God is truly the central priority and focus of our lives, such that we have centered our faith, fellowship, obedience, and service toward Him. They must be able to observe that we really possess a spirit of hope with meekness (that is – humility in relation to others) and fear (that is – reverence toward the Lord our God). Then as they are able to observe our hope, they will be moved to ask us concerning the reason that we are able to maintain such a hope. Even so, then we should be ready to give them the reason for our hope – The Lord Jesus Christ in us as our eternal Savior (See Colossians 1:27 & 1 Timothy 1:1)

<hr />

318. We must maintain a Christ-like willingness to suffer for righteousness' sake in refusing to join in with the fleshly lusts of this world.

1 Peter 4:1-5 – "***Forasmuch then as Christ hath suffered for us in the flesh, arm yourselves likewise with the same mind****: for he that hath suffered in the flesh hath ceased from sin; that he no longer should live the rest of his time in the flesh to the lusts of men, but to the will of God. For the time past of our life may suffice us to have wrought the will of the Gentiles, when we walked in lasciviousness, lusts, excess of wine, revellings, banquetings, and abominable idolatries: wherein they think it strange that ye run not with them to the same excess of riot, speaking evil of you: who shall give account to him that is ready to judge the quick and the dead.*"

Just as our Lord Jesus Christ maintained a willingness to obey the will of God the Father in suffering for us sinners and for our salvation, even so we are to maintain the same mindset of willingness to obey the will of God our heavenly Father in suffering for Christ's sake and for righteousness' sake. Yet the explanation of 1 Peter 4:1-5 provides more understanding concerning this instruction. Even so, verses 1-2 reveal that when we maintain a mindset of willingness to suffer for Christ's sake and for righteousness' sake, we will be able to walk in spiritual victory over sin. Indeed, when we maintain a mindset of willingness to suffer for Christ's sake and righteousness' sake, we will be able to walk in spiritual rejection of the fleshly lusts of this world and in faithful obedience unto the holy will of the Lord our God.

Even so, verses 3-5 provide a further explanation, saying, "For the time past of our life may suffice us to have wrought the will of the Gentiles, when we walked in lasciviousness, lusts, excess of wine, revellings, banquetings, and abominable idolatries: wherein they think it strange that ye run not with them to the same excess of riot, speaking evil of you: who shall give account to him that is ready to judge the quick and the dead." Indeed, before we were saved through faith in Christ, we walked according to the fleshly lusts of our own hearts and of this wicked world. However, now that we are saved through faith in Christ, we are called to walk in newness of life, that is – in submission and obedience unto the will of the Lord our God and heavenly Father. Yet when we refuse to walk after the fleshly lusts of this world and choose rather to walk after the holy will of the Lord our God, this spiritually lost world will speak evil and reproachful things against us. Therefore, it will be necessary for us to maintain a mindset of willingness to suffer for our Lord's sake and for righteousness' sake, if we shall faithfully walk after our Lord's will in the face of this world's reproach.

319. We must not behave so as to suffer punishment as a murderer, thief, evil doer, or "busybody in other men's matters."

1 Peter 4:15 – "*But let none of you suffer as a murderer, or as a thief, or as an evildoer, or as a busybody in other men's matters.*"

On the one hand, suffering for righteousness' sake should be viewed as a positive opportunity of the Christian life. On the other hand, suffering for unrighteousness' sake is something that we should seek to avoid by not engaging in unrighteous behavior.

320. When we suffer for righteousness' sake, we must "commit the keeping of our souls" unto the Lord our God "in well doing," completely trusting in His everlasting faithfulness and almighty power.

1 Peter 4:19 – "*Wherefore let them that suffer according to the will of God commit the keeping of their souls to him in well doing, as unto a faithful Creator.*"

First, when we suffer for righteousness' sake, we must commit ourselves and our case unto the Lord our God. He is the Savior and Keeper of our souls; therefore, we must trust Him to engage in the keeping of our souls. Second, when we suffer for righteousness' sake, we must continue "in well doing," and not become weary therein. Trusting in our Lord to keep our souls, we must continue in serving Him. Third, when we suffer for righteousness' sake, we must maintain a heart-trust that the Lord our God is "a faithful Creator." Herein we must set the trust of our hearts upon two characteristics of our Lord God's holy nature. In the first place, we must set the trust of our hearts upon our Lord God's faithfulness, that His faithfulness is an everlasting faithfulness that never fails. In the second place, we must set the trust of our hearts upon our Lord God's power, that He is the almighty Creator who created the entire creation by the word of His power. Indeed, we must maintain the heart-trust that the Lord our God will engage in the keeping of our souls because He is all faithful, and that the Lord our God can accomplish the keeping of our souls because He is almighty.

321. Those believers who are younger in age must submit themselves unto the spiritual maturity and wisdom of those believers who are older in age.

1 Peter 5:5 – "*Likewise, ye younger, submit yourselves unto the elder. Yea, all of you be subject one to another, and be clothed with humility: for God resisteth the proud, and giveth grace to the humble.*"

322. We must be diligent to grow forward unto spiritual maturity through the development of virtue, knowledge, temperance, patience, godliness, brotherly kindness, and charity.

2 Peter 1:5-7 – *"And beside this, giving all diligence, add to your faith virtue; and to virtue knowledge; and to knowledge temperance; and to temperance patience; and to patience godliness; and to godliness brotherly kindness; and to brotherly kindness charity."*

Herein we find seven spiritual characteristics that we are diligently to develop into the character of our hearts and lives. First, we are to develop "virtue," which means a heart commitment unto righteousness. Second, we are to develop "knowledge," which means a Biblical discernment for living. Third, we are to develop "temperance," which means a Holy Spirit guided restraint of our desires. Fourth, we are to develop "patience," which means a spiritual endurance against temptation, trouble, and tribulation. Fifth, we are to develop "godliness," which means a faithful walk with and for the Lord our God. Sixth, we are to develop "brotherly kindness," which means a gracious heart of service toward our brethren in Christ. Finally, we are to develop "charity," which means a godly love of self-sacrifice for others.

Unto this 2 Peter 1:8-9 adds the promise and the warning, saying, *"For if these things be in you, and abound, they make you that ye shall neither be barren nor unfruitful in the knowledge of our Lord Jesus Christ. But he that lacketh these things is blind, and cannot see afar off, and hath forgotten that he was purged from his old sins."* Then verses 10-11 reiterate the instruction and deliver a promise, indicating that this diligence to grow forward unto spiritual maturity is the means to have a strong ("sure") Christian walk in this life and to obtain abundant reward in the life to come – *"Wherefore the rather, brethren, give diligence to make your calling and election sure: for if ye do these things, ye shall never fall: for so an entrance shall be ministered unto you abundantly into the everlasting kingdom of our Lord and Saviour Jesus Christ."*

323. We must remember that our Lord's longsuffering in not yet returning is because He is concerned for the repentance and salvation of lost souls.

2 Peter 3:15 – "***And account that the longsuffering of our Lord is salvation;*** *even as our beloved brother Paul also according to the wisdom given unto him hath written unto you.*"

Within the immediate context, this instruction is built upon the truth of 2 Peter 3:9, wherein God's Word states, "*The Lord is not slack concerning his promise, as some men count slackness; but is longsuffering to us-ward, not willing that any should perish, but that all should come to repentance.*" Our Lord does not "stall" His promised return because He is unfaithful in keeping His promises. Rather, our Lord "stalls" His promised return because He does not desire for souls to perish in hell. Even so, He "stalls" His promised return through a motive of longsuffering, that more and more souls might come unto repentance and eternal salvation. Thus as we look for His promised return, we must ever remember the reason that He has not yet returned according to His promise – because "the longsuffering of our Lord is salvation."

324. We must beware that we not be "led away with the error of the wicked," and thereby fall away from our steadfastness in walking with and for our Lord.

2 Peter 3:17 – "***Ye therefore, beloved, seeing ye know these things before, beware lest ye also, being led away with the error of the wicked, fall from your own stedfastness.***"

325. We must walk after the example of our Lord Jesus Christ's walk, ever obeying God's Word and will in everything.

1 John 2:6 – "***He that saith he abideth in him ought himself also so to walk, even as he walked.***"

How then did our Lord Jesus Christ walk? In John 4:34 our Lord Jesus Christ gave the answer – "*Jesus saith unto them, My meat is to do the will of him that sent me, and to finish his work.*" Again in John 8:29 He gave the answer, saying, "*And he that sent me is with me: the Father hath not left me alone; for I do always those things that please him.*" Yet again in John 17:4 our Lord Jesus Christ prayed unto the Father, saying, "*I have glorified thee on the earth: I have finished the work which thou gavest me to do.*" Even so, in John 15:10 our Lord Jesus Christ revealed the promise and the example, saying, "*If ye keep my commandments, ye shall abide in my love; even as I have kept my Father's commandments, and abide in his love.*" So then, our Lord Jesus Christ walked so as always to do the will of the Father, and thereby always to please and to glorify the Father; and we ought ourselves "also so to walk, even as he walked." We ought ever to obey our Lord God's Word and will in everything. Even so, 1 John 2:3-5 presents the following truth, "*And hereby we do know that we know him* [that we are walking in fellowship with Him]*, if we keep his commandments. He that saith, I know him, and keepeth not his commandments, is a liar, and the truth is not in him. But whoso keepeth his word, in him verily is the love of God perfected: hereby know we that we are in him.*"

326. We must not love the world around us or the principle of selfishness that governs the world around us.

1 John 2:15-17 – "***Love not the world, neither the things that are in the world.*** *If any man love the world, the love of the Father is not in him. For all that is in the world, the lust of the flesh, and the lust of the eyes, and the pride of life, is not of the Father, but is of the world. And the world passeth away, and the lust thereof: but he that doeth the will of God abideth for ever.*"

Herein we are instructed not to love the world or "the things that are in the world." Yet in this context "the things that are in the world" are not defined as material things, but as motivational things. Herein all of "the things that are in the world" are defined as "the lust of the flesh, the lust of the eyes, and the pride of life." As such, all of "the things that are in the world" are revealed to be all of the motivational principles that govern this world; and all of the motivational principles that govern this world can be condensed into the singular motivational principle of selfishness. Even so, we must not set the love of our hearts upon this world or upon the motivational principle of selfishness that governs all of this world's system. Yea, we must not give our hearts and lives unto the motivational principle of selfishness. This motivational principle of selfishness is not of God our heavenly Father, but is of this present evil world. This motivational principle of selfishness is the opposite of love for God our heavenly Father. This motivational principle of selfishness and all that it obtains will pass away, "but he that doeth the will of God abideth for ever."

327. We must not be deceived into thinking that a person can be right with the Lord while walking in sin.

1 John 3:7 – *"Little children, let no man deceive you: he that doeth righteousness is righteous, even as he is righteous."*

The surrounding context of 1 John 3:4-10 provides an expanded teaching on this instruction and truth, saying, *"Whosoever committeth sin transgresseth also the law: for sin is the transgression of the law. And ye know that he was manifested to take away our sins; and in him is no sin. Whosoever abideth in him sinneth not: whosoever sinneth hath not seen him, neither known him* [that is – whoever is walking in sin is not right with Him and is not walking in fellowship with him]. *Little children, let no man deceive you: he that doeth righteousness is righteous, even as he is righteous. He that committeth sin is of the devil* [that is – whoever is walking in sin is walking after the character and ways of the devil]; *for the devil sinneth from the beginning. For this purpose the Son of God was manifested, that he might destroy the works of the devil. Whosoever is born of God doth not commit sin; for his seed remaineth in him: and he cannot sin, because he is born of God. In this the children of God are manifest, and the children of the devil: whosoever doeth not righteousness is not of God, neither he that loveth not his brother."* So then, we must not deceive ourselves concerning our own walk; and we must not be deceived by others concerning their walk. If we ourselves or those others are walking in sin and not in righteousness, then we ourselves or those others are not right with the Lord our God and are not walking in fellowship with Him.

---

328. We must not believe every teaching or teacher, but must test every teaching and teacher by the doctrine of God's Word, whether they are the truth of God or the error of the antichrist.

1 John 4:1-6 – "***Beloved, believe not every spirit, but try the spirits whether they are of God***: *because many false prophets are gone out into the world. Hereby know ye the Spirit of God: Every spirit that confesseth that Jesus Christ is come in the flesh is of God: and every spirit that confesseth not that Jesus Christ is come in the flesh is not of God: and this is that spirit of antichrist, whereof ye have heard that it should come; and even now already is it in the world. Ye are of God, little children, and have overcome them: because greater is he that is in you, than he that is in the world. They are of the world: therefore speak they of the world, and the world heareth them. We are of God: he that knoweth God heareth us; he that is not of God heareth not us. Hereby know we the spirit of truth, and the spirit of error.*"

Herein we find both a negative and a positive instruction. On the one hand, we are not to believe every spirit, that is – not to believe every teaching, every teacher, every message, every preacher. On the other hand, we are to try (test) every spirit (every teaching, teacher, message, preacher) to determine whether they are truly of God, or not. The reason that we must do this is because there are many false prophets, false teachers, and false preachers who have gone forth into this world. Such false prophets, false teachers, and false preachers are actually motivated by the spirit of antichrist; and we should certainly desire not to have any part with them. So then, how may we discern whether a teaching, teacher, message, or preacher is truly of God, or not? By what standard may we judge the difference between "the spirit of truth" and "the spirit of error"?

In 1 John 4:1-6 we are given a two-fold standard. The first of these concerns the doctrine of the gospel – If an individual teaches and preaches the doctrine of Jesus the Christ and Savior with Biblical accuracy, then that individual holds unto the true gospel of God. However, if an individual teaches and preaches contrary to the doctrine of Jesus the Christ and Savior in any way, then that individual is not of God, but is motivated by the spirit of antichrist and of error. Then the second standard for truth concerns all other Biblical doctrine – If an individual teaches and preaches the ideas and philosophies of this world, the multitudes of this world will follow after him. Yet he is not a teacher or preacher of God, but of the world. However, if an individual teaches and preaches in accord with the apostles, as recorded in the divinely inspired Scriptures, those who walk in fellowship with the Lord will follow after him, while those who are of the world will reject him. Even so, he is a preacher of God, who is motivated by "the spirit of truth." Yet are we believers truly able to discern between "the spirit of truth" and "the spirit of error"? Yes, we will be able to do so, if we submit unto the guidance of the indwelling Holy Spirit of truth. We believers are indwelt by the Spirit of truth; and greater is the Spirit of truth that is in us, than Satan the deceiver that is in the world.

329. When we see a fellow believer in sin, we must pray for his or her repentance, in order that he or she might be restored unto the abundant life.

1 John 5:16-17 – "*If any man see his brother sin a sin which is not unto death, he shall ask, and he shall give him life for them that sin not unto death. There is a sin unto death: I do not say that he shall pray for it. All unrighteousness is sin: and there is a sin not unto death.*"

Herein we are instructed concerning what to do when we notice a fellow believer's sinning "a sin which is not unto death." We are to engage in pray for that fellow believer, asking that the Lord our God might give life unto that fellow believer. Now, since that fellow believer has not sinned a sin unto physical death, the life for which we are to pray is not that of physical life. Rather, the life for which we are to pray is the abundant spiritual life. Furthermore, since the only way for a sinning believer to be restored unto abundant spiritual life is through broken-hearted repentance of sin, the focus and burden of our praying is that the fellow believer might come to repentance in order that he or she might be restored unto the abundant spiritual life.

330. We must not follow the example of believers who are evil, but must follow the example of believers who are good.

3 John 1:9-12 – "*I wrote unto the church: but Diotrephes, who loveth to have the preeminence among them, receiveth us not. Wherefore, if I come, I will remember his deeds which he doeth, prating against us with malicious words: and not content therewith, neither doth he himself receive the brethren, and forbiddeth them that would, and casteth them out of the church. Beloved, follow not that which is evil, but that which is good. He that doeth good is of God: but he that doeth evil hath not seen God. Demetrius hath good report of all men, and of the truth itself: yea, and we also bear record; and ye know that our record is true.*"

We understand that the instruction in the first half of the verse not to follow "that which is evil," but to follow "that which is good" concerns the example of others because the truth in the second half of the verse speaks concerning people who do good or who do evil. So then, we are not to follow the evil example of believers like Diotrephes, who loved to have preeminence, who spoke malicious words against other men of God, who would not show godly love toward other men of God, and who forbade others from showing such godly love. However, we are to follow the good example of believers like Demetrius, who maintained a testimony of goodness toward all, and who walked in the truth of God's Word.

331. We must "earnestly contend for the faith which was once delivered unto the saints," that is – for the sound doctrine of God's Word.

Jude 1:3 – *"Beloved, when I gave all diligence to write unto you of the common salvation, it was needful for me to write unto you, and exhort you **that ye should earnestly contend for the faith which was once delivered unto the saints**."*

The reason for this instruction is given in Jude 1:4, *"For there are certain men crept in unawares, who were before of old ordained to this condemnation, ungodly men, turning the grace of our God into lasciviousness, and denying the only Lord God, and our Lord Jesus Christ."* False teachers abound in the world and will even find their way deceptively into churches. Such false teachers will be ungodly in their character, will teach that God's grace allows for us to do our own thing, and will teach contrary to the Lordship authority of God the Father and Jesus Christ in our daily living. Because of this, we must not only hold fast unto the sound doctrine of God's Word to govern our own lives, but must also contend earnestly for the sound doctrine of God's Word to govern our churches. We must not allow false teachers and false teaching to get a hold upon our homes and churches, but must earnestly contend for the sound doctrine of God's Word to maintain its place of priority in our homes and our churches.

332. We must repent of leaving our priority love for the Lord, and must return unto a faithful walk therein.

Revelation 2:5 – "***Remember therefore from whence thou art fallen, and repent, and do the first works***; *or else I will come unto thee quickly, and will remove thy candlestick out of his place, except thou repent.*"

In Revelation 2:4 our Lord Jesus Christ rebuked the church at Ephesus, saying, "*Nevertheless I have somewhat against thee, because thou hast left thy first love.*" Thus in verse 5 our Lord Jesus Christ instructed them to repent and return. Even so, whenever we leave our priority love for the Lord, we also must repent of our sinful failure and return unto a right priority.

333. We must repent of allowing false teachers to have freedom to teach their falsehood within our churches.

Revelation 2:14-16 – "*But I have a few things against thee, because thou hast there them that hold the doctrine of Balaam, who taught Balac to cast a stumblingblock before the children of Israel, to eat things sacrificed unto idols, and to commit fornication. So hast thou also them that hold the doctrine of the Nicolaitans, which thing I hate.* ***Repent****; or else I will come unto thee quickly, and will fight against them with the sword of my mouth.*"

Even so, whenever we have allowed false teachers to have freedom within our church to teach falsehood, we must repent thereof.

334. We must repent of becoming spiritually dead, and must pursue spiritual revival in our lives.

Revelation 3:1-3 – "*And unto the angel of the church in Sardis write; These things saith he that hath the seven Spirits of God, and the seven stars; I know thy works, that thou hast a name that thou livest, and art dead. Be watchful, and strengthen the things which remain, that are ready to die: for I have not found thy works perfect before God.* **Remember therefore how thou hast received and heard, and hold fast, and repent.** *If therefore thou shalt not watch, I will come on thee as a thief, and thou shalt not know what hour I will come upon thee.*"

Revelation 3:15-20 – "*I know thy works, that thou art neither cold nor hot: I would thou wert cold or hot. So then because thou art lukewarm, and neither cold nor hot, I will spue thee out of my mouth. Because thou sayest, I am rich, and increased with goods, and have need of nothing; and knowest not that thou art wretched, and miserable, and poor, and blind, and naked:* **I counsel thee to buy of me gold tried in the fire, that thou mayest be rich; and white raiment, that thou mayest be clothed, and that the shame of thy nakedness do not appear; and anoint thine eyes with eyesalve, that thou mayest see.** *As many as I love, I rebuke and chasten:* **be zealous therefore, and repent.** *Behold, I stand at the door, and knock: if any man hear my voice, and open the door, I will come in to him, and will sup with him, and he with me.*"

Even so, when we enter into a walk of spiritual deadness and self-deception, we also must be zealous to repent thereof, and to return unto the Lord, and to remember, and to be watchful, and to hold fast, and to strengthen ourselves again in the walk of revival and fellowship with our Lord.

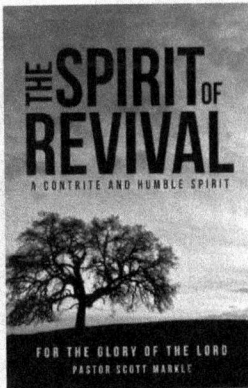

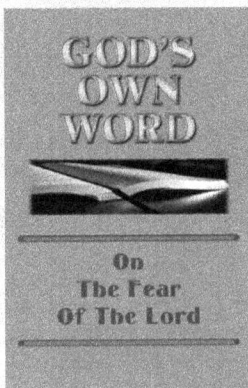

GOD'S OWN WORD
On The Fear of the Lord

Chapter Contents
(82 pages)

The Fear of the Lord
The Terror of the Lord –
Because of His Glory
The Fear of God's People –
Because His Hand Is with Them
Learning to Fear the Lord
The Benefits of Fearing the Lord
If You Will Not Fear the Lord
The Terror of the Lord –
Because of Our Sin

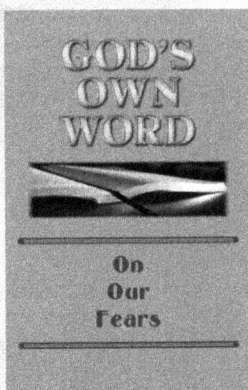

GOD'S OWN WORD
On Our Fears

Chapter Contents
(80 pages)

Fear Thou Not
Fear in the Midst of Affliction
I Will Fear No Evil
Afraid of Man
Delivered from Fear
Fear as a Judgment from the Lord